THE TURBULENT WORLD OF MIDDLE EAST SOCCER

JAMES M. DORSEY

The Turbulent World
of Middle East Soccer

OXFORD
UNIVERSITY PRESS

OXFORD
UNIVERSITY PRESS

Oxford University Press is a department of the
University of Oxford. It furthers the University's objective
of excellence in research, scholarship, and education
by publishing worldwide.

Oxford   New York

Auckland   Cape Town   Dar es Salaam   Hong Kong   Karachi
Kuala Lumpur   Madrid   Melbourne   Mexico City   Nairobi
New Delhi   Shanghai   Taipei   Toronto

With offices in

Argentina   Austria   Brazil   Chile   Czech Republic   France   Greece
Guatemala   Hungary   Italy   Japan   Poland   Portugal   Singapore
South Korea   Switzerland   Thailand   Turkey   Ukraine   Vietnam

Oxford is a registered trade mark of Oxford University Press
in the UK and certain other countries.

Published in the United States of America by
Oxford University Press
198 Madison Avenue, New York, NY 10016

Library of Congress Cataloging-in-Publication Data is available
James M. Dorsey.
The Turbulent World of Middle East Soccer.
ISBN: 9780199394975

Printed in India on acid-free paper

"Some people believe football is a matter of life and death. I am very disappointed with that attitude. I can assure you it is much, much more important than that."

Legendary Liverpool FC manager Bill Shankly

"Sport is a powerful political weapon. We should never surrender it into enemy hands."

Claudio Tamburrini, Argentinian philosopher, writer and former goalkeeper

"Football can be a means of domination and a means of resistance."

Daniel Künzler, Sociologist

"Football is like democracy: twenty-two people play and millions are watching."

German comedian Klaus Hansen

CONTENTS

Acknowledgements   ix
Chronology   xi

Introduction   1

1. Bearing the Scars of Battle   11

2. The Battle for Greater Freedom   25
    Scoring Political Goals   25
    Politics is in soccer's DNA   30
    The Stadium: Soccer's Grunt School   37
    Upholding Dignity: Breaking the Barrier of Fear   59
    Soccer: Barometer of Morsi's Political Fortune   69

3. Islamists Fight over Soccer   93
    Soccer vs Jihad   93
    Islam vs Islam   114

4. Struggling for Nationhood, Battling for Change   149
    Bridging Divides   149
    Playing for Nationhood   169
    Sectarianism Trumps Soccer   182
    Controlling Soccer is Mastering Politics   197

5. Shattering Taboos   213

6. Competing on the World Stage   237
    Soccer: An Alternative National Defence Strategy   237
    (West) Asian Soccer: A Cesspool of Government Interference, Struggles
        for Power, Corruption and Greed   262

Epilogue   283

Notes   289
Index   321

ACKNOWLEDGEMENTS

The penny dropped with the arrival of an email. "You've got a book," the sender, Steven Solomon, a successful author, journalist and avid soccer player and fan, said. He was referring to an article I had written positioning politics as an impediment to Middle Eastern and North African soccer performance. Steven is this book's midwife. He was there with solid advice throughout the process. When I wrote the article, I would have declared "nuts" anyone who would have predicted that years later I would be writing a book and still looking at the Middle East and North Africa through the prism of soccer. Yet, Steven launched me on a path I had been struggling to find: an original and different way of viewing, analysing and understanding ever more tumultuous and dramatic events in a region I have been covering for more than forty years.

I am equally indebted to Singapore in more ways than I can recount. An invitation to become a senior fellow at the Middle East Institute of the National University of Singapore, followed by an appointment at Nanyang Technological University's renowned S. Rajaratnam School of International Studies (RSIS), offered me a platform and an unrivalled intellectual environment. I cannot thank enough two of Singapore's top diplomats, RSIS Dean Barry Desker, and Bilahari Kausikan, one of the Foreign Ministry's greatest, beloved guiding lights, whose support was invaluable. Ever the diplomat in everything but professional designation, RSIS Deputy Executive Chairman Ong Keng Yong and Dean Joseph Chinyong Liow's door, like those of Barry and Bilahari, was always open, even when my research and investigative reporting landed me in hot water. There are too many other MEI and RSIS colleagues to mention, amongst them Peter Sluglett, Ali Alawi, Mushahid Ali and Leonard

ACKNOWLEDGEMENTS

Sebastian. Their friendship, insights and comments in multiple conversations sparked and stimulated my thinking. This is equally true for two great lights of the study of sports, Harald Lange of the Institute of Sport Science of the University of Würzburg, who by inviting me to co-direct with him the Institute of Fan Culture exposed me to a broader world of fandom in ways I may not have had access to without him, and Paul Verweel, who by fighting for my acceptance as a doctoral candidate at the University of Utrecht added a key dimension to an academic and think tank career that I had discarded almost half a century earlier in favour of journalism.

I owe Teresita Cruz-Del Rosario my recognition of the utility of a doctoral degree to my late-in-life career broadening, best described by BBC foreign correspondent turned communications professor James Rodgers as "hackademia". But reducing my debt to Tess at that alone would be an enormous understatement. She was there for me with crucial advice, unquestioned support, and invaluable guidance in the world of academia. I thank her for her insight and theoretical understanding of, and practical experience in, protesting against and toppling autocratic leaders, as well as the inevitable Leninist process of consolidation that follows successful revolts, and am grateful for much else besides.

The names of those across the Middle East and North Africa and beyond who spared time and shared their knowledge and experience, as well as offering me a platform to speak and debate, are far too numerous to list here. Many, for obvious reasons, would prefer to remain anonymous. Nevertheless, their contribution is central to the writing and publishing of this book.

That is no truer than for the one person I do want to name: Prince Ali Bin Al Hussein. I have benefitted immensely from Prince Ali's wisdom and knowledge and learnt from his strategic depth and deliberate and considered approach to problem solving. But most importantly, I have been honoured and enriched by his friendship.

Last but not least, this book would not have been published without the quiet, unobtrusive encouragement of Michael Dwyer and his dedicated staff at Hurst Publishers.

The long and short of this all is: thank you. Without all of you, this book would have never been written.

CHRONOLOGY

Late 1800s	British troops, businessmen and sailors introduce soccer in various Middle Eastern and North African nations, notably Egypt whose instant love affair with the game started when they first saw British colonial troops play in 1882.
1899	Turks challenge the Sultan's ban on soccer with the founding of the All-Turkish Black Stockings (Siyah Çoraplılar) club.
1903	Founding of Beşiktaş Jimnastik Kulübü by sons of senior officials in the Ottoman Sultan's palace.
1907	Egyptian nationalists establish Al Ahly [The National] SC as a club, initially for Egyptians only, in response to the British sports clubs that barred Egyptians. Al Ahly quickly becomes an anti-colonial, anti-monarchist, nationalist rallying-point.
1911	Founding of Zamalek SC as the club of Egyptian royalists and pro-British forces.
1919	Al Ahly SC serves as launch pad for a revolution that forces Britain to recognize Egypt's independence in 1922.
1920s	Shah Reza Khan of Iran orders his armed forces to play soccer. Egyptian sports journalism exploits anti-British fervour by covering British–Egyptian matches in military jargon.
1926	The Iranian parliament authorizes construction of Iran's first soccer pitch.

1928	FIFA grants membership to the Palestine Football Federation, grouping Jewish, British and Palestinian clubs.
1930s	Zionists use sports events as cover for illegal Jewish immigration to Palestine.
1931	Zionist efforts to co-opt sports in the nationalist struggle prompt Palestinians to establish their own, short-lived sports governing body, the Arab Palestine Sports Federation (APSF).
1932	Founding of Al Faisali SC, widely viewed as representing Jordan's East Bankers.
1936	Founding of Beitar Jerusalem FC.
1940s	Nationalist Palestinian media campaign to convince religious and educational authorities to see sports as part of their nation's national struggle.
1945	Founding of Tehran's Esteghlal FC as the Shah's club, and of Lebanon's Nejmeh SC.
1952	Egypt's post-revolution leaders—Gamal Abdel Nasser, Field Marshal Abdelhakim Amer, and General Abdelaziz Salem—occupy top positions in Egyptian and African soccer.
June 1954	At the World Cup in Switzerland the Algerian National Liberation Front (FLN) announces the onset of its armed struggle for independence from France.
1956	The FLN announces a boycott by Arab and Berber clubs of the Algerian leagues and orders club members to join the rebels.
1956	Founding of Al Wehdat SC in a Palestinian refugee camp in Amman where Yasser Arafat's Palestine Liberation Organization (PLO) was headquartered until its expulsion from Jordan in 1970. Founding of the Saudi Arabian Football Federation after clergy drops its opposition to soccer in the Kingdom.
November 1956	Lebanon, Iraq and Egypt boycott the Melbourne Olympics in protest against the tripartite British–French–Israeli attack on Egypt.
1958	Some ten Algerian players who were likely to play

	in the French team in the World Cup desert France to tour the world on behalf of the FLN, playing matches during the Algerian War of Independence in support of their country's struggle.
1963	Founding of Tehran's Persepolis FC, widely viewed as the team of Iran's lower classes.
1 October 1963	Authorities ban Egyptian players from visits to Aden after they instigate pro-Nasser demonstrations.
1964	Israel blocks attempt by Israeli Palestinian nationalist group Al-Ard to establish a league of independent Israeli Palestinian clubs.
June 1967	Egyptian President Gamal Abdel Nasser bans soccer matches and popular music after the disastrous 1967, Six-Day War in which Israel conquered the West Bank, the Gaza Strip, Sinai and the Golan Heights.
17 September 1967	Forty-two people die and 300 others are injured in fighting at Kayseri's Ataturk Stadium in one of Turkey's worst sporting incidents, sparked by political, geo-political and commercial rivalries, violence, corruption and match-fixing.
1968	The slogan "Death to Israel" is chanted for the first time in an Iranian football stadium.
5 September 1972	Palestinian gunmen take hostage and kill eleven Israeli athletes at the Munich Olympics.
1976	Beitar Jerusalem wins its first Israel Cup.
1979	Iranian clergy debates soccer's compatibility with Islam.
1980	Turkish military leader General Kemal Evren changes rules governing soccer leagues to ensure the promotion of the Turkish capital Ankara's MKE Ankaragücü.
1981	Fans of arch rivals Esteghlal and Persepolis, in a rare show of unity, meet to protest against an Iranian crackdown on soccer, aimed at reducing the game's importance.
1982	Founding of militant Turkish soccer fan group Beşiktaş Çarşı Grubu.

February 1982   The Syrian government turns the stadium at Hama into a mass detention centre after troops brutally crushed an uprising by the Muslim Brotherhood, killing at least 10,000 people.

16 September 1982   Israeli-backed Christian militia use a soccer pitch for a four-day massacre in the Beirut Palestinian refugee camps of Sabra and Shatila.

1984   Iranian Prime Minister Mir-Hossein Mousavi, seeks to distract attention from soccer following a riot that demonstrated the pitch's potential as a release valve for discontent.

1985   Turkish President Turgut Özal seeks to garner votes by promoting midseason the teams of Anatolian towns Bursa and Konya to the premier league.

1986   Jordan temporarily shuts down Al Wehdat football club after its fans chant slogans against the monarchy.

1987   Beitar Jerusalem wins its first Israeli championship.

Late 1980s   Anti-government protests dominate Algerian soccer matches. Berbers assert their non-Arab identity in stadiums. Iranian spiritual leader Ayatollah Ruhollah Khomeini increases television coverage of soccer to curb the influence of more conservative clerical forces.

1990s   The Taliban use Kabul's Ghazi Stadium as a public site for executions, amputations and floggings. Sahar Al-Hawari builds the Arab world's first association women's soccer team and regional women's soccer championship.

1991   Rival, heavily armed, Istanbul soccer fan groups declare a truce to prevent further deaths.
Founding of Bnei Sakhnin FC in Israel.

1993   Uday Hussein, Iraqi sports czar and scion of Saddam Hussein, lifts a ban on Iraqi players playing for foreign teams provided they pay him a percentage of their salaries.

1994	Iran drops plans to admit women spectators into stadiums.
29 November 1997	Celebrations of Iranian defeat in World Cup qualifier turn into anti-government protests.
1998	Palestine becomes the first nation without a state to be granted FIFA membership. US–Iran soccer friendly turns terraces into battlefield between proponents and opponents of the Islamic Republic. Qatari funding helps Sepp Blatter become president of FIFA.
15 June 1998	Osama Bin Laden targets England–Tunisia World Cup match.
2000	Al Saadi Qaddafi orders destruction of Al Ahly Benghazi SC's 37-hectare headquarters after anti-government protests. Galatasaray becomes the first Turkish club to list on the Istanbul Stock Exchange.
6 April 2000	Two Leeds United fans stabbed to death in a soccer brawl in Istanbul.
2001	US troops play an Afghan soccer team to highlight the changes they are bringing to the war-ravaged country in the wake of the overthrow of the Taliban. Lebanese government intervention in a murky match-fixing scandal allows Lebanon's sectarian leaders to restructure the soccer association along sectarian lines.
2002	Celebrations of Iranian soccer victory manifest opposition to strict Islamic social norms.
2003	The Coalition Provisional Authority (CPA) disbands the Iraqi National Olympic Committee and prioritizes construction and rehabilitation of soccer stadiums and clubs. Egyptian soccer enthusiasts forge contacts with organized militant soccer fans in Serbia, Italy and Argentina. Hamas suicide bombers can be traced to mosque soccer team.
June 2003	Militant Turkish soccer fans play central role in worst anti-government protests in a decade.
2004	Bnei Sakhnin FC wins Israel's State Cup. Al Saadi

Qaddafi, president of the Libyan Football Federation, takes command of key Libyan military unit. Supporters of Turkish–Kurdish guerrilla group PKK found Dalkurd FF, a rising force in Swedish soccer.

March 2004   Syrian troops kill six people in Qamishli in an attack on Syrian–Kurdish supporters of Al Jihad SC, who were waving Kurdish flags and pictures of US President George W. Bush during a match against predominantly Arab Al Fatwa SC from Deir-ez-Zor.

2005   Founding of militant Beitar Jerusalem fan group La Familia. Al Saadi Qaddafi reportedly tortures and kills Libyan national team player and coach Bashir Al-Ryani. A fatwa by militant Saudi clerics denounces soccer as an infidel invention and redrafts its International Football Association Board (IFAB) approved rules to differentiate the game from that of the heretics. Militant Turkish soccer fans join Greenpeace in protests against the installation of a nuclear power station in the Black Sea city of Sinop. Turkish Prime Minister Recep Tayyip Erdoğan, in a bid to curry favour in the Black Sea town of Trabzon, pumps funds into Trabzonspor FC and appoints a former club player as his minister of public works. Devout Israeli–Palestinian Muslim Abbas Suan achieves what politicians in more than half a century have not: uniting Israelis and Palestinians by securing with a last minute equalizer against Ireland—Israel's first chance in thirty-five years to qualify for a World Cup. Lebanon imposes multi-year ban on spectators attending soccer matches after a car bomb kills Prime Minister Rafik Hariri.

2006   Celebrations of Iranian soccer victory again manifest opposition to strict Islamic social norms. Berlin's predominantly Turkish BSV Al Dersimspor becomes first foreign women's soccer team to play in post-revolution Iran. Iranian conservatives thwart President Mahmoud Ahmadinejad's efforts to relax the ban on women attending soccer matches in stadiums. Jihadist Syrian scholar Abd-al Mun'em Mustafa Halima Abu Basir, better known as Abu Basir al-Tartusi, breaks ranks with his militant brethren by endorsing soccer as a "means of entertainment" but forbidding the watching of World Cup matches. Founding of Hapoel Katamon Jerusalem FC, Israel's only fan-owned club.

2007   Militant Egyptian soccer fans, or Ultras, make their debut during a match between Zamalek SC and Sudanese club Al Hilal FC (Omdurman) Vatican creates the Clericus Cup as an international tournament for priests and seminarians to bring the church closer to believers. Militant Turkish soccer fans oppose the demolition of the landmark Muhsin Ertugrul Theatre on Istanbul's Taksim Square. Iraq wins Asian Cup after fifty soccer fans are killed in a Baghdad bombing.

2008   Palestine plays its first ever international match on home ground. Abu Dhabi ruling family acquires Manchester City.

2009   Iranian national soccer team players wear green arm bands in solidarity with the opposition Green Movement. Egyptian President Hosni Mubarak and his sons fan the flames of nationalism after Egypt loses its chance to qualify for the 2010 World Cup, sparking riots on two continents.

17 July 2009   Al Faisali supporters chant slogans denigrating the Palestinian origins of Queen Rania and Crown Prince Hussein bin Al Abdullah during a match against Al Wehdat SC.

October 2009   Hamas organizes the Gaza Dialogue and Tolerance Cup.

2010   Iraqi military says it has arrested a dissident Saudi military officer for being part of an Al-Qaeda plot to attack the World Cup in South Africa. Ramazan Kizil, chairman of Swedish soccer team Dalkurd

FF, sentenced in Turkey in absentia to ten months in prison for giving a speech in his native Kurdish and campaigning on behalf of a pro-Kurdish political party. Kuwait lifts ban on women's soccer; Islamists denounce Kuwaiti national team's first international appearance.

July 2010

Two people are killed and thirty detained during Al-Shabaab raid in Somalia on a home where people had gathered to watch a World Cup match. Al-Shabaab kill seventy people in bombing two cafes in the Ugandan capital of Kampala where people had gathered to watch the 2010 World Cup final. Saudi Arabia's religious police roll out mobile mosques on trucks and prayer mats in front of popular cafés where men gather to watch World Cup games.

November 2010

Riots at a match between Amman arch rivals Al Wehdat SC and Al Faisali SC in which 250 people, including thirty police officers, are injured, highlight widespread discontent in Jordan

2 December 2010

FIFA awards Qatar the right to host the 2022 World Cup. Emergence in Egypt of the Black Bloc—vigilantes reminiscent of soccer hooligans and anarchists in Europe and Latin America, made up of Ultras, leftists and some Islamists who dressed in black T-Shirts emblazoned with a "Fuck the System" slogan and masks. Tunisia suspends soccer matches to prevent stadiums from becoming anti-government rallying points.

2011

Militant soccer fans play a key role in toppling Egyptian President Hosni Mubarak after protests in Tahrir Square. Syrian military uses stadiums in Latakia, Dera'a and Baniyas as mass detention centres in its bid to quash anti-government revolt. Bahrain arrests and/or fires 150 athletes and sports officials, including three national soccer team players, for their alleged participation in anti-government protests. Researchers at Cairo's

Ain Shams University conclude that divorce rates in Egypt are highest in families where the men are avid soccer fans. A Belgian court convicts Tunisian soccer player Nizar Trabelsi for planning an Al-Qaeda attack on NATO headquarters. Israeli–Palestinian Maccabi Haifa striker Mohammed Ghadir challenges Beitar Jerusalem's refusal to hire Palestinian and Muslim players by publicly offering to join the club. FIFA and UEFA pressure persuades Israel to release Palestinian soccer player Mahmoud al-Sarsak from prison after a 92-day hunger strike. Syria targets goalkeeper Abdelbasset Saroot after he emerges as a leader of the anti-Assad uprising in Homs. FIFA bars Syria from competing in the 2014 World Cup after the national team fields an ineligible player in a qualifying match against Tajikistan. Fear of defections prompts Syrian refusal to send athletes to the Arab Games. FIFA disqualifies Iranian women's soccer team and two Jordanian players for wearing a hijab on the pitch. Qatar purchases Paris Saint-Germain FC. International trade unions threaten boycott if Qatar fails to bring workers' living and working conditions in line with international labour standards.

January 2011	Egypt suspends all soccer matches to prevent stadiums being used as anti-government rallying points.
February 2011	Iran suspends Tehran soccer matches to prevent celebrations of the anniversary of the Islamic Republic being marred by protests.
March 2011	Al Faisali supporters chant anti-monarchy slogans after Jordanian nationalists and security forces attack pro-democracy demonstrators in Amman.
May 2011	A commemoration of an Iranian soccer player in Tehran's Azadi stadium turns into a mass protest against the government of Mahmoud Ahmadinejad. FIFA suspends its vice president and Asian Football

Confederation (AFC) president Mohammed Bin Hammam, a Qatari national, on suspicion of bribery; Bin Hammam withdraws his candidacy for the FIFA presidency.

July 2011   Mohammed Bin Hammam banned for life from all soccer-related activities by a five-member panel of the FIFA Ethics committee.

November 2011   Palestinians defy Islamists by publicly supporting their national women's soccer team. Protesters occupy Cairo's Tahrir Square demanding the resignation of the transitional military government. Almost a week of fierce clashes between soccer fans and security forces on nearby Mohammed Mahmoud Street leave more than forty people dead and 1,000 wounded.

2012   Algerian soccer fans demonstrate their disdain for the fate of President Abdelaziz Bouteflika as he recovers from a stroke in a Paris hospital in May 2012 by cheering their team for days in the streets of Algiers in advance of an upcoming championship. The International Olympic Committee (IOC) forces Saudi Arabia, Qatar and Brunei to field their first ever women athletes at an international sports tournament. Unprecedented fan pressure forces Prince Nawaf bin Faisal, a member of the Saudi ruling family, to resign in 2012 as head of the Saudi Football Association. Human Rights Watch accuses Saudi rulers of kowtowing to assertions by the country's powerful conservative Muslim clerics that female sports constitute "steps of the devil" that will encourage immorality and reduce women's chances of meeting requirements for marriage. Saudi government announces plans to allow girls physical education in private schools. Stadiums in Algeria re-emerge as rallying points for anti-government protest. Al-Shabaab targets Somali players, officials including former Somali Olympic Committee vice-president Abdulkader Yahye Sheik Ali and Somali

Football Association president Said Mohamed Nur, and sports journalists. Turkish match-fixing scandal puts Islamist power struggle between Prime Minister Recep Tayyip Erdoğan and cleric Fethullah Gülen centre stage. Israel detains Palestinian soccer players Mohammed Nimr and Omar Abu Roweis on charges of having been involved in a shoot-out with Israeli troops. Syrian soccer player Ahmed al Sheban is killed in Homs in suspicious circumstances. In the spring, the UAE withdraws its ambassador to Tehran after President Mahmoud Ahmadinejad pays a controversial visit to disputed islands close to the Strait of Hormuz. The bad blood leads the UAE to cancel a soccer match against Iran. FIFA lifts ban on Muslim women soccer players wearing a headdress.

February 2012	Seventy-four soccer fans are killed in a politically loaded riot in the Suez Canal city of Port Said; Egyptian soccer matches are suspended indefinitely.
April 2012	Bahrain's Formula 1 race is again overshadowed by anti-government protests.
July 2012	Lausanne-based Court of Arbitration of Sports (CAS) overturns FIFA's life ban on Mohammed Bin Hammam's participation in association soccer.
2013	West Asian Football Federation (WAFF) puts women's soccer on a par with the men's game, legally speaking. Prominent Saudi clerics meet King Abdullah to express opposition to the corruptive effects of women's sports.
January 2013	First verdicts in the Port Said soccer brawl trial spark popular revolt in Suez Canal cities as well as mass protests in Cairo.
April 2013	Bahrain's Formula 1 race overshadowed by anti-government protests.
May 2013	Asian Football Confederation (AFC) elects Bahrain Football President Sheikh Salman Bin Ibrahim Al

	Khalifa as its president. Turkish police tear gas soccer fans approaching Prime Minister Recep Tayyip Erdoğan's Istanbul office.
June 2013	Rival soccer fans unite to spearhead mass anti-government protests on Istanbul's Taksim Square.
July 2013	Twenty members of Istanbul's Beşiktaş JK Çarşı supporters group are indicted on charges of being members of an illegal organization.
August 2013	Turkish governments bans political slogans in stadiums.
November 2013	Al Ahly SC bans prominent striker Ahmed Abd El Zaher for expressing support for outlawed Muslim Brotherhood.
December 2013	Bahrain detains scores of soccer players and athletes.
2013/2014	Soccer fans form the backbone of mass student protests against the regime of Egyptian President Abdel Fattah Al-Sisi.
March 2014	Authorities arrest Al Ahly SC chairman Hassan Hamdi on corruption charges. Egyptian ultras demand withdrawal of security forces from all stadiums.
April 2014	United Nations Special Rapporteur on the human rights of migrants calls on Qatar to abolish *kafala*, its labour sponsorship system. Islamic State uses soccer to recruit foreign fighters.
May 2014	An Egyptian court sentences twelve militant soccer fans to five years in prison on charges of organizing an illegal gathering and vandalism.
June 2014	The World Cup in Brazil sparks debate among Islamists, Salafis and jihadists about the rectitude of the world's most popular sport.
July 2014	Qatar invests in Israeli–Palestinian soccer cubs as Gaza war erupts. The Qatar Foundation calls for radical overhaul of Gulf state's labour recruitment system.
September 2014	International Olympic Committee (IOC) president Thomas Bach acknowledges for the first time that sport and politics are inextricably intertwined.

October 2014	A British court lifts the immunity of Prince Nasser bin Hamad al-Khalifa whom Bahraini human rights groups accuse of being responsible for the arrest of hundreds of sports executives and athletes, including national soccer team players who allege that they were tortured.
January 2015	An Asian Football Confederation executive supports a ban on Iranian women attending soccer matches in stadiums.
February 2015	Twenty soccer fans die in Cairo stampede engineered by Egyptian security forces.
April 2015	Clashes in Ahwaz between soccer fans and security forces highlight mounting resentment against discrimination of Iranians of Arab descent.
May 2015	Bahraini Sheikh Salman Bin Ebrahim Al Khalifa elected president of the Asian Football Confederation (AFC) for a second term and vice president of world soccer body FIFA despite allegations that he was involved in the arrest and torture of soccer players and his quashing of enquiries into corruption in the soccer body. Swiss authorities investigate the integrity of Qatar's 2022 World Cup bid.

INTRODUCTION

Mexico's national soccer team didn't know what to expect when it toured the Middle East and North Africa for the first time in advance of the 1986 World Cup. It was a journey into the unknown for the team, as it was for me. I was not a soccer fan then and am not today. But I was asked to accompany the team by United Press International and Mario Vázquez Raña, the Mexican press baron and then-vice president of his country's Olympic Committee, who was at the time acquiring the financially troubled global news agency.

The tour introduced me to the inextricable intertwining of politics and soccer in the Middle East and North Africa and its key role in the development of the region since the late nineteenth century, even if it took me more than two decades to connect the dots between the tour's various vignettes: an Arc de Triomphe-like entrance to the stadium in the Libyan city of Benghazi dominated by a quote from Moammar Qaddafi, "Sports and weapons belong to the people"; police fighting players and fans on the pitch in Cairo; a stadium bereft of spectators in Sharjah; and an arena in Damascus controlled by the military.

Connecting these dots made me realize that no study, analysis or history of modern society is complete without a focus on the nexus of sport, society, culture, politics and development. The power of this nexus is nowhere more evident than in soccer—the world's most global cultural practice. Players, managers and fans define their shared identity, often in opposition to other groups, through their everyday involvement in soccer and this is especially the case in the Middle East and North Africa.

Soccer figures prominently in the region's life. The pitch is often the indicator of things to come. Militant soccer fans played a key role in the

1

years building up to the toppling of Egyptian President Hosni Mubarak in 2011, the subsequent years of transition and the protests against the regime of Egyptian general-turned-president Abdel Fattah Al-Sisi, as well as in the protests in 2013 against then Turkish Prime Minister Recep Tayyip Erdoğan. Unprecedented criticism of ruling families in Saudi Arabia, Qatar and Jordan occurred within the wider milieu of soccer and ongoing protests against Algeria's military autocrats were held in in the country's stadiums. For years, many in autocratic regimes viewed the weekly match as their sole safety-valve, so much so that disruption of meagre family budgets by expenditure by husbands on tickets for games sparked a sharp increase in the divorce rate in Egypt. Conversely, across the Middle East and North Africa in autocratic nations and countries that have witnessed recent popular revolts, women often see the stadium as an important venue to assert their rights in defiance of conservative clergymen and a traditionally-minded society.

Qatar has led the other Gulf states in spending massively to position itself as a global hub punching above its weight, increasing its diplomatic and economic influence and employing soft power to embed itself in the international community and to enhance its security, branding and access. In doing so, it has challenged the traditional wisdom that a state's ability to project power is at least partly dictated by its size. And Qatar, with a minis-cule population and a resource-dominated economy, is competing to be the region's foremost sports hub alongside Turkey, a nation with strategic depth, a significant population, a highly diversified and developed econ-omy and the region's most modern industrial infrastructure.

"The study of sports, and football in particular, arguably the most popular form of cultural performance in Egypt and the rest of the Middle East, has much to add to our current understanding of the social, political and cultural history of the region," commented the historian Shaun Lopez as he lamented the failure of specialists on the Middle East to write about sports.[1] Lopez argued that the lack of research into sports was all the more stunning given "the seminal importance of football and other sports in the region or the central role athletics plays in the forma-tion of national identity in most Middle Eastern and North African countries."[2] And as soccer has become increasingly popular, it has also become a vehicle for social and political change fuelled by the emergence of sports publications and discussions among fans in the stands and club-houses. Paul Aarts and Francesco Cavatorta have noted that the "real protagonists of the Arab Spring do not come from the usual suspects within established and formal civil society but from sectors of society that have been largely under-explored."[3]

In fact, the influence of politics on, and the political influence of, the region's soccer is so pervasive that it has shaped teams formed in Europe and elsewhere by Middle Eastern and North African immigrant communities. For example, Sweden alone has three professional immigrant teams that are products of Middle East politics.

This book builds on the work of those who have positioned soccer as a pillar of popular culture, and thereby a focal point of politics,[4] a social construct shaped by those involved in the game,[5] and a reflection of how a society models political, philosophical and social issues.[6] Unlike other regions such as Latin America, Africa, Europe and Asia[7] where many scholars and authors have addressed soccer, the Middle East and North Africa has been the subject of only very limited research by a few academics and journalists. There is a long and dramatic history of intersection between sport and politics across the globe—in the boycott by sports people of apartheid South Africa and Nelson Mandela's engagement with rugby to promote post-apartheid racial harmony, for example. Sport's role in challenging sexist, patriarchal and racist attitudes is similarly global. Sporting competitions can be global platforms for peaceful and violent protest as well as the struggle for human, labour and gender rights. Coining the phrase "corporate diplomacy", a shift from traditional inter-state diplomacy to economics-driven diplomacy, sports sociologist Steven J. Jackson argues that sport throughout history has been a vehicle to demonstrate a nation's ideological, political and military superiority, and more recently to drive tourism. "Today, international sport organizations such as the International Olympic Committee (IOC) and Fédération Internationale de Football Association (FIFA) occupy strategic positions as global arbiters between governments, major media corporations and corporate sponsors," Jackson says.[8]

The incestuous relationship between sports and politics is also evident across the Middle East and North Africa. The Formula 1 motor races held in Bahrain in 2012 and 2013 were intended to obscure a fiercely suppressed popular revolt but turned into a public relations disaster as the media focused on mass anti-government demonstrations. Qatar's triumph at winning the 2022 World Cup has been dashed by the worst scandal in soccer history and pressure to bring its restrictive regime for foreign workers in line with international standards after reports of large numbers of deaths during infrastructure construction projects,

The International Olympic Committee (IOC) used the 2012 London Olympics to force three reluctant Muslim nations—Saudi Arabia, Qatar and Brunei—to field women athletes for the first time at a global sporting event. The 2013 election as president of the troubled Asian Football Confederation of a Bahraini soccer executive who refused to condemn the arrest and torture of national soccer team players who took part in anti-government demonstrations highlighted the intimate relationship between sports and politics and the hypocrisy of international sports management.

In 2009 Iranian players wore green bands in solidarity with brutally suppressed pro-opposition protests. The Palestinian Black September Organization made headlines around the world when they kidnapped and killed eleven members of the Israeli team at the 1972 Munich Olympics. And as far back as 1956, Lebanon, Iraq and Egypt boycotted the Melbourne Olympics in protest against the tripartite British-French-Israeli attack on Egypt. The marriage of sport and politics reverberates in derbies in Amman, Tehran, Riyadh and Cairo, home, at least until Mubarak's downfall, to the world's most violent soccer rivalry.

Hisham Sharabi's concept of neo-patriarchy, in which an autocrat projects himself as a father figure who franchises his authority at different levels of society, is a useful way of examining how, in Middle Eastern and North African contexts, the soccer pitch becomes a battlefield.[9] It builds on Michel Foucault's notion that institutions of power turn the public into active participants in their own subjugation, making revolt inconceivable.[10] Neo-patriarchism, and the notion of the leader as the father of a nation, hark back to the Arab struggle for independence in the early twentieth century. Leaders then as now projected themselves as parents obliged to raise their children.[11] Saad Zaghloul, the leader of Egypt's nationalist Wafd party, and a founder of Cairo soccer club Al Ahly SC, a bastion of anti-monarchical republicanism, was his country's "father". His wife Safiyya was Egypt's mother in the years that Saad was exiled by the British. And Saad's club, Al Ahly, was the launch pad for the 1919 revolution sparked by his exile. Three years later Britain was forced to grant Egypt independence.

As in Franco's Spain, where soccer's mass appeal and a lack of cheap alternative entertainment[12] positioned the beautiful game as a lightning rod for dissent, in the Middle East and North Africa soccer has for many years been the only major institution alongside Islam able to offer a public space for dissent. Away from the glare of the international media, soccer has provided a venue to release pent-up anger and frustration and to struggle for political, gender, economic, social, ethnic and national rights. By the time the Arab popular uprisings erupted in December 2010, soccer fans had emerged as a key non-religious, non-governmental institution capable of successfully confronting repressive regimes and militant Islamists:

"In authoritarian regimes with a repressed or largely absent civil society, football has remained one of the few if not the only arena open for exposure of social and political identities, and the football arenas are where political messages are first communicated and struggle with authorities initiated."[13]

In countries where social mobility and economic advancement have depended largely on regime-related nepotism, the soccer pitch has been a rare meritocratic exception in which talent and performance have weighed more heavily. Soccer players, more often than not from lower-class families, become celebrities due to their skill, not because of who their father was. And despite clashes with militant fans, the stadium is also one venue where security forces have often sought to uphold the rules of the game, not bend them in the ruler's favour. It is also the sole space where the public are, at least ostensibly, the judges of performance and the experts on the game. The soccer pitch, Adel Iskandar has written, is "the ultimate meritocracy that defies the omnipresent *wasta* (connections)."[14]

Soccer stadiums became arenas of political agitation and social protest in countries like Algeria[15] and Egypt[16] as repression spread there from popular neighbourhoods. "The sport stadiums were next to register the heat of social discontent. At every match, there were riots and youth demonstrations," wrote Said Chikhi[17] in his description of the protests that swept through Algeria in the late 1980s. Attempts by autocrats to co-opt soccer to improve their tarnished images and deflect attention from unpopular policies have turned the game into a high-stakes political cat-and-mouse contest between fans, despots and Islamists for control of the pitch and a counterbalance to jihadi employment of soccer as a bonding and recruitment tool. All participants in the contest bank on the fact that only soccer can capture a similar deep-seated emotion, passion and commitment evoked by Islam among a majority of the local population.

Soccer fans foreshadow what may be the most fundamental change underlying the popular revolts against autocratic rule in the Middle East and North Africa: a shift in mood from subservience and acceptance to a determination to question and challenge authority, to decide for oneself. This can be true across the political and social spectrum: for liberals interrogating and resisting religious precepts, children questioning their parents, and young Islamists challenging their ideological elders. But the process is volatile and often violent: "These things take time and they are done through conflict, trouble and confrontation and then they unfold."[18]

Militant, highly politicized, violence-prone fans, or "Ultras",[19] are "early risers" who test and expose a state's increased vulnerability to collective challenge.[20] Tunisia, Egypt, Libya, Syria and Algeria have all at one time suspended soccer leagues to prevent the pitch from becoming an opposition rallying point. In doing so, they have followed in the footsteps of Gamal Abdel Nasser, the twentieth century's most prominent Arab leader, who as president of Egypt banned soccer matches and popular music after the disastrous 1967 Six Day War.

Nasser succeeded in averting anti-government protests. His successors did not. The twenty-first century has seen fans play a key role in eroding the climate of fear cultivated by neo-patriarchal autocrats,[21] a barrier internalized and reproduced at virtually every level of society to ensure keep these regimes permanently in power. Years of confrontation with security forces in stadiums turned soccer fans in Egypt, the only civic group apart from the Bedouin of the remote Sinai desert to have consistently confronted the regime, into a major threat to the authorities. That experience in stadiums moulded the fans into an organized, battle-hardened force. Their resistance intensified as labour, neighbourhood and professional groups staged incidental protests of their own.

Taken together, the actions of fans, the Bedouin resistance and the involvement of other groups challenges the notion that the popular revolt in Cairo's Tahrir Square, the city's historic venue for expression of dissent, owed everything to Tunisia's successful overthrow of its autocrat, Zine El Abidine Ben Ali. Theirs was a hard-fought, home-grown, long-in-the-making battle that while it gained momentum from Tunisia's successful toppling of Ben Ali was certainly brewing without it.

The harsh response of Egypt's security forces played a key part in fomenting revolution. Virtually every sector of Egyptian society had felt its hand when on 25 January 2011 demonstrators gathered in Tahrir

Square for an eighteen-day protest that forced Mubarak from office. The Ultras were the first urban group to demonstrate the protesters' ability to change the balance of power. For four years, they had stood their ground, repelling the regime's efforts to control the one public venue where the populace could express dissatisfaction.

Militant soccer fans in the Middle East and North Africa display elements of both the dramaturgical[22] and the grievance[23] models. Dramatic support of clubs with a choreography of banners, slogans, chants, dance, flares and fireworks brought fans into confrontation with security forces, fuelling a sense of abuse and mistreatment that resonated with experiences in their daily lives. Finding strength in numbers, they survived regular confrontations with the security forces and in so doing demonstrated the latter's vulnerability and the limits of the regime's repression—a prerequisite for successful revolts.[24] Their achievement emboldened them to believe that protest could precipitate change, if not the downfall of the regime.

There were other challenges associated with the battles taking place in Egypt's soccer stadiums. The assertion of masculinity associated with the male-dominated pursuit of soccer complicated the fans' struggle first to topple the autocratic figure whose power derived to a large extent from his patriarchal status, and then dismantle the regime he established, which gave the rights of women and minorities short shrift. "The worst and the most damaging form of the persistence of the *ancien régime* is when it persists in the very lives, behaviour, habits and decisions of the revolutionaries themselves," remarked the prominent Syrian intellectual Sadik Al Azm.[25] And yet fan action, despite the internalization of masculine values, challenged gender prejudice in asserting women's rights to play soccer despite legal restrictions, social pressure and religious dress codes. And it was a cornerstone of efforts by the stateless—Palestinians and Kurds, for example—to obtain a state of their own, or by minorities like the Berbers, Iranian Azeris and Israeli Palestinians to assert their identity.

George Orwell described sport as "war minus the shooting."[26] In the spirit of Orwell, I aim to take the reader on a journey into the colourful, hair-raising, little-known world of the region's soccer. It's a journey from Afghanistan to Algeria; from the Palestinian–Israeli conflict to soccer stadiums in Afghanistan and Iraq littered with bodies; from the sectarian strife that forced Lebanese squads to play in empty stadiums and deprived Iraq's victorious, multi-ethnic, post-Saddam team of a place in the World Cup, to Europe's failed integration of Muslim immigrants and the related self-destruction of the French national team during the 2010 World Cup. Soccer's unique vantage point brings to life the aspirations and divisions of a turbulent and volatile region.

The Middle East and North Africa, despite their turbulence, form a soccer powerhouse. Arab nations have won eleven of twenty-seven African Cup tournaments and boast twelve of the continent's top twenty clubs, seven of the eighteen most successful Asian national teams, ten of Asia's top soccer players in the last twenty years and twelve of its top twenty-four clubs. Iraq proved the region's potential by winning the Asian Cup in 2007, a year in which the country witnessed some of its worst sectarian violence. Egypt won the African cup for an unprecedented third time in a row in 2010. Meanwhile Qataris are grooming the next generation of soccer stars by offering world-class training to the three best youth players to emerge each year from a competition it sponsors among 500,000 promising kids in Africa, Asia and Latin America. The Gulf states, like other resource-rich Middle Eastern nations, are buying high profile European, African and Latin American players and coaches to beef up their national teams while sheikhs are acquiring European premier league teams.

Although Qatar won the right to host the 2022 World Cup, at the time of writing their successful bid is the subject of American and Swiss investigations into corruption in the Fédération Internationale de Football Association (FIFA), the body that governs association soccer. These investigations include credible assertions that Qatar won its World Cup bid through a combination of massive vote-buying and backroom political and commercial deals.[27] Qatar's woes serve notice to the region's regimes of the risk of murky, international deal-making and abuse of human rights as governments try to project themselves on the international stage. Qatar's migrant labour regime has been subjected to widespread criticism by human rights and trade union activists as well as FIFA, its corporate sponsors, soccer players and fans, while the United Arab Emirates was already in the firing line for similar shortcomings in its treatment of foreign workers.[28]

Assuming Qatar retains the right to host the 2022 World Cup, the tournament might encourage the national teams of the MENA region to strive to ensure that they are well represented in the competition. Such a feat will take more than skill and endurance on the part of the players involved. Soccer is part and parcel of the Middle East's unruly and often bloody struggle between revolution and counterrevolution, sectarianism, the redrawing of its political geography, the rise of jihadism, and stalled transitions away from autocracy to greater democracy. In Egypt professional soccer has been either suspended or closed to the public since the popular revolt that ousted President Hosni Mubarak in 2011. More than one hundred fans have died in politically motivated soccer riots and anti-government protests. Militant soccer fans, or "Ultras", have been banned as terrorist organizations. Prominent soccer figures have been targeted on charges that they supported the outlawed Muslim Brotherhood. The Syrian national team's players continue to compete internationally, afraid that the regime would retaliate against their families if they defect. Jihadists in Iraq, Syria, Somalia and Nigeria target stadiums, players and sports journalists. The 2022 World Cup is still years away, but so are the prospects of greater security and stability in the Middle East and North Africa.

BEARING THE SCARS OF BATTLE

"Military police, you are dogs like the Interior Ministry. Write it on the prison's walls: down, down with military rule."

Egyptian Ultras' chant

In the Middle East and North Africa stadiums serve as the arenas for political and social battle. They bear the scars of such encounters and memorialise the brutality employed to suppress expressions of dissent or punish players' failure to perform. And they stand as monuments to challenges, sporadic or sustained, to regime attempts to control all public space. The very nature of the stadium—an enclosed space that holds a large number of spectators—shaped the way militant fans expressed support for their team and, by claiming title to the venue, challenged the authority of authoritarian regimes.[1] That claim offered those who felt marginalized or excluded from society a sense of ownership.[2]

Dingxin Zhao[3] employed Sewell's theory of the impact of a built environment on contentious politics[4] to argue that the ecology of a particular venue, along with organization and networking, strengthens bonds within a group, in this case referring to student mobilization during the 1989 protests on Beijing's Tiananmen Square as well as to popular protest during the French revolution. That ecology—defined as the impact of a venue's architecture and layout on those who visit it, as well as on spatial distribution and activities that shape human interaction through passive encounters and active networking—can produce an environment that sustains a high rate of participation. It also facilitates what Sewell describes as "the formation of many ecology-dependent strategies" that shape a group's dynamics.[5]

Zhao focuses primarily on the ecology of university campuses. His argument builds on scattered references in social movement theory to the impact of infrastructure on mobilization by student groups in the United States,[6] Russia,[7] and China[8] as well as riots in densely populated urban American ghettos in the 1960s. To Zhao the impact on mobilization on the ecology of infrastructure is more significant than the response of governments to defeat protest movements. He was doubtless influenced by the fact that the authorities refrained from entering the walled campuses of Beijing's universities to prevent further alienation of already restless students. In Zhao's example, Chinese security forces initially adopted an approach that was part of a soft strategy which involved public denunciation of the protesters. This backfired in that it encouraged rather than dissuaded the student activists, after which the Chinese reverted to hard-headed obstruction and repression of dissent and protest.

Absolute control of stadiums was crucial for Middle Eastern and North African rulers. It was there that the ruler shared with the public the kind of deep-seated passion that was paralleled only by religion. That moment of unification was broadcast on television and magnified in state-run media. It was a tool to polish an image often tarnished by regimes' inability to solve nations' economic and social problems and by their repressive nature. Soccer was important, said state-owned *Al-Ahram Weekly Online*, because it is "one of the threads that comprises the social fabric of Egyptian culture."[9] Hassan Khater, a member of the Muslim Brotherhood, lamented that Israel would not have dared annex and populate predominantly Palestinian East Jerusalem if Arabs were as passionate about the fate of the Al-Aqsa Mosque, Islam's third most holy shrine, as they were about the beautiful game.[10]

Demonstrative punishment of players who failed to perform was another feature of the autocrats' association with soccer. A poor performance on the pitch deprived the ruler and his offspring of an opportunity. Thus Uday Hussein, the son of Saddam Hussein, showered expensive gifts on the Iraqi team when they won, but humiliated and tortured players for a missed penalty or an errant pass. Former Iraqi national soccer team coach Ahmed-Rahim Hamed recalls generous rewards in the form of real estate, cars and cash as well as punishments that included electrocution, being forced to play barefoot with a concrete ball in 130°F (55°C)[11] heat or having their heads publicly shaved in Baghdad's Stadium of the People[12] when the team failed to qualify for a World Cup. A striker in the Iraqi national team that competed in the 1986 World Cup in Mexico, Hamed admired former English coach Kevin Keegan. "I had a perm like him. After one game, Uday shaved everybody's hair. That's when I lost my perm," he recalls. Soccer legend and former Iraqi goalkeeper Hashim Hassan describes being forced to lie with his whole team on the stadium's grass where they were beaten by Uday's goons on their feet and backs with sticks before being imprisoned for a week because they lost a 1997 World Cup qualifier against Kazakhstan.[13] Only in 1993 did Uday allow Iraqi players to play for foreign teams and only if he could collect a percentage of their salaries. Players going abroad were warned that their families would pay with their lives if they failed to live up to their obligations.

One of the first moves of the Coalition Provisional Authority (CPA) that governed Iraq after the US invasion was to dissolve the Iraqi National Olympic Committee (INOC) as part of its de-Baathification program—a bid to loosen the grip of the former regime's supporters on the country's sport and a recognition of the role the US hoped that sport would play in the country's transition to democracy. The CPA prioritized the construction and rehabilitation of soccer stadiums and clubs. In 2005, it allocated 22.4 billion Iraqi dinars (approximately US$16 million) to sports, and 93.2 billion dinars (US$64 million) in 2006. US General David Petraeus, the commander of allied forces in Iraq, repeatedly pointed to the proliferation of makeshift soccer fields on which boys and men would play in the evening when the searing heat cooled off as a mark of how the country had changed. US troops packed soccer balls into their Humvees to hand out to kids in the days before anti-American and sectarian violence forced them to restrict their movements. "Soccer stars are more highly regarded than government leaders. That's why sporting events are so important. It will bring this society back to life," said Donald Eberly, a former deputy director of the White House's Faith-Based and Community Initiatives who served as a senior advisor to the Iraqi youth and sport ministry in the wake of the dissolution of the INOC.[14] Eberly and other coalition officials also saw soccer and sports as a way of thwarting efforts by militant Islamic groups and criminal gangs to recruit idle youth. "If they are not at school or playing sports they will be targeted by terrorist organisations, religious fundamentalists or other criminals," warned the former Scottish rugby player and lawyer Mark Clark who supervised the rebuilding of sports infrastructure on behalf of the CPA until 2008.[15]

Colonel Qaddafi's son, Al Saadi, who took command in 2004 of a key unit of the Libyan armed forces that played a crucial role in his father's fight for survival in 2011, made soccer an arena of confrontation between supporters and opponents of the regime long before Libyans rose up to topple it. The colonel set the stage by adorning the country's stadiums with quotes from his Green Book[16] that explained his idiosyncratic theories of democracy, including the notion that weapons and sports belong to the people, and derided fandom.

Qaddafi wrote that:

as the era of the masses does away with the instruments monopolizing power, wealth and arms, it will, inevitably, destroy the monopoly of social activity in such areas as sports, horsemanship, and so forth... Public sport is for all the masses. It is right of all people for their health and recreational benefit. It is mere stupidity to leave its benefits to certain individuals and teams who monopolize these while the masses provide the facilities and pay the expenses for the establishment of public sports. The thousands who crowd stadiums to view, applaud and laugh are foolish people who have failed to carry out the activity themselves. They line up lethargically in the stands of the sports grounds, and applaud those heroes who wrest from them the initiative, dominate the field and control the sport and, in so doing, exploit the facilities that the masses provide. Originally, the public grandstands were designed to demarcate the masses from the playing fields and grounds; to prevent the masses from having access to the playing fields. When the masses march and play sport in the centre of playing fields and open spaces, stadiums will be vacant and become redundant. This will take place when the masses become aware of the fact; that sport is a public activity which must be practised rather than watched.

Al Saadi, "notoriously ill-behaved," according to a 2009 US diplomatic cable,[17] cruelly applied his father's logic. Interpol had a red notice arrest warrant out for him "for allegedly misappropriating properties through force and armed intimidation when he headed the Libyan Football Federation." Al Saadi was extradited from Niger to Libya where he is on trial for the murder of national team player and coach Bashir Al-Ryani. A prominent Qaddafi critic, Al-Ryani was tortured and killed in 2005. "Two years before he was killed he told Saadi he was part of a dictatorship and had corrupted Libya. After that he was beaten and left outside his house," according to Dr Hussein Rammali, a former teammate of Al-Ryani. Rammali said Al-Ryani's family had last seen him four days before the player's body was delivered to their home at a seaside villa belonging to Al Saadi.[18]

A pile of rubble in Benghazi, symbolizing the Libyan leader's tense relations with the city, stood as a memorial to the price the city's soccer club played for being a platform of dissent. The ruins were what remained of the headquarters of the Al Ahly Benghazi soccer club, a testimony to an extraordinary show of resistance. Al Ahly's battle with the Qaddafis goes a long way towards explaining why Benghazi emerged as the fulcrum of the revolt against them. It is also the story of Al Saadi, who headed the Libyan soccer federation, and the horrific manner in which he exacted revenge for Al Ahly's expressions of dissent.

Al Saadi's efforts to bury the historic club were thorough, to say the least. Its red and white colours were banned from public display. Scores of its supporters were imprisoned, some of whom were sentenced to death for attempting to subvert the Qaddafis' rule. It was a heavy price to pay for challenging the ruling family in a country in which sports broadcasters were forbidden to identify players by name to ensure that they did not become more popular than their rulers. Al Ahly was particularly vulnerable because its Tripoli namesake was owned and managed by Al Saadi who also captained the team and was referred to as 'player number one.' Libyans recall opposing defenders peeling away whenever Al Saadi approached his opponent's goal with the ball in his possession.

Soccer in Libya was as much a political match as it was a sports competition in which politics rather than performance often dictated the outcome. For Al Saadi, it was also personal. His prestige, and with it that of the regime, were on the line whenever Al Ahly Tripoli laced up their boots. Al Saadi made sure the team blossomed by enabling it to buy the best players and bribe and bully referees and linesmen to rule in its favour.

At the turn of century, Al Ahly Benghazi fans had enough. They booed him and his team during a national cup final in front of visiting African dignitaries and dressed up a donkey in the colours of Al Ahly Tripoli. Al Saadi went ballistic. "I will destroy your club! I will turn it into an owl's nest!" the *Los Angeles Times* quoted Khalifa Binsraiti, Al Ahly Benghazi's then chairman, who was imprisoned in the ensuing crackdown, as being told by an irate Al Saadi immediately after the match.

A penalty in a subsequent Al Ahly Benghazi match against a team from Al-Baydah, the home town of Al Saadi's mother and the place where the first anti-government demonstrations were staged in 2011, again so outraged Benghazi fans that they invaded the pitch, forcing the match to be abandoned. Things came to a head when Al Saadi sought to engineer Al Ahly Benghazi's relegation to the second division by instructing a referee in a match against Libyan premier league team Al Akhdar to call a questionable penalty. Al Ahly's coach confronted the referee, allegedly shoving him. Militant fans stormed the pitch. The game was suspended and Al Ahly's fate was sealed.

Al Ahly Benghazi fans didn't leave it at that. They headed to downtown Benghazi shouting slogans against Al Saadi, burnt a likeness of his father and set fire to the local branch of his national soccer federation. "I was ready to die that day, I was so frustrated," the *Los Angeles Times* quotes 48-year-old businessman Ali Ali, who was among the enraged crowd, as saying. "We were all ready to die."

It did not take long for Libyan security men to respond. Al Ahly's 37-hectare clubhouse and facilities were razed to the ground as plain-clothesmen visited the homes of protesting soccer fans. Some eighty were arrested; thirty of them were brought to Tripoli to stand trial on charges of vandalism, destruction of public property and having contacts with Libyan dissidents abroad, a capital offence in Libya. Three people were sentenced to death, but their penalties were commuted to life in prison by the Libyan ruler. They were ultimately released after serving five years in jail. Public outrage over the retaliation against Benghazi forced Al Saadi to resign as head of the soccer federation, only to be reinstated by his father in response to the federation's alleged claim that it needed him as its leader.

The dreadful murder of Al Ahly precipitated Al Saadi's inglorious attempts at making it in Italian soccer. He signed up with the Maltese team Birkirkara, but never showed up. Three years later, he resigned from the board of storied club Juventus in which Libya had a 7.5 per cent stake to join Italy's AC Perugia but was suspended after only one game for failing a drug test. The incident earned him the reputation of being the Italian Serie A's worst ever player. In a statement, Perugia owner Luciano Gaucci said that "[Italian Prime Minister Silvio] Berlusconi called me up and encouraged me. He told me that having Qaddafi in the team is helping us build a relationship with Libya. If he plays badly, he plays badly. So be it."

Al Saadi's dismal record did not stop him from enlisting in 2005 with Italy's Udinese, where he was relegated to the role of bench warmer except for a ten-minute appearance in an unimportant late-season fix-ture. Riccardo Garrone, the president of Sampdoria and head of the oil company Erg, subsequently invited Al Saadi to train with his team in the hope that it would open the door to Libyan oil contracts. Libyans joke that Al Saadi was the only soccer player who paid to play rather than was paid to play.

Middle Eastern and North African autocrats have often used stadiums as mass detention centres and killing fields when their regimes are threat-ened. In the first year of the armed rebellion against Syrian President Bashar al-Assad in 2011, the security forces herded anti-government protesters into stadiums in Latakia, Dera'a and Baniyas.[19] Their use evoked memories of the government's 1982 assault on Hama when it crushed an uprising by the Muslim Brotherhood in which at least 10,000 people were killed. A 1983 Amnesty International report charged that the city's stadium was used to detain large numbers of residents who were left for days in the open without food or shelter.[20] Islamist rebels fighting the Assad regime were three decades later ensconced in the stadium of Raqqa, the Syrian capital of the jihadist Islamic State, from where they ran the municipality. On any given day, armed rebels would watch over residents waiting to resolve rent disputes or legalize marriage contracts in a waiting room with a tactical board for a forthcoming match.[21] Similarly, the stadium in the northern Lebanese city of Tripoli, once the finest in the country's soccer infrastructure, is a shadow of itself since the Lebanese army used it as a staging ground against Islamists located within a Palestinian refugee camp.

US and Iraqi forces discovered mass graves in several Iraqi stadiums after the overthrow of Saddam. In Afghanistan, shortly after their 2001 overthrow of the Taliban, US-led international forces played soccer against an Afghan team in Kabul's Ghazi Stadium to highlight the change they were bringing to the war-ravaged country. The stadium had been used by the Taliban for public executions, stonings and amputa-tions. Afghans believe it is still haunted by the dead and are often afraid of entering the stadium after dark. Even the night watchmen limited for years their patrols to the stadium's perimeter.[22]

Memories of the punishments meted out in the stadium are never far beneath the surface. Afghan filmmaker Sedigh Barmak remembers not only those who lost their lives at the hands of the Taliban but also the 2,500 films they burnt in the stadium. Zaidullah, an Afghan journalist, pointed during festivities for the reopening of Ghazi Stadium after it was refurbished with US funding, to a corner in the pitch's penalty area where "there was a thief who stole something from his village … they cut his hand, right here. A man and a woman were having illegal sexual relations. They were caught, brought here, given 100 lashes each and told to marry each other … I also saw people beheaded and shot. Afghans will never forget these bad memories."[23]

In an interview with Agence France Presse, Daud, a driver, remembered the execution in 1999 of Zarmeena, a woman accused of killing her husband. Dressed in a blue burqa, she was made to kneel on the pitch. "The Taliban got the Kalashnikov, put it behind her head and shot her two times. She fell down on the ground. The crowd went very quiet. It was a strange and dangerous atmosphere. People were shocked and scared. Sometimes I remember that woman, I even dream about it," he said.[24]

Christian militiamen responsible for the 1982 massacres in the Beirut Palestinian refugee camps of Sabra and Shatila, to which Israeli invasion forces turned a blind eye, converted a local soccer pitch into a staging ground. Somali jihadists once used the capital of Mogadishu's stadium— one of East Africa's most impressive, crammed with 70,000 passionate fans during games—as an Islamist training and recruitment centre.

Yet, the same stadiums that bear the scars of abuse also served to celebrate soccer's popularity and successes in their bid to benefit from the passion evoked by the sport and the political opportunities it created.

Ali Abdullah Saleh, the toppled Yemeni leader, highlighted soccer's importance for autocrats by meeting his country's national youth team barely 36 hours after returning in 2012 to Sana'a from almost four months of medical treatment in Saudi Arabia, further to a failed assassination attempt against him. Algerian President Abdelaziz Bouteflika's National Liberation Front populates its Facebook page with soccer news rather than the party's proposals to solve the country's mushrooming social and political problems.

President Mubarak would congratulate players and place medallions around their necks after each of Egypt's triumphs in the African Cup of Nations. In doing so, the team's victories became an expression of the success of his nationalist leadership, which he used to counter the growing popularity of the Muslim Brotherhood, the country's main Islamist opposition. Mubarak's effort peaked in 2009 when he and his sons fanned the flames of nationalism after Egypt lost its chance to qualify for the 2010 World Cup in South Africa. The nationalist fervour they whipped up brought the world to the brink of a soccer-inspired conflict for the first time since the 1969 'Soccer War' between Honduras and El Salvador,[25] with violent clashes erupting between Egyptian and Algerian fans on three continents.[26] It was a dispute that exploited the two countries' soccer rivalry to distract attention from mounting domestic discontent and enhance Mubarak's prestige as a nationalist leader. It also constituted a battle about which country had the historic and cultural credentials to represent the Arab world on the global pitch: Egypt, the Arab world's most populous nation and traditional leader, or Algeria wearing a revolutionary badge earned in its horrendous war of independence against France.

Egypt recalled its ambassador to Algeria while Algeria slapped then Egyptian-owned Orascom Telecom's Algerian operation with a tax bill of more than US$500 million. Libyan leader Qaddafi intervened to prevent the dispute from escalating. Algiers was draped in the colours and flag of its national team, while traffic turned into a choir of honking cars whose passengers cheered their country and its soccer squad. Soap operas from Egypt, the region's Bollywood, were boycotted. Advertisements for Egypt Air and Djezzy, the Orascom-owned telecoms operator that sponsored major Algerian soccer clubs, were torn down. Material damage to businesses was estimated at US$64 million. The Egyptian international striker Amr Zaki refused to move to English Premier League team Portsmouth, owned at the time by Saudi businessman Ali al-Faraj and UAE real estate investor Sulaiman Al-Fahim, because there was "no way I could play for Portsmouth with an Algerian in their ranks," a reference to Portsmouth defender Nadir Belhadj, an Algerian national.[27] "The violence expressed years of depression of a population that constantly witnesses social, financial and political failure. Soccer is their only ray of light," remarked Ahmed Al Aqabawi, a psychology professor at Al Azhar University, the world's most prestigious institution of Muslim learning, and a member of Egypt's Muslim Brotherhood.[28]

For a brief moment, frustrated and humiliated Egyptians forgot Arab and Muslim solidarity and their hatred of US support for Israel and Mubarak's regime when they cheered the American infidels in their 2010 World Cup match against Algeria. Yet Egyptians and Algerians, despite their longstanding soccer rivalry, were ultimately angry about the same issues: they resented their lack of freedom and economic prospects and despised the omnipresent security services that kept their power-hungry, long-serving presidents in office.

Government support of soccer and political management of stadiums were designed to control the game. The post-Mubarak Egyptian strongman General Abdel Fattah Al-Sisi, head of the armed forces, who in July 2013 toppled the country's first democratically elected president, Mohammed Morsi, commemorated the restoration of Egyptian military pride in Cairo's military-owned Air Defence Stadium. Celebrities and pop singers lavished praise on the military in a televised extravaganza complete with dancers and an elaborate fireworks display. At least fifty-one anti-military protesters were killed as artists pumped up pro-military, nationalist fervour in the stadium and a procession on Tahrir Square. "Watch out, this isn't any Egypt. This is Egypt the victorious, the Egypt we carry in our hearts and minds," crooned the Lebanese pop star and sex symbol Nancy Ajram, performing together with dancers wearing Egypt's state seal on their chests. Lyrics echoing statements by Al-Sisi such as "Egypt is the mother of the world and is destined to be as big as the entire world" were lit in flames in a section of the stadium.

In Tunisia, the post-revolt sports minister, Tarak Dhiab, a former soccer player, charged that Slim Chiboub, the son-in-law of toppled Tunisian President Zine El Abidine Ben Ali, together with the security forces, had controlled sports, incited violence in stadiums and corrupted competitions.[29] In soccer-crazy Egypt about half of the Premier League's sixteen teams are owned by the military, the police, government ministries or provincial authorities. Military-owned construction companies built twenty-two of Egypt's soccer stadiums. They were exploiting what journalist Mohamed El-Sayed called Egyptians' instant love affair with soccer that started in 1882 when they first saw British troops play what seemed initially an odd game.[30] Similarly, Iran's Revolutionary Guards have in recent years taken control of a number of prominent soccer teams. In the time of the late King Hassan II, Moroccan federations and clubs were long presided over by either members of the royal family or senior military officers. In the Gulf, soccer association and club boards are populated by royals. The Syrian military and police own and operate two of the country's most important teams with Al Jaish [The Army], long virtually synonymous with the country's national team, and Al Shurta [The Police]. Al Jaish's senior executives are military officers, its training ground an off-limits military zone.

Nonetheless, the popular revolts that swept the Middle East and North Africa challenged the notion of autocratic control. Saudi Arabia's circling of the wagons as part of its effort to insulate itself from the wave of change failed when it came to soccer. The game has emerged as one focal point of dissent alongside minority Shiite Muslims and relatives of imprisoned government critics. Unprecedented fan pressure forced Prince Nawaf bin Faisal, a member of the ruling family, to resign in 2012 as head of the Saudi Arabian Football Association following Australia's defeat of the Kingdom in a 2014 World Cup qualifier.[31] Nawaf was succeeded for the first time by a commoner, Ahmed Eid Saad Alharbi, a lanky former Saudi soccer midfielder and proponent of women's soccer, who won the association's first ever election.

Nawaf's resignation broke the mould in a nation governed as an absolute monarchy. It also marked the first time that a member of a ruling elite in the region saw association with a national team's failure as a risk to be avoided rather than one best dealt with by firing the coach or, as in extreme cases like Saddam Hussein's Iraq or Moammar Qaddafi's Libya, brutally punishing players.

Nawaf's resignation was followed by a Facebook page entitled Nasrawi Revolution demanding the resignation of Prince Faisal bin Turki, the owner of renowned Riyadh club Al Nasser FC and a burly nephew of King Abdullah who sports a moustache and beard. A YouTube video captured Faisal seemingly being pelted and chanted against as he rushed off the soccer pitch after rudely shoving a security official aside. The resignation of Nawaf and the campaign against Faisal gained added significance in a nation in which the results of Premier League clubs associated with various members of the kingdom's secretive royal family are seen as a barometer of their relative status, particularly at a time that its septuagenarian and octogenarian leaders were preparing for a gradual generational transition. The demand that Prince Faisal step down was in part a protest against princes who micromanage clubs as their personal playgrounds, often phoning mid-game their team's coaches with instructions on which players to replace.

In another incident, fans and an official of Riyadh's Al Hilal SC tweeted and chanted racist remarks against players of Al Ittihad SC of Jeddah, which has a number of dark-skinned Saudi players. "The last match between Al-Hilal and Al-Ittihad clearly revealed the indecency of Al-Ittihad players through two movements—one from 'the monkey' Fahd

Al-Muwallad who did not stop proceeding when Muhammad Al-Qarni was injured in a jostle with him. Secondly, [they] did not fulfil the commitment to Majed Al-Murshidi, and did not greet or thank him," Saud Al-Sahli, assistant director of public relations and announcer at King Fahd International Stadium in Riyadh, commented on Twitter. Al Hilal fans chanted "Nigger, Nigger" during the match. Al-Muwallad and Al-Qarni are both dark-skinned.

Saudi newspapers warned that racist incidents threaten to rekindle religious sectarianism, tribalism and regionalism in the kingdom, in part a reference to Shiite Muslim protests in the oil-rich Eastern Province. "The racist and sectarian utterances of sports fans should not be punished by fines alone, as some heads of the sports clubs are immensely rich and can pay the fines against their fans without feeling any burden. There should be harsher punishments, including a ban on the fans from entering the stadiums, reducing the club's league points or even downgrading it to a lower division," stated the *Saudi Gazette* in an editorial.

Mounting dissent on the soccer pitch has prompted Saudi authorities, already concerned about growing discontent in the kingdom, to seek advice on how to deal with fans. Summing up the mood among fans and many other Saudis, a Saudi journalist said: "Everything is upside down. Revolution is possible. There is change, but it is slow. It has to be fast. Nobody knows what will happen."

"The Saudis are extremely worried. Soccer clubs rather than the mosque are likely to be the centre of the revolution," added Washington-based Saudi dissident Ali al-Ahmad, who heads the Gulf Institute. "Kids go more to stadiums than to mosques. They are not religious, they are ruled by religious dogma." Al-Ahmad was referring to the power of clerics preaching Wahhabism, the puritan interpretation of Islam developed by the eighteenth-century preacher Mohammed ibn Abdul Wahhab. Saudi Arabia's ruling Al Saud family established the kingdom with the help of the Wahhabis who in return were granted the right to ensure that their views would dominate public life.

Sources in the Kingdom claimed that the authorities were seeking to reduce soccer's popularity by emphasizing other sports such as athletics and handball in policy and fundraising while at the same time preparing to professionalize and further commercialize the sport using the English Premier League as a model. "They are identifying what talent is available in the kingdom. Football is a participatory sport. They want to emphasize the social aspects of other sports. Football won only one medal in the last Asian Games. They think they can score better in other sports. There are parallel agendas with competition about who gets the visibility," said one source.

2

THE BATTLE FOR GREATER FREEDOM

"When we came, football was full of lies and deception: it was a distraction, and a mask for the authority. They try to polish it and make it the country's preoccupation: they forgot the stadium, filled with thousands. Kill the idea continuously. Injustice is everywhere. I will never forget your past, you were the regime's slave."

Egyptian Ultras' chant

Scoring Political Goals

In many ways, the political struggle on the pitch mirrored the essence of soccer: control of as much of the opponent's territory as possible. The battle between autocrats and fans was steeped in a history of soccer that much like cricket made it highly political from the day British officials, soldiers, businessmen and sailors—arguably modern history's greatest promoters of Western sports[1]—introduced it[2] as a tool to co-opt local elites. As a result, many clubs in the Middle East and North Africa associate their founding with politics. The struggle between autocrats and fans positioned soccer and stadiums, in the words of French sociologist Christoph Bromberger, as "powerful catalysts for protest, by awakening rather than anaesthetizing political consciousness."[3]

Much of what Sewell and Zhao identified as the impact of the ecology of a venue is also applicable to stadiums and militant soccer fans and stadiums in the Middle East and North Africa. As on campus, the stadium "facilitated the spread of dissident ideas before the movement and

25

the transmission of news."[4] It nurtured networks that constituted "the basis of mutual influence, even coercion, among students and, therefore, sustained a high rate of ... participation. It shaped students' spatial activities" that "became centres of ... mobilization" and "facilitated the formation of many ecology-dependent strategies of collective action. Those actions patterned the dynamics of the movement."[5]

The experience of the protests in 2010 and 2011 in Tunisia and Egypt also highlighted a factor that was even more important than the ecology of a venue: how a regime responds to the challenges of protestors, especially as regards law enforcement, is more likely to determine how and whether a game-changing confrontation unfolds. In Tunisia, it was the humiliation of a fruit vendor by an individual police officer in late 2010 that went viral and sparked mass demonstrations that toppled President Zine El Abidine Ben Ali; in Brazil and Turkey heavy-handed police tactics turned small demonstrations into nationwide mass protests that altered the political landscape.

Repression is impossible to avoid in most Middle Eastern and North African autocracies and stadiums were public spaces that these regimes were not prepared to surrender. Confrontation between security forces and fans claiming that space as their own was inevitable, and repeated encounters prepared militants for eventual clashes in less contained venues such as Cairo's Tahrir Square. The militants perceived themselves as the shock troops and defence force of a broader protest movement as opposed to the Beijing students who saw going to Tiananmen Square as "a common pastime and a fun activity."[6]

The experience of the Ultras in the Middle East and North Africa raises the question of what comes first, the chicken or the egg. Arguably, mobilization in the case of the Ultras was driven by a passion for soccer and a belief that as the only truly altruistic supporters of the club they were entitled to claim ownership of a stadium. The stadium itself provided the opportunity rather than the driver for mobilization: it was a ready-made, relevant space with an appropriate audience that potentially would demonstrate support for a club irrespective of whether that entailed a clash with the authorities. Ultimately, however, it was the nature and routine of the game, depth of passion and self-definition of fans that dictated how such public spaces were contested. As a result, the Ultras hark back to social movement concepts[7] that emphasize formal and informal ties facilitating communication and solidarity. In doing so, they challenge the universality of Zhao's notion that ecology plays a key role in social movement mobilization in autocratic regimes that repress freedom of association.

Similarly, the Ultras offer a different perspective on Sewell and Zhao's argument that venues influence patterns and intensity of mobilization. Soccer's popularity in the Middle East and North Africa meant that it populated multiple aspects of people's lives. Its impact was magnified by the importance regimes attributed to the game and the fact that it affected households and domestic life.

A 2011 study[8] by Hamdi Abdul Azeem and Mona el-Sayyed Hafez, concluding that divorce rates in Egypt are highest in families where the men are avid soccer fans suggests, however, that at least in certain circumstances social factors rather than space are key vectors. The study found that the more husbands watched soccer matches, particularly within recently married couples where the wife has no interest in the sport, the more likely it was that they would ultimately break up. Azeem asserted that the highest risk for divorce was in families "in which the wife does not like football and the man engages in watching soccer matches and following up news of soccer players on a daily basis" and may be part of an activist support group. Implicitly, the study spoke to the gendering of the stadium that was populated primarily by men whose passion for the game cut across social classes.

Azeem's co-author reinforced the point by quoting Um Mohamed, a Cairo mother of two, that her husband had divorced her after she had refused to let him watch Al Ahly play. "Watching football matches led to daily arguments between me and my husband, who finally divorced me," she said, adding that the couple had quarrelled for four years because she had not supported his soccer team and did not enjoy watching matches. Her husband had insulted her and had become physically abusive. The abuse was worst when Al Ahly lost a match. Hafez noted that divorce rates tended to spike during the Premier League season: "The divorce rate [in Egypt] is still higher than in most other Arab countries particularly during the soccer league season." She observed that emotions were heightened during the season and soccer-addicted husbands were in need of psychological help, which they seldom sought. "Such excessive love for football by husbands brings about a state of panic to the whole household where the wife suffers from the pain of divorce."

The study concluded that husbands' expenditure on soccer paraphernalia and match tickets was a major irritant in marriages where husband

and wife failed to share the same passion for soccer. "Such expenditures tighten the budget of families to the point that they are barely able to meet their basic needs, and therefore leaving no money for recreation. In addition, a man and his wife need to communicate in order to stay strong, but unfortunately soccer-instigated tension means that spousal violence is getting the better of people," Azeem wrote. He said that husbands tended to cancel summer vacations to be able to watch matches and afford tickets in a bid to escape their economic, marital and personal problems. "It is a reality today that millions of husbands have no choice but to stay home, seeking entertainment from watching soccer matches. In doing so, families barely talk to each other anymore and their feelings are always tense," he wrote.

Stadiums in the Middle East and North Africa, like university campuses in Beijing, have a layout that simplifies mobilization. Yet, if the latter facilitated the transmission of dissident ideas by sparking the emergence of multiple small dormitory-based student networks, which sustained a high level of student participation and encouraged inter-university competition for activism, stadiums in the former offered protesters bound by a virtually all-consuming passion for the game strength in numbers. This was because security forces could not detain thousands of supporters and the matches were often broadcast live, risking the regime's repression being put on public display. In contrast to Beijing, rivalry between Middle Eastern and North African soccer groups increased mutual animosity that was only overcome once protests spilled beyond the stadiums.

Beyond at times temporarily burnishing their image, soccer allowed autocrats to divert attention from simmering social discontent. "We play to forget our sorrow," complained Nobel Prize-winning novelist and soccer fan Naguib Mahfouz to fellow author Gamal al-Ghitani after Egypt bagged yet another African championship.[9] It also enabled autocrats to employ sports as a policy tool while controlling the "fun" element. More progressive forces, including leaders of post-colonial revolutionary regimes, invoked Islamic concepts of a Muslim's obligation to engage in physical exercise in order to introduce sports to conservative segments of society as a means of regimenting rather than liberating it.

The autocrats' identification through patronage and micromanagement with soccer emulated the use of games and sports by Roman emperors to solidify their power.[10] Arab autocrats, however, unlike their Roman predecessors, were determined to prevent soccer clubs from becoming arbiters of political power. The Greens and the Blues and their fans in fifth-century AD games were the Roman predecessors of today's Middle Eastern and North African soccer fans who expressed similarly deep-seated passions. In Rome, a new ruler had to be acclaimed by one of the two factions to be installed in power, which would have been unthinkable for Arab autocrats because it would have given the public a degree of sovereignty and undermined their role as the authoritarian father. Thus the Roman notion of the stadium as a listening post that allowed the Emperor to take early note of public grievances[11] was anathema to Arab autocrats. They understood the risk the Byzantine Emperor Justinian I shouldered when in 532 AD Blues and Greens fans rioted for a week, sacking Hagia Sophia and almost persuading him to vacate his throne.[12]

Such neo-patriarchy is what makes Arab authoritarianism different from dictatorships in other parts of the world, Sharabi has argued.[13] Arab society was built around the "dominance of the father [patriarch], the centre around which the national as well as the natural family are organized. Thus between ruler and ruled, mediated in both the society and the family by a forced consensus based on ritual and coercion." In other words, Arab regimes franchised repression so that society, the oppressed, participated in their repression and denial of rights. The regime is in effect the father of all fathers at the top of the pyramid. The Egyptian journalist, writer and activist Salam Moussa recalls that Nasser's handler would order students at schools he visited to address the leader as *baba* or father. "It was an overt and expensive act of defiance for a boy to use the more traditional *Siadat El Rais* [Mr. President] as a greeting, even if beaming while shaking the nicotine-stained fingers," Moussa reminisces.[14]

The notion of the father figure—the Za'im who built the nation—filled the statements of ousted leaders such as Tunisia's Ben Ali, Egypt's Mubarak and Libya's Qaddafi in the weeks before their demise. It took the 2011 revolt for an Egyptian prime minister to answer unscripted questions on television after President Anwar Sadat in 1977 responded angrily to questioning by two student activists saying: "How can you talk to me like that? I am the president of the family, the president of the country." In his last televised speech before resigning on 11 February 2011, Mubarak, speaking as their father, addressed Egyptians as "my sons, the youth of Egypt, and daughters." He said his was "a speech from the father to his sons and daughters. I am telling you that I am very grateful and so proud of you for being a symbolic generation that is calling for change."[15] In response, protesters on Cairo's Tahrir Square articulated their discontent as a rejection of neo-patriarchy. "How dare he talk to us like naughty children? He must go immediately," insisted protester Abdallah Moktar.[16]

Politics is in soccer's DNA

Politics is written into the DNA of soccer across the Arab and non-Arab Middle East and North Africa, playing a key role in the region's struggle for independence. The history of the Algerian national team originates with the escape from France in 1958 of ten Algerian players, some of whom were likely to play in the French team in the World Cup, in order to act as revolutionary goodwill ambassadors touring the world, playing matches during the war of independence on behalf of the National Liberation Front (FLN). This team won the vast majority of its matches in North Africa, the Middle East, Eastern Europe, and Asia, garnering international support for Algeria's independence struggle. The team's song, "Kassaman" (We Pledge), became Algeria's national anthem. The defection of these players constituted a repudiation of French policy to recruit Algerian and other African sportsmen to play for France rather than their colonized countries of origin. The team's success built on Algerian soccer pitches becoming as far back as the 1920s venues for nationalist, anti-French protest. The FLN used the 1954 World Cup in Switzerland to announce the launch of its armed struggle. Two years later, it ordered sports clubs to freeze their activities and instructed their members to join the rebels. The FLN campaign was steeped in the Algerian Arab nationalist use of sports to express nationalist sentiment dating back to the establishment of a centre for sports and politics in 1926.[17]

In response to the FLN's mobilisation of soccer for liberation, FIFA banned its players and excluded teams that agreed to play them. After independence, the national soccer team was used to rebuild the nation, helped it break with its colonial past, created the image of the new, socialist and nationalist Algeria, countered regionalism and projected the country's socialist model on the international stage. Palestine and Kurdistan's use of soccer to project nationhood and achieve statehood is modelled on Algeria's success, on the premise that "football is the continuation of war by other means" in the words of *The Times*, paraphrasing Clausewitz's maxim that war is the continuation of politics by other means.[18]

Celebrated clubs like Cairo rivals Al Ahly SC and Zamalek SC, Tehran foes Persepolis SC and Esteghlal SC, Amman's storied Al Faisali SC and Al Wehdat SC, a club founded in and named after a Palestinian refugee camp, or Israel's notorious Beitar Jerusalem trace their origins to either republican, royalist or nationalist aspirations. Founded in 1907 by nationalists[19] as a club initially for Egyptians only, in response to British sports clubs that barred Egyptians, Al Ahly [The National] quickly became an anti-colonial, anti-monarchist, nationalist rallying point as opposed to Zamalek, originally the club of the royalists and pro-British forces. Similarly, Esteghlal was the Shah of Iran's club in contrast to Persepolis, widely viewed as the team of Iran's lower classes.[20] In Tehran, as in Cairo, historian Shiva Balaghi observed that "under the spell of football, complex ideological, political and economic divides seem to fade, before resolving again into the clear, tangible line between the reds and the blues—the colors of the most popular Iranian teams."[21] For all practical purposes, Al Ahly offered rebellious nationalist student unions the base and cover they needed to organize protests against colonial rule.

The embrace of soccer in more recent years by Mubarak and other republican and royal autocrats harked back to the ideology of the founders of clubs like Al Ahly. Its president, Abdel Khaliq Sarwat Pasha, who went on to become prime minister, expressed that ideology in a speech in 1919 to the club's general assembly. Speaking on the eve of student demonstrations that together with Zaghloul's exile sparked Egypt's first nationalist revolution, Sarwat said the club had been founded to foster a sense of political solidarity among mostly anti-colonial students as well as to create opportunity for physical exercise.[22]

Similarly, the continuous reporting of the interest in soccer expressed by Arab autocrats and their families on the front pages reflected the politicization of state run sports media coverage in its early days. Egyptian sports pages in the 1920s exploited anti-British fervour by reporting British-Egyptian matches in military jargon. Similarly, autocrats like Mubarak used soccer to rally the public around the flag and their regime. "From its inception … the sports page in *Al-Ahram* linked the Egyptian national football team (and itself) with both politics and the masses," historian Shaun Lopez wrote referring to the country's foremost state-run media.[23] *Al-Ahram*'s post-Mubarak soccer coverage echoed much the same themes:

government leaders and politicians' political interest in the game, soccer as an indicator of the nation's progress, and the corrupt nature of its institutions. Describing *Al-Ahram*'s initial coverage, Lopez observed that "first, writers often noted the interest of Egypt's political leaders in the Egyptian football team's performance in both 1924 and 1928. Second, success on the pitch was often attributed to (and served as proof of) Egypt's march towards European modernity … Third, *Al-Ahram*'s sportswriters often criticized Egypt's Football Federation, citing it as a microcosm of Egyptian political corruption and representative of the absence of democracy in all aspects of Egyptian political life."[24]

The political origins of soccer are still visible today. Al Ahly players dress in the red colours of the pre-colonial Egyptian flag. Established three years later, Al Ahly's arch rival Zamalek SC was founded initially as Qasr al-Nil bil-Jazira, then renamed Al Mukhtalaf [The Mix] before it changed its name to that of the despised, reigning monarch, Farouk. It was forced to refashion itself after Zamalek island in the Nile when the Nasserites toppled the monarchy in 1952.[25] The British authorities' founding of Zamalek mimicked their effort throughout much of their empire to employ soccer as a means of introducing concepts of discipline, obedience and order.[26]

Following in the footsteps of the European colonial rulers, the leaders of the newly independent, post-colonial states of the Middle East and North Africa saw soccer as a symbol of modernization. Reza Khan, the Shah of Iran, ordered his armed forces to play the game as far back as the 1920s, while parliament authorized the construction of Iran's first soccer pitch in 1926.

Nasser was named Al Ahly's honorary president after the 1952 coup; Field Marshal Abdelhakim Amer, Egypt's military commander, became president of the Egyptian Football Association; and General Abdelaziz Salem was named head of the Cairo-based African governing body, the Confederation of African Football. Mohammed Heikal, a prominent Egyptian journalist with close ties to Nasser, recalled that the revolutionary leader would attend matches even though he wasn't interested in soccer as a game.[27] Nasser nevertheless recognized soccer's political, economic and financial utility, With the realization that soccer would also allow Egypt to project itself internationally, Nasser pushed in 1957 for the creation of the Africa Cup of Nations. Soccer was so important that match results were frequently discussed in Cabinet meetings. In a 1999 interview with an Egyptian journalist, Major-Gen. Abdulmohsen Kamel Murtaja recalled being suddenly ordered by Nasser to take over the management of Al Ahly in order to reverse the club's sudden run of defeats.[28]

Similarly, Nasser saw the Egyptian national soccer team as a tool to propagate his vision of Arab nationalism and to agitate against the remnants of British colonialism and the feudal rulers of the Gulf. In a confidential memo to the British colonial secretary Duncan Sandys accompanied by Aden Colony Police reports, the British High Commissioner in Aden, Sir Gerald Trevaskis, reported on 1 October 1963 that Egyptian players would be barred from further visits after they had instigated pro-Nasser demonstrations, denounced police forces as dogs and "proved an embarrassment to the police" during a tour the previous month. The tour occurred three months before an anti-British uprising erupted in Aden inspired by Nasser's pan-Arabism and against the backdrop of Egyptian-backed guerrilla groups fighting the colonial power.[29]

The appointment of revolutionary leaders to senior positions in sports symbolized the Nasserites' tight political grip in which they even defined daily prayers as a form of exercise. Mohammed Naguib, Egypt's first republican president, stressed a year after coming to power that the Prophet Mohammed had advocated swimming and archery.[30] He sought to redefine sports as benefitting the nation rather than only the individual and saw them as a tool to shape a cultural agenda and promote public health. In a letter in 1953 to a newly established sports magazine, Naguib expressed the "hope that the magazine will fulfil its task by creating a physically strong and healthy generation vigorous in its beliefs, mentality and spirit for the purpose of creating a strong internal united and organized front." A pro-Nasserite publication, *Al-Abtal*, declared sport a force that would be capable of coping with "all aspects of life of peace and war."[31] Similarly, the Shah of Iran saw soccer as a way to improve public health, and encourage cooperative attitudes that would help industrialization and social cohesion.[32]

The identification of men like Mubarak, former Iranian president Ahmadinejad and ousted Yemeni leader Saleh—as well as Libyan leader Colonel Moammar Qaddafi's son, Al Saadi al Qaddafi, with their country's national teams turned the squads' successes and failures into barometers of how their regimes were faring. Players and coaches found themselves in the firing line whenever their teams' performance failed to live up to the political expectations of their bosses, invariably autocratic leaders, their families and associate As a result, soccer players and officials in the region are by and large typical products of Sharabi's concept of neo-patriarchy. To them the popular revolts that erupted in 2011 symbolized patricide, or the death of the father.[33]

In Egypt and Tunisia, most players and officials remained on the sidelines of the momentous events, with some declaring their support for the embattled autocratic leader. "I kissed Mubarak's hand when he honoured Egypt after the 2010 African Cup of Nations as I saw him as a father of all Egyptians," recalled Egyptian striker Mohamed Zidan.[34] Similarly, it took four months of mass protests that morphed into civil war for a group of Libyan players to join the rebel forces aligned against Qaddafi. At the same time, a former captain of the team called the anti-Qaddafi rebels rats and dogs.

The divide between players' and fans' attitudes towards political upheaval exacerbated the emerging gap between the two groups. Egyptian fans responded by unfurling a banner at one of the first matches following Mubarak's overthrow that read: "We followed you everywhere but in the hard times we didn't find you."[35] Another put the fans further at odds with their clubs and star players who resisted a proposed capping of transfer fees and salaries for coaches and players. It read: "You're asking for millions and you don't care about the poverty of Egyptians."[36] The slogan reflected the mounting calls for social justice that were rampant on internet soccer forums in which fans vented their anger against the transition military government's handling of the post-Mubarak period. Fuelling the growing gulf between fans and players was what sociologist Ian Taylor described as resistance to and rejection of the upwardly mobile movement of players from their working-class origins to a middle-class status with a jet set lifestyle. "The player has been incorporated into the bourgeois world, his self-image and behavior have become increasingly managerial or entrepreneurial, and soccer has become for the player, a means to personal (rather than sub-cultural) success," Taylor wrote in his analysis of British soccer violence.[37]

As a result, relations between fans and players have, much like Egyptian politics, been on a rollercoaster since the fall of Mubarak. Early tensions made way for reconciliation in the wake of a politically loaded soccer riot in February 2012 in Port Said in which seventy-four militant fans of Cairo's champion team Al Ahly SC were killed in the worst incident in Egyptian sporting history.[38] The catastrophe prompted three Al

Ahly players who were part of Egypt's national squad to retire from the game. Within days Al Ahly militants, responding to an outpouring of sympathy from across Egypt including militants of their arch Cairo rival Zamalek SC, apologized on a specially created Facebook page named "We are sorry Shika" to Zamalek winger Mahmoud Abdel-Razek aka Shikabala, widely viewed as one of Egypt's top players, for routinely abusing him verbally during their clubs' derbies. The abuse frequently led to Shikabala and Al Ahly fans trading insults in heated exchanges.[39]

Responding in an interview on the Zamalek club's website, Shikabala welcomed the apology. "Despite the cruelty of what happened in Port Said, this disaster played a role in uniting the fans of all clubs. It might be a turning point in ending intolerance and hatred in Egyptian football. I will go to the Ahly club along with my teammates to offer our condolences to the families of Port Said martyrs. The fans of Ahly are my brothers. I hope Ahly and Zamalek fans can sit together in the stands without barriers," he said.[40]

Breaking with the tradition of players hovering on the sidelines of popular revolts, if not supporting the region's autocratic leaders, the star striker Mohamed Abou-Treika announced in September 2012 that he would not be joining his fellow Al Ahly SC players in a Super Cup match against ENPPI, Egypt's first domestic fixture following the lifting of a seven-month ban on professional soccer.[41] His decision symbolized the struggles in virtually every Egyptian institution between post-Mubarak reformers and supporters of the Mubarak-era status quo ante. In doing so Abou-Treika, one of Egypt's most popular players, sided with Ultras Ahlawy, the club's militant support faction. The Ultras opposed the resumption of soccer as long as justice had not been seen to be done for the seventy-four fans killed in Port Said and spectators were banned from attending matches. The rift among players and between players and fans was highlighted when Al Ahly defender Mostafa Younes accused Abou-Treika of supporting "outlaws."[42]

Abou-Treika's puncturing of the neo-patriarchy that underlay the attitudes of most players symptomised Egypt's convoluted transition from autocracy to an as yet undefined form of a more open society that was being waged in virtually all of the country's institutions. Egypt expert Nathan J. Brown argues that "after [the fall of Mubarak in] February 2011, internal battles took place in all state institutions—with some people advocating greater autonomy, others gravitating toward the

SCAF [the Supreme Council of the Armed Forces that ruled Egypt until Morsi's election in July 2012], and old leaders hanging on ... Many critical Egyptian institutions are still undergoing slow but portentous internal struggles, generally away from the headlines."[43]

Those battles culminated two and a half years after Mubarak's fall in the July 2013 military coup that deposed Mohammed Morsi. Soccer fans who in 2011 were in the forefront of the revolt against Mubarak were as organizations conspicuously absent from the mass protests in 2013 that preceded the overthrow of Morsi. While endorsing participation of their members in ongoing protests the fans, like their counterparts in Turkey who were prominent in the demonstrations against then Prime Minister Erdoğan, retreated to their traditional public stance: that they are apolitical organizations but do not stop their followers from engaging politically. It was a position designed to minimize their vulnerability as groups and shield them from being politically cornered and was identical to the public statements issued by Egyptian Ultras on the eve of the eighteen days of mass protests that forced Mubarak to resign after thirty years in office.

The coup in Egypt and the sustained resistance of the Brotherhood to the overthrow of their leader constituted a dilemma for the Ultras whose members populate the full spectrum of politics in the country. They nurture a deep-seated distrust of the military and the security forces who have since re-emerged in full strength. By the same token, many Ultras opposed Morsi because of his perceived attempt to undermine the goals of Egypt's popular revolt and his failure to reform the security sector. This tactical retreat and re-calibrated organizational focus exclusively on soccer by fan groups in Egypt and Turkey followed incidents in both countries ostensibly designed to intimidate them and curb their activism. Meanwhile efforts to reign in the Ultras led in Egypt to the formation by militant soccer fans of anti-coup groups such as Ultras Nahdawy and Students Against The Coup, who became the backbone of anti-Sisi protests on university campuses and local neighbourhoods.

In Egypt it was the politically loaded riot in Port Said in which more than seventy Al Ahly fans lost their lives; for Çarşı, the popular militant support group of Istanbul's Beşiktaş JK, it was the indictment of twenty of its members on charges of being part of an illegal organization because of their role in the anti-Erdoğan protests. Both incidents were designed to undermine and criminalize fans and protesters. In Egypt, the Port Said massacre constituted an attempt to teach the Ultras a lesson that got out of hand. For Erdoğan, it was a bid to cater to a traditionalist and conservative base and distinguish himself from the more modernist façade of his Islamist rival, Fethullah Gülen, a powerful, self-exiled, 76-year-old imam with strong popular and media support and influence in state institutions like the police and the judiciary.

"The anti-Erdoğan demonstrations have shown that rival soccer fans can work together. The demonstrations have put Erdoğan on notice. But that's not all. They also send a message to Gülen," said a Turkish soccer fan. His words were echoed by an Egyptian Ultra: "We may have opted to pull back as organizations. But we are no less opposed to the military and the security forces. We have learnt that united we stand stronger. We understand our power and need to wield it intelligently."

The Stadium: Soccer's Grunt School

"You can crush the flowers, but you cannot stop the spring from coming."

Ultras' graffiti quoting Pablo Neruda

Soccer stadiums across the Middle East and North Africa became a "grunt school" (training ground) for fans from Algeria to Iran as they cut their teeth resisting autocrats' attempts to impose political control on the game. They served as venues of expression of pent-up anger and frustration, assertion of national, ethnic and sectarian identity and demands for women's rights, and breeding grounds for politically and socially motivated violence. They enabled young soccer fans to operate independently of their more often than not overbearing, patriarchal fathers. Their resistance measured the heat of social discontent in the countries of the region, all of which have disproportionately high numbers of young people.

Almost twenty years after Iran's Islamic revolution, patterns of life in Tehran were reversed in 1997, if only briefly, after the Iranian national team defeated Australia and the Islamic Republic qualified for the first time in two decades for the World Cup finals. Conservative clerics who had denounced the game as a colonial leftover lined up to congratulate the squad, attributing its success to God's will. Thousands poured onto the streets to celebrate in a country in which the Islamic revolution had turned religious devotion into a public fixture and pushed joy and entertainment into the confines of private homes.

The public celebrations quickly turned into protests. They erupted barely a month after the election of Mohammed Khatami as president

37

held out the promise of a less restricted society. Men and women honked their car horns, waved Iranian flags and danced in the streets together to blacklisted music and sang nationalist songs. They did so again six months later when Iran defeated the United States.

The protesters chanted, "Death to the Mullahs."[44] Some 5,000 women stormed Tehran's Azadi stadium where the team that defeated Australia was being welcomed in protest against their banning from attending soccer matches and in defiance of calls in the media for women to watch the ceremony on television at home. Punctuated by seventeen qualifiers, an unusually high number for a World Cup, the national team's arduous road to competing in the finals constituted a metaphor for what it would take to return isolated Iran to the international community as a respected and honoured member. It also was a harbinger of ethnic tension. Azeris, Arabs and an Armenian were among the team's key players who made it by playing for Tehran clubs. Yet to their communities in the provinces of Eastern Azerbaijan and Khuzestan they were symbols of a national identity that was not purely Persian.

The victory over Australia could not have come in a politically more important year. Soccer was the sport of the regime's liberals, wrestling that of its conservatives—a tussle that played out in the presidential elections in 1997 in which Khatami, a reformer, defeated in a landslide Ali Akbar Nateq Nuri, who was backed by the conservatives and the wrestling community. Iran's dismal performance in World Cup qualifiers prior to its victory against Australia catapulted soccer to the forefront of political debate in parliament. Liberals blamed the national team's poor performance on its coach, Mayeli Kohan, a conservative who barred Iranians playing abroad from joining the national team because he considered them traitors. They ensured that Kohan was replaced by Valdeir Viera, the Brazilian coach of Iran's Olympic team, who led Iran to its defeat of Australia.

Bahrain's defeat of Iran four years later in a World Cup qualifier again sparked mass protests against a backdrop of mounting disappointment with Khatami's inability to implement change. Shouting anti-government slogans, soccer fans attacked banks and public offices and clashed with security forces. Khatami's younger brother, the deputy speaker of parliament, warned that the protests reflected popular frustration with unemployment and low standards of living and a rejection of the regime's "excessive interference in people's private lives."[45] The unrest ignited heated debate in parliament and on the pitch about where the Islamic republic was heading.

An Iranian sports journalist asserted that "in terms of freedom of expression, soccer stadiums are nearly as important as the internet in Iran now. The protest is more secure there because the police can't arrest thousands of people at once. State television broadcasts many matches live and the people use it as a stage for resistance. They're showing banners to the cameras and chanting protest songs, which is why some games are broadcast without sound now."[46] The historian Shiva Balaghi argues that Tehran's Azadi [Freedom] stadium "has become a rare social space where Iranian youth can transcend boundaries of authority and express themselves with relative lack of inhibition."[47]

The 1998 World Cup served as a catalyst for simmering discontent. Together with the election of a reformist president, it narrowed the gap between Iranians resident in Iran and the country's significant diaspora community largely opposed to the regime. This was highlighted by the appointment of Jalal Talebi, a California-based exile, as the Iranian national team's coach. "For 25 years, the Iranian diaspora and Iranians inside the country didn't have a common cause to cheer for. Football gave them a chance to do that," said Iranian striker Hamid Estili, whose header contributed to that year's decisive 2–1 defeat of the United States in a game-changing World Cup qualifier.[48] Together with the eruption of Iranian cinema onto global screens, soccer contributed to an ultimately unexploited mellowing of Iranian-US relations. "Our people are looking for something to fill the void in their lives. Our national football has become a uniting factor of our people all over the world," remarked national team captain Ali Daei after being signed by German club Hertha Berlin FC.[49]

As soccer is a barometer of rising discontent, frustration and pent-up anger, Algeria is another country where fans' protests are mounting amid uncertainty about the future as the regime's ageing leadership. They demonstrated their indifference towards the 76-year-old President Abdelaziz Bouteflika as he languished in a Paris hospital by expressing riotous support for the national team in Algiers ahead of a championship. Similarly, fans interrupted a minute's silence to commemorate the deaths of two former presidents, Ahmed Ben Bella and Chadli Benjedid, and that of Ali Kafi, who served as a transition leader in the early 1990s when the military fought Islamist forces in a civil war of incredible savagery that left some 100,000 people dead, even though it was the Islamists who had prevailed at the ballot box.

The demonstrations constituted a rejection of Bouteflika's effort, true to Sharabi's concept of neo-patriarchism, to re-assert himself as father of the revolutionary Algerian nation. In a message distributed on state-run television on 30 April, the day before the Algeria Cup derby between rivals Mouloudia Club d'Alger (MCA), which traces its roots to the Algerian liberation movement, and Union Sportive Médina d'Alger (USMA), Bouteflika said: "It is very difficult for me to find myself in a hospital abroad for health reasons and not to be, for the first time, with the Algerian people to celebrate … and attend the finals of the Algeria Cup … Irrespective of the circumstances, I share the joy of my country's daughters and sons on this day."[50] The protests also were a rejection of Mouloudia's call on Bouteflika to run for a fourth term in presidential elections scheduled for 2014.

The championship final was laden with political symbolism that went beyond Bouteflika's faltering attempt to shore up his image. It also was a reflection of the government's economic liberalization policy in the 1990s that sparked the privatization of Algerian soccer clubs from which prominent businessmen with close links to the regime benefitted. In doing so, the government sought to encourage professionalization of the sport, while at the same time retaining a degree of control. As a result, many clubs remain financially dependent on the sports and youth ministry and local authorities rather than on private sector investment, sponsorship and the proceeds of merchandising and broadcast rights.

To many Algerians, the match between MCA and USMA was a competition between MCA owner Sonatrach, Algeria's state-owned oil and gas giant, and its controversial, unpredictable manager Omar Ghrib on the one hand, and USMA proprietor Ali Haddad, Algeria's largest contractor and a media mogul, on the other—two men who had ostensibly benefitted from close ties with the regime. Ghrib demonstrated a degree of independence, however, at the end of the match when his defeated Mouloudia players refused to accept medals that were being handed out by Prime Minster Abdelmalek Sellal on live television. The embarrassing incident put a spotlight on mounting criticism of corruption and nepotism in Algeria; even Mouloudia later apologized, saying its players had rejected the awards as a protest against unfair decisions by the referee.

These multiple incidents suggested that Bouteflika's stroke could mark a turning point after two years in which the memory of the civil war in the 1990s and the military-dominated regime's liberal social spending had taken the wind out of the demonstrators' sails and persuaded them in 2011 to shy away from staging a full-fledged revolt. "If there is not real democratic transition, there will be an uprising ... we will return to the violence of the 1990s," warned Chafiq Mesbah, a former member of Algeria's intelligence service and now a political analyst, in an interview with the Associated Press.

The various protests occurred as Algeria witnessed an upsurge in soccer-related violence from 2012 onwards. The disturbances suggested that increased wages and government spending were failing to compensate for frustration with the failure of the country's gerontocracy to share power with a younger generation, create jobs and address housing problems. "Violence in Algeria has become ordinary and banal. *Hogra*, the word Algerians use for the government's perceived contempt for ordinary citizens, has planted a sickness in Algerian society. People feel that the only way to get anything done is to have connections or threaten the peace. It is a system where *hogra* and social injustice rule. Social violence has become the preferred mode of communication between the citizen and the republic—today in our country everything is obtained through a riot," commented psychologist Mahmoud Boudarene.[51]

Dozens of people, including a player, were injured in late 2012 when supporters of Jeunesse Sportive de la Saoura (JSS) stormed the pitch during a Premier League match in their home stadium in Meridja in the eastern province of Bechar against Algiers-based Union Sportive de la Médina d'El Harrach (USM). The incident followed a massive brawl between players and between fans after a Libya-Algeria Africa Cup of Nations qualifier. In April of that year supporters of MC Saida stabbed six players of Union Sportive Médina d'Alger (USM), including international Abdelkader Laifaoui. Albert Dominique Ebossé Bodjongo Dika, a 25 year old Cameroonian, who played for Algerian club JS Kabylie (JSK), was killed in 2014 by a rock believed to have been thrown by a JSK supporter upset that his team had lost a match. Hamza Bencherif, a midfielder and friend of Ebossé, told BBC World Football that Algerian players ran risks whenever they ran on to the pitch. "Every time we lose a game, [there are] some rocks. ... Death is not far when a risk like that is taken. ... It's hard to see what [the soccer authorities] can do because they allow so much freedom in the way the stadiums are controlled. If they continue that way there is absolutely nothing they can do."[52]

The protesters' retreat into the stadiums amounted to a tacit under-standing between Algerian soccer fans and security forces that supporters could express their grievances as long as they did so within the confines of the stadiums. "Bouteflika is in love with his throne, he wants another term," is a popular anti-government chant in stadiums. Moreover, stadiums have long been an incubator of protest in Algeria. A 2007 diplomatic cable sent by the US embassy in Algiers and disclosed by WikiLeaks linked a soccer protest in the desert city of Bou Saada to demonstrations in the western port city of Oran sparked by the publication of a highly contentious list of government housing recipients. The cable warned that "this kind of disturbance has become commonplace, and appears likely to remain so unless the government offers diversions other than soccer and improves the quality of life of its citizens." Seven fans were killed between 2009 and 2014 in soccer-related violence and more than 2,700 wounded, according to Algerian statistics. The protests and violence were a far cry from the 1960s and 1970s when fans chanted endorsements of government policies. This shift also predated the popular revolts. It was rooted in the initial assertion in stadiums in the 1980s by Algerian Berbers, who constitute at least 20 per cent of the population, of their non-Arab identity.

Algeria's domestic fragility is highlighted by almost daily smaller pro-tests in towns across the country sparked by anger over lack of water, housing, electricity, jobs and salaries. Protests led in 2011 to the suspen-sion of soccer matches. Soccer was also suspended during legislative elections in 2014. A sense that the government may revert to strong arm tactics rather than reform if protests swell was reinforced when General Bachir Tartag was recalled from retirement in 2012 to head the Directorate for Internal Security (DSI). Gen. Tartag, who is believed to be in his sixties, made a name for himself during the civil war against the Islamists as one of Algeria's most notorious military hardliners. The appointment initially positioned him as a potential successor to the aging spy chief Gen. Mohamed 'Tewfik' Mediene. Tartag was dismissed in 2014 in an internal power struggle and succeeded by Ali Bendaoud, reportedly a relative of Bouteflika.

In countries like Algeria, Jordan and Egypt, the soccer pitch was a harbinger of things to come. It was often where political taboos in terms of confronting the regime were first broken, opening the door to broad segments of society publicly to express sentiments that until then were at best only articulated in the privacy of one's home. Tensions between tribal East Bankers and urbanized, more affluent Palestinians in Jordan, the only Arab country to have granted citizenship to refugees fleeing Palestine during the 1948 war that cemented Israel's creation, spilled on to the soccer pitch in the capital of Amman a month before the self-immolation of a young vegetable vendor in Tunisia sparked popular revolts across North Africa as well as in Yemen, Bahrain and Syria. The incident at a match between Amman arch rivals Al Wehdat SC and Al Faisali SC in which 250 people, including thirty police officers, were injured, foreshadowed the tensions marking discontent in the kingdom.

Al Faisali is widely seen as an East Bank team while Al Wehdat symbolizes both urbanized Palestinians as well as some 1.8 million Palestinians who live as refugees in the kingdom, often in camps like Al Wehdat on the southern edge of Amman, to which the soccer club traces its origins. The expulsion from Jordan of Yasser Arafat's Palestine Liberation Organization (PLO) in 1970 heightened the symbolism of Al Wehdat whose green, red, and black shirts with a white stripe are the colours of the Palestinian flag. Al Wehdat's emergence as one of Jordan's most successful clubs became a symbol of national pride on both banks of the Jordan River. Its victories stood out against the failure of Palestinian and Arab leaders to secure Palestinian rights. Al Wehdat's success in competing head to head with Al Faisali, the foremost team of the East Bankers, was also a reflection of East Bank fears that its people could lose control of a country that had no symbols or treasures post-dating its creation in 1946 and was reliant on the Hashemites tracing their lineage back to the Prophet Mohammed. It challenged Jordan's efforts to emphasize Jordanian identity at the expense of a Palestinian identity, even though Jordanian Palestinians were increasingly defining themselves as a Palestinian-Jordanian blend. That trend was fuelled both by improvement in economic circumstances as well as the United States' 1988 recognition of the PLO and the subsequent Israeli-Palestinian peace process that forced Palestinians who hailed from 1948 Israel and their descendants to accept that they would not be returning to their pre-Jewish state homes. The Palestinian–East Bank soccer rivalry nevertheless served the monarchy's interests in projecting its family history as pan-Arabist. It also helped to ensure that Palestinians and East Bankers would not work together to challenge its legitimacy.

Citizenship enhanced the Palestinians' ability to find employment and eased their graduation into the middle class. Nevertheless, Palestinians in

Jordan maintain that they suffer discrimination in employment in the public sector and the military, both East Banker strongholds. They also charge that the electoral system is designed to ensure that East Bankers have a majority in parliament. East Bankers, empathetic to the plight of the Palestinians who in 1948 fled across the Jordan River, traumatized and bitter about Arab military failure, welcomed them but were concerned that they might eventually challenge their control of security and politics in the kingdom. Their demographic concerns were heightened by Jordan's 1948 incorporation of the predominantly Palestinian West Bank into the kingdom, an act which turned East Bankers into a minority. Over time, the Palestinians' increasing affluence and commercial success reinforced that concern. Surveillance and discrimination was the East Bankers' defence, particularly with the emergence of the PLO as a nationalist guerrilla movement. Those tensions exploded in 1970 when the PLO, headquartered in Al Wehdat, was forced in a bloody war that Palestinians refer to as "Black September" to leave Jordan for Lebanon. Jordanian forces bombarded the camp during the hostilities.

The rivalry between Al Wehdat and Al Faisali, which owes its name to Hashemite King Faisal who was the first King of Syria and then of Iraq in the 1920s and 1930, reflected the tensions rooted in the Palestinian influx. Al Faisali is controlled, according to a US embassy cable disclosed by WikiLeaks,[53] by the prominent East Bank Udwan tribe even though its founder, Suleiman Nabulsi, was Palestinian, and Palestinians are among its players. Similarly, Al Wehdat boasts East Bankers as members of its team. The underlying tension was nevertheless highlighted by repeated fighting between the supporters of the two teams and the sentencing in absentia to two years in prison of the Al Wehdat president and well-known businessman Tareq Khouri for insulting a police officer during an earlier Al Wehdat–Al Faisali match. Khouri voiced Palestinians' complaints in his November 2009 election campaign, which failed to return him to parliament. He did so at a sensitive moment in East Bank-Palestinian relations. A new Israeli government had just come to office whose foreign minister, Avigdor Lieberman, advocated a territorial separation of Jews and Muslims. Lieberman's proposal sparked fears that Israel would force Palestinians in areas under its control to cross the Jordan River and effectively turn the kingdom into a Palestinian state.

The delicate balance embedded in Amman's soccer rivalry threatened to get out of hand by the late 2000s. The US cable described the anti-

Palestinian hooliganism and Al Faisali slogans denigrating the Palestinian origins of Queen Rania and Crown Prince Hussein bin Al Abdullah during a 17 July 2009 match between the two teams as "a new low" in their often violent rivalry. The match was cancelled mid-game. The slogans, an offence punishable with up to three years in prison, were particularly divisive and controversial because they were directed at members of the royal family, the cable reported. In contrast to 1986, when Al Wehdat was temporarily shut down after its fans chanted against the monarchy, Al Faisali was not penalized. The cable nevertheless quoted an embassy contact as describing "the 'increasingly explicit and provocative' Faisali slogans as proof that status quo-oriented East Bankers are uncomfortable with the increasing pressures for reform that will inevitably lessen their near-monopoly on political and social power." Throwing bottles at Al Wehdat players, the Al Faisali fans chanted: "Divorce her you father of Hussein, and we'll marry you to two of ours," symbolism of a separation of East Bankers and Palestinians and preservation of the alliance between the monarchy and the tribes. Taunting the Palestinians, the fans shouted: "Wehdat youth are all guerrillas." To which Wehdat supporters responded: "We don't want wheat or sardines, give us explosives."[54]

The riot and the slogans harked back to the 1980s, when fighting between Al Wehdat and Al Faisali supporters was a fixture of Jordanian soccer. But the boot is now on the other foot. Wehdat slogans no longer emphasize a purely Palestinian identity nor glorify their people's armed struggle. Wehdat players may dress in Palestinian colours but the club and its fans fly the Jordanian flag; Al Faisali's slogans, by contrast, are more political and according to the US cable "have over time become a popular barometer of tensions between East Bankers and Palestinians." The cable noted that "there is broad recognition throughout Jordan that the Faisali–Wehdat incident exposed the uncomfortable gap between East Bankers and Palestinian-origin Jordanians—one that most would rather keep well-hidden for the sake of political stability. The connection between this rift and the Hashemite monarchy, including the newly-appointed Crown Prince, makes the incident even more unsettling. Even our most forthcoming contacts are reluctant to talk with us about the issue, recognizing that it strikes at the core of Jordanian identity politics."

The Al Faisali slogans reappeared in March 2011 when nationalists and security forces attacked pro-democracy demonstrators in Amman. Al

Faisali militants had opened the door to unprecedented criticism of the royal family becoming part of mainstream political discourse. Scores of Jordanian tribal leaders issued a statement a month earlier and only weeks after popular revolts toppled the Tunisian President Zine El Abidine Ben Ali and Egypt's Hosni Mubarak, accusing Queen Rania, who had adopted a high-profile global role, of corruption.[55] The thirty-six tribal leaders, backed by retired military officers opposed to constitutional reform, charged that the queen, together with "her sycophants and the power centres that surround her," were dividing Jordanians and "stealing from the country and the people."[56] They compared Rania to Ben Ali's hated wife, Leila, who stood accused of enriching her family with publicly held assets and funds, and alleged that she was enhancing her public image at the expense of ordinary Jordanians. The leaders demanded that those accused of corruption, irrespective of status, be put on trial. They called on King Abdullah "to return lands and farms given to [the queen's] Yassin family. The lands belong to the Jordanian people." They warned that if the king failed to tackle corruption and introduce reform, "similar events to those in Tunisia and Egypt and other Arab countries will occur," with the risk of another civil war. Internet and satellite television had made it impossible for regimes to stifle public access to information about events in the region, said the leaders' statement.

A play by Jordanian satirist Kamel Nuseirat that opened to great acclaim in Amman in the spring of 2013 added to the breaking of the taboo of discussing publicly tensions between East Bankers and Palestinians. In *Neither East nor West* the identities of a mixed Palestinian-East Bank couple, Zarifeh and Jaber, play out in their rival support for The Boss and The Green Giant, Al Faisali vs. Al Wehdat and their preferences for food. Their fierce debates symbolically reverberate in their home's curtains: some Faisali blue, others Wehdat green, and in their headdress, Jaber's East Bank Bedouin red and white chequered kaffiyeh vs. Zarifeh's black and white headdress popularized by Yasser Arafat who wore it folded on his forehead in the shape of the map of Palestine. Similarly, Jaber prefers *mansaf*, a traditional East Bank dish of lamb cooked in yogurt and served with rice and nuts. He refuses to eat Zarifeh's *mulukhiyeh*, a dense soup made from corchorus leaves.

Their rivalry notwithstanding, the play is as much about the differences between East and West Bankers as it is about the game's contribution to bonds between them. When the couple's home is emptied by thieves aided by Jaber, who hopes that it will help him emerge from their rivalry on top, reality dawns on him. "We lost everything!" he cries in remorse. "It is easy to destroy a wall, but it is better to bring down the barriers inside our hearts," he says. "Get me mansaf and mulukhiyeh on one table. I miss both dishes."

The spectre of ethnic strife on the soccer pitch was not unique to Jordan. Syrian troops fired on Syrian Kurdish supporters of Al Jihad SC in 2004 as they waved Kurdish flags and pictures of US President George W. Bush during a match against predominantly Arab Al Fatwa SC from Deir-ez-Zor in the town of Al Qamishli near Syria's border with Turkey. Six people were killed and another three died in a stampede to escape the stands. Fighting between fans of the two teams spilt into the streets after Deir-ez-Zor supporters shouted insults at Iraqi Kurdish leaders Massoud Barzani and Jalal Talabani and brandished portraits of the deposed Iraqi leader Saddam Hussein whom Kurds blame for the death of more than 100,000 of their brethren in a targeted campaign. "We will sacrifice our lives for Bush," the Kurds shouted back.

Anger erupted again a day after the match when security forces fired on the funerals of the supporters. The unrest spread to neighbouring towns and villages. Protesters chanted anti-government slogans, toppled a statue of Bashar al-Assad's father, Hafez al Assad, and destroyed of the Baath Party. Up to thirty Kurds were killed and more than a hundred were wounded in fighting before Syrian troops were able to regain control of the city in a dry run of Bashar's response to anti-government protests seven years later that provoked Syria's bitter civil war.[57] The fighting sparked protests among Kurds in Damascus where hundreds of riot police surrounded Damascus University and in the suburb of Dummar, home to thousands of Kurds.

In Egypt, politics was pushed into the mosque and onto the soccer pitch due to a sense that little had changed in an authoritarian system that has shaped the country since the 1952 revolution and which gave the Egyptian military and security services effective control of the country. Assad, a leader of Al Ahly's Ultras observed: "Soccer is bigger than politics. It's about escapism. The average [Cairo club Al] Ahly fan is a guy who lives in a one bedroom flat with his wife, mother-in-law and five kids. He is paid minimum wage and his life sucks. The only good thing about his life is that for two hours on a Friday he goes to the stadium and watches Ahly. That's why it is such an obligation to win every game. It makes people's lives happy."[58]

Former Al Ahly board member Khalid Motagi, scion of the club's first post-revolution chairman, adds that "people suffer, but when Ahly wins they smile."[59] Al Ahly has indeed given its fans multiple reasons to smile. It has won Egypt's championship thirty-seven and Africa's titles nineteen times; rival Zamalek secured the Egyptian title eleven and Africa's titles nine times. The Ultra self-definition comes closest to the scholars such as Taylor[60] and Clarke[61] who argued that British hooligans were the product of unemployment and urban decay, a "subcultural agent"[62] abandoned by parents, government and soccer club management. Rejection of traditional authority, and the ACAB principle—All Cops are Bastards—are written into the DNA of the North African Ultras, who pride themselves in being a group that shape character, ensure discipline and encourage fraternity.

The Ultras are renowned for their fanatical support of their teams. "They don't simply stop at football. They actually have a philosophy and stand for a number of values and are not just simply football hooligans. Theirs is a way of life, a subculture, with its own rules, music and art. That makes them very unique," said political pundit Mahmoud Salem, better known as Sandmonkey, the name of his widely read blog. With elaborate displays of fireworks, flares, smoke guns, loud chanting and jumping up and down during matches, the Ultras hope to create an atmosphere in the stadium that encourages their team and intimidates opposing players and supporters. Like many of their counterparts in Europe and elsewhere, they are fiercely independent, with bans on outside funding. They abide by strict rules that oblige them to attend every match. As in many countries, the rank and file of Middle Eastern Ultras are composed largely of young working-class men who embrace a culture of confrontation—against opposing teams, against the state, and against expressions of weakness in society at large. This culture manifests itself in acts of political rebellion.[63] They are often led by educated, Westernized intellectuals and professionals.

According to Mohamed Gamal Beshir, author of *Kitab al-Ultras* [The Ultras Book], who is widely seen as the godfather of the Egyptian Ultras and was a leader of the Ultras White Knights (UWK), the militant Zamalek support group:

> I made my first steps into politics in 2000. I was against corruption and the regime and for human rights. Radical anarchism was my creed. Ultras ignore the system. You do your own system because you already own the game. We see

ourselves as organizers of anarchy. Our power was focused on organizing our system ... We were the first graffiti movement to use graffiti to discuss police brutality, and freedom of expression and the spread of the Ultras movement before the revolution. The battle we fought was against the tear gas and rubber bullets that the security forces launched at us prior to the revolution when we were prevented from cheering and supporting our team with our banners, flares and TiVo (choreographed cheering) activities. This was a battle we had to fight during the January revolution to end the war between the police and us. So it wasn't about football, it was about fighting for freedom ... Things escalated to the point when one of our songs became a rallying cry of the revolution. The song expressed the protesters' worry that the revolution was threatened by the police's return to oppressive behaviour. For the first time an Ultras song was being sung by non-Ultras. That was important because it spread Ultras culture and made activists and intellectual realize that we are not simply a bunch of crazy guys. People recognized that we have a philosophy.[64]

Surfing the internet in the mid-2000s, some Ultras contacted like-minded militant fan groups in Serbia, Italy, Russia, and Argentina, developing friendships and in a few instances even long-distance relationships. They also contacted Ultras groups in Tunisia and Morocco that had emerged several years earlier. Their affinity with Serbia—where Yugoslav president Slobodan Milosevic and gangster turned-government hit man Zeljniko Rajnatovic, aka Arkan, mobilised soccer fans in the 1990s to spark war with Croatia and later moulded them into an anti-Croatian and anti-Muslim paramilitary ethnic cleansing force in Bosnia Herzegovina and Kosovo—was focused on soccer rather than political ideals.

The first Middle Eastern and North African groups of Ultras emerged in Tunisia in the middle of this century's first decade. They were associated with Espérance Sportive de Tunis and Club Africain Tunis. Morocco, which today has some forty groups with tens of thousands of members, quickly followed suit. Egyptian Ultras trace their history to a match in 2007 in Cairo between Zamalek and Sudanese club Al Hilal FC (Omdurman) whose militant fan group has won acclaim for its choreography.

"Ultras across the globe are one. The internet has helped cooperation between individuals and groups of different race and trends and the forging of international friendships. They help each other. It is like a school where everyone learns the same principles and approaches," Bashir said. "No one can doubt the love and loyalty of groups of Ultras. It isn't just supporting a club through thick and thin. For Ultras it goes deeper. They are united by love and a sense of group solidarity. They belong to a class, Ultras, which they see as a model of belonging, loyalty and hard work aimed at achieving success. Theirs is a way of life in and outside of the stadium."

Indeed, the concerns of the Ultras across North Africa were the same, with one difference: while Tunisian and Egyptian Ultras were determined to topple their autocratic leader, Moroccans were willing to give King Mohammed VI the benefit of the doubt. While Ultras on Tahrir Square chanted "*Irhal, Irhal*" [Leave, leave], those in Morocco sang:

Hate the government,
We have only one king, Mohamed VI,
Others are thieves, they have contempt for us,
They fill their bags with the money of the poor,
In North Africa oh oh oh, the situation is the same.

The Ultras saw themselves as distinct from the mass of fans who were either on the payroll of the clubs or one of the players or who viewed the Friday game as pure entertainment and escape from the drudgery of daily life but attached no social or organizational importance to their support. For the Ultras, support of their club was all-consuming; it was the core of their existence, to be or not to be. They emerged at a time when Egyptian soccer was becoming profitable, there was money going round and pockets could be filled. Like elsewhere, the Ultras were determined to defy the norms by what they viewed as their joyful and colourful expression of support for their team. Their dynamism, organizational ability, rebellious attitude, dress and flexibility were geared towards rejecting their club's tutelage that they associated with patriarchism and elitism and confronting the security forces and the media, both of which they perceived as hostile.

The Egyptian Ultras knew what they were up against—the security forces, the corporate sponsors, the state and the soccer establishment—and made that obvious in their literature, art, graffiti and stadium choreography. Their former Yugoslav counterparts had demonstrated that soccer fans can change the course of history. A plinth on a statue of three soldiers in front of Dinamo Zagreb's Maksimir Stadium reads: "To the fans of the club, who started the war with Serbia on this ground on May 13th, 1990," a reference to pitched battles between supporters of Dynamo and Arkan's Serb nationalist Red Star Belgrade, the worst incident in former Yugoslavia's sporting history and widely viewed as the prelude to a decade of war in the Balkans. Supporters of both clubs, armed with rocks and acid, arrived at the stadium prepared for battle. Dynamo's Bad Blue Boys, aided and abetted by Croatia's newly elected nationalist president Franco Tudjman, a former Yugoslav general and director of federalist Partizan Belgrade, swelled the ranks of the fledgling Croatian army when fighting with Serbia erupted shortly after the game. They wore their club emblem alongside their military insignia.

Ahmed Fondu, a UWK co-founder, was drawn into the movement by what he discovered in the former Yugoslavia. "Soccer is a way of life for me. I made my transition to the Ultras on the internet. I encountered the fans' movement. They were about bringing the game back to the fans. I talked to them every day for three or four years, and I'd check the newspapers every day," said Fondu, who met his Serbian girlfriend through his connections with Belgrade.[65]

At the same time, the Egyptian Ultras refrained from adopting the right-wing ideology of some of their counterparts overseas, or the nihilistic violence common to European soccer hooligans. According to Fondu, "We are normal people. We love our country, our club and our group. We are fighting for freedom. That was the common thing between the revolutionaries and the Ultras. We were fighting for freedom in the stadiums. The Egyptian people were fighting for freedom. We invested our ideas and feelings in revolution."

The Ultras organized themselves in the stadiums of Cairo in sections led by a *kabo*, the Arabized equivalent of the Italian *capo*, and named after the city's teeming, popular neighbourhoods. What bound them together was an assertive, urban and tough masculinity in which men where perceived to stand up for their principles. New recruits swore to uphold the group's unity and discipline. They adopted often Westernized *noms de guerre*. Each one of them was assigned a place and a role whether in the stadium or on the street. He knew the importance of timely coordination and aggressive assertion.

The Mubarak regime, unlike the monarchy in Morocco, which effectively negotiated terms under which Moroccan Ultras operated, refused to concede public space to a group whose mounting credibility it sought to undermine by denouncing them as drug addicts and junkies.[66] Leaders of the group were often randomly arrested. Nevertheless, their regular clashes with security forces set a dangerous precedent. They demonstrated that the security forces were not invincible; that determined, motivated youth who were passionate about something like soccer could defeat the police; and in doing so carve out a space of their own that put the regime on the back foot. Moreover, the clashes turned the Ultras into a force to be reckoned with and positioned them at a key moment in Egyptian history at the vanguard of a people's uprising.

The rise of the Ultras coincided with a period in which foreign diplomats and intelligence services feared that the Mubarak regime was becoming increasingly out of touch with public opinion and more and more corrupt and heavy-handed. Ali al-Din Hilal Dessouki, a former Mubarak Cabinet minister, advised an American diplomat in 2009 that "widespread, politically motivated unrest was unlikely because it was not part of the 'Egyptian mentality.'"[67] He said that threats to daily survival rather than politics was the only thing that would prompt Egyptians to stage mass protests.

The ranks of the police and security forces meanwhile swelled as ever more recruits were brought in to expand surveillance. Illegal detention and torture became commonplace, no longer a tactic reserved for Islamists and other opponents of the regime. Security was stepped up with a notable increase in armoured vans on Tahrir Square—historically the venue where victories on the soccer pitch were celebrated, the deaths of national celebrities were mourned or discontent was expressed. Rows of black-clad police encircled groups whenever they arrived on the square as they did stadiums in advance of matches. The expanded repression showed that the regime was no longer effectively gauging public opinion, as was obvious in the confrontations with security forces in the stadiums, who responded with demonstrable violence when engagement would have produced better results.

"The police are the police. They regard the citizens with a look of superiority and misappropriate their personages and human dignity. The police's loyalty is to their leaders and the powers-that-be, not to the law," observed the Egyptian journalist Karim Yahya.[68]

The choice in Cairo of Tahrir Square reflected a sense of confidence among youth and soccer groups that their time had come. The size of the square meant that their protest needed to be sizeable not to be marginalized by the vastness of the venue. The choice of the square, given the fact that it is accessible by wide avenues, also meant that protesters would be more vulnerable to attack by police and security forces who could reach it just as easily as the protesters and for whom deployment would be far easier than in a warren of narrow streets in a Cairo neighbourhood. The success of the youth and soccer groups in attracting tens of thousands of people on 25 January 2011, the first day of the anti-Mubarak protests, guaranteed that their protest could not be simply dismissed, and that it would enjoy significant media exposure.

That confidence reflected in part the Ultras' sense of empowerment as a result of years of resistance in the stadiums. Moreover, a culture that emphasized visibility and being conspicuous worked to their advantage. As Italian sociologists Alessandro Dal Lago and Rocco De Biasi observe, Ultras "travel in large groups and often, when there is trouble, they adopt strategies very similar to the types of fight evident in political riots."[69]

Tahrir Square's topography, dominated by constant reminders of a repressive regime as well as a statute of national hero Omar Makram who led the resistance against Napoleon, made it the obvious place for protests once they left the stadium. The same was true for Tunis' Avenue Habib Bourguiba, a wide avenue in the heart of the city that hosts the interior ministry and was the headquarters of the hated secret police.

The multi-storey headquarters of Mubarak's National Democratic Party that were burnt in the early days towered over Tahrir. On the south side of the square stands the Mugamma, a brooding fourteen-floor structure reminiscent of Soviet architecture that houses the government's central administration, symbolizing Egypt's infuriating impenetrable, corrupt and crushing bureaucracy. Pedestrians used to hurry past the Mugamma, their eyes focused on the pavement to avoid the glare of plainclothes security men monitoring the building's surroundings.

Opposite the Mugamma to the north stands the National Museum designed to reinforce the autocratic regime's narrative of historic legacy and national triumph. Just beyond the square lie the headquarters of the ineffective Arab League, the US embassy and the hated interior ministry. For the Ultras, moving from the stadium to the square amounted to expanding their claims to ownership of public venues to the core of Cairo in an implicit assertion that they belonged to them rather than to a corrupt and repressive regime. Those claims are further expressed in the murals and graffiti that adorn streets near the square.

The square and the avenue moreover bolstered the fact the protests were more than simple demands for the departure of Mubarak and Ben Ali. They constituted a rejection of a system in which established opposition parties or groups compromised their demands for democratic reform and were rewarded by the regime with limited gains like a license to establish a party or a limited number of seats in a parliament dominated by the ruling party. As a result, many activists and Ultras viewed party politics with a degree of suspicion as long as the goals of their revolt, including reform of the security sector, had not been achieved. Their suspicion hampered the post-autocratic regime transition from contentious to electoral politics.

Weekly battles in stadiums with security forces and rival fan groups had politicized the Ultras and prepared them for the clashes in Tahrir Square.[70] These clashed forced them to develop skills that were alien to the middle class and most other segments of Egyptian society, but also came in handy as a daily survival mechanism beyond the stadium. Nevertheless, they more often than not refused to frame their radicalization in political terms. "We steer clear of politics. Competition in Egypt is on the soccer pitch. We break the rules and regulations when we think they are wrong. You don't change things in Egypt talking about politics. We're not political, the government knows that and that is why it has to deal with us," said one Egyptian Ultra in 2010, after his group overran a police barricade erected to prevent it from bringing flares, fireworks and banners into a stadium.[71]

Assad, an Ultras Ahlawy leader, stated:

> The old [Mubarak] regime was very suspicious of everything organized. They tried to control the unions, they tried to control the student unions in the universities and they tried to control the political life. Suddenly they found in front of them a bunch of young people organizing themselves in football. That's why we had so many problems. They just weren't happy with the fact that you have 20, 25 guys who have gathered 500 people in two hours. For them, now they are speaking about football, tomorrow they will be speaking about politics and funnily enough, for us, we had no political intention at any moment. They made of us what they were afraid, repressing us when they started like fighting us, people started to hate them because we were fighting for our freedom, for what we believe we had the right to achieve and the right to establish.[72]

As in Egypt, anti-government protests on the soccer pitch preceded the mass demonstrations that erupted in Tunisia in December 2010, forcing President Zine El Abidine Ben Ali to resign and sparking the "Arab Spring". Tunisian fans jeered the Confederation of African Football (CAF) president Issa Hayatou in November during the Orange CAF Champions League return final between Espérance Sportive de Tunis and TP Mazembe from the Democratic Republic of Congo. In the first encounter between the two teams in Congo, in which Espérance lost, the fans charged that the Togolese referee had been corrupt, and waved banknotes at Hayatou. The protests led to clashes between the fans who, like their counterparts in Egypt, had become street battle-hardened.

Rival Cairo Ultras on Tahrir Square set aside their deep-seated animosity grounded in the history of Al Ahly and Zamalek, that continues to this day despite Egyptian independence, the demise of the monarchy and the erosion in differences between their fan bases. Their joining of forces resembled an earlier, similar alliance in Tehran between arch enemies Persepolis and Esteghlal, still named Taj at the time, whose supporters came together in 1981 in a rare show of unity to protest the Islamic regime's crackdown on soccer in an initial failed bid to reduce the game's importance.

The rivalry between Ahly and Zamalek, the Arab world's foremost sporting competition, went beyond soccer. In the perception of the fans and officials it was about more than pride; theirs was a struggle about concepts of nationalism, class and escapism. Al-Ahly's liberal republicans perceived themselves as representing the devout, the poor and the proud while Zamalek projected itself as the club of the conservative royalists and bourgeois middle class. Former Zamalek board member Hassan Ibrahim, a man who was born fourteen years after the abolition of the monarchy, noted that "Zamalek is the biggest political party in Egypt. We see the injustice of the Football Federation and the government against whatever once belonged to the king. The federation and the government see Zamalek as the enemy. Zamalek represents the people who express their anger against the system. We view Ahly as the representative of corruption in Egypt."[73]

It is a perception that lives on despite the fact that it no longer reflects a reality in which the social differentiation of the supporter base of the two teams has faded and the teams' representation of political trend or social group is imagined rather than real. The two teams' militant fan groups are similar to those in Italy, who pioneered concepts of the Ultras' autonomy and giving priority to the group's survival, if need be at the expense of their club. "The Ultras' style of support has never been dominated by any particular social stratum or any specific youth style. The unifying element for the youth of Italian *curvas* [stadium ends or terraces] has always been support itself, and not social consumption, or class status, or political belief, or musical fashion etc.," Dal Lago and De Biassi write.[74]

So deep-seated was the Al Ahly–Zamalek rivalry that the Mubarak government insisted that matches be played on neutral ground with European referees flown in to manage the game. Their derby, one of the most violent in the world, divides the city and the country. Hundreds of black-clad riot police, soldiers and plainclothes security personnel, worried about what the teams' Ultras may have in store, surround the stadium on game day. The police are tasked as much with keeping the fan groups apart as they are with preventing the Ultras from claiming the stadium as a space of their own beyond the reach of the regime, even if only for ninety minutes or less. Routes to and from stadiums are strictly managed so that opposing fans don't come into contact with one another before or after the match. "Soccer is a massive thing in Egypt. It is like religion. In most countries you are born Jewish, Muslim or Christian. In Egypt you were born Ahly and Zamalek. People would not ask your religion, they would ask whether you were Ahly or Zamalek," said Adel Abdel Ghafar, Sarwat's great-grandson, and a PhD student at the Australian National University.[75]

The divide between Ahly and Zamalek mirrors Jason Cowley's description of the ardent soccer fan as a function of the father-son relationship that involves:

> both an affirmation (a commitment to a cause) and an escape (from the everyday reality). For this reason the bond between fan and club is irrational: you can change your wife and job, even the shape of your nose, but, if you're a true fan, you can never change the club to which you committed emotionally at a young age, no matter how much frustration and unhappiness it brings. You are bound helplessly to the mast of your own obsession. Most of us men who like and watch football, and those who write about it, do so because of our fathers. The experience of being a fan is bound up with that of being a son; of how you were first introduced to the game and conducted into its codes and rituals.[76]

The social and economic fallout of soccer passions and rivalries was first revealed in a study in the 1960s in São Paulo that showed how productivity rose by 15 per cent when the city's soccer team won and dropped by 12 per cent when it lost.[77] Gary Armstrong and Rosemary Harris argued that humiliating rivals constituted a core element of being a militant soccer fan: soccer "is primarily a game that aims to humiliate rivals and oblige them to recognize the challengers' superiority; to achieve this aim, however, there has to be a willingness to turn the game into a blood sport, like foxhunting…"[78]

Dal Lago and De Biasi note that rival Ultras share a "fighting culture" in which each group "fights to impose its symbolic strength in terms of the beauty and impressiveness of the choreography ... and in terms of displaying courage" and "before or after the match regards the end, the stadium and the open spaces surrounding the stadium (including under-ground stations, railway stations, and so on) as its exclusive territory to be defended against the enemy's raids ... In order to defeat the enemies on the field, Ultra groups try to adopt urban guerrilla tactics (particularly setting ambushes near to stations and involving the police)."[79]

The combined skills of the two Ultras groups coupled with their street battle experience were evident in the organization and social services as well as the division of labour established on Tahrir Square as tens of thousands camped out for eighteen days until Mubarak was left with no choice but to step down. The Ultras stood on the dividing line that would determine the revolt's fate. They mastered hit-and-run tactics, came pre-pared to resist tear gas, understood the need to rotate those manning the front line and the art of tactical withdrawal to avoid panic and stam-pedes, and appreciated the mobilizing impact as well as the communica-tion advantages of beating drums. Much in the way that a municipality would organize services, protesters were assigned tasks such as the collec-tion of trash. They wore masking tape on which they were identified by their role, medic or media contact, for example. Their organization mimicked that of similar Italian groups and had its roots in models found among militants in Italy. As Dal Lago and De Biasi write: "the firmly structured organizational dimension of some extremist political youth associations has been adopted, as shown by the following features: the presence of a *Direttivo*, a sort of political bureau, the assembly-like or democratic style of decision-making in the Ultras groups; the strong commitment of some members during the week (meetings, preparations of banners and choreography, distribution of leaflets); and even the use of flagpoles as weapons. All these are elements which were already pre-sent in political extremism."[80]

The Ultras—often committed anarchists who oppose hierarchical systems of government—joined those patrolling the perimeters of the square and controlling entry. Dressed in skinny jeans, neck scarves and hooded sweatshirts pulled tight over their heads, they manned the front lines in clashes with security forces and pro-government supporters. Their faces were frequently covered so that the police, who had warned them to stay away from Tahrir Square, would not recognize them. They marched under huge, professionally prepared banners, chanted to the thudding beat of a bass drum and with military precision clapped their hand over their heads. "The Ultras are here. I know that because they're the only ones facing the CSF [Central Security Force] with force while singing their hymns," tweeted protester and photographer Mosa'ab Elshamy on the first day of clashes. "The Shabaab (youth) r doing fantastic job @ the barricades, security is well run on all exits. Bless them," added the blogger and activist Hossam el-Hamalawy.[81]

The Ultras' experience benefitted them in the struggle for control of the square when the president's loyalists employed brute force in their bid to dislodge them. The Ultras' battle order included designated stone throwers, specialists in turning over and torching vehicles for defensive purposes and a machine-like quartermaster crew delivering projectiles on cardboard platters with logistical efficiency. Some described as *sayaadin* [hunters] hurled tear gas canisters fired by the police back into the ranks of the law enforcers. "At Kasr el Nil Bridge, we have taken complete control Gaza style with just rocks against gun fire," marvelled activist Gigi Ibrahim in a 2 February 2011 tweet.[82] Almost two hours later, blogger Mosa'ab Elshamy added: "We're now using burnt CSF trucks for protection & blockade and pushing them [the security forces] away."[83] Added blogger Amr Gharbeia: "The resistance I witnessed in Tahrir last night is humbling. We all owe it to the bravery of last night's Museum Battle in #Egypt."[84] Elshamy camped out on Tahrir Square noted: "Remember this is a nation that only waved the flag during football games and was labelled by its last PM 'not yet ready for democracy.'"[85]

For the youth and soccer fans this was a battle in which they had nothing to lose and everything to gain. Their weekly stadium battles with the police and rival fans were a zero-sum game for ownership of a space they saw as theirs as a result of defining themselves as the only true club loyalists. Club executives, in their eyes, were regime pawns while players were hired guns who were in it only for the money. A blacklist of Mubarak supporters that circulated immediately after the president's fall included national team coach Hassan Shehata, former goalkeeper Ahmed Shobeir, who was accused of participating in the abuse of political prisoners, and Zamalek's Ibrahim. Similarly, Tunisian fans forced Ben Ali's sports minister to flee his office through the back door and demanded the resignation of club boards.

Gerry P. T. Finn has argued persuasively that fans have:

> an emotional and cognitive identification with the club, another imaginary community, for fans see themselves as the real *supporters* of the club. They see themselves as providing finance by their gate-money and believe themselves to uphold the traditions of the club: fans are the self-perceived moral custodians of the club, albeit custodians who feel exploited and frustrated at their lack of access to most club decision-making ... The belief that the club belongs to the fans appears a distortion of economic reality, but is more a statement of the intensity of feelings fans have for their team and an expression of their belief that they are genuinely part of it.[86]

In a similar vein, Gary Armstrong and Malcolm Young reason that to militant soccer fans "the game and its metaphoric language is all about aggressively defeating an enemy—an 'other'—who must be shown to be inept, bungling, untalented and certain to be thrashed. The social process has always required them to be antagonistic, offensive and abusive."[87]

Much like hooligans in Britain, whose attitudes were shaped by the decaying condition of stadiums, Egyptian and Tunisian Ultras were driven by the regime's attempt to control their space by turning it into a virtual fortress ringed by black steel. The struggle for control produced a complete breakdown, social decay in a microcosm. If the space was expendable, so was life. As a result, militant fans would confront the police each weekend with total abandon in a phenomenon in stadiums that Pratt and Salter describe as "a meeting point for a variety of social conflicts, hostilities and prejudices."[88] As Dal Lago and De Biassi conclude in their analysis of Italian Ultras: "The intensification of police control inside and outside the stadia led the Ultras to adopt a mode of military organization and a war-like attitude against the police. As a result football hooliganism qua social problem has to be regarded as the legacy of such policing."[89]

Upholding Dignity, Breaking the Barrier of Fear

> *"When the revolution erupted, we took to the streets all over the nation: we died for Freedom and the fall of the heads of corruption. We are not done yet, as the regime is still kicking: the dogs of the interior police and injustice are everywhere. Kill the revolution more and more. The word "Freedom" drives you crazy! No matter how brutal the warden is, he's a chicken against my voice."*

Egyptian Ultras' song

In Egypt, less than two weeks after Tunisian Ultras and other protesters forced Ben Ali to leave the country in early 2011, Egyptian Ultras and youth groups followed suit. The first major protest in Egypt was planned for Cairo's Tahrir Square on 25 January 2011. The day before the protest, the two leading groups of Ultras in Cairo issued statements on Facebook stressing that they were non-political organizations, but that their members were free as individuals to participate in the protests. "The group emphasizes that its members are free in their political choices," said the statement by the Ultras Ahlawy.[90]

Privately, both groups told their followers that the demonstration was what they had been working towards in four years of almost weekly clashes with security forces in the stadiums of Cairo. The Ultras, unlike most other groups in Tahrir Square, were braced for violent confrontations. Daring cat-and-mouse tactics by Ultras, often teenagers or men in their early twenties, and steadfastness at front-line barricades under tear gas and rubber bullets, wore the police down. "We fought for our rights in the stadium for four years. That prepared us for this day. We told our people that this was our litmus test. Failure was not an option," said Ahmed Fondu, a founder of Zamalek's Ultras White Knights, who proudly described how several days into the mass protests he captured camel-mounted Mubarak loyalists attacking the demonstrators and held them captive in the Sadat metro station near Tahrir Square.[91]

"We were in the front line. When the police attacked we encouraged people. We told them not to run or be afraid. We started firing flares. People took courage and joined us, they know that we understand injustice and liked the fact that we fight the devil," added Muhamed Hassan, a 20-year-old, softly-spoken computer science student, aspiring photographer and a UWK leader.[92]

Nagat Ali, a doctoral student in literature at Cairo University, recalled joining a crowd outside a mosque that was headed for Tahrir Square on 28 January, the third day of protests against Mubarak:

> I suddenly noticed in the crowd many were Ultras from the Zamalek team and Ahly. From the first moment I viewed the Ultras with a terrified eye and considered them a threat because of my fear of the violent groups of Ultras I had seen at soccer matches—in terms of their strength in numbers and organization. I found myself marching with the Ultras and repeating their chants. I noticed how they swept through the streets; they were not afraid of security forces. Just the opposite, they knew how to deal with them. Like a team, their movement was disciplined and they chanted in rhythm. I felt this demonstration had transformed into an orchestra; they were clever musicians. Like pied pipers, they were trying to draw people from their buildings with their chants:

One, two, where are the Egyptian people?
Why are you watching from far away? You're Egyptian, aren't you?
Raise. Raise the voice. He, who chants will never die.[93]

Marching from the Cairo neighbourhood of Shubra, Muhamed, a small-framed man with carefully trimmed three-day stubble, led a crowd that grew to 10,000 people; they marched through seven security barricades to Tahrir Square on 25 January, the first day of the protests. Ultras on rooftops hurled Molotov cocktails at security forces blocking off popular neighbourhoods in a bid to prevent residents from making their way to the square. This was the day Muhamed and the Ultras had been preparing for in the past four years, honing their fighting skills in running battles with the police, widely viewed as Mubarak's henchmen, and with rivals from other teams. Years of battle had taught him and his cohorts how to be one step ahead of the security forces. They, like the youth groups, would call publicly for protesters to gather in the early afternoon at well-known landmarks and intersections in an effort to lure security to those locations but would start their march at noon elsewhere in popular neighbourhoods. "Hey government, tomorrow you will be cleansed by the people's hands. Hey stupid regime, when will you understand that what I demand is freedom, freedom, freedom?" they chanted.

A group of UWK Ultras, including Muhamed, sought at one point to break through a police barrier to reach the nearby parliament building. "When I see the security forces, I go crazy. I will kill you or I will be killed. The Ultras killed my fear. I learnt the meaning of brotherhood and got the courage of the stadium," he said. He pointed to a scar on the left side of his forehead from a stone thrown by police who stymied the fans' early attempt to break through to parliament. As blood streamed down his face, he heard internal walls of fear crumble as cries rose from the crowd behind him: "They are our brothers. We can do this." Nora Shalaby, an archaeologist, tweeted: "Those protesters that have remained in the streets despite the latest police brutality against us are really brave."[94] Some of those who opted for safety above struggle conceded to having feelings of guilt afterwards. "I did not take part in the violence, which is a real moral dilemma for me right now for its people who did who saved me," tweeted blogger Amr El Beleidy.[95]

An iconic video clip posted on YouTube on 25 January exemplified the role of the Ultras.[96] A young man believed to be an Ultra dressed in a black jacket and white scarf single-handedly, if temporarily, stopped a water cannon from progress near Tahrir on Qasr al-'Ayni Street by defiantly blocking its way with his hands on his hips. His defiance reflected a widespread perception among the Ultras: defeating the police amounted to defeating the Mubarak regime. "The Ultras remained in the square fighting for some three days. You couldn't miss them. They're easy to identify because of their use of Molotov cocktails, uniform dress, courage and recklessness, and their chants," recalls one protester. "The security forces would have succeeded in pushing us out of Tahrir if the Ultras had not been there," said another.

The Ultras' role was instrumental in defeating what Salwa Ismail describes as "fear and the culture of fear that continuous monitoring, surveillance, humiliation and abuse have created."[97] As John Chalcraft has noted, for ordinary Egyptians the state is "in the detention cells, in the corrupt police stations, in the beatings, in the blood of the people, in the popular quarters."[98] In fact, it was everywhere. The police and security forces effectively constituted the regime's administrative arm. It did not matter what the issue was—official documents like passports, drivers' licences or birth and death certificates; local conflicts, elections and election fixing, vetting of public sector appointments, labour issues or stadium and mosque security—it was the police and security forces that were responsible. They also often depended on a high level of bribery in a bid to supplement their meagre incomes.

A "culture of impunity," in the words of successive annual US State Department human rights reports and former US ambassador to Egypt Margaret Scobey, enjoyed by the police and the security forces was reinforced by their structural cooperation with criminal groups dating back to Mubarak's continuation of his predecessors' effort to strengthen them at the expense of the military. Intimidation of groups likely to vote against the ruling party or professional associations critical of the government was outsourced to criminals and thugs. Brawls provoked by thugs provided the police and security forces with the pretext to step in and arrest opposition figures at polling stations. By the same token, the police's use of criminals gave them licence to extort protection payments from individuals and businesses and often sexually harass women. Police and security officials' adaptation to criminal practices meant that not only activists and opposition figures but increasingly ordinary citizens risked arbitrary arrest and abuse. Physical abuse of detainees became part of young recruits' induction to the police and security forces. The police's impunity was officially enshrined when its slogan was changed from "The Police in the Service of the People" to "The Police and the People in the Service of the State."

"Contacts attribute police brutality to poor training, understaffing and official sanction. Human rights lawyer xxxx speculated that officers routinely resort to brutality because of pressure from their superiors to solve crimes. He asserted that most officers think solving crimes justifies brutal interrogation methods, and that some policemen believe that Islamic law sanctions torture. Xxxx commented that a culture of judicial impunity for police officers enables continued brutality. According to xxxx, 'Police officers feel they are above the law and protected by the public prosecutor.' Human rights lawyer xxxx attributed police brutality against common criminals, including the use of electric shocks, to the problem of demoralized officers facing long hours and their own economic problems. He asserted that the police will even beat lawyers who enter police stations to defend their clients," Scobey wrote in 2009 in a classified diplomatic cable to the State Department.[99]

A popular Ultras Ahlawy song, "Oh Nesting Crow", captured the popular perception of the police and security forces having been transitioned from servant to master of the people:

Oh crow nesting at our home, who has always been a failure in life,
In high school, he barely scored fifty percent.
Through bribes, his "excellency" obtained an education and a degree worthy of a hundred colleges.
Oh crow nesting at our home,
Why are you destroying the joy of our lives?
We will not do as you want,
So please save us your grace.
Go ahead and contrive a case since this is what the *Dakhliya* [Ministry of Interior] usually does.
I was arrested and charged with international terrorism when all I did was wave a torch and chant "Ahly."[100]

The breaking down of the barrier of fear meant that government coercion was rendered ineffective, a key pre-condition, according to Charles Tilly,[101] for a revolution to occur. The effectiveness of government coercion declines, he argued, "when the character, organization, and daily routines of the population to be controlled change rapidly."[102] Four years of battles in the stadiums coupled with years of labour unrest and youth groups that harnessed new media as an organization tool meant that the Mubarak regime in early 2011 was dealing with a different civic society, one that was emboldened and less intimidated. Degradation of police capacity, added Chalcraft, was "in some ways ... the sine qua non of breaking the culture of fear and being able to perform a rejection of the regime."[103]

It was also a civic society that was learning the lessons—in the run-up to Mubarak's downfall and in the initial post-Mubarak transition period—of the failures of revolutionaries like the prominent Syrian poet Ali Ahmad Said Asbar, better known as Adonis and Yasin Al-Hafiz in the heyday of Arab nationalism, whose Marxist thinking was at the core of the Syrian Baath Party's ideology but was rendered impotent by autocracies that stymied critical, independent thinking.

"We aspire as revolutionary Arabs, to lay the foundations for a new era for the Arabs. We know that institutionalizing a new era requires from the very beginning a total break with the past. We also know that the starting point of this founding break is criticism, the criticism of all that is inherited, prevalent and common. The role of criticism is not limited to exposing and laying bare whatever prevents the creation of a new era but involves its destruction," Adonis wrote in a manifesto first published in the late 1970s.[104]

Al-Hafiz cautioned some two decades later that "a critique of all aspects of existing Arab society and its traditions as well as a strict scientific, secular critique and deep, penetrating analysis is a fundamental obligation of the Arab revolutionary socialist vanguard ... Exploring the traditional frames of Arab society, will accelerate the creation of a completely modern Arab society. Without such an explosion, the chances for a systematic, speedy and revolutionary development of the traditional intellectual and social structures of the Arab people will be questionable if not impossible."[105]

The military and later Egypt's first and only freely elected president, the Muslim Brotherhood's Mohammed Morsi, nevertheless quickly created the conditions for a potential second revolution. The military, which took over from Mubarak with a promise to lead the country to free elections within six months, demonstrated that its agenda differed radically from those who had toppled him. Determined to retain its political, economic and security privileges, the armed forces worked to enhance the country's democratic façade, without touching the very structures crucial to maintaining power. As a result, it refused to engage with the movement that had toppled Mubarak, which it accused, along with the soccer fans, of being foreign agents who had been trained militarily in

Serbia. Against the backdrop of repeated clashes with security forces and pro-regime thugs, the military banned all protests in June 2011 and ordered demonstrators to leave Tahrir. Whoever disobeyed would be treated as an agitator and foreign agent seeking to destroy Egypt, the military warned, foreshadowing its bloody crackdown on the Brotherhood two years later.

Confrontation was again evident in the November 2011 clashes between security forces and Ultras eager to settle old accounts in the streets of the Abdin neighbourhood east of Cairo's Tahrir Square that lead to the interior ministry. They were joined by some Muslim Brotherhood youths with whom the Ultras, the second largest civic group in Egypt after the Brothers, together with the *wilad sis*—unemployed and underemployed, uneducated young men from sprawling informal neighbourhoods who were bristling for a fight—had formed bonds in their eighteen days on Tahrir Square in early 2011. Taking a break from the fighting, a young Ultra said it was all par for the course. "Ours is a way of life. One doesn't simply join the Ultras, one is born an Ultra. Our time has come. We are not the first ones to attack. But we stand up whenever and wherever we see injustice. There are no free lunches. We suffer and sacrifice to achieve justice," he added, his eyes wandering in the direction of the clashes.[106]

In the instinctive spirit of Adonis and Al-Hafiz, the Ultras alongside other youth groups were determined in the months leading up to the first post-Mubarak elections to foil the military's attempts to operate on the principle of the emperor is dead, long live the emperor. The military's mishandling of the transition, with its crude attempts to undermine a democratic process and employ intimidation, sparked the November protests and five days of pitched battles between security forces and Ultras-led protesters demanding the military's return to barracks in which forty-two people were killed. "Cairo's Tahrir Square is in a certain sense the paradigm for all the other Tahrir Squares in the Arab world in their resistance to persistent efforts by ancien regimes to effectively retain some degree of power," said the prominent Syrian intellectual Sadik Al-Azm.[107]

Protesters reoccupied Tahrir on 18 November 2011, demanding the resignation of the transition military government in one of the largest protest gatherings since Mubarak's demise. By mid-afternoon the next day, phone calls from the square requested the Ultras to shield them from an imminent attack by security forces. The calls were made just as Al Ahly and Zamalek Ultras, aware of the imminent security operation, decided that they could not stand by idly as innocent protesters were being targeted. "We can deal with poverty, but not tolerate repression. Social justice is one of our key demands," insisted an Ultra who was part of the decision to join the protesters in the square. However, what began as a human barricade created to protect protesters from the security forces bent on clearing the area escalated into a battle with its own dynamics. Police faced off with protesters, who were armed with rocks, Molotov cocktails and homemade explosive devices using teargas and at times live ammunition. As the frontline in the so-called Battle of the *Dakhliya* [interior ministry], or alternatively the Battle of Mohammed Mahmoud Street, moved at times closer to and then further away from the ministry, Chinese-made motorcycles carried the wounded to safety. *Shamarikh*, the coloured fireworks employed by the Ultras during soccer matches, and burning garbage bins lit up the sky at night replacing street lights that had been turned off. More than forty people were killed and more than a thousand injured with many losing one or both eyes.

State-run media and officials calling into television talk shows charged that the Ultras and youth had been incited by thugs funded by supporters of the Mubarak regime. The allegation reflected an initial effort by the military, and later by Morsi's Brotherhood, to shift responsibility for the country's problem to third parties, including foreign agents, *baltageyya* or thugs and *fulul*, remnants of the Mubarak regime. Yet the struggle of the Ultras, the youth groups and the *wilad sis* was as much a battle for *karama* or dignity—albeit one that was predominantly instinctive, masculine resistance—as it was part of the fight to hold the military to its pledge to lead the country to democracy. Their dignity was vested in their ability to stand up to the *Dakhliya*, the knowledge that they no longer could be abused by security forces without recourse and the fact that they no longer had to pay off each and every policemen to stay out of trouble. Yet it was also a battle for the sake of the battle. "We knew what would happen, we wanted the fight," said one young man his face covered with a handkerchief.

In doing so, the Ultras nevertheless built on a perception perpetuated by repressive security forces in popular neighbourhoods and in the stadiums of their arbitrary use of force. In the words of Eduardo P. Archetti and Amilcar G. Romero, police and security forces' "use of physical force aided by arms of some kind … [was] exclusively destined to harm, wound, injure, or, in some cases, kill other persons, and not as an act intended to stop unlawful behaviour that is taking place or may take place."[108] Official foot-dragging in holding security officers accountable added to that perception, giving "police power ... the aura of omnipotence" that "at the same time lost all legitimacy both in moral and social terms,"[109] they argued—a development reinforced in post-revolt Arab societies such as Egypt by the failure to date to reform the security forces. "The police in the stadia, therefore, are perceived not as neutral and shallow actors but as central and active participants. To resist and to attack the police force is thus seen as morally justified," they wrote. For their part, the police defined "the fans as a political. Stadiums were converted into open political arenas."[110]

Yet at the same time parallel events in Abdin and on Tahrir Square reflected developing faultlines between those protesters demanding achievement of the popular revolt's goals and those for whom the ongoing demonstrations offered an opportunity for payback. The square was populated by a cross-section of Egyptian society, activists and ordinary citizens. Abdin was the territory of militant, marginalized, young men united by their hostility to the security forces and, in the case of the Ultras, loyalty to their club. There was nevertheless a symbiotic relationship between the two. The square was dependent on the Ultras' protection, while the Ultras' ability to exact revenge was to raise the stakes in their battle with the security forces.

Ironically, on Mohammed Mahmoud Street there was nevertheless an unspoken, shared sense among both the security forces and the Ultras that for the first time in five years of on-going battles it was the interior ministry's forces rather than the soccer fans that were fighting for their own survival. The police's tarnished image as the regime's enforcers remained unchanged and, if anything, was reinforced by the refusal of the government to hold police officers accountable for their excesses despite pressure from the public as well as reform-minded security personnel. The battles with the Ultras, as was the case when the military unleashed the security forces in the summer of 2013 against the Brotherhood, provided opportunities for the police and other elements of the security sector to act out their frustration and anger at their public humiliation in the post-Mubarak era as the evil face of the regime. Their status of being a law unto themselves, inextricably tied to the autocracy, had been under threat since Mubarak's fall and was only reasserted with the military's toppling of Morsi in July 2013. It was also a payback for the setbacks they had suffered in the lead-up to Mubarak's overthrow when they had been unprepared to deal with a massive popular uprising. The security forces had hoped to quell the uprising on its third day by cutting off all internet and mobile communications. That might have worked if it had not been a Friday, the public day of rest on which many Egyptians go to the mosque for midday prayers. Any doubts about joining the protesters or returning to Tahrir Square were erased by imams in the mosques denouncing the dictatorship. The security forces' humiliation was sealed when their second line of defence—live fire, snipers, tear gas, water cannons, mass arrests and driving armoured vehicles into crowds—failed equally miserably. Emboldened protesters with Ultras in the lead had worn the security forces down. They were defeated, and left with no choice but to withdraw.

The blurring of Ultras and *wilad sis* was already evident shortly after the ousting of Mubarak. In April 2011 during an African championship match between Zamalek and Tunisia's Espérance Sportive de Tunis, less ideologically motivated UWK members led by Said Moshagheb, a mesmerizingly charismatic, under-educated and unemployed orator, took the lead in storming the Cairo International Stadium's pitch in the ninetieth minute of the game. The storming was part of a tug of war within the group between members committed to the principles of the global Ultras' movement and inspired by anarchism and those who wanted hooliganism to dominate the group. UWK leaders, who had put on a well-oiled display of support for Zamalek with flares, fireworks, seventy-metre-long banners and smoke guns, estimated that the disruption reflected the growing influence of *wilad sis* within the group.[111]

The storming represented an unexpected milestone in the Ultras' settling of accounts with security forces, but one in which they believed that they had walked into a trap. Despite having phoned UWK members on the eve of the match to warn them that they would not be allowed to take their fireworks, flares and banners into the stadium, the security forces were virtually absent on the day of the game. Their absence contrasted starkly with past practice in which security forces surrounded the stadium and operated multiple checkpoints to prevent fans from bringing anything into the stadium. The police opted not to stand by their warning to avoid a confrontation with the Ultras, a group that had enhanced its credentials during the overthrow of Mubarak at a time that the security forces were seeking to shed their image as henchmen of the ousted leader. Moreover, the storming of the pitch allowed the security forces to cite the disruption as evidence that they were needed to prevent a break-down of law and order. At the same time, UWK founders conceded that the group had attracted large numbers of frustrated, uneducated young men who lacked their kind of commitment. They described a conflict within the group between highly politicized members and those for whom politics was reduced to a view of the interior ministry and its security forces as evil incarnate.[112] That war was in many ways a reflection of their success in what Tilly described as the ability to demonstrate that they were "worthy, united, numerous and committed."[113]

The Ultras, unlike their brethren known as *barras bravas* in Argentina—who have evolved into criminal gangs engaged in illegal businesses such as drug trafficking, often in cahoots with club officials, politicians and police or who are hired as bodyguards—saw themselves first and fore-most as fervent supporters of their clubs and the shock troops of a revolution engaged in non-formalized politics, a form of instinctive resistance that rejected political dominance and horse trading by established groups. Opting for contentious political tactics was one way the Ultras hoped to fend off attempts by the authorities and parties to manipulate them. It also constituted the Ultras' retort to the military's argument in the run-up to the 2012 elections that the revolution had achieved its aims and that the time had come for Egypt to return to normal and move on.

Soccer: Barometer of Morsi's Political Fortune

> *"In Port Said, the victims saw treachery before death. They saw a regime that presents chaos as its only alternative. That regime thought its grip would make it untouchable. And make the revolutionary people kneel to the military rule. Not anymore! Unleash more of your dogs and spread chaos everywhere. I will never trust you, nor let you control me one more day."*

Egyptian Ultras' song

It was a match that would reshape Egyptian politics, erase whatever credibility Egypt's security forces had left, revitalize revolutionary movements, further fracture the country and close the door on further direct military rule. As Al Ahly prepared in February 2012 for a clash in the Suez Canal city of Port Said with another of its arch rivals, Al Masry SC, emotions were running high. Trouble was brewing, yet security men refrained from searching spectators as they entered the stadium. Supporters of both clubs had traded death threats on Twitter before the match but few believed it was anything more than bluster. The long-standing rivalry between the clubs had gained an additional dimension with the overthrow of Mubarak. Ultras Ahlawy prided itself as a leader of the revolution. Al Masry's Green Eagles were latecomers, having initially sat on the fence in a city that was not one of the engines of the popular revolt.

Kick-off was hardly auspicious. Al Masry fans on the pitch forced a thirty-minute delay. They stormed the pitch again at half time. When the referee blew his whistle to end the game with an unexpected Al Masry 3–1 victory thousands invaded the pitch. They were armed with knives, bottles, clubs and stones. Al Ahly Ultras were unprepared. They ran for the exits, but those were locked from the outside. Seventy-four Ultras died, stabbed and beaten to death, thrown off the stands and trampled in the stampede. Al Ahly coach Manuel José de Jesus and the club's superstar, Mohammed Abou-Treika, saw their supporters dying in the dressing room. The scenes of horror were broadcast live on television; video footage showed police standing by. "It was my dream to see you before I die, now that I did, I know I will die," said an Al Ahly fan as he sighed his last breath in Abou-Treika's arms.[114]

"We found ourselves like say 800 people all stuck inside this tunnel, 60 square metres. We started to fall down on each other, there were like five levels of people all on each other ... All you could see was half of a human. You could see just the upper part, you could see the head and the body is buried under other bodies. You could see the hand, just one hand of our friends, just trying to say help or something. The cops didn't do anything, they were just watching. The army were guarding this gate and they were just watching," recalled an Al Ahly fan who survived the incident.[115]

The violence quickly spread to Cairo. Protesters set fire within minutes of the Port Said incident to the Cairo Stadium after a match between Zamalek and Ismailia. The Zamalek coach Hassan Shehata cancelled the match during halftime. As the magnitude of the disaster in Port Said emerged, the Egyptian Football Association (EFA) suspended the league. "This is a war that was planned and premeditated," said a visibly shaken Ehab Ali, the Al Ahly team's doctor.

Few doubt that the riot was planned and politically inspired. Many read significance into the fact that it occurred almost to the day a year after the Ultras took centre stage in Tahrir Square's infamous Battle of the Camels, fending off attacking Mubarak supporters mounted on camels and donkeys. Similarly, there is little doubt that the intended thrashing got out of hand, leaving an indelible stamp on the country's already volatile transition. "Is what is happening in Port Said a message to the revolution?" tweeted Essam Sharif, an academic who participated in the Tahrir Square protests against Mubarak and then served for eight months as the military's ceremonial prime minister until his resignation in November 2011.

Others linked it to the military's efforts to persuade the Islamist-dominated parliament to maintain emergency rule, a hangover from the Mubarak era. Social democratic MP Ziad al-Elaimy argued that the incident occurred a day after the military had visited parliament and amidst a string of armed robberies that he said were designed to bolster the argument of Field Marshall Mohamed Hussein Tantawi, head of the ruling Supreme Council of the Armed Forces (SCAF), that lifting emergency rule would only increase thuggery.

"This is not normal. This is the result of a malicious and sinister plan, carefully plotted and expertly perpetrated, and we all know by whom. This past year has seen obvious attempts at destabilizing the nation, and we have remained silent through them all. We were silent as our institutions were burned to the ground, we were silent as our women were publicly dragged and beaten. We cannot remain silent any longer," said Nader al-Sayed, a sports show host, former goalkeeper and one of the few players to have joined the anti-Mubarak protests on Tahrir Square.

The backlash from the worst incident in Egyptian sporting history could not have been greater. The ranks of the revolution's martyrs swelled. The Ultras' resolve was firmer than ever. The military and the security forces were on the defensive. When Morsi took power six months later, he quickly proved incapable of dealing with the crisis he had inherited. The aftermath of Port Said exposed his inexperience and haughtiness. Instead of reaching out to his critics, he followed in Mubarak's footsteps, hoping that the security forces could restore a semblance of order. It was a strategy that emboldened Ultras already knew how to counter. Adding insult to injury, Morsi postponed the one thing that could have helped deflate the tension: reform of Egypt's 1.7 million strong police and security force, the executors of the Mubarak era's repression and the country's most despised institution. Little more than a year after the incident, Morsi was forced to replace security forces with military troops to prevent revolts in three cities along the Canal sparked by the deadly match's aftermath from getting further out of hand.

Official investigations and court proceedings established what happened in the stadium, but left key questions at best unsatisfactorily answered: was the incident premeditated, why and by whom? What were the politics that led to the brawl? "It wasn't just about killing, it was about humiliating. When you see someone with two broken legs and stabbed in the face just like that and stabbed in his stomach, you're not just killing, you're humiliating before killing," insisted a fan.[116]

Perceptions that the Port Said incident was not spontaneous were fed by a belief that many of the post-Mubarak clashes constituted what Mohammed Elshahed termed fabricated urban crises.[117] His notion identified the government and the security forces, who repeatedly used instigated violence to defeat their opponents, rather than the Ultras and the youth groups, as the main actors in Egypt's unfolding crisis. As evidence, he pointed among other things to the fact that Cairo's Mohammed Mahmoud Street, the scene of vicious confrontations between the Ultras and security forces months before Port Said, does not lead directly to the interior ministry and that other streets would have been more appropriate sites if attackers were indeed targeting the ministry. Similarly, he quotes witnesses as saying that security force refrained from intervening in September 2011 when Ultras and youth groups attacked the Israeli and Saudi embassies in Cairo until the incident had been televised.

Morsi's Muslim Brotherhood publicly linked the Port Said incident to anti-Brotherhood demonstrations in Cairo. Members of the Ultras alleged that Port Said was the result of the Brotherhood's betrayal of the popular anti-Mubarak revolt by cutting a deal with the ruling SCAF in advance of presidential elections scheduled for later that year. That sense was reinforced by the demand by the Freedom and Justice Party (FJP), the Brotherhood's political arm, that the military take responsibility for reform of the security forces. In its condemnation of the Port Said bloodshed, the FJP blamed "domestic parties and dubious forces" rather than the military and the security. The condemnation reflected the instinctive perception of the Brotherhood, shaped by its long history of clandestinity, of the Ultras as counterrevolutionary thugs who were doing the bidding of an invisible force, the deep state, determined to destabilize Egypt and derail the legitimate political process.[118]

The failure of the police might be explained by the fact that law enforcement had been largely off Egyptian streets since the fall of Mubarak. The security forces' prime concern was to shed their image from the Mubarak era which had made them the country's most despised institution. To that end, they avoided where possible high-profile confrontations with popular groups. The street battles in late 2011, aimed at preventing rioting Ultras and youth groups from reaching the interior ministry that controlled the security forces, were the exception. Law enforcement hoped that the deterioration in public security would re-establish it as the force that stood between Egypt and chaos and anarchy. Yet even so, questions lingered: why had advance indications that violence could occur, including threatening Twitter traffic, been ignored? Why were the stadium doors locked? Why were the fans not searched as they came in carrying knives and flares and clubs as had been the case in past clashes between the two clubs? Why were the stadium lights turned off when the fighting began? What explains the contradiction that soccer violence is usually initiated by supporters of the losing rather than the winning team, unlike what occurred in Port Said?

Reinforcing soccer's key role in politics, the Port Said incident put the ruling SCAF, its successor Morsi and the security forces in a no-win situation. The legal proceedings initiated against seventy-three defendants, including nine mid-level security officials, were destined to upset either the Al Masry or the Al Ahly fans, highlight the fact that two years after the overthrow of Mubarak no security official had been held accountable for the deaths of more than 800 protesters since January 2011, and to propel the need for security sector reform to the top of the country's agenda. "26 January—punishment or chaos" was the slogan of the Al Ahly Ultras in advance of the initial verdict for some of the individuals standing trial in support of their demand that those responsible for the incident be held accountable. The Black Bloc—vigilantes reminiscent of soccer hooligans and anarchists in Europe and Latin America, made up of Ultras, leftists and some Islamists who dressed in black T-Shirts emblazed with a "Fuck the System" slogan and whose faces were concealed by black masks, a tactic used by the fans during the revolt against Mubarak—attacked the Cairo Stock Exchange, paralyzed the metro system and blocked main thoroughfares in support of their call for justice.

In the end, the verdicts announced in two batches in January and March 2013 sparked a popular uprising in Port Said and other Suez Canal cities and mass protests in Cairo. The initial sentencing of twenty-one Al Masry fans to death on charges of voluntary manslaughter moreover tapped into a deep-seated vein of resentment in Port Said,

Egypt's third most important economic hub, against the central government in Cairo. An appeals court in 2015 reduced the number on death row to eleven. In response to the first verdict, thousands, some armed, rampaged through Port Said, attacked the prison where those on death row were being held and looted shops. Denunciation of the protesters as thugs by state-run media, senior government officials, opposition leaders and Al Ahly Ultras fuelled local animosity.

The protests harked back to the city's tradition of resistance rooted in opposition to the British in the late nineteenth century when it was founded as a predominantly European town. It had also witnessed nationalist demonstrations in the run-up to Egypt's 1919 popular revolt, anti-government protests in the early 1950s and against its role as a military base in the 1956 and 1973 Middle East wars as well as in the Egyptian-Israeli war of attrition in the late 1960s. Port Said's perception of itself as a city that made sacrifices for an ungrateful nation was reinforced by the Mubarak regime's failure to forge a national identity rooted in citizenship rather than servitude. The city's history fostered a sense of entitlement and regional identity that at times played out in Port Said's soccer rivalry with Cairo. Al Ahly fans provoked Al Masry on the eve of the disastrous soccer match by describing their initial reluctance to join the 2011 anti-Mubarak demonstrations as the result of a "rotten city that does not produce men." In response, Al Masry's Green Eagles praised their city's history of resistance and promised Al Ahly fans they would meet their maker.

In sharp contrast to Port Said, Al Ahly fans were initially euphoric about the sentencing to death of Green Eagles activists. That euphoria, however, quickly gave way to resentment that seven security officials were acquitted, reinforcing a sense that the real culprits—the military and law enforcement's top command—had got off scot-free. The resentment spilled onto the streets despite a call for restraint by the leaders of Ultras Ahlawy. "They can go to hell. They have no choice but to join us," said a young Al Ahly militant in response to his leaders' call as smoke billowed in March from the nearby headquarters of the Egyptian Football Association and the Police Club set on fire by his fellow Ultras.

Nevertheless, some analysts argued that with the verdict the alleged goal in Port Said of neutralizing Ultras Ahlawy, one of the most militant groups, had been achieved. They suggested that the Brotherhood had successfully infiltrated the Cairo Ultras in the year between the incident and the verdicts. They noted that the groups had remained relatively quiet since the initially split response to the verdicts and that the language of Ultras Ahlawy had at times taken on religious overtones. Leila Zaki Chakravarti has pointed to the unprecedented praise of the judiciary by the group's leadership after the verdicts were announced. She further highlighted the group's adoption of the slogan Retribution or Blood, "Al-Qissas aw al-Damm".[119] "Qissas" is a term employed in Islamic law for equitable retribution based on the principle of an eye for an eye and harsh punishment. It rules out clemency or compensation. It contrasted starkly with the more secular slogan adopted by Al Masry's Green Eagles, "Al-adl aw al-mawt", Justice or Death. In a similar vein, the Egyptian journalist Wael Eskander noted that during a protest in February 2013, three weeks after the Port Said death sentences, Ahlawy leaders went out of their way to persuade demonstrators to refrain from attacking Morsi and the Brotherhood.[120] The seeming shift in attitude followed weeks of debate on Facebook and other social media. An attempt to remove a Ministry of Defence sign once the protesters reached their destination pitted the leadership of the Ultras against some of their rank and file as well as members of youth groups. Fighting erupted as the Ultras turned on those chanting against Morsi. "Protesters left with more questions than answers as to what drove the Ultras to adopt such a position. Were they convinced that justice could be attained under the rule of the Muslim Brotherhood? Were they infiltrated? Were they placated by the court verdict, which sentenced twenty-one individuals to death for involvement in the Port Said massacre?" Eskander asked.

The Brotherhood had at best succeeded at only temporarily neutralizing the Cairo Ultras whose judgements were less bound by ideology than by an instinctive distrust of authority and a pragmatic response to events as they unfolded. Yet, there was a logic to their madness. The Port Said verdicts went some way to satisfy their demand for justice. The Morsi government's increasingly evident failure and its authoritarian reliance on the security forces nevertheless revived the aforementioned Black Bloc, which let it be known that its adapted goal was to protect protesters against attacks by the police, pro-Mubarak thugs and Brotherhood heavies. In a statement on Facebook, the Black Bloc claimed responsibility for an arson attack on the office of the Muslim Brotherhood's official website and a well-known restaurant in Cairo believed to be owned by a Brotherhood associate. "We declare our revolution ...

until Egypt and its people get their rights back. We are not thugs or sabo-
teurs, but rather we defend Egypt against the criminality of the Muslim
Brotherhood," the statement said. By the same token, the importance of
resistance to oppression and injustice among Ultras is what persuaded
many of them seemingly to change course when in July 2013 they joined
mass pro-Morsi protests against his overthrow by the military. Prosecutor
General Tal'at Abdullah denunciation of the Black Bloc as a terrorist
group whose members should be arrested anticipated the military's justification for its coup and the banning of Ultras groups two years later
with the argument that the Brotherhood was inciting violence, endanger-
ing national security and associated with terrorism.

Three weeks into the Suez Canal revolt, thousands of mourners carried the body of 23-year-old Mahmoud al-Nahas through the streets of
Port Said. Al-Nahas was the forty-fifth person to be killed by security
forces in violence that turned the city into a war zone. A civil disobedi-
ence campaign and mass protests sparked by perceptions that Port Said
was being scapegoated for the soccer killings reflected deep-seated
antagonism towards central government, the product of decades-long
failure to develop the city's infrastructure and to make good on development promises made as far back as thirty years before. The neglect of
Port Said highlighted the Mubarak regime's nepotism. Mubarak cronies
bypassed the city, building high-end housing and tourism projects such
as Porto Sokhna, a 2.2 million-square metre holiday development fifty
kilometres outside of Port Said owned by Mansour Amer, a former
member of parliament for the ousted president's National Democratic
Party. Conspiracy theorists believed that Mubarak's refusal to live up to
his promises and the fact that he visited the city only twice in his thirty
years in office were revenge for a failed attempt on his life during his first
visit in 1999.

Rather than listening, Morsi unleashed his security forces as soon as
protests erupted against the sentencing to death of the lower-class Al
Masry fans. More than thirty people were killed on the first day alone of
the uprising. To calm the situation, he replaced the police with military
troops in a move that further exacerbated his relations with the armed
forces and made the commander of the Second Army Division, General
Ahmed Wasif, rather than the president the man who earned the city's
respect. Fearing that the military's still significant popular support, reinforced by its refusal a year earlier to suppress the revolt against Mubarak,

would be weakened if it confronted protesters in Port Said, top commanders let it be known they would protect strategic installations like the port but would not get involved in repressing demonstrations. If there was one thing that the Green Eagles, the Al Masry Ultras who were in the forefront of the Port Said revolt, and Ultras Ahlawy agreed on, it was the culpability of the security forces and subsequently the judiciary.

While Morsi shied away from security sector reform, he insisted on an overhaul of the judiciary. His relations with the judiciary, in sharp contrast to six years earlier when the Muslim Brotherhood supported judges protesting against Mubarak's attempts to force them to endorse rigged elections, had deteriorated sharply within months of his coming to office. Unlike the security forces, Morsi saw the judiciary as a major obstacle because of the Supreme Constitutional Court's ruling that the newly elected and Islamist-dominated parliament should be dissolved due to irregularities in the election law. He viewed that decision as a sneak attack on the people's rightfully elected representative authority. Egypt's new controversial constitution, drafted by Islamists and signed into law by Morsi despite objections from liberals and secularists who complained that it potentially limited basic freedoms and constituted a basis for Islamization of the country, gave him the upper hand. It allowed him to reduce the number of judges on the High Court from eighteen to eleven and empowered him to appoint members of the court. Morsi's most vocal critics were among the judges who were retired. A proposal in the Senate to reduce a judge's retirement age from seventy to sixty was designed to engineer the departure of a further 3,000 judges.

The attack on the judiciary was also intended to appease the Ultras and other youth groups who saw it as complicit in efforts to shield security personnel from prosecution, even though the judges' hands were often bound because police and security forces had sabotaged due process by destroying or holding back evidence. Morsi's efforts backfired. His failure to enact security sector reform, tackle systemic corruption and act in the interests of the victims of the Mubarak regime as well as his burial of government reports documenting abuse, painted him as a leader who had reduced the judiciary's independence and politicized it rather than ensuring that it would guarantee justice and greater freedom.

The Port Said revolt brought together two groups with working-class roots that played key roles in the toppling of Mubarak: militant, highly politicized, battle-hardened soccer fans and the labour movement. The fans fought police and security forces in the stadiums while workers in industrial towns like Al-Mahalla al-Kubra organized strikes against his economic liberalization policy and corrupt and nepotistic privatization of state-owned assets. In fact, the workers were the first to breach the barricade of fear with a series of economic and social strikes starting in late 2006 to which security forces responded harshly.[121] It took, however, changing attitudes among the majority of Port Said's people to bring fans and workers together. In doing so, Morsi failed where Mubarak succeeded: keeping powerful critics divided.

Militant soccer fans first reached out to the workers' movement during protests a year earlier immediately after the soccer deaths by acknowledging in a song that workers were among those who lost their lives in Egypt's popular revolt. Ramy Essam, the singer who made his name with *Irhal* [Leave], the song that became Tahrir Square's anthem during the anti-Mubarak protests, claimed in his post-Port Said song, "Ya Magles Ya Ibn El-Haram" ["Oh Council, You Son of a Bitch"] referring to SCAF: "And they've killed the finest of youth, some were engineers, some were factory workers and also youngsters." As Ultras-led protest marches passed government buildings and factories in Port Said, public-sector workers poured into the street swelling the demonstrators' ranks.

The deaths in Port Said and the Ultras' militancy, courage, devotion and creativity moved groups across society to adopt their brand. Groups across the political and social spectrum established themselves as Ultras: Ultras Bassem Youssef, supporters of Egypt and the Arab world's Jon Stewart, a heart surgeon-turned-comedian who gained international acclaim after being charged in 2013 with disturbing public peace and security; Ultras SpongeBob, fans of the animated American television series SpongeBob SquarePants; Ultras Salafi, followers of a militant Islamic trend that wants to emulate as far as possible life as it was in the time of the Prophet Mohammed and his four immediate successors; and Ultras Nahdawi, the first group of militant soccer fans that was not tied to a club and whose initial ties to the Brotherhood positioned itself publicly as a political entity. Nahdawi members jumped up and down like Ultras in a stadium chanting: "Morsi, Morsi, Morsi, Morsi, Morsi, Oh-o, Oh-o, Oh-o, Morsi, Morsi, Morsi, Morsi" in songs modelled on the soccer fans' original repertoire. In mimicking the Ultras, the Brotherhood argues that it illustrates its popularity among the youth and affinity with its concerns.

The leaking in early 2013 of the prosecutor's report of its investigation into the Port Said incident[122] together with a human rights report,[123] reinforced the conviction that the security forces were responsible for the deadly encounter as well as the need for reform of the police and security forces. The 200-page prosecutor's report asserted that police were as responsible as Al Masry fans for the deaths in Port Said but evaded the question of whether police in the stadium had been acting on instructions from higher up. It concluded that the police had failed to search fans entering the stadium for weapons but did not explain why. It cited several Al Masry fans who told investigators they had noticed that one of the gates had been welded shut when they entered the stadium. The report confirmed that the stadium's lights had been turned off when the fighting began, allegedly at the behest of an Al Masry leader.

Based on interviews with fans of Al Ahly and Al Masry, journalists who reported on the match, stadium lighting experts and police, as well as autopsy reports and videos, the report suggested that the Port Said brawl was planned two days before the match at a meeting of a support group called Super Green that was sanctioned by the club. The meeting was, according to the report, attended by some of the twenty-one fans sentenced to death. It made no mention of the fact that police and security monitor meetings of Ultras in advance of a match and often contact the fans by phone during such meetings, more often than not in a bid to pre-empt violence.

The report noted further that militants of both Al Masry and Al Ahly had issued threats on social media in advance of the fatal match. "Port Said is waiting for you with knives and pistols," one of the messages read, according to the report. "If you are coming to Port Said, write your mother a will because you will die for sure," read another.

The report said the meeting of the Al Masry Ultras had been chaired by Mohammed Adel Mohammed, a 21-year-old known as "Hummus", who was among those condemned to death and had become a symbol of the Port Said uprising with calls for his release plastered on walls across the city. "Defendants premeditated the killing of some of the Ahly club fans [Ultras] to retaliate for previous disputes between them and to show off their strength. For this purpose, they used weapons [knives and sticks] and explosive materials, such as flames, and rocks and other items to assault people."

The report further pointed out that Al Masry Ultras began ambushing the Al Ahly team at its hotel even before the match with rocks and insults.

The taunting continued at the stadium with several Al Masry fans changing their clothes and weapons to make it harder to identify them in security videos. Throughout, the Port Said police "didn't interfere in any way, which was seen on the videos," the report said. As the match ended with the unexpected Al Masry victory, Al Masry Ultras attacked Al Ahly fans in the seating section area reserved for them. They threw Molotov cocktails, bricks and chairs at the visitors from Cairo. "Al Mando was seen taking a blade from his mouth on video," the report stated, referring to an Al Masry Ultra by his nickname. "Hummus" admitted to investigators that he had thrown rocks at Al Ahly fans, claimed the prosecution. Others told the prosecution that they saw him also carrying Molotov cocktails, knives and sticks.

A police officer, identified only as Defendant 70, testified that he could not find the keys to the gates when the stampede began, according to the report. Defendant 70 offered contradictory explanations for his inability to find the keys and his disappearance during the incident. At one point, he said he did not unlock the gate at the request of Defendant 64, another officer. He told someone else that the crowds were too big for him to confront. For his part, Defendant 64 said he never gave such orders and could not find his fellow officer when the attack began. "The prosecution found the keys with [Defendant 70] during the investigation. He said that he is the one who locked the doors, and he kept the keys with him until he handed them in to the prosecution. The prosecution made sure of that by trying the keys on the locks on Gates 2 and 3 and they opened the locks."

The security forces' laxity was repeated a year later when they were unprepared for the unrest that the verdicts in the Port Said case sparked and responded with a degree of brutality that left more than forty protesters in Port Said dead, forced Morsi to declare emergency rule in the city and elsewhere and ultimately prompted the president to replace security forces with the military in Al Masry's hometown.

The security forces' handling of the protests appeared to reaffirm the Egyptian Initiative for Personal Rights (EIPR) report's conclusions. "The Egyptian police continue to systematically deploy violence and torture, and at times even kill. Although the January [2011] revolution was sparked in large part by police practices and vocally demanded an end to these practices, accountability for all offenders and the establishment of permanent instruments to prevent their recurrence, two years after the revolution the situation remains unchanged," the EIPR stated.[124]

Similarly, four-metre high walls made of huge, rounded concrete cubes across the very streets around Tahrir that witnessed some of the worst clashes between the security forces and the Ultras initially symbolized the failure of the military while in government to retain support as it sought to lead the country from autocracy to democratic elections. Built to protect key institutions such as the interior ministry and the parliament, the walls and monuments to the military, coupled with the elected president's failure, reflected Morsi's increased reliance on law enforcement and lack of consideration for popular concerns. The walls turned once bustling thoroughfares in downtown Cairo into stagnating back streets. "Parts of Cairo actually look like occupied territory with streets blocked with barbed wire, military checkpoints, and stonewalls," noted ElShahed, in Cairo for his doctoral research.[125] "They perpetuate the gap between the rulers and the ruled," added Mohamed Elshahed, the editor of *Cairobserver*, an online urban space journal.

Cairo's visual images and relations between the government and the public became even more convoluted with Morsi and the Muslim Brotherhood's refusal to listen to criticism and advice that sparked the popular revolt against them in July 2013. The revolt paved the way for a military coup that removed him from office and a brutal crackdown on the group. The polarization between a military-backed mass movement opposed to Morsi and a substantial segment of Egyptian society that supported him posed an initial dilemma for the Ultras who lacked ideological and political coherence.

As a result, they cheered Morsi's June 2012 presidential election defeat of Ahmed Shafiq, a Mubarak associate, yet also chanted "Yasqut hukm al-murshid" [down with the rule of the Muslim Brotherhood's supreme guide], signalling the fact that Morsi was on probation. The battle in the summer of 2013 shifted away from stadiums, empty because soccer competitions had largely been suspended and fans barred from the few international matches that were allowed, to Tahrir Square where anti-Morsi demonstrators gathered in great numbers and eastern Cairo where protesting Brothers and their supporters had occupied Rabaa al-Adawiya Square.

Popular attitudes among the Ultras towards the military and the security forces differed in 2013, for a host of reasons. Ranking high among those is the fact that the Egyptian military is a very different institution from the one that first took power sixty-four years ago. This evolution explains why the military bungled its seventeen months in power and why a smooth transition towards a civilian-led democracy in Egypt in the coming years is unlikely. Nasser's military was highly politicized. Its officer corps, particularly in the artillery and cavalry, was reformist and favoured democracy.[126] Nasser's defeat of the reformists set the stage for the police state created under President Anwar Sadat and perfected by Mubarak. It was, and is, a state with a built-in rivalry between the military and the security forces. As in the early 1950s, the security forces have much to lose in a transition towards democracy, while the military has much to gain from liberalization provided it can retain its perks and privileges. The security forces had the upper hand in 1954; they retained significant influence in 2013 because the military needed them.

The emergence of Mubarak's police state was built on the de-politicization of the military that effectively insulated it from politics. As a result, the military has proven to be politically naïve and inexperienced. Under Mubarak, the power balance between the military and the security forces had shifted. Egypt's standing army counts 500,000 men; its security forces have ballooned to an estimated 1.5 million and are better connected to politics and crime syndicates. That allowed the military to rely on the security forces to prevent the destruction of what Egyptian sociologist Hazem Kandil terms the "dam of autocracy."[127] The security forces rather than the military thus became the face of repression under Mubarak, Morsi and the military-backed government that replaced the Islamist president. They ensured that protests in favour of social justice and greater freedoms did not produce anarchy.

Neither the military nor the anti-Morsi protesters—despite expressions of support by the armed forces—had any illusions about the nature of their relationship and its inherent contradictions. The military's authoritarian and patriarchal nature and goal of preserving the status quo ante to guarantee its privileges were in direct conflict with the protesters' aims of a more open, transparent, accountable and just society. The two sides were opportunistically using one another and playing a dangerous game that could only end in failure, if not renewed strife. The millions, including many Ultras, who signed the petition calling for the removal of the Brotherhood government, hence paving the way for the intervention by the armed forces, signed up for new elections rather than a return of the military to politics.

The fiasco of the short-lived Morsi government was compounded by the failure of the security forces to formulate a vision of their own in a post-revolt environment. Instead, they opted to lie low so as not to provoke further animosity. They hoped that their absence and a decline of law and order would position them as the force that stood between Egypt and the abyss. The failure of the security forces' leadership to redefine itself in a post-revolt environment was encouraged by the military's opposition to real reform and calls for independent police trade unions, improved accountability and rules governing promotion and training by reformist officers who—if acknowledged—could have sparked a similar development within the armed forces.

One reason why the police, unlike the military, had reformists within its ranks was the fact that military personnel enjoyed economic and financial perks that lower-level police offices lacked, making them on the one hand more corrupt, dependent on getting *baksheesh* for their services and more connected to the criminal networks that were often employed to do the Mubarak regime's dirty work.

The military's popularity, however, was not unconditional. The Ultras may have stood aside as huge numbers of Egyptians demanding Morsi's downfall set the stage for the July 2013 coup against the country's first democratically elected president. Yet it did not take long for many Ultras to revert to their instinctive distrust of the authorities. These premonitions were borne out when the military and the government it installed cracked down on the Brotherhood, arresting hundreds, closing Islamist media and targeting businesses associated with the group. The return of Mubarak-era officials and the revival of the security forces' feared department in charge of combatting extremism and monitoring political and religious activities left little doubt of the military's intentions. "We are going back to square one. Morsi was a disaster. He failed to honour the mandate we Egyptians gave him. However, if we do not stand up now, we will have lost everything," said a young Ultra, one of many who as in 2011 joined the pro-Morsi protesters chanting and jumping in a tacit understanding that they would not remain neutral even if, as a group, self-protection as well as internal divisions persuaded them to remain officially aloof.

"We want your head, you traitor Tantawi. You could have carved your name in history, but you were arrogant and you believed Egypt and its people could take a step back and forget their revolution," said an Ultra group addressing Egypt's top Mubarak-era military commander who Morsi replaced with Al-Sisi, on its Facebook page in the wake of Port Said. That sentiment extended quickly to Al-Sisi, with opponents of Morsi—

despite the general's near-cult status—increasingly wondering whether they had swapped one problem for another as the military and its government revived the pillars of the old order. The animosity harked back to slogans that had echoed through stadiums for much of the seventeen months that the military had been in office. The slogan "military police, you are dogs like the Interior Ministry. Write it on the prison's walls, down with military rule," reverberated in Egyptians' living rooms as they watched those matches that were not suspended on their televisions.

Egypt's deep polarization in the summer of 2013 as the Muslim Brotherhood fought for its survival on the streets, as well as the crisis in Egyptian soccer that was accelerated by the deadly brawl in Port Said, did not leave the militant soccer fans unscathed. While the Ultras as organizations had refrained from joining the fray, many of their members' and leaders' participation reflected the gamut of political views in their ranks. In a twist of irony, many UWK members joined the pro-Morsi protests. The Black Bloc sided with the police in the crackdown on the Brotherhood. The UWK's arch-rivals, Ultras Ahlawy, fans of Al Ahly SC, historically the nationalist club, issued their first anti-Brotherhood statement six weeks into the post-Morsi crisis. By refraining from attacking the government, the group had hoped that harsh verdicts would be served in the trial of those responsible for the deaths in Port Said. It got only partial satisfaction. While twenty-one supporters of Port Said's Al Masry SC club were sentenced to death, seven of the nine security officials were acquitted. On appeal, the number of death sentences was reduced to eleven. "The Ultras have become fascists. Like Egypt, they have collapsed. They have no values and no real beliefs," stated a former Ultra leader who left his group in disgust at the political turn it had taken.[128]

In a perverse way, the Ultras' dilemma was not dissimilar from that of the Brotherhood. Neither could decide what it really stood for. The Brotherhood had yet to make up its mind what it is: a social or a political movement. Similarly, the Ultras refused to acknowledge that they were as much about politics as they were about soccer. Their battle for freedom in the stadiums and their prominent role in the toppling of Mubarak, the opposition to the military rulers that succeeded him and the Morsi government made them political by definition. Yet those who comprised their rank and file were united in their support for their club and their deep-seated animosity towards the security forces but nothing else.

The impact of Said Moshagheb's 2011 coup during the Zamalek-Espérance Sportive de Tunis match became evident in the aftermath of the military overthrow of Morsi two years later on the embattled campuses of Egyptian universities and in poorer neighbourhoods of Egyptian cities, focal points of protest against the military. It was also evident in the evolution of the UWK as a group and that of Moshagheb personally, which were symptomatic of a generation that had progressively lost hope and was potentially prone to radicalisation. Their histories served as warning signs that frustration sparked by the success of the military and the security forces in rolling back the achievements of the 2011 revolt, coupled with Al-Sisi's even more repressive policies, was fuelling radicalisation rather than returning Egypt to stability.

Moshagheb finalized his takeover of the UWK months after the pitch invasion by brutally pushing out the UWK's founders, some of whom were attacked and injured by his knife-wielding followers. "All the old people have left. There was a fight within the group. Some were kidnapped and held for three days. We were attacked with knives. People were injured. Their leader is enormously charismatic," said a founder of the group referring to Moshagheb. "This is a new generation. It's a generation that can't be controlled. They don't read. They believe in action and experience. They have balls. When the opportunity arises they will do something bigger than we ever did," he added.

The founder cautioned against repeating the mistake of the Mubarak era when policymakers and analysts underestimated the groundswell of anger and frustration among youth that was bubbling at the surface.[129] "Standing up to the regime amounts to suicide. The question is how long that perception will last. The closing of the stadiums shuts down the only release valve. Things will eventually burst. When and where nobody knows. But the writing is on the wall," the founder said.[130]

Moshagheb's case lifted the veil on a process of radicalisation at the fringe of the Ultras fuelled by the Al-Sisi government's policies. It also put into perspective the war waged against the UWK by Zamalek president Mortada Mansour, a larger than life figure who after twice failing persuaded an appeals court to outlaw the Ultras as a terrorist organization on the grounds that the group tried to assassinate him. Mortada, who identified Ultras with the Brotherhood, prided himself on having requested police action against fans in front of Cairo's Air Defence Stadium in February 2015. This sparked a stampede in which twenty UWK members died. In late June 2015, Mortada withdrew his complaint against 20 of the 21 UWK members on trial for attempting to kill him but maintained his charge against Moshagheb. Denying that they had tried to kill the Zamalek president, the UWK dubbed Mansour "the regime's dog."

Moshagheb was further suspected by authorities of having been involved in violent resistance to the Al-Sisi government. The UWK leader had been under surveillance for some time during which he had been smuggling arms into Cairo from Sinai, the setting for an armed insurgency. AK-47s were allegedly found in the homes of friends of Moshagheb some two weeks before his arrest.[131]

Moshagebh was arrested after he and another Ultra, Hassan Kazarlan, allegedly set fire to a Cairo convention hall. Sixteen people were injured in the incident. Kazarlan fled to Turkey after the arson attack.[132] He was persuaded to return to Egypt after security forces detained his father as a hostage and was immediately detained upon his arrival. Kazarlan told authorities that he had wanted to travel from Turkey to Syria. He provoked security force ire by accusing his interrogators of being infidels.[133]

If he had made it to Syria, Kazarlan would have followed in the footsteps of Rami Iskanderiya, a former leader of Ultras Ahlawi in Alexandria, who joined the Islamic State and married a Syrian woman in the group's Syrian stronghold of Raqqa.

Tarek M. Elawady, a lawyer for the UWK, said Mr Kazarlan had led security forces to Moshagheb when he revealed his whereabouts under torture. Elawady was careful to insist that he represented the UWK and Moshagheb only in as far as his legal problems were related to the Ultras.

"Mortada wanted to drive a wedge between the UWK rank and file and its leaders who may have had political affiliations. Mortada provoked them to be violent… His actions are part of a government plan to weaken any youth group that opposes the state… The problem is that Mortada is playing the security forces' game. He acts as their agent provocateur," Elawady said, speaking in his office close to the brooding headquarters of the Mukhabarat, the term broadly used for intelligence and law enforcement, that is surrounded by grimy walls, barbed wire and watch towers.[134]

The targeting of Ultras was evident not only in Mansour's campaign as well as the judicial crackdown on militant soccer fans but also in the military where conscripts are asked after being drafted whether they are members of an Ultras group. Those that respond affirmatively are singled out. "They were immediately ordered to do 100 push-ups during which an officer shouted at them: 'You are the lowest creatures. You sacrifice yourselves for your club, not for your religion or country,'" a source recounted.[135]

Attacks on the Ultras in state-owned Egyptian media in the two years before the banning of the soccer fan groups suggested it was only a matter of time before the government and its allies would move against them. *Al Ahram*, long a mouthpiece for the government, asked: "Will the Ultras be shown the red card after crossing the red line? Are they digging their own grave? Football Ultras of soccer powerhouse Egyptian clubs Ahly and Zamalek have become a dangerous phenomenon… These days the Ultras are a symbol of destruction, attacking the opposition and sometimes their own kind," the paper said.[136]

In late January, around the fourth anniversary of the revolt that toppled Mubarak, Moshagheb had hoped to escalate protests in Cairo neighbourhoods like Matareya, a stronghold of the outlawed Brotherhood. Some seventeen of the seventy-four Ultras Ahlawy members killed in the Port Said stadium hailed from Matareya, the scene of multiple anti-government protests that is known for its stockpiles of illegal arms, drug dealing and high crime rate.[137]

Moshagheb failed to escalate the protests in Matareya into an armed confrontation. Flash protests have also largely moved from campuses to neighbourhoods after Friday prayers because of security force control of universities, reflecting efforts by better educated Ultras to maintain pressure on the government while preventing mounting frustration and anger from sparking nihilistic violence. Their dilemma echoed calls by younger members of the Brotherhood, to whom many politicized Ultras were close, for the adoption of more confrontational, potentially violent, tactics against the Al-Sisi regime summarized in the slogan, "Anything but Bullets."

"We don't like violence but we are not weak. Hope keeps us going. We believe that there still are options. We created options on Tahrir Square. This regime is more brutal but there still are options. Success for us is our survival and ability to keep trying. The government wants to provoke us to become violent. Two years later, we are still active. Politics is about making deals; revolution is putting your life on the line. We are the generation that staged the revolution. The new generation no longer cares. Our role is to get the new generation to re-join the revolution. The government markets itself with promises and the power of the state. We can promise only one thing: we will stay on the street. To us football is politics, politics is in everything. That's why we tackle politics," said Ahmed, the alias of a leader of Ultras Nahdawy, a member of the Brotherhood, and a fugitive after he was expelled from university and convicted twice in absentia to long-term jail sentences. Ahmed moves around Cairo in a protective cocoon, speaks in a low voice to avoid being overheard, and looks furtively over his shoulder as he organizes instant protests against the Al-Sisi regime. "It's likely to be the quiet before the storm. I don't know a single young person who voted in the presidential elections. Even my parents, simple people who are not Islamists, do not believe in what is happening. People will lose faith in the military. They are losing faith in everything," said another former Ultra.[138]

Instead of casting their vote in the elections, men like Ahmed, a member of an Ultras group that played a key role in the 2011 Tahrir Square revolt, and Yusuf Salheen, a 22-year old Islamist leader of Students Against The Coup who professes not to be a Brother, endorsed calls by scores of clerics to defeat the Al-Sisi regime by all "legitimate means."[139] Their views were reflected in criticism in 2015 of Mahmoud Ghozlan, a senior Brother who argued weeks before his arrest that the group's rejection of violence was one of its principles.[140] Echoing the views of many younger Brothers, Hazem Said, a long-standing member of the group called in response to Ghozlan for "projecting force" and the targeting of individuals who had "killed or raped". Said asserted that "the Egyptian military which is now killing us and the criminal police are not our kin" and asked: "how can you ask for non-violence given the military coup's army, police and judiciary?"[141]

Ahmed, Salheen and other leaders of Nahdawy, with its 67,000 followers on Facebook[142] and Students Against The Coup, groups that grew exponentially after the bloody suppression of the Raba'a al-Adawiya Square sit-in, in which security forces killed more than 600 people, saw themselves as forces trying to offer disaffected youth with a glimmer of hope. "Many of us are Islamists. I am a member of the Brotherhood, but that is not why we supported the Brotherhood. We don't want to be inside the Brotherhood or the system. We supported Morsi not because he was a brother but because we wanted a revolutionary force to be in government. The Brotherhood was the only revolutionary force that had a candidate and popular support and was part of the (2011) revolution," Ahmed said.

Some seventeen members of Nahdawy that has branches in most Egyptian universities were killed in clashes with security forces in the first two years after the coup against Morsi. "We are looking for alternatives outside the campus. We have managed to do so in neighbourhoods and smaller universities that are less controlled. We're looking at new strategies and options given that the risk is becoming too high. We are absolutely concerned that if we fail things will turn violent. Going violent would give the regime the perfect excuse. We would lose all public empathy. We hope that Egyptians realize that there are still voices out there that are not giving up and are keeping protests peaceful despite all that has happened," Salheen said.

Steeped in the history of the politicized, militant soccer fans, the student movement and the Brotherhood, men like Ahmed and Salheen see themselves not only as opponents of what they view as a dictatorial regime but also as agents of change within the Islamist movement. They base themselves on the history of soccer fans and students that since the crackdown on the Brotherhood by President Nasser were the Brotherhood's catalyst for adaptation and revival.

"The Muslim Brotherhood of the early 1970s was a shell of its former self. Many of the surviving activists, numbering barely one hundred members, were not even certain that they wanted to resurrect the organization's mission upon their release from prison. The real story of this era revolves around a vibrant youth movement based in Egypt's colleges and universities. Even as they rebelled against the tenets of Nasserism, the youth of this period were the products of its socioeconomic policies, from increased urbanization to greater access to education. They found in their Islamic identity a response to the post-1967 crisis, even as they adopted the modes of popular contention that had emerged under Nasser. The student movement was notable for the fluidity it displayed on the ideological level and the dynamism it exhibited on the organizational front," says historian Abdullah Al-Arian, author of *Answering the Call, Popular Islamic Activism in Sadat's Egypt*, in an interview with Jadaliyya.[143]

He goes on to say that his book examines critical moments where these forces intersected and traces the path taken by the bulk of the student movement's leadership as it ultimately 'graduated' to take on the Brotherhood's mission and adopt its organizational model. One of his key findings is that, "even as they attempted to reassert the Brotherhood's traditional hierarchical structure, senior figures like Mustafa Mashhur, Kamal al-Sananiri, and Umar al-Tilmisani could not help but adapt their mission to the changing landscape of Islamic activism."

For men like Ahmed and Salheen it was less about the Brotherhood and more about aligning Islamists and revolutionary forces that run the gamut from liberal to conservative, from left to right and from secular to religious in a united front against autocracy. "It's not about Morsi, we have bigger fish to fry than Morsi. Most of us no longer believe in the slogan in returning Morsi to office. Thousands are suffering. I don't give a damn about Morsi. Anything is better than this regime. There are two approaches, the reformist and the revolutionary one. We have seen dramatic shifts since 2011. Both Tahrir Square and Sisi's junta were dramatic twists. I and many like me believe that another twist is possible even if that will take time," Salheen said.

Ahmed and Salheen were the first to admit that the odds were stacked against them. Their space to manoeuvre was increasingly being curtailed while their effort to stem radicalization and keep the momentum of peaceful protest was being stymied by the policies advocated by Al-Sisi, who projects himself as a bulwark against jihadism.

This is not an appraisal shared by Robert Kagan and Michele Dunne:

> Unfortunately the idea that Sisi will be an effective ally against Islamic terrorists is misguided. He has, in fact, become one of the jihadists' most effective recruiting tools. The simple truth is that, since Sisi took power, the frequency of terrorist attacks in Egypt has soared; there have been more than 700 attacks over 22 months, as opposed to fewer than 90 in the previous 22 months. Harder to measure is the number of young people radicalized by Sisi's repression, but we can assume it is significant and growing... In this environment, is it surprising that reports surface regularly about the trend of radicalization of Egyptian youth, including previously peaceful Islamists? Sisi's brutal actions speak far louder than his few words about reforming Islam; to believe that he, or the religious institutions of his government, can have a positive impact on young people susceptible to radicalization is beyond wishful thinking. It would be laughable if it were not dangerous self-delusion...[144]

Radicalization is both a product of the brutality of an unreformed security force and a military whose brutal tactics have turned a local Bedouin population into allies of militants influenced by the Islamic State and other jihadist groups. "In Cairo, the police are idiots. They have perfected the art of ensuring that people hate them. One is told in the military that we are the good guys and the police are the bad guys. But in the Sinai, the military is under siege, it moves in convoys that are focused on self-protection and not being blown up by improvised explosive devices. Locals no longer wear traditional Bedouin dress and don western clothing to avoid being detained and harassed by the military who sees the Bedouin as the enemy. Locals used to inform on the jihadists, they no longer do, they look the other way. There is no solution. It's a battle till death," said a soccer fan shortly after returning from northern Sinai.[145]

The post-Mubarak failure to push for security sector reform granted the security forces time to regroup and exploit instability, deteriorating security, and increased political violence to ensure their immunity to calls for change. Egypt "presents the most egregious example of the consequences of failing to undertake far-reaching security sector reform," Yezid Sayigh noted in a study of the politics of police reform in the two post-revolt countries.[146]

"Ministries of interior remain black boxes with opaque decision-making processes, governed by officer networks that have resisted meaningful reform, financial transparency, and political oversight, Until governments reform their security sectors, rather than appease them, the culture of police impunity will deepen and democratic transition will remain impossible in Egypt and at risk in Tunisia," Sayigh said.

The death of the UWK members in the Cairo stadium and the reported presence of scores of unknown men armed with identical batons among those that attacked the Ahly supporters in Port Said three years earlier[147] fit a pattern of senior security officers and governors employing *baltageyya* to cooperate with security forces.

This backfired not only in its inability to stymie radicalization but also because militant soccer fans and students who took to the streets often were joined by locals. "Take Alf Maskan," said an Ultra and student activist. "Alf Maskan is a traditionally conservative, Islamist (Cairo) neighbourhood. Youth have nothing to look forward to. They are hopeless and desperate. They join our protests but their conversation often focuses on admiration for the Islamic State. They are teetering on the edge. We are their only hope but it's like grasping for a straw that ultimately is likely to break."[148]

3

ISLAMISTS FIGHT OVER SOCCER[1]

"People will spend hundreds and thousands of pounds for this religion of theirs, travelling to other parts of the world in support of their team ... showing affection, supporting and caring about ... They will jump down the throats of those who so much as even dare to criticize their god, rising to defend it at all costs."

The Saved Sect

Soccer vs Jihad

First there was a bright flash, than the sky turned grey as if it was raining. Lori Ssebulime felt broken glass and plastic all around her. Everything seemed to be swirling. She heard screaming from everywhere, tasted blood in her mouth and felt burning sensations on her body. Her table in the Ugandan capital of Kampala's popular Ethiopian Village restaurant had exploded. Minutes later, another bomb wrecked the Kyadondo Rugby Club across town. More than seventy people died in the twin blasts timed to coincide with the 2010 FIFA World Cup final.[2]

Lori and five of her Christian missionary friends had arrived early at the restaurant for a good seat to watch the match between the Netherlands and Spain. A Selinsgrove, Pennsylvania, school teacher, she and her friends were in Uganda to complete a wall that would keep intruders out of a church-school compound that their Christian community was funding. Six of Lori's fellow missionaries were among the seventy wounded in the attacks claimed by Harakat Al-Shabaab Al-Mujahidin, or

"Mujahidin Youth Movement", the Al-Qaeda affiliate known more widely as Al-Shabaab, which was fighting Uganda-led African peace-keepers in Somalia.

In his hiding place in the mountainous border region between Afghanistan and Pakistan, the late Osama Bin Laden, an Arsenal FC fan, must have cringed when he heard about his jihad's latest Ugandan strike. The world's most notorious terrorist, Osama shared with Al-Shabaab as with the Taliban an austere Islamist worldview that proscribes music, gender mixing, women's education, gambling, drinking, homosexuality and the shaving of beards as well as the belief that rule by Sharia'a [Islamic] law can only be achieved in a holy war against the infidels.

But when it came to soccer, Bin Laden and Al-Shabaab parted ways. They represented two sides of militant Islam's love-hate relationship with the game. Islamist leaders like Bin Laden and Hamas Gaza leader Ismail Haniyeh occupied a middle ground in the theological debate about soccer that runs the gamut. Their enthusiasm and endorsement of the game put them at odds with more radical jihadists as well as with more conservative Salafi clerics who condemn the sport. Men like Bin Laden and Haniyeh were comfortable with more nuanced Salafi and mainstream scholars who argued that the Prophet Mohammed advocated physical exercise to main-tain a healthy body. These scholars, who like all Salafis favour the Muslim world's emulation of life at the time of the Prophet Mohammed and his immediate successors, criticize the effects of the commercialization of soc-cer and the fact that it distracts from the performance of religious duties but acknowledge that there is nothing in Islamic law that would justify banning the sport or imposing restrictive conditions.

Bin Laden's passion did not, however, stop him from authorizing a plan by Algerian jihadists to attack the 1998 World Cup, pinpointing a match between England and Tunisia scheduled to be played in Marseille as well as US matches against Germany, Iran and Yugoslavia as targets.[3] The England-Tunisia match was expected to attract a worldwide televi-sion audience of half a billion people while the US match against Iran was already highly political because of the strained relations between the two countries. "This is a game that will determine the future of our planet and possibly the most important single sporting event that's ever been played in the history of the world," said US player Alexi Lalas, sarcastically remarking on the furore that had been whipped up by the media of both countries.[4]

The plot, that bore hallmarks of the Palestinian assault on the Israeli team at the 1972 Munich Olympics and also included an attack on the Paris hotel of the US team, was foiled when police raided homes in seven countries and hauled in around a hundred people for questioning. Some terrorism experts believe that the failure of the plot persuaded Al-Qaeda to opt instead for the bombing of US embassies in Dar es Salaam and Nairobi in the summer of 1998 in which 224 people were killed. Similarly, purported messages by the Malaysian-born, Al-Qaeda-affiliated bomb-maker Noordin Mohammed Top, claimed that the 2009 bombings of the Ritz Carlton and Marriott hotels in the Indonesian capital of Jakarta were intended to kill the visiting Manchester United team. Nine people were killed and fifty-three others wounded in the attacks. The bombs exploded two days before the team was scheduled to check into the Ritz and prompted it to cancel its visit. Noor said in one of three online statements that one aim of the attacks was "to create an example for the Muslims regarding Wala' [Loyalty] and Baro' [Enmity], especially for the forthcoming visit of Manchester United Football Club at the hotel. Those [soccer] players are made up of salibis [Crusaders]. Thus it is not right that the Muslim ummah [community] devote their loyalty and honour to these enemies of Allah."[5] A variety of other jihadists allegedly targeted soccer stadiums over the years in a number of foiled or aborted plots, including that of Manchester United and Jerusalem's Bloomfield in 2004, Melbourne's MCG in 2005 and a stadium in the US in 2010. The Iraqi military reported that it had arrested a dissident Saudi military officer for being part of an Al-Qaeda plot to attack the 2010 World Cup in South Africa.

Soccer also figured prominently in Bin Laden's imagery. Speaking to supporters about the 9/11 attacks on New York and Washington, he drew an analogy with soccer. "I saw in a dream, we were playing a soccer game against the Americans. When our team showed up in the field, they were all pilots! So I wondered if that was a soccer game or a pilot game? Our players were pilots," he said according to a video released by the US Defence Department.[6] Al-Qaeda spokesman Suleiman Abu Ghaith recalls in the video that a television programme about 9/11 "was showing an Egyptian family sitting in their living room, they exploded with joy. Do you know when there is a soccer game and your team wins, it was the same expression of joy? There was a subtitle that read: 'In revenge for the children of Al Aqsa, Usama Bin Ladin executes an operation against America',"[7] said Abu Ghaith, referring to Islam's third most holy site, the Al Aqsa mosque in Jerusalem.

In many ways the debate among jihadists and clerics about soccer mirrors similar concerns among Christian clergymen. Soccer fans outnumber churchgoers in several West European countries. Greek Orthodox Metropolitan Hierotheos Vlachos of Nafpatkos warned shortly after the 2010 World Cup in South Africa that soccer had become a religion that promoted superstition:

> For many people, soccer is a religion, a worship. Several expressions used are taken from religion. Spectators sit in the stands and their 'gods', the soccer players, contest as another twelve/eleven gods in the field for Victory. Since soccer is considered by many as a new worship, there is certainly their own god, the god of soccer. They pray to this non-existing god ... The first prize for superstition goes to the English, who for many years now have been worshipping Beckham as the thirteenth Apostle, and this is why they built him a huge statue in Trafalgar Square, to worship in his shadow and pray. The fans of all teams respect the customs of superstition—they cross themselves, they murmur hocus-pocus, they tie their fingers, they pray to Allah. But whatever their religion or their soccer god, after all they remain faithful to the doctrine of self-idolatry.[8]

Similarly, Monsignor Keith Barltrop of Britain's recently dismantled Catholic Agency to Support Evangelisation praised the Brazilian international Ricardo Kaka, a devout Christian, who has the words "God is faithful" stitched on his boots and tears off his jersey to reveal a T-shirt that boasts "I love Jesus," saying "it is good to have positive role models." Barltrop worried that the excitement generated by pop stars and sporting celebrities "leads to a life of hedonism."[9] For its part, the Vatican, much like the Islamic Movement in Israel and Saudi clerics who developed rules for what they described as an acceptable Muslim form of soccer, created in 2007 The Clericus Cup, an international tournament for priests and seminarians, aimed at bringing the Church closer to believers and "reinvigorating a sporting tradition within the Christian community." And like mosques that sponsor soccer teams, up to a third of Britain's Premier League clubs were founded in association with a church and with the help of the clergy. By the same token, Islamic clerics endorse expressions of religiosity on the pitch and rejection of Western vices by some of Europe's most prominent Muslim players.

The Jordanian-born Palestinian Sheikh Mashhoor Bin Hasan Al Salman summed up the Islamic clerical divide over soccer in a treatise published in 1998. The treatise is long on articulating militant arguments against soccer citing a slew of Saudi clerics and rulings, including Sheikhs Hamoud al-Tuwayjuri,[10] Abdulaziz bin Abduallah ibn Baz, Abdul Razak Afifi, Abdullah bin Ghudayan and Abdullah bin Qu'ud;[11] Abdul Halim Uways,[12] Shukri Ali al Tawil;[13] Abdul Aziz as Salman;[14] and Ahmad Shalabi,[15] but short on countering them. While Salman appears to agree with many of their arguments, he makes clear that he believes that soccer also contains elements and values that put it in line with Islamic morals and standards.

"Football training is in the realm of the permissible, as we do not know of any proof that prohibits it. The origin of a thing is that it is permissible (a principle in *fiqh* [Islamic jurisprudence]) is that there is nothing that distances it from permissible actions as long as a Muslim does it in order to strengthen the body and use it as a means for strength, exercise and vitality. In fact, the legislation allows it for reasons that will strengthen one's body, for the purpose of striving in the path of Allah. It is verified that the Messenger of Allah (*sallallaahu alayhi wassalam* [Peace be upon Him]) stated: 'The strong believer is better and more beloved by Allah than a weak believer even though there is good in both of them,'" Salman concluded.[16] Distancing himself from interpretations of jihad to justify terrorism, Salman relied on Al-Tuwayhari's referral to the fourteenth-century Islamic scholar Taqi ad-Din Ahmad ibn Taymiyyah,[17] widely viewed as a co-founder of the Hanbali school of Islamic legal thought and an inspiration for contemporary militant Islamists and jihadists. Al-Tuwayhari quoted Ibn Taymiyyah as saying that "ball games are good as long as the intention of the one practising it is for the benefit of training horses and men, so as to help them in attacking and retreating, and in entering, withdrawing and performing similar actions during jihad. The purpose is to secure help during jihad, which Allah and his Commander (Peace be upon Him) commanded. However, such games are forbidden if they have any detrimental effect on horses and men."[18]

Salman interpreted Ibn Taymiyyah's statement as detrimental to anything that would distract a Muslim from performing his religious obligations. He argued on the basis of opinions of Saudi scholars that soccer is forbidden if it "becomes a common habit that commands too much of a person's time," involves clothing that exposes thighs or anything above it or allows spectators to watch players whose bodies are exposed in ways that violate Islamic dress code.[19] In a later treatise, however, Salman's thinking appeared to have evolved to conclude that soccer was distracting believers from their religious obligations. "Football now has become one of the destructive hoes which our enemies are using in order to destroy the Islamic Ummah [community]," he said. Salman's conclusion was prompted by his observation that thousands of Muslims give priority to supporting their team during a match above going to daily prayers if the two coincide in time.[20]

In his original treatise, Salman quoted extensively the banning of soccer by Muhammad ibn Ibrahim Al Sheikh, a late grand mufti of Saudi Arabia, the country's highest religious authority, but proceeded to take issue with the ban itself. Al Sheikh, who was in office until his death in 1969, sought to stop the institutionalization of soccer by banning the establishing of leagues, associations and governing bodies. Al Sheikh warned that "the nature of the game sparks fanatical partisanship, troubles and the emergence of hate and malice," which contradict Islamic notions of "tolerance, brotherhood, rectification and purification of hearts and sows resentment, grudges, and discord that exist among losers and winners of the game." He cautioned further that soccer can spark violence. "So from this, soccer is prohibited ... Soccer does not serve the goal of things that justify allowing sport activities under the divine law of Islam such as exercise of the body, training in fighting or the curing of chronic illness," Al Sheikh ruled. In addition, he argued that soccer leads to the postponement of prayers for which there "is no legal excuse" and encourages gambling and betting in violation of Islamic law.[21]

Salman countered Al Sheikh by reasoning that "within the context of Islam and its way of building societies, soccer is among games endorsed by Islam as is the study of it. Soccer involves studying lessons in unity as opposed to splitting, mutual love as opposed to hatred and animosity." He defined soccer as a game that emphasizes those values and whose "values cannot be realized but through teamwork (in which) the team is greater than the individual."[22]

The debate about soccer is reminiscent of clerical opposition to the introduction of the game in the early twentieth century In Turkey and in Iran immediately after the 1979 Islamic revolution that overthrew the shah. Once popularized, religious forces in Iran recognized the game's political advantages and were quick to embrace them. The debate is also reflected in advice rendered to believers on the official fatwa website of Saudi Arabia operated by the General Presidency of Scholarly Research and Ifta (Fatwa) that effectively endorsed the game but banned competitions[23]—an approach that has been ignored by the government with a member of the royal family overseeing the country's leagues.

The presidency in a ruling tells a merchant to close his shop and go to the mosque to pray because a television set in his store that broadcasts soccer matches distracts people from their religious obligations. It justifies its advice with a quote from Allah: "O you who believe! Let not your properties or your children divert you from the remembrance of Allah. And whosoever does that, then they are the losers." Another fatwa, permitting soccer but banning competitions read: "Contests are only permissible when they can be sought for help in fighting Kuffar [disbelievers] like that of camels, horses, arrows and the like of other fighting machines such as planes, tanks and submarines, whether they are held for prizes or not. Whereas if these games are not sought for help in wars like football, boxing and wrestling, it is impermissible to take part in them if the contests include prizes for winners."[24] Yet another fatwa cautions that "attending football matches and watching them is unlawful for a person who knows that they are played for a reward, for attending such matches involves approving of them."[25]

The twisted rulings of the more radical Egyptian and Saudi clergy meanwhile provided the theological underpinnings of militant groups like the Taliban, informed Al-Shabaab's recruitment drive in Somalia and inspired some players to become fighters and suicide bombers in foreign lands. They also fuelled a debate about the participation of three Muslim nations—Saudi Arabia, Iran and Tunisia—in the 2006 World Cup. Militant clerics denounced the tournament as a "plot aiming to corrupt Muslim youth and distract them from jihad" and as "a cultural invasion worse than military war because it seizes the heart and soul of the Muslim." They dubbed the World Cup the "Prostitution Cup" because of the influx of prostitutes into Germany in advance of the games.[26] Writing under the name Abu Haytham, one cleric asserted that "while our brothers in Iraq, Palestine and Afghanistan are being massacred in cold blood by the Crusaders and the Jews, our young people will have their eyes riveted on depraved television sets which emit the opium of soccer to the extent of overdose."[27] In a similar vein, Hamid bin Abdallah al-Ali, a prominent Kuwaiti Salafist, issued a fatwa on his website that was widely circulated on jihadist forums declaring that "it is illicit to watch these matches on corrupt television channels while our nation is decimated night and day by foreign armies."[28] A British pan-

Islamist website advocating the creation of an Islamic state in the United Kingdom, banned in 2006, asserted that soccer promotes nationalism as part of a "colonial crusader scheme" to divide Muslims and cause them to stray from the vision of a unified Islamic identity. "The sad fact of the matter is that many Muslims have fallen for this new religion and they too carry the national flag," it said.[29]

Militant clerics differed about the fatwas and Salafi campaigns in fierce debates on Islamist websites. More moderate religious leaders and government officials weighed into the discussion about the role of soccer in society. Syrian scholar Abd-al Mun'em Mustafa Halima Abu Basir, better known as Abu Basir al-Tartusi, who is widely viewed as a spiritual jihadist influence, broke ranks with his militant brethren in 2006 by declaring that there is "no objection to soccer, playing sports as a means of entertainment" but that it was forbidden to watch World Cup matches because they distract believers from the abuses of Arabs in Iraq, Palestine and elsewhere. Al-Tartusi asserted that on the day of the opening of the Cup in Germany, billions of people clung to television screens while "the Zionist Jews bombed civilians."[30] Radical Islamists also posted a video of their own World Cup on the internet showing scenes of the 11 September 2001 attacks, the killing and torture of Palestinians, the Guantánamo Bay detention facility in Cuba and the abuse of Iraqi inmates by US forces in the notorious Abu Ghraib prison. In its introduction, the video stated that "at a time when pro-Zionist Arab media are busy broadcasting the World Cup to divert Muslims away from their religion and from jihad … we offer you the three other cups which those media are trying to hide from our nation."[31] One Islamist, Sa'ad al Wissi, who identified himself as "an extremist", insisted that he could "find no problem in watching the matches. Your calls to boycott the World Cup are doomed to fail," said Al Wissi.[32]

A controversial 2003 ruling[33] by anonymous militant clerics in Saudi Arabia, the world's most puritanical Muslim nation, is believed to have motivated three Saudi players to join the jihad in Iraq. Published as the Saudi national team prepared to compete in the 2006 World Cup, the fatwa denounced the game as an infidel invention and redrafted the country's International Football Association Board (IFAB) approved rules to differentiate it from that of the heretics. It banned words like foul, goal, corner and penalty. It ordered players to wear their ordinary clothes or pyjamas instead of shorts and T-shirt and to spit on anyone who scored a goal. It did away with the role of referees by banning the drawing of lines to demarcate the pitch and ordering that fouls and disputes be adjudicated on the basis of the Sharia rather than by issuing yellow or red cars. "If you … intend to play soccer, play to strengthen the body in order to better struggle in the way of God on high and to prepare the body for when it is called to jihad. Soccer is not for passing time or the thrill of so-called victory," argued the fatwa. It dictated that the game should be played in anything—"one half or three halves"—but the internationally accepted two halves of 45 minutes each, "which is the official time of the Jews, Christians and all the heretical and atheist countries." The ruling was based on an earlier fatwa issued in 2002 by radical Saudi cleric Abdullah al-Najdi,[34] a descendant of one of the companions of Mohammed ibn Abdul Wahhab, the eighteenth-century warrior priest who founded Wahhabism, Saudi Arabia's austere school of Islamic thought. Echoing Al Najdi, the Egyptian-born Sheikh Abu Ishaaq Al Huweni commented on YouTube (the video has since been deleted): "All fun is bootless except the playing of a man with his wife, his son and his horse … Thus, if someone sits in front of the television to watch football or something like that, he will be committing bootless fun … We have to be a serious nation, not a playing nation. Stop playing."[35]

Saudi officials and columnists responded by denying that soccer violated Islamic law. They accused the issuers of anti-soccer fatwas of misleading Saudi youth and called for a re-examination of the kingdom's religious discourse and the prosecution of those who had decreed soccer as un-Islamic. Authorities should "prosecute those involved in the publishing of these fatwas in a Sharia court for the crime they have committed," Saudi mufti Sheikh Abdel Aziz Ibn Abdallah Al-Sheikh was quoted as saying.[36] Justice ministry advisor Sheikh Abdel Muhsin Al-Abikan argued that "the rules of the game and the prohibition against using terms such as foul, out, penalty kick, etc. is misguided, since even the Prophet Muhammad used non-Arabic expressions in the hadith [the sayings of the Prophet], and even Allah used some non-Arabic words in His book the Qur'an … There is nothing wrong with the lines, the referee, and the soccer rules. All things that come from the West but are not unique to it are permitted. Soccer has become a world sport and does not belong only to the non-believers."[37] To reinforce the message, the municipality of Mecca, Islam's most holy city, announced the construction of sixty soccer pitches that would be managed by a local club and the World Assembly of Muslim Youth (WAMY), a group that in the past was investigated for alleged links to militant Islamist groups.[38]

The Iranian filmmaker Mazar Bahari documented ambiguous Shiite Muslim clerical attitudes towards soccer while sharing a taxi in Tehran with a clergyman. The cleric gave his assessment of Iran's performance in an Asian Cup tournament. Asked about his fundamental view of soccer, the cleric scowled and said "it's a waste of time." He explained his following of the Asian Cup as relaxation in between his religious studies.[39] His attitude was rooted in religious opposition to attempts to promote soccer by Iranian ruler Reza Shah starting in 1940. Religious leaders at the time denounced the game as evidence of the moral corruption of the Pahlavi regime.[40] Similarly, the Islamic republic following the 1979 overthrow of Reza Shah's son waged an initial campaign against soccer, which it viewed as a "royalist tool of manipulation,"[41] a violation of Islamic values and law, a diversion from more pressing political issues and a threat because it involved the gathering of large numbers of people.

The vision of more nuanced scholars like Salman, let alone the views of mainstream scholars and officials, had little impact on Al-Shabaab, jihadist rebels in northern Mali, or, for that matter, on the Taliban's image of a Sharia-based society. Al-Shabaab banned the game in the large chunks of war-ravaged Somalia that it long controlled on the grounds that it distracted the faithful from worshipping Allah, competed with the militants for recruits and lent credence to national borders at the expense of pan-Islamist aspirations for the return of the Caliph who would rule the world's 1.5 billion Muslims as one. It also celebrated peaceful competition and undermined the narrative of an inevitable clash of civilizations between Islam and the West. Pakistani journalist Muhammed Wasim recalls the arrest by the Taliban of a Pakistani soccer team during a visit to Kandahar because they were wearing shorts. As punishment, the players had their heads shaven before being sent home. "They were arrested because they violated the Islamic dress code, which forbids exposing any parts of the body," Wasim quoted Taliban spokesman Maulvi Hameed Akhund as saying.[42]

The risks of playing soccer were far greater in Somalia, but so were the opportunities.

Mahad Mohamed was eleven when he joined an Islamist militia. By the time he realized that doing a jihadist warlord's bidding to give meaning to his life in a country savaged for two decades by civic strife and brutal militias was not what he expected, he was three years older. Now he dreams of being a soccer coach, a pilot and a computer teacher and plays in the defence in his country's Under-17 national soccer team.

"People were afraid of me when I had an AK-47; now they love and congratulate me. I thank the football federation, they helped me," he said.[43] "I just drifted into being a soldier; it is hard to say how it happened. Some friends of mine ended up being fighters and they used to tell me that it was a good and exciting life and much better than doing nothing or being on the streets. After I spent some time doing that, I understood that it wasn't like that at all and I was happy to get out."

The opportunity to leave the militia presented itself after three years of fighting government troops, rival jihadists and warlords and African Union peacekeepers when the warlord he served as a bodyguard was killed. Mahad ran away and returned home to play soccer in an open field. A Somali soccer association scout spotted him and offered him a chance to play on its youth team.

Mahad's shift from boy killer to soccer star stood out in Somalia, a soccer-mad Arab country that straddles Africa's strategic Gulf of Aden, along which Al-Shabaab had at the time draconically imposed an austere lifestyle. Supporters of a fiercely austere interpretation of Islam that made puritan Saudi Arabia seem liberal, they banned soccer as satanic and un-Islamic while Mahad was still a fighter. At the time, Al-Shabaab were on the ascendancy. The then US-backed head of Somalia's transitional government, Sheik Sharif Sheikh Ahmed, was hanging on to power by the skin of his teeth. The jihadists had reduced his authority to a few blocks around his embattled presidential palace in the crumbling, battle-scarred capital of Mogadishu. Supported by African Union and Kenyan troops, Somali forces have since regained control of much of the country with the jihadists declaring a tactical retreat.

Like the Taliban in Afghanistan, Al-Shabaab was a product of a failed foreign invasion that did little but exacerbate Somalia's political, social and tribal faultlines. US-backed Ethiopian forces crossed the Somali border in 2006 and ousted the hardline Islamic Courts Union barely six months after the militia had driven the warlords out of Mogadishu on the eve of the 2006 World Cup in a bid to restore law and order. One of the militia's first decrees banned the watching of World Cup matches. Much like the US effort a decade earlier recounted in Ridley Scott's war movie *Black Hawk Down*, the Ethiopian invasion and toppling of the Islamists sparked the emergence of even more radical forces and an uptick in violence. Tens of thousands of people have been killed since the invasion; another 1.8 million fled their homes to become refugees.

Mahad exemplified the serious challenge soccer posed to the jihadists' dire worldview. The scout who discovered him was on no ordinary recruitment drive. His slogan was "Put down the gun, pick up the ball." He was part of a Somali Football Association (SFA) campaign, backed by FIFA, soccer's world body, and local businessmen to throw down a gauntlet for the jihadists by luring child soldiers like Mahad away from them. "However difficult our situation is, we believe football can play a major role in helping peace and stability prevail in our country, and that is what our federation has long been striving to attain. Football is here to stay, not only as game to be played but as a catalyst for peace and harmony in society," said Shafi'i Moyhaddin, one of the driving forces behind the campaign.[44]

Mahad was one of hundreds the association assisted in swapping jihad for soccer, the only institution that competed with radical Islam in offering young Somalis the prospect of a better life. "If we keep the young generation for football, Al-Shabaab can't recruit them to fight. This is really why Al-Shabaab fights with us," remarked Somali soccer association head Abdulghani Sayeed.[45] To shield himself from threats by Al-Shabaab, Sayeed lived in and operated from a heavily guarded Mogadishu hotel. Yet he refused to move the association's headquarters out of Mogadishu's Al-Shabaab-controlled Suuqa Bakaaraha to avoid giving the jihadists a further excuse to attack its members. An open-air market in the heart of the city, Suuqa Bakaaraha was famous for its trade in arms and falsified documents and as the crash site of one of two downed US Black Hawk helicopters in the 1993 Battle for Mogadishu.

Middle Eastern and North African soccer fans insist that their sport is more than just a game; it is a matter of life and death. From Mahad and Sayeed's perspective, that was no exaggeration. Nowhere did enthusiasm for the beautiful game involve a greater act of courage and defiance than in their native Somalia under Al-Shabaab where the sport had developed its own unique thrill—a high-stakes game of cat and mouse between enthusiasts and jihadists and a struggle for a trophy grander than the world's largest sports event, the FIFA World Cup: the future of a country and perhaps even a region. It was the world's most important match: soccer versus jihad.

Somalia was the pitch, battle-hardened kids like Mahad were the ball. Players and enthusiasts risked execution, arrest and torture. Militants in their trademark green jumpsuits and chequered scarves drove through towns in southern Somalia in Toyota pickup trucks mounted with megaphones. Families were threatened with punishment if their children failed to enlist as fighters. Boys were plucked from makeshift soccer fields. Childless families were ordered to pay Al-Shabaab US$50 a month, the equivalent of Somalia's monthly per capita income. Local soccer club owners were detained and tortured on charges of misguiding youth. "I don't go anywhere. I just stay at home with my family so that the Shabaab don't catch me," said Mahad who ran a double risk as a teenager and a deserter.

Sheikh Mohamed Abdi Aros,[46] a militant cleric who doubled as head of operations of Hizbul Islam, a jihadist group that in 2010 merged with Al-Shabaab, condemned soccer as "a waste of money and time" and "an inheritance from the primitive infidels." His campaign reached a crescendo every four years during the World Cup—a moment when most of the world is glued to the television and much of Somalia risks public flogging and execution to catch a glimpse of the game. Somalia had the sad distinction of being the only country where the world's most popular game was a clandestine, life-threatening activity. To Sheikh Mohamed, whose warlords once were soccer's most powerful supporters and providers of security, the World Cup was the equivalent of Karl Marx's opium for the masses. In his mind, soccer diverted the Muslim faithful from jihad; the World Cup offered youth a stark reminder that watching games and waging battles on the pitch is a lot more fun than the austere life of a fighter who defies death in street battles.

To mark the kick-off of the 2010 World Cup in South Africa, Sheikh Mohamed cautioned "all Somali youth not to dare watch these World Cup matches ... They will not benefit anything or get any experience by watching semi-nude madmen jumping up and down and chasing an inflated object ... we can never accept people to watch it." During the match between Germany and Australia, Sheikh Mohamed's fighters raided a private home in the town of Afgoye, 20 km south of Mogadishu. Of the tens of fans clustered around one of the country's relatively few satellite TVs, one eye on the game with the volume turned off to avoid drawing attention, the other on the door in case of a raid, two were killed and thirty detained among whom were fourteen teenagers. In the village of Suqa Holaha north of Mogadishu, another cleric, Sheik Abu Yahya Al Iraqi, warned a crowd that "soccer descended from the old Christian cultures and our Islamic administration will never allow watching what they call the FIFA World Cup. We are sending our last warning to the people," he said hours before a match between Nigeria and Argentina.[47]

Soccer allowed Mahad to forget the tragedies that dominate life beyond the pitch. He took pride in flying the Somali flag at international matches and showing the world that there is more to his country than wild-eyed fanatics, suicide bombers and pirates. Yet, his transition from child solider to national star was not easy. "I lost everything when I was a fighter, I had nothing." Soccer training for Mahad and his fighter-turned-player team mates involved far more than just gearing up for the next match. Psychologists helped him transit back to a semblance of normal life in a country that is stumbling from bad to worse.

They were aided by the fact that the soccer association constituted an island of relative normalcy. Buoyed by its success in wrenching child fighters from the clutches of the Islamists, the association upped the stakes in its battle with the militias. In the spring of 2010 it revived for the first time in three years the country's soccer championships at a ceremony on the well-protected grounds of the Somali police academy in Mogadishu. It also launched a tournament for primary and secondary school students.

The jihadists were quick to respond to the association's challenge. "If we kill you, we will get closer to God," they said in an email sent to the association. Several days later, they sent a second mail: "This is the last warning for you to take the path of Islam. If you don't, you have no choice but to die. Do you think the non-believer police can guarantee your security?"[48]

Al-Shabaab have since been driven out of virtually all Somali cities. Soccer is one measure of the success of the drive to defeat them. Their loss of influence is evident in the fact that for the first time in more than two decades, matches are being played at night, teams travel in relative safety within the country and war-ravaged sports facilities, including Mogadishu's national stadium, once one of East Africa's most impressive filled with 70,000 passionate fans (which was used by Al-Shabaab as an arms depot and training facility), are being refurbished. Scores cheered Somalia's Under-17 national team after it defeated Sudan in September 2012 in an African youth championship, playing without its goalkeeper, Abdulkader

Dheer Hussein, who was assassinated in April of that year as part of an Al-Shabaab murder campaign that increasingly targets not only athletes and officials but also sports journalists, who glorify "satanic" games.

The campaign illustrated that Al-Shabaab may be down and out as it loses control of territory but is far from defeated. Al-Shabaab has adjusted to a new reality by shifting gears to focus on hit and run guerrilla tactics. For much of the last two years, Al-Shabaab's targets were senior government officials as well as players like Hussein and Under-20 international Abdi Salaam Mohamed Ali as well as former Somali Olympic Committee vice-president Abdulkader Yahye Sheik Ali, killed in July 2012, and SFA president Said Mohamed Nur, who spearheaded the campaign to win back child soldiers and was murdered in April 2012.

Fourteen sports journalists were killed in the first nine months of 2012 alone, including Abdirahman Mohamed Ali whose decapitated body was dumped next to a restaurant a day after he was kidnapped; Hassan Yusuf Absuge, shot that same day by masked gunmen as he returned home from work; and Mahmoud Ali Buneyste, killed in August while filming a soccer match in Mogadishu hours after he attended the funeral of a murdered colleague Yusuf Ali Osman. Al-Shabaab claimed responsibility for their deaths with a militant leader telling a Somali radio station that "God is great. We have killed spy journalists. They were the real enemies of Islam." Their demise, he said, constituted "one of the victories that Islam gained, and such operations will continue." Despite such statements, the facts in lawless Somalia remain murky and it is not impossible that they may have been victims of personal feuds or rogue armed groups. Irrespective of who is responsible for the killing of journalists, Al-Shabaab's ability to target senior political and soccer officials demonstrated its continued ability to strike and the importance of soccer in its effort to impose its moral and social code if not by territorial control then by a campaign of fear and terror.

By contrast, Al-Shabaab mentor and Taliban ally Bin Laden, like various other leaders of militant Islamist political movements, worshipped the game as only second to Allah. So did many of their subordinates. "The day [Egyptian President Anwar] Sadat was killed [in 1981] was one of the happiest of my life along with the day when Ahly football club—fielding only youth players and substitutes—beat Zamalek's first team by three to two," recalled (in his autobiography) Khaled al-Berry, a teenage member of a militant Egyptian Islamist group who went on to study medicine and become a London-based writer.[49] These men recognized soccer's useful bonding and recruitment qualities.[50] It bought recruits into the fold, encouraged camaraderie and reinforced militancy among those who had already joined. Soccer fans like jihadists live in a world characterized best by US President George W. Bush's us and them response to 9/11: "You are either with us or against us." The track record of soccer-players-turned suicide bombers proved his point. "I had full confidence in those who were ready to take up the challenge," said Al-Berry referring to his older jihadi peers, "those who were capable with their honesty, their self-sacrifice, and their faith. They wre the ones whom I played soccer with and prayed with, and at whose hands I studied. They were the ones who, when I was in their midst, made me feel safe and protected, the one, who should I fail to show up, would ask about me as though my mere absence was an event of significance."[51]

Soccer was perfect for the creation and sustenance of strong and cohesive jihadist groups. It facilitated personal contact and the expansion of informal networks which, in their turn, encouraged individual participation and the mobilization of resources. These informal individual connections contributed to jihadist activity in a variety of ways. First, they facilitated the circulation of information and therefore the speed of decision-making. In the absence of any formal coordination among jihadi organizations, recruitment, enlistment and cooperation focused on individuals. Another important function of multiple informal individual relationships was their contribution to the growth of "feelings of mutual trust," commented Indonesian security consultant Noor Huda Ismail, a consultant on the impact of religion on political violence. "Recruitment into most jihadi groups is not like recruitment into the police or army or college. Indeed, previous formal or informal membership in action-oriented groups such as soccer or cricket teams, and other informal ties, may facilitate the passage from radicalization into jihad and on to joining suicide attack teams."[52]

Nonetheless to Bin Laden as well as to more mainstream, non-violent, ultra-conservative Muslims, the beautiful game also posed a challenge. In a swath of land stretching from Central Asia to the Atlantic coast of Africa soccer was the only institution that rivalled Islam with its vast network of mosques in creating public spaces to vent pent-up anger and frustration. During the 2010 World Cup in South Africa, Saudi Arabia's religious guardians, afraid that believers would forget their daily prayers during matches broadcast live on Saudi TV, rolled out mobile mosques on trucks and prayer mats in front of popular cafés where men gathered to watch the games.[53]

Much like with Arab autocrats, soccer posed both an opportunity and a challenge to religious conservatives. The emergence of soccer clubs in Palestinian villages and towns in Israel, for example, challenged traditional social structures.[54] They competed with the sway of conservative Muslim clergymen who saw the clubs as dangerous attempts at modernization and innovation. In a bid to co-opt soccer, Israel's Islamic Movement created a league of its own operating independently of Israel's governing soccer body, the Israel Football Association (IFA).

Underlying the debate about soccer is a more fundamental view among militant Islamists that fun, not exclusively but often associated with sports, is a potential threat to political and social control. Witness restrictive sports policies adopted by Saudi Arabia, Iran, the Taliban, Al-Shabaab and some Salafis in Egypt. Youth are often the main targets because of their sheer number and disruptive potential, meaning in the words of Asef Bayat that the:

> youth habitus is characterized by a greater tendency for experimentation, adventurism, idealism, drive for autonomy, mobility, and change ... Whereas the elderly poor can afford simple, traditional, and contained diversions, the globalized and affluent youth tend to embrace more spontaneous, erotically charged, and commodified pleasures. This might help explain why globalizing youngsters more than others cause fear and fury among Islamist (and non-Islamist) anti-fun adversaries, especially when much of what these youths practice is informed by Western technologies of fun and is framed in terms of "Western cultural import" ... In other words, at stake is not necessarily the disruption of the moral order, as often claimed, but rather the undermining of the hegemony, the regime of power on which certain strands of moral and political authority rest ... The adversaries' fear of fun, I conclude, revolves ultimately around the fear of exit from the paradigm that frames their mastery; it is about anxiety over loss of their "paradigm power."[55]

That principle was at times extended beyond the realm of nations or territories under Islamist rule. Former Egyptian national coach Hassan Shehata maintained an unwritten rule in the first decade of the twenty-first century that allowed only practising Muslims to join the Egyptian national soccer team. Players prayed before games for God's intervention and offered up prayers of thanks for goals and victories. To join the team, players had to pass a religious litmus test; "pious behaviour" alongside soccer skills was a primary criterion for making the team. "Without it, we will never select any player regardless of his potential," confirmed Shehata, who dumped a talented player for visiting a nightclub in London rather than a mosque: "I always strive to make sure that those who wear the Egypt jersey are on good terms with God."[56]

For Palestinians—locked into Gaza by Israeli and Egyptian travel restrictions in an economic siege that isolated the Strip from the outside world and helped Hamas reinforce its conservative social and political mores—soccer, too, constituted a rare space for relaxation and a safe outlet for pent-up emotions. That is as long as one steered clear of the Strip's politically controlled clubs. Young Gazans who gathered in a Gaza restaurant to watch the 2010 World Cup qualifying match between Egypt and Algeria discussed the significance of soccer during halftime. "There is sense of despair and there is a mistrust in the leadership whether in the West Bank or in the Gaza Strip," said a young spectator only weeks before soccer played its part in the Arab revolt that would rewrite the region's political map.[57]

Bin Laden and Haniyeh's political interest in soccer stemmed from the fact that jihadists often start their journey as members of groups organized around another activity like soccer. The perpetrators of the 2004 Madrid subway bombings played soccer together. Saudi players Tamer al-Thamali, Dayf Allah al-Harithi and Majid Sawat attended a Qur'an group twice a week alongside their regular soccer training. Silently they made their way to Iraq as the Al-Qaeda-led insurgency gained steam. Tamer and Dayf died as suicide bombers; Majid's father recognized his son when Iraqi television broadcast his interrogation by authorities.[58]

Both Haniyeh and Bin Laden learnt the significance of soccer early on. As a child, Bin Laden organized soccer games in poor parts of Jeddah, his hometown. As if in anticipation of later rulings by radical Muslim clerics that ranged from condemning the game as a satanic invention of the infidels to seeking to provide it with an Islamic gloss, Bin Laden played centre forward wearing his headdress and long trousers so as not to expose parts of his body.[59] He used the matches as a platform to preach his conservative view of Islam during breaks and rewarded co-players who correctly answered trivia questions about the Qur'an and the teachings of the Prophet Muhammed.[60]

In the 1990s, when Bin Laden based Al-Qaeda in Sudan, the group had its own soccer league with two competing teams that maintained regularly scheduled training and played weekly matches after Friday prayers.[61] Back in Afghanistan during the US-backed Islamist war against the Russians, the Afghan guerrillas and their foreign fellow travellers dealt with jihadi ennui in between battles with their own World Cup; fighters competed in soccer teams representing their countries of origin. Once the Russians withdrew and foreign jihadists returned home, soccer matches were an opportunity to stay in touch.[62]

Soccer often served as the lure militant Islamists employed to draw teenagers like Bin Laden and young men into their circle. A high school friend of Bin Laden's in Jeddah recalls being attracted to an extracurricular Qur'an class in the school held by a Syrian instructor who promised his students that they would play soccer after learning verses of the Qur'an. Initially, "we'd sit down, read a few verses of the Qur'an, translate or discuss how it should be interpreted, and many points of view would be offered. Then he'd send us out to the field. He had the key to the goodies—the lockers where the balls and athletic equipment were kept. But it turned out that the athletic part of it was just disorganized, an add-on. There was no organized soccer. I ended up playing a lot of one-on-one soccer, which is not very much fun," the schoolfriend recalled.[63] He left the group a year later, feeling trapped and bored, while Bin Laden became increasingly committed to it. As the year progressed, the group moved from memorizing verses of the holy book to reading and discussing hadiths, the sayings of the Prophet, to listening to the instructor's increasingly mesmerizing but violent stories. The story that prompted Bin Laden's friend to leave the group was "about a boy who found God—exactly like us, our age. He wanted to please God and he found that his father was standing in his way. The father was pulling the rug out from under him when he went to pray," he recalled. The Syrian instructor "told the story slowly, but he was referring to 'this brave boy' or 'this righteous boy' as he moved toward the story's climax. He explained that the father had a gun. He went through twenty minutes of the boy's preparation, step by step—the bullets, loading the gun, making a plan. Finally, the boy shot the father." The instructor concluded his story with the words: "Lord be praised—Islam was released in that home." The schoolfriend said that he watched in the years after leaving the group how Bin Laden and others adopted the appearance and ideas of an Islamist by growing their beards, shortening the length of their trousers, wearing unironed shirts and advocating the Arab world's return to strict Islamic law.

Similarly, the former Tunisian soccer player Nizar Trabelsi was an unlikely candidate for Islamic militancy given his record of petty crime and drug abuse. A one-time promising player for Germany's Fortuna Düsseldorf and Wuppertaler SV, he was quickly dropped by Borussia Dortmund when it emerged that he had a cocaine habit and a criminal past. A seemingly integrated immigrant from North Africa, Trabelsi drifted until he was finally persuaded by Djamel Beghal, a French Algerian who was released from prison in 2011 after serving time for planning to attack the US embassy in Paris, to go to Afghanistan to join a European cell. When he returned to Europe he consorted with jihadists in London and Brussels as well as the group that assassinated the Dutch filmmaker Theo van Gogh. Convicted in 2001 of intending to attack NATO's headquarters on the edge of Brussels, he said in court that a picture of a baby Palestinian girl killed in the Gaza Strip had convinced him to become a suicide bomber. "I intended to go in with the picture of the little Palestinian girl and press the detonator," he admitted, describing the logistics of his foiled mission.

Six Palestinians involved in a wave of Hamas suicide attacks in 2003 traced their roots to a mosque-sponsored soccer team in the conservative West Bank town of Hebron, much like members of a soccer team in southern Thailand, who two years later joined a militant Islamist group seeking the independence of Pattani Province that killed 112 people in a series of attacks on the police. Israeli intelligence believes Hamas saw the team as an ideal recruitment pool—a tight-knit group that shared a passion for soccer, a conservative, religious worldview and deep-seated frustration with Palestinian impotency in shaking off Israeli occupation.[64] Considered one of the best teams in the West Bank's most traditional city, they played on Fridays on a pitch made of asphalt just down the street from the Jihad mosque located above a local grocer and a car repair shop. Green banners shuttering in the wind on its rooftop indicated the mosque's affiliation with Hamas, in a city then governed by a Hamas mayor.

"A tightly knit group that communicates face-to-face rather than on a mobile phone like this soccer team is a tough nut to crack," according to Eran Lerman, a former senior Israeli intelligence official, describing the difficulty counterterrorism forces often have in monitoring soccer-related jihadist groups. Israeli forces killed Abdullah Qawasmeh, the 43-year-old alleged Hamas mastermind behind the soccer team more than half a year after his recruits executed their grizzly assignments. Israeli officials claimed that Qawasmeh, a member of Hamas' military wing, the Izzedin al-Qassem Brigade, had recruited in total more than a dozen players from different clubs.

At the time of Qawasmeh's assassination, Israel also rounded up the remaining players of the Jihad mosque team founded six years earlier by Muhsin Qawasmeh, another member of Hebron's most powerful clan. Like the legendary Egyptian player and trainer Hassan Shehata, Muhsin, the team's coach who doubled as a player, attributed equal importance to soccer skills and religiosity. He demanded that members of his team pray five times a day and that they wear the club's blue-and white strip inscribed with its slogan: "Al-Jihad: Be Prepared for Them." Muhsin was arrested in the spring of 2002 in an Israeli sweep of Hebron aimed at breaking the uprising's backbone. He was sentenced to six months in prison. Many of his fellow inmates were supporters of Hamas. Israeli officials and relatives believe the Intifada and his detention radicalized him and convinced him of the virtues of martyrdom. His prison sentence was extended by three months after he allegedly attacked a prison warden.

Resistance to Israeli occupation of the West Bank became an early part of the Jihad soccer team's ethos. Players participated in the second Intifada against Israel barely two years after the team's creation. Two players were killed in demonstrations by Israeli soldiers. Mohammed Yagmur, another player, became the team's first member to die in a suicide mission when he attacked a Jewish settlement in 2002. A fourth player, Hamzi Qawasmeh, was shot to death several months later after he killed a settler and wounded three others in an attack on Kharsina, an Israeli outpost northeast of Hebron. The losses undermined the team's game but fuelled a longing for revenge among its remaining members. Barely three months after Hamzi's death, Muhsin and another Qawasmeh smuggled themselves into Kiryat Arba just north of Hebron where they shot dead a couple sharing a Sabbath dinner and wounded three others before they were killed by Israeli soldiers. Almost simultaneously, two other players were shot and killed as they tried to enter the settlement of Negohot. Two months later, Fuad Qawasmeh and fellow player Bassem al-Taquri launched separate suicide attacks in Hebron itself and in East Jerusalem.

Several years later, heavily armed members of Hamas' military wing provided security in Gaza for the 2009 Gaza Dialogue and Tolerance Cup, organized less than a year after a nineteen-day Israeli assault on the strip in which more than 1400 people, including three prominent Palestinian

113

soccer players, were killed. Rather than retreating to their dressing rooms at half time, players and spectators crowded the pitch to pray. The tournament was intended to revive Gaza's soccer league following its demise two years earlier when the Islamists seized control of the strip, the world's most densely populated sliver of land sandwiched between Israel and Egypt, from their arch rival Al Fatah. To underscore the importance he attributed to the game, the de facto Hamas prime minister Haniyeh handed the cup's trophy to the captain of the winning club.

Haniyeh, like Bin Laden and Hezbollah's Hassan Nasrallah, has a soft spot for the game and understands the political benefits it offers, the organizing force it possesses—and the threat it poses. As a youngster, he played as a defender for Al Shasta, his neighbourhood team made up of members of Hamas as well as Al Fatah and the only soccer team associated with the West Bank group established by Yasser Arafat that survived Hamas' takeover of the Gaza Strip in 2007. As a political leader, Haniyeh harnessed soccer's power. In one of its first moves after its power grab, Hamas and its military wing took control of Gaza's soccer clubs. In doing so, Haniyeh was in good company. Further north, Hezbollah's leader Nasrallah engineered funding for Al Ahed, one of Lebanon's most successful clubs, and sponsorship by Al Manar, its popular TV outlet. Hamas' Islamist rival, Islamic Jihad, organized camps on Gaza's Mediterranean Sea beaches for disadvantaged children who were offered a game of soccer or volleyball, swimming and a hefty dose of slanted history that portrayed the Israeli-Palestinian dispute as a religious rather than a national conflict and Israelis as hell-bent on killing Arabs. "The purpose is to counter their anger, fear and sorrow. They play soccer and other games in the morning. In the afternoon we discuss the need to sacrifice. We tell them how the Jews persecuted the prophets and tortured them and how they kill Arabs and Palestinians. They learn that this conflict is about religion, not land," said one of the camps' organizers.

Islam vs Islam[65]

"You can use your tear gas bombs, you can use your tear gas bombs. Have courage if you are a real man, take off your helmet and drop your batons, then we'll see who the real man is."

Turkish Ultras' chant taunting the police

If there is one lesson Turkish President Recep Tayyip Erdoğan, a former soccer player with an athlete's swagger, should have drawn from the popular revolts that toppled four Arab leaders and sparked civil war in Syria since 2011, it was that police brutality strengthens protesters' resolve and particularly that of militant, street-fighting soccer fans.

Heavy-handed police tactics, involving the use of pepper spray, tear gas and water cannons, prepared the ground in early June 2013 for mass anti-government protests, the largest in modern Turkey's history, on Istanbul's iconic Taksim Square and in cities across the country. Militant soccer fans knew what to expect on the square as they found themselves at the core of battles with security forces in what was the most serious challenge to Erdoğan's rule in his decade as prime minister.

As police, backed by armoured vehicles and helicopters on the first day of the protests unleashed their tear gas and water cannons on demonstrators opposed to the planned destruction of a historic park on the square, thousands of fans from rival Istanbul clubs Beşiktaş JK, Galatasaray SK and Fenerbahçe SK, widely viewed as Europe's most fanatical soccer supporters, were united for the first time in decades despite deep-seated soccer and political rivalries as they arrived to protect the protesters and raise morale. The police operation earned Erdoğan the nickname "Chemical Tayyip," a reference to Chemical Ali, the senior Iraqi official under Saddam Hussein responsible for the use of chemical weapons against Kurds in northern Iraq.

In a replay of the events on Cairo's Tahrir Square that toppled Egyptian president Hosni Mubarak, thousands of physically fit, often unshaven fans took up positions bristling for a fight. They were led by Çarşı, the left-wing fan group of Beşiktaş, modern Turkey's oldest club. Çarşı was the most politicized of Turkish soccer supporters' groups. The Ultras dug up pavement stones erected barricades, handed out gas masks, helped protesters deal with the effects of the police's tear gas and pepper spray, applied first aid to the injured, lit the sky with their flares, counterattacked the police and threw tear gas canisters straight back into the ranks of the security forces. They knew when to confront the police and when to urge protesters to remain calm. In one instance, soccer fans wearing surgical and Guy Fawkes masks as well as safety helmets and waving Turkish flags employed a hotwired bulldozer from a construction site near Beşiktaş' İnönü Stadium to confront police.[66] "The police are attempting to intimidate us. It doesn't work. I and my friends have repeatedly been beaten by the police. We are not afraid," said one Beşiktaş fan.

"It was a critical moment. Supporters of all the big teams united for the first time against police violence. They were more experienced than the protesters, they fight them regularly. Their entry raised the protesters' morale and they played a leading role," added Bagis Erten, a sports reporter for Eurosport Turkey and NTVSpor.

Initial comparisons between Taksim and Cairo's Tahrir Square, which had come to symbolize the ability of the street to topple a government, were tempting. The two squares shared experiences of the unification of rival soccer fans despite a history of fighting one another; the occupation of a main city square; and the violent police crackdowns. The tactics of the Turkish government and police, moreover, displayed an uncanny resemblance to those of their Egyptian counterparts and the Bahraini security forces. Erdoğan vigilantes attacked demonstrators and opposition offices. Police gassed protesters seeking refuge from tear and pepper gas in a luxury hotel lobby. Protest leaders were especially sought out in a widespread crackdown. Doctors treating the injured, lawyers representing the detained, and human rights activists supplying food and medicine to protesters were arrested.

As the drama in Istanbul and Cairo unfolded over the summer, the similarities, however, increasingly outweighed the differences. Erdoğan introduced draconian measures to prevent protests from moving from the square into stadiums and onto university campuses. His controversial moves fuelled the spectre of Turkey reversing political liberalization in favour of illiberal democracy, the outcome of Egypt's military coup. Erdoğan, a product of multiple coups in his own country, failed to see the contradiction between his fervent and often emotional condemnation of the intervention of the military in Egypt and the policies he was implementing at home. His stance ignored the fact that both the protests in stadiums in both countries and on Taksim as well as the demonstrations on Tahrir against Morsi amounted to battles for control of public space in which significant segments of Turkish and Egyptian society with soccer fans in the front lines were telling their leaders they wanted more inclusive, consultative, transparent and accountable government. In contrast to Morsi, Erdoğan was in the enviable position of being told that his critics were willing to give him the opportunity to mend his ways; Tahrir's message to Morsi was one of game over, there was no hope that he could change, it was time for him to go.

What started out as an effort to save trees in İnönü Gezi Park, a dilapidated area on Taksim named after modern Turkey's second president who lived in the vicinity, had evolved into a crisis that put at risk

Erdoğan's sweeping reforms. A former Istanbul mayor, Erdoğan was Turkey's first prime minister in decades to have swept three elections with enough votes to form a one-party government. Yet he has turned Turkey into a country that outranks China, Iran and Eritrea in the number of journalists it has incarcerated. And while the gap between secular and conservative segments of society initially narrowed under his rule, Erdoğan's more recent hubris, haughtiness and lack of transparency, coupled with Islamist-tinted measures and efforts to limit people's freedoms, renewed secular suspicion of his true intentions. Saving the trees amounted to opposition to Istanbul's decades of uncontrolled growth and a municipal policy that catered more to conservatives, big business, developers and contractors than environmentalists seeking to preserve its threatened historic and cultural sites.

For the secularists, Gezi Park was the straw that broke the camel's back, a defining moment in what social anthropologist Jenny White describes as an ongoing process of redefinition of Turkishness that de-emphasized nationalist core values in favour of more pluralistic and at times more socially conservative choices.[67] The explosion of discontent allowed secularists to turn the protests into manifestations against the alleged Islamization of society. They pointed to restrictions on the sale and consumption of alcohol, Erdoğan declaration that *ayran*, made of yoghurt, was Turkey's national drink, his denunciation of anyone who drinks as an alcoholic, the reform of the education system to increase compulsory lessons in Sunni Islam, the boosting of specialized religious Imam Hatip Liseleri training schools, tightened restrictions on alleged un-Islamic content of television programmess, the use of courts to block access to over 25,000 websites and the naming of a third, controversial Istanbul bridge spanning the Bosporus after Yavuz Sultan Selim, or Selim the Grim, the Ottoman sultan widely blamed for the massacre of Alevis in the early sixteenth century. The naming reinforced discomfort among Alevis, who account for an estimated 20 per cent of Turkey's population, over Erdoğan's support for Syria's Sunni Muslim rebels. Their unease, rooted in longstanding disregard for their concerns, tapped into widespread popular criticism of the government's active opposition to Syrian President Bashar al-Assad, criticism that is shared by Turks of all opinions. Alarm was further boosted when two bombs ripped through the border town of Reyhanlı weeks before the Gezi Park protests, killing fifty-two people. The bombing reinforced a sense of impotence among

Erdoğan's critics who saw it as pro-Assad retaliation for Turkey's support of Islamist rebels in Syria.

Turkish support for Syrian Sunni rebels, possibly including jihadist groups, was but one of a series of statements and policies that reeked of a combination of an imposition of Islamic values and unilateral urban megalomania gone wild. It came on top of the alcohol restrictions, the bridge controversy and other grandiose infrastructure plans like a third Istanbul airport, a vast land-reclamation project in the Marmara Sea and a shipping canal parallel to the Bosporus. Protests stymied Islamist efforts to ban outdoor café and restaurant tables where customers consumed alcohol in the vicinity of Taksim. The adoption of restrictions on the sale of alcohol coincided with the Justice and Development Party's (AKP) advocated ban of over-the-counter sales of morning after pills. Erdoğan had earlier enraged liberal and secular women when he declared in 2008 that every Turkish family should have at least three children. His statement four years later that abortion constituted homicide sparked demonstrations against a government bill that would have restricted abortion rights. An announcement at the Kurtulus metro station in Ankara weeks before the Taksim protests urging youth to uphold morality in public sparked a kiss-in at the subway stop organized on social media sites. Deputy Prime Minister Bülent Arınç appeared to backtrack on Erdoğan's three-child policy in late June 2013 as mass anti-government protests continued. At a circumcision ceremony for the son of one of his aides, he declared: "Our intention is not to tell families how many children they should have, and I just want to wish happiness to everyone and hope couples have healthy kids. It does not matter how many kids they have."[68]

The protests illustrated Erdoğan's limited ability to alter the legacy that Mustafa Ataturk, the visionary who in 1923 carved modern Turkey out of the ruins of the Ottoman Empire, had created in Turkish history and culture in a bid to turn the country irreversibly westwards. Ataturk replaced the Arabic alphabet with a Latin one and Ottoman with modern Turkish. He abolished the Caliphate, pushed religion out of public life, outlawed Sufi brotherhoods, imposed Western dress and headwear instead of the traditional fez, secularized the education system and enforced gender equality. Interest in Ottomania revived under Erdoğan and as a corollary to Turkey's emergence as a superpower in lands once ruled by the Ottomans. Ottoman-era dramas and soap operas dominate Turkish television programming. Turks of all walks of life embrace the empire's architecture, fashion and food. Turkey's biggest budget ever movie, *Conquest 1453*, dramatizing the Ottoman conquest of Constantinople, is the country's highest grossing film.

The protests also signalled that Erdoğan's initial success in building bridges between the country's virtually segregated conservative and secular communities by introducing democratic reforms and propelling economic growth was wearing thin. Increasingly, the prime minister's definition of a new Turkish identity appeared to liberal and secular Turks to be exclusive rather than inclusive and failed to take into account the diversity and pluralism of Turkish society. In many ways, however, it was far more a reflection of a struggle for power in his own backyard. To counter Fethullah Gülen, a powerful 76-year-old, self-exiled, Pennsylvania-based preacher who was both an ally and a rival, Erdoğan's tough line towards the protesters, his portrayal of them as pawns of an ill-defined foreign effort to undermine Turkey's rise, his effort to criminalize militant soccer fans, his adoption of more conservative social mores and his attempt at micromanaging Turks' lives constituted an appeal to a conservative, nationalist constituency. It was a bid to differentiate himself from Gülen's more modernist urban appeal, stressing the appeal of Ottoman-era tolerance and science and logic rooted in the teachings of Bediüzzaman Said Nursî, a twentieth-century Muslim revivalist who was repeatedly imprisoned for his Islamist activism.

"Erdoğan and Gülen are like Ottoman sultans. They are the new Ottomans. They need each other. They love each other. But they kill each other. Both want to dictate people's lives. Erdoğan focuses on lifestyle, Gülen on control of institutions. Their once close relationship has been replaced by paranoia about one another. It's a unique relationship between an elected government and an elusive powerhouse, a government with an invisible coalition partner," remarks a well-placed journalist, Mustafa Hoş, like Erdoğan a fervent Fenerbahçe supporter who wears the club's wristband as a piece of jewellery. He is referring to Gülen's economic, media, finance, health and educational empire with schools in 140 countries commonly known as Cemaat, the Community, which constitutes one of Turkey's largest conglomerates, operates globally and is estimated to be worth US$20 billion. Gülen owes his movement's rise and financial muscle to its support of the 1980 military coup, the subsequent period of economic liberalization under Prime Minister Turgut Özal and the military's ousting in 1997 of Erdoğan's predecessor,

Islamist Prime Minister Necmettin Erbakan. The staunchly secular military's refusal to distinguish between the Gülenists and other Islamists prompted it to forge an alliance with Erdoğan's AKP.

A one-time government-employed imam, Gülen has long advocated obedience to the state. He supported secularist Turkish leaders like former prime ministers Tansu Çiller and Mesut Yılmaz in the 1980s because he saw the electoral success of Necmettin Erbakan's Refah Party, where Erdoğan first got his political grounding, as a threat to his strategy of preparing for control of the state through gradual infiltration of the military, the police and other state institutions. Gülen's strategy is similar to the Muslim Brotherhood's adoption of the 1960s German student leader Rudi Dutschke's "long march through the institutions" in pre-revolt Egypt. His gender-segregated schools produce loyal graduates who build their careers in the police force, the judiciary and the media and have helped Gülen gain significant influence.

"Fethullah's main project is the takeover of the state. That is why he is investing in education. They believe the state will just fall into their lap because they will be ready for it, they will have their people in place. That is their long-term plan," claimed Soli Özel, a prominent political scientist. Hüseyin Gülerce, a pro-Gülen journalist, argued with a degree of exaggeration that electoral politics gain Islamist parties less than 50 per cent of the vote while "we reach 100 per cent through education and the media." He went on to argue that "we have to decide what we want to be. We as a people have forgotten Islam. Men in Anatolia no longer take their children into their arms the way the Prophet did." A media colleague and close Gülen associate adds that "Fethullah Hoca does not want to impose anything now." Arguing that the Prophet Mohammed banned alcohol gradually instead of in one fell swoop, he says, "That is the best way to effect change in society."

Gülen, a diabetic with a heart ailment who often dresses in crumpled sports jackets and slacks and sprinkles his slow and deliberate speech with Ottoman rather than modern Turkish words that are regarded as quaint by many Turks, encouraged his millions of followers to join the civil service in what his detractors elleged is a long-term effort to Islamize Turkey by gaining control of the state through infiltration of its key institutions. Yet the multi-storey Istanbul headquarters of his influential *Zaman* newspaper initially had no toilet facilities for women. To accommodate female visitors, a male member of the staff was sent to check whether a men's room was free. With the issue of women's rights at the cutting edge of differences between militant Islam and the West, Gülen's writings, statements and institutions aim to put a modern face on fundamentally traditional views.

A series of pictures published in the media in 2007 showing police officers in the Black Sea town of Samsun posing with the 17-year-old killer of the prominent Armenian newspaper editor Hrant Dink fuelled suspicions of Gülen's true intentions among liberals and secularists. A Human Rights Watch report a year later alleged that abuse by the police, in which Gülen wielded influence, was a regular occurrence in and outside of formal custody. The report asserted that there was a pattern of police shootings, ill-treatment and excessive use of force and a culture of violence during the policing of demonstrations.[69] The US State Department's 2012 report on human rights in Turkey quoted activists as asserting "that LGBT persons, particularly gay men, were subject to abuse and harassment by police on 'moral' grounds."[70] LGBT activists had reported three months earlier that police had employed pepper spray in the resort town of Antalya to prevent bystanders from helping a sex worker after she was assaulted on a street and had her throat cut.[71]

The secular governments that preceded Erdoğan as far back as that of Özal, who in the 1980s introduced economic and political reforms, emphasized Ataturk's French *laïcité*-based secularism at the expense of more conservative segments of society. In his rivalry with Gülen, Erdoğan reversed this course by bringing conservative elements of society, including more religiously inclined Anatolian businessmen, back into the fold. "We are working to bring back history that has been destroyed ... We will unite Taksim with its history," Erdoğan asserted, defending his development plan for Gezi Park. For the secularists, Erdoğan's equation of lifestyle and politics, his insistence on legislating morality, his belief in the right of the majority to impose its will on the minority and his refusal to acknowledge the rights of cultural and political dissenters amounted to a form of state authoritarianism.

In a diplomatic cable in early 2004, the US ambassador to Turkey, Eric S. Edelman, cautioned on the eve of a visit to Washington by the prime minister that:

> Erdoğan has traits which render him seriously vulnerable to miscalculating the political dynamic ... and vulnerable to attacks by those who would disrupt his equilibrium. First, overbearing pride. Second, unbridled ambition stem-

ming from the belief God has anointed him to lead Turkey ... Third, an authoritarian loner streak which prevents growth of a circle of strong and skilful advisors, a broad flow of fresh information to him, or development of effective communications among the party headquarters, government, and parliamentary group. This streak also makes him exceptionally thin-skinned. Fourth, an overweening desire to stay in power which, despite his macho image, renders him fearful and prone to temporizing even at moments which call for swift and resolute decisions. Fifth, a distrust of women which manifests itself not only in occasional harsh public comments but also in his unwillingness to give women any meaningful decision-making authority.[72]

In a follow-up cable almost a year later, Edelman noted that:

inside the party, Erdoğan's hunger for power reveals itself in a sharp authoritarian style and deep distrust of others: as a former spiritual advisor to Erdoğan and his wife Emine put it, "Tayyip Bey believes in God ... but doesn't trust him." In surrounding himself with an iron ring of sycophantic (but contemptuous) advisors, Erdoğan has isolated himself from a flow of reliable information, which partially explains his failure to understand the context ... and his susceptibility to Islamist theories. With regard to Islamist influences on Erdoğan, DefMin [Defence Minister] Gonul, who is a conservative but worldly Muslim, recently described [President Abdullah] Gul associate [Foreign Minister Ahmet] Davutoglu to us as 'exceptionally dangerous.' Erdoğan's other foreign policy advisors (Cuneyd Zapsu, Egemen Bagis, Omer Celik, along with Mucahit Arslan and chef de cabinet Hikmet Bulduk) are despised as inadequate, out of touch and corrupt by all our AKP contacts from ministers to MPs and party intellectuals. Erdoğan's pragmatism serves him well but he lacks vision. He and his principal AKP advisors, as well as FonMin Gul and other ranking AKP officials, also lack analytic depth. He relies on poor-quality intel and on media disinformation. With the narrow world-view and wariness that lingers from his Sunni brotherhood and lodge background, he ducks his public relations responsibilities. He (and those around him, including FonMin Gul) indulge in pronounced pro-Sunni prejudices and in emotional reactions that prevent the development of coherent, practical domestic or foreign policies. Erdoğan has compounded his isolation by constantly traveling abroad.[73]

The disproportionate, random and brutal use of force against militant soccer fans in stadiums and other demonstrators by the police, who after a purge during military rule in the early 1980s were dominated by right-wing nationalists and religious conservatives, encouraged the growth of the protests in a society almost evenly split between secularists and conservatives. Erdoğan's efforts to improve law enforcement's human rights record, including the introduction of cameras in interrogation facilities and the conviction of police and prison officers on charges of violence and killings, failed to erase lingering questions about the police's loyalty to Gülen. The brutality of the police's response to the Gezi protests left Erdoğan with little choice but to embrace and praise the police in a move that initially strengthened Gülen's position. It also exposed the degree to which Gülen and Erdoğan's popular base were intertwined, making it difficult for both men to simply go their separate ways.

Besides soccer fans, the police's brutal use of force brought together environmentalists, urban purists, hardline secularists, Kemalists, communists, liberals, anarchists, secular businessmen and bankers, trade unions, gay rights activists and nationalists. Some saw Erdoğan's intransigent insistence on replacing the park with a shopping mall on a historically contested political space as an effort to impose authoritarian rule and further his Islamist agenda. Others believed it was a means to deflect criticism of his peace negotiations with the outlawed Kurdistan Workers' Party (PKK) that has waged an intermittent thirty-year guerrilla war in southeast Turkey in which more than 40,000 people were killed. It may have been all of the above, but it also reflected the rise of a religiously conservative movement after decades of repression by a militantly secular military and the failure of secularists, whose commitment to democracy had been at best skin-deep, to hear their often justified grievances. Erdoğan's arrogance was part character trait, part response to decades of demonization that allowed the country's military, political and social elite to ignore social cleavages and societal change. His urban projects were both projections of Islamist modernism and monuments to a past the elite had chosen to ignore or straightjacket into its rewriting of Turkish history.

The Gezi Park mall was to be modelled on the nineteenth-century Orientalist-style Halil Pasha Artillery Barracks built by Sultan Selim III, who was known for a passion for large scale military projects. The barracks was severely damaged in 1909 when under the Ottomans the Young Turks, a group of reformist-minded military cadets and students, defeated the Hunter Brigades, religiously conservative soldiers who called for the introduction of Islamic law. Their defeat led to the demise of Sultan Abdulhamit II and the purging of the Islamists. Ultimately the barracks was replaced first by a soccer pitch where official matches were played and then by a park that was originally built with marble from a nearby Armenian cemetery.

Tension between the Turkish police and the soccer fans mounted in the months before their entry into Taksim Square in June 2013. Police using tear gas—or perfume as Çarşı members called it—attacked Çarşı as the fans marched in May 2013 after a final league match to celebrate the end of the season and the fact that the stadium was closing for renovation. The clash was sparked by the fact that the fans were getting too close to Erdoğan's Beşiktaş office near the club's 32,000-seat İnönü Stadium. With thousands in the stadium on match day, traffic stalled along the water and the adjacent tree-lined boulevard and Çarşı chants ringing in the air, the distance between the stadium and Erdoğan's office virtually evaporated. "The police were brutal. They gassed our children. They treat us like animals. They see football fans as uneducated garbage. Turks don't trust the police. This has been true for decades and predates Erdoğan and Gülen," said Çarşı lawyer Mehmet Derviş Yıldız, a chubby man with a blue baseball cap and large, dark sunglasses that gave him a John Belushi quality as he sipped coffee in the warren of streets with small shops, bars and restaurants to which the group owes its name.

While the European Union and human rights groups criticized the government's crude tactics, research by the anthropologist Elif Babül showed that EU programmes designed to bring the Turkish police into line with European standards had served to enhance law enforcement's capabilities and better package heavy-handed responses rather than reduce its disproportionate use of force. The brutal response of the police to the Gezi Park demonstrations turned a small environmental protest into mass anti-government action with thousands of militant soccer fans on the front line. Babül's sombre analysis suggested that violence was inevitable in future confrontations between the government and hardened soccer fans determined to stand their ground.

> My research on human rights training programs for Turkish state officials has taught me that the meetings and workshops organized to improve the capacity of Turkey to become a member of the EU are far from unproductive, useless sites of whitewashing that help the government continue business as usual. On the contrary, these workshops, projects, and other tools of harmonization actually serve as platforms for government actors to manage the terms of EU membership, and the governmental standards that they entail.[74]

"It is by conducting projects that state officials come to learn what these standards are really about. They are place-holders for democracy and the rule of law that are supposed to be managed strategically in order to reduce liability and perform a level of development. For instance, it is by interacting with the British police at experience-sharing meetings that the TNP officers learn what it takes to become 'security experts,'" she went on to say.

Rather than installing mechanisms to fight impunity within the organization, they learn that what they need is "better policing" that can be attained by building crime databases or by setting up high-tech labs to better conduct forensic investigation ... Scholars who are critical of democratization and development industries have shown that programs for economic and political transition continue to produce unexpected outcomes in a variety of places, leading to more accentuated forms of exclusion, inequality, and authoritarianism. The contradictions between the stated goals and actual outcomes of these projects are inherent to the world of development.

Beşiktaş' İnönü Stadium is filled to the brim when the team plays. Çarşı members shout and chant profanities against their opponent from the moment the national anthem ends and the game kicks off. For the players, the match is a professional game; for Çarşı, it is the core of their existence, an event for which they are willing to put their lives on the line. Çarşı's philosophy is that being a fan involves an all-consuming relationship with the club. A survey by Turkish sports sociologist Ahmet Talimciler concluded that two-thirds of Turkish fans ranked soccer third after family and country while one-third stated that it was more important to them than anything else. Little wonder that authorities are constantly on the alert at match time with security, fire engineds and ambulances in place should Çarşı decide to attack police barricades, the opposite side's fans or the buses carrying their opponent's players. Some 2,000 fans, including students, workers, government officials, private security personnel, police officers and journalists, have been banned from stadiums since 2010 for bringing proscribed substances into the stadium, shouting profane slogans or entering a stadium without a proper ticket, according to interior minister Muammer Güler.[75]

The 2013/14 soccer season, the first after the Gezi Park protests, posed a particular challenge to the government. In an attempt to prevent stadiums from re-emerging as platforms for anti-government protests and to undermine the power of Çarşı and other support groups it banned the chanting of political slogans weeks before the opening of the season. "We are adding bad political and ideological slogans to the list of illegal demonstrations in football stands, or behaviour not complying with sporting ethics," Güler told an Istanbul sports conference. Beşiktaş was furthermore ordered to force spectators to sign a pledge not to chant political slogans before they were allowed to attend a match. Failure to abide by the pledge could result in the cancellation of their season tickets. Plainclothes policemen would be deployed in those areas of stadiums where militant soccer fans gather, and a tender for the installation of cameras was being issued, Güler said. The government feared the chanting of anti-Erdoğan slogans in the Istanbul stadium named after him where Beşiktaş would be playing while its own stadium was being renovated. The ban followed the indictment of ninety-four Gezi Park protesters, including members of Çarşı, who were charged with membership of an illegal organization. Much like the Egyptian military that sought to demonize the Muslim Brotherhood as a terrorist organization after the toppling of elected President Mohammed Morsi, Turkey's Anti-Terrorism Office issued a video cautioning the public that "our youth, who are the guarantors of our future, can start with small demonstrations of resistance that appear to be innocent, and after a short period of time, can engage without a blink in actions that may take the lives of dozens of innocent people."[76] The video featured a young woman who in 55 seconds went from demonstrator to suicide bomber while displaying the cautionary words: "before it is too late."

The parallel between Egypt and Turkey extended to efforts to criminalize politicized, militant soccer fans. In December 2014 the government indicted 35 members of Çarşı on charges of belonging to an armed terrorist organization and seeking to overthrow the government. In a statement, the Istanbul Bar Association denounced the proceedings against Çarşı as belonging to the "fantasy world" of prosecutors.[77] "What they are trying to do here is to dilute the concept of a coup in order to spark fear in people, justify police violence that may occur in the future, and intimidate a nation. The law cannot be manipulated for such purposes. Prosecutors' right to open a case must be restricted by logic and rules of law," the statement said.

Basing his charges on wiretaps, Adem Meral, Istanbul Terrorism and Organized Crime Unit prosecutor, charged that the soccer fans had not been driven to join the protests by environmental concerns and opposition to plans to replace the historic Gezi Park with an Ottoman-style shopping mall. Instead, Meral said in his 38-page indictment: "It is understood that they were trying to overthrow the democratically elected

Turkish government and to facilitate this objective, they were attempting to capture the Prime Ministry offices in Ankara and İstanbul". In line with Erdoğan's assertions at the time of Gezi Park protests, the prosecutor asserted that the protests were a foreign conspiracy.

The indictment cited as evidence statements by various defendants in tapped telephone conversations. One defendant allegedly said he was "not interested in the construction of the mall or the demolition of trees," but wanted to "topple the government." Another supposedly suggested that the protests could lead to civil war, adding that "we will today occupy the prime ministry's residence." Others were said to have suggested attacking the police to fuel public anger.

In a repetition of the Gezi Park protests when rival fan groups in a rare demonstration of common purpose came together to confront police, fans from Istanbul's three major competing clubs gathered together with trade unionists, opposition politicians and activists outside the court house on the first day of the trial to chant "shoulder-to-shoulder against fascism," "Çarşı is conscience and cannot be judged," and "Çarşı will never walk alone," according to participants in the protest. Fans in Europe expressed solidarity with supporters of Germany's Borussia Dortmund displaying placards during a match that called on Çarşı to "never give up," urged it "to fight for your way" and demanded "freedom to Ultras and Turkey." The protests and flimsy evidence ultimately persuaded prosecutors to advise the court in September 2015 to drop the charges against Çarşı.

The distrust of the police and the judiciary and Çarşı's ingrained empathy with underdogs forged the basis for rival fan groups to join forces on Taksim Square. "What happened on Taksim is incredible, it is unbelievable. Two weeks ago we were discussing how divided we were, how intolerant fans of Galatasaray, Fenerbahçe, Beşiktaş, Trabzonspor and others were. We felt the culture of football was deteriorating. Occupation Gezi Park has changed that," a Turkish soccer militant remarked.

He was referring to gangland wars in the 1980s between the three main Istanbul supporter groups that often erupted into vicious street battles, lynching and raids on each other's facilities. Their rivalry started on the eve of the 1980 military coup when Beşiktaş fans, led by the late Çarşı founder and history teacher Mehmet Işıklar aka Optik Baskan, fought hard with sticks and knives to keep supporters of rival clubs out of the covered areas of their İnönü Stadium. It was a period when all club matches were played there because the city's other stadiums were being renovated. Within a matter of years, the fans graduated to the use of Molotov cocktails and firearms in a country where passengers at the entrance to the domestic air terminal were requested to surrender their weapons for safekeeping during the flight. A truce arranged at a gathering of heavily armed rival supporters after a Beşiktaş fan was trampled to death in 1991 by his Galatasaray adversaries reduced but did not put an end to the violence. Two Leeds United fans in Istanbul for their team's match against Galatasaray were stabbed to death in 2000 during a riot on Taksim. Stray bullets fired into the air to celebrate the Turkish team's victory killed a third person and wounded four others. Çarşı members forced supporters of Galatasaray and Fenerbahçe who frequent Beşiktaş, a popular downtown destination, in their clubs' colours to take off their shirts whether it was winter or summer. The former Manchester United manager Sir Alex Ferguson recalled his team's 1993 match in Istanbul against Galatasaray as involving "as much hostility and harassment as I have ever known on a football expedition."[78] Eighteen years later, the *Guinness Book of Records* awarded the club the honour of having produced the world's "loudest crowd roar at a sport stadium."[79]

The differences between the support groups have long had little to do with outdated perceptions of their class differences that classified Beşiktaş' support base as working-class and left-wing intellectual, Galatasaray as more upmarket middle-class because of its origins in Galatasaray Lyceum, a French-language elite school founded under the Ottomans, and Fenerbahçe as right-wing, *nouveau riche* and nationalist. "There is much that we have in common. We are fighting to carve out breathing space. We have common ambitions. We want to advance professionally. We want to interact with the outside world. If Erdoğan has his way, Turkey would go in the opposite direction. Erdoğan has done much for Turkey, but now it's time for a change," said a Fenerbahçe fan. Gezi Park united the fans at the moment that their twenty-year old tacit truce was fraying at the edges.

A couple of weeks earlier, Fenerbahçe fans taunted Ivory Coast Galatasaray striker Didier Drogba with racist chants. Two men wearing Galatasaray shirts stabbed a Fenerbahçe fan to death. The sociologist Ahmet Talimciler views the killing as an indication of the brutalization of Turkish society. "Football is only a reflection. It doesn't stem from football. When we face violence at home, in schools and in traffic; it is impossible not to see it in stadiums, too. We don't have a football culture; thus, people cannot learn how to behave in a football environment. Our football culture was shaped on the basis of destroying the opposing fans. This has reached such an extent that whereas in the past the fans would tease each other, now they want to destroy each other," he concluded. Violence is not the exclusive domain of fans. Competing managers and players often stop just short of physical confrontation.

Çarşı and other groups trace their roots to that environment of violence. The 1980 military coup and the brutal repression that came with it were designed to put an end to escalating political violence that left up to thirty bodies a day of people killed in the streets of Istanbul. As across the Middle East and North Africa, stadiums emerged as the one place where people could rally and express their identity and anger. Militant fans greeted visitors to their stadium with the words, "Welcome to Hell," a reference to their deliberately aggressive and intimidating support for their clubs.

On Taksim Square, weeks after the nineteen-year-old Fenerbahçe supporter Burak Yıldırım was stabbed to death by two Galatasaray fans following their team's defeat, fans of all Istanbul three clubs threw their arms around one another, taunted the police together and chanted in unison:

> You can use you tear gas bombs, you can use your tear gas bombs,
> Have courage if you are a real man,
> Take off your helmet and drop your batons,
> Then we'll see who the real man is.

The chant became the protesters' anthem. It rang across the square whenever police employed tear gas.

Protesters with a sense of humour carried signs saying: "Send the water tanks, we haven't showered in three days." In one instance, a Beşiktaş fan surrounded by friends put his phone on speaker mode as he dialled the police emergency number. "Hello, police? It's Beşiktaş. We've got some food but there's no pepper. Send us some pepper. Some pepper gas," he said. Çarşı's sense of irony and wit meshed perfectly with the carnivalesque mood of other protesters who cleverly employed humour to turn Erdoğan's attempts to discredit them against him. "Our sense of humour is our survival," remarked Çarşı lawyer Yıldız.

Çarşı's home ground, Beşiktaş, is a central, gentrified working-class neighbourhood that stretches inland from the European bank of the

Bosporus dividing Europe and Asia. It hosts Barbarossa's tomb and Istanbul's most important government building, the Ottoman-era Dolmabahce Palace, home to the Ottoman Empire's last six sultans as well as to Ataturk, who carved modern Turkey out of its ruins. Beşiktaş is a stronghold of Turkey's main opposition party, the Kemalist Republican People's Party (CHP), and is the frequent scene of resistance against the police.

Beşiktaş' public spaces are the groups' meeting points. Statues of prominent Turkish politicians, journalists and authors wore gas masks in the neighbourhood's Abbasaga Park after police pushed the protesters out of Taksim and Gezi Park. The park, like scores of parks across the city, had become a Hyde Park-style gathering point for protesters. They publicly discussed their options while organizers announced musicians' performances and artists put up installations. Residents in the park's neighbourhood banged pots and pans on their balconies in solidarity. "Taksim is everywhere, resistance is everywhere," was the motto of the nightly gatherings. The underlying tone was one that resembled the breaking of the Arab world's barrier of fear. United in a desire for greater freedom, protesters from diverse worldviews and walks of life displayed a humour-laced irreverence of power with chants, jokes and art. Çarşı members wearing their club's black-and-white strip often moderated the deliberations. They insisted that their sole ideology was opposition to repression and inequality, quoting the group's slogan, *Çarşı, her seye karsi!* Çarşı is against everything!

Çarşı's claiming of Abbasaga Park, like the protesters' occupation of parks elsewhere in the city, was a rebuke of the city government's definition of who was entitled to enjoy the public spaces. At a ceremony to mark the reopening of Gezi Park in early July attended by senior officials Istanbul's governor Hüseyin Avnni Mutlu warned that protests would not be allowed. "We invite our folks, our people, our children, the elderly and families to visit the park … Parks are for children, their families, the old, and the young," he said. His implicit message was that families were the unit in society entitled to claim public space, not various sub-groups such as gays who had frequently gathered in the park prior to the protests. "If certain groups claim to be the public and argue that 'this park belongs to us, we're the owners of this park,' we will not allow that," warned Mutlu.

Çarşı had the wherewithal to challenge the governor's notion. It had garnered a huge following far beyond Istanbul that stretched across the country. Many of its core members, however, have emerged from various left-wing organizations, including Dev-Sol, the Revolutionary People's Liberation Party-Front, which in the late 1970s and 1980s targeted Turkish security personnel and US interests. Çarşı members, who see their club as Turkish soccer's underdog, frequently embrace liberal and left-wing causes. In its logo Çarşı replaced the A with a red symbol of anarchism. They take pride in the group's slogans that do justice to its contrarian spirit, "Çarşı is against everything!" and "One day peace, 364 days war," its frequent references to Che Guevara, its identity as revolutionary souls proudly describing themselves as hooligans and chants like:

> Got no money, no car, not even a slut to fuck,
> But I don't care,
> Because we are Çarşı, Kings of the World.

Çarşı opposes the commercialization of the sport, participates in Labour Day marches, helps the disabled and the poor and protests against the government's nuclear policy. The group's egalitarianism is highlighted by the fact that one of its spokesmen, Alen Markaryan, is a squat 47-year-old Armenian goldsmith-turned-restaurant owner who was shot and wounded in 2013 in a fight with a rival leader of the group. Wearing black and white shirts, scarves and hats, its members are notorious for their fighting skills, profanity and nostalgic poetry. Çarşı's political activity—its protests against urban renewal, its cooperation with Greenpeace against the installation of a nuclear power station in the Black Sea city of Sinop and its opposition in 2007 to the demolition of Taksim Square's landmark Muhsin Ertugrul Theatre—are prime time news. Çarşı's leaders are frequently invited to parliament hearings and political events. Like its counterparts in North Africa and elsewhere in the world, Çarşı spokesmen deny that they have a hierarchic organization with appointed leaders but do concede that there is an inner group of men, supporters of Beşiktaş since childhood, who bear the scars of past battles, who provide direction. These men represent the one third of Çarşı's original founders that are still alive. Of the 15 founders, five died in battle while five others passed away of natural causes.

Çarşı was joined on Taksim Square by Galatasaray's UltrAslan, a group also formed by left-wingers that has since attracted large numbers of nationalists and Islamists, as well as by Fenerbahçe's Outside Left. Outside Left are Fenerbahçe's odd men out. They are left-wingers who earned the respect of the club's conservative pro-government majority as a result of their key role in mobilizing Fenerbahçe fans during a major match-fixing scandal that centred on the club. The groups joined the protests independently but found themselves fighting the same enemy. When the protests expanded from Taksim to Beşiktaş, Galatasaray and Fenerbahçe fans stood alongside Çarşı to defend Beşiktaş' heartland. "We are one heart today," Galatasaray tweeted. "We would sacrifice everything for Çarşı," said a Fenerbahçe banner. And in contrast to North Africa, where most players stayed on the sidelines as fans joined popular revolts, prominent players, including Galatasaray's top scorer Burak Yilmaz and its foreign stars Didier Drogba and Wesley Sneijder, tweeted messages of support.

Nevertheless, differences between the fan groups remained. Some resisted embracing Çarşı's political agenda. In a statement on its website UltrAslan said it was "saddened to see [that] political action has begun to emerge along with the Gezi Park protests. Attempts aiming at raising the issue to a political level and attempts to hijack the protests by some movements are unacceptable for us." It stressed that "no one should attempt to categorize and use UltrAslan in favour of a political movement."

Challenge and political controversy has been the key to Turkish soccer since, like elsewhere in the Middle East and North Africa, it was introduced by British residents of the Ottoman Empire in the late nineteenth century. With Ottomans of Turkish descent banned from embracing the sport, soccer was initially the game of the empire's European, Jewish, Greek and Armenian minorities.

It took little more than two decades, however, for Turks to challenge the ban with the emergence in 1899 of the Black Stockings (Siyah Çoraplılar), the first club formed by Turkish players and headed by a Naval Academy student. Its English name was intended to persuade security forces that it was a British club and spare it the invasion of pitches and arrest of players. Such measures constituted a doomed effort to halt the soccer wildfire that erupted with the emergence of various Istanbul-based clubs, including Kadikoy FRC, Moda FC, Elpis and Imogene FC established by staff working on a British embassy yacht of that name, as well as similar teams in the port city of Izmir.

"In Turkey, football has long been a metaphor for life," noted Al Jazeera Türk reporter Eylam Kaftan. In a documentary she plays excerpts of a decades-old Turkish black and white film. "Brothers and sisters, be my referee. This is like a match. Play on the pitch of life. We are the players. The ball is our conscience. Tell me, is this not a goal?" asks an emotional, moustachioed soccer fan. Turning to a judge, he adds: "I take refuge in your justice. Your honour, is this not a goal?" The judge bangs his hand on the table. "It's a goal," he says as the court room applauds and the film switches to a soccer match.[80]

The turn-of-the-century ban by Sultan Abdulhamit II, who viewed public gatherings of more than three people as a threat, reflected the then Ottoman elite's animosity towards Western modernity, which it viewed as a menace to indigenous and Islamic culture as well as a potential political challenge by highly educated urban Turks who were enamoured of the game. In a foretaste of modern-day opposition to soccer by segments of the militant Islamist community, Ottoman clerics denounced it as a distraction from the study of the Qur'an, promoting inappropriate dress and the display of naked flesh and symbolizing blasphemy because it resembled the kicking round of the severed head of the Prophet Mohammed's grandson Hussein by his killers in 680 CE.

The tide began to change, however, towards the end of the first decade of the twentieth century as the sultan's power increasingly made way for the rise of the reformist Committee for Union and Progress or Young Turks. Turkish clubs joined the league established in 1904 while educational institutions attended by Muslims and non-Muslims gave birth to some of modern Turkey's foremost clubs: gymnastics club Beşiktaş JK, elite French school Galatasaray's Galatasaray Spor Kulübü and St. Joseph's Fenerbahçe Spor Kulübü.

The publication in that period of Istanbul's first sports magazine bore witness to the explosion of the city's repressed passion for soccer. In the words of Cem Emrence,[81] the newly established Turkish clubs served "to support the nationalist project under the auspices of the intelligentsia" as the empire neared its demise. They were tools in the effort of the Young Turks to "bolster popular Turkish nationalist sentiment and challenge non-Muslim cultural supremacy"[82] as well as European prerogatives. Not unlike present day Arab autocrats who view soccer as a threat as well as an opportunity, the Young Turks saw it not only as a policy tool but also as a potential political rallying point. As a result, they focused on the sport as physical education rather than a way to align nationalist sentiment and reduce the risk of political and social mobilization.

This first defining period was followed by the post-World War Two emergence of soccer as a tool of expression of competing economic, ethnic and religious regional identities that often challenged the supremacy of Istanbul's three dominant clubs—Beşiktaş, Fenerbahçe and Galatasaray. Anatolian clubs frequently did so from the position of the underdog given the Istanbul clubs' greater access to resources.

Despite making it to the World Cup finals for the first time in 1954, Turkey's initial march to glory began only in the late 1950s with a first wave of professionalism. That did not prevent the political, geo-political and commercial rivalries and associated violence, corruption and match-fixing that underlay Turkish soccer from exploding in the deaths of forty-two people and wounding of 300 others in 1967 in the central Anatolian city of Kayseri in one of the worst incidents in Turkish sporting history. The incident occurred against the backdrop of local, often more pious Anatolian political and economic bosses organized around communal and religious networks who manipulated soccer for their own purpose and as a way of challenging the country's dominant political elite.[83]

The emergence of provincial teams highlighted competing efforts by Anatolian cities to wield political and economic influence as regional centres, to establish a civic and local identity of their own and to integrate the mass influx of rural migrants. Competition between Kayseri and Sivas, dating back to the early days of the modern Turkish republic, was particularly fierce with Kayseri viewed as the wealthier, more developed and economically dominant of the two. Fighting erupted in the stands during a match in 1967 between Kayseri's Kayserispor and Sivas' Sivasspor following a controversial decision by the referee to cancel a red card he had shown to a Kayseri striker. Hundreds of primarily Sivas fans were crushed, unable to exit tunnels because the gates were locked.

By the same token, the Black Sea city of Trabzon, once a thriving Ottoman port, saw soccer as a way of ensuring that it did not become a backwater. Maritime trade was in decline since the rise of the Soviet Union and Eastern Europe's turn to communism. New railroad construction bypassed the city and distanced it from its hinterland. The Turkish sports historian Sevecen Tunc argues that municipal leaders believed that soccer could restore the city's civic pride and ensure that it remained a player on the national stage.[84]

If politics dominated soccer in the provinces, it also was dominant nationally, never more so than in the last quarter of the twentieth century. After staging a military coup in 1980, General Kemal Evren, determined to have Ankara represented among Turkey's top teams, changed rules governing the leagues to ensure the promotion of the capital's MKE Ankaragücü. Similarly, in 1987 President Turgut Özal hoped to garner votes by promoting midseason the teams of Anatolian towns Bursa and Konya to the premier league. A 2005 US embassy cable disclosed by WikiLeaks reported that Erdoğan appointed a close associate, Faruk Nafiz Ozak, as chairman of the Black Sea club Trabzonspor, and also paid the club millions of dollars from a prime ministerial slush fund. Erdoğan dismissed the allegations as gossip. The move was designed to counter the town's opposition mayor who benefitted from the fact that he, like Erdoğan, was a prominent local soccer player but unlike the prime minister, who publicly declared himself a Fenerbahçe fan, supported Trabzon's club. Erdoğan also appointed a former star Trabzonspor player as his minister of public works.[85]

Professionalism and commercialization further deepened the wedge between Istanbul and much of the rest of the country. Clubs located in Turkey's more globalized commercial hubs, with Istanbul in the forefront, pulled ahead by attracting a wealthy benefactor, often a businessman who made his fortune in construction or the media, forcing those that could not follow suit to compete by becoming more and more dependent on funding from local government.[86] The new wealthy owners ran their clubs much like their family-owned business as their personal fiefdoms. They used the clubs to increase their own public recognition as well as that of politicians, leveraging ownership to create new business opportunities. The club often served to launch the political career of the new owner who counted on fans grateful for his coming to the rescue of their club voting for him.

Controversial media and communications industry mogul Cem Uzan, for example, scion of a family viewed either as robber barons or the Turkish equivalent of the early, rough playing Rockefellers, established his own political party partly with the support of fans of two long neglected historic clubs, Istanbulspor and Adanaspor, acquired by his family. The soccer holdings helped him boost his media properties with the repeated winning of the broadcast rights of the Turkish Super League and the European Champions League. Ultimately however, the two clubs suffered the fate of their owners. They went into bankruptcy in 2005 after the Uzans became embroiled in multi-billion dollar law suits with their communications industry partners, Motorola and Nokia, and had many of their companies confiscated. Uzan's father and brother evaded arrest by fleeing the country. Cem Uzan's right-wing, nationalist Genç [Youth] Party emerged a strong contender from the 2002 elections having won the third largest number of votes. Those were, however, insufficient for the party to cross the 10 per cent threshold needed for a seat in the Turkish parliament.

In contrast to North Africa where militant soccer fan groups emerged relatively late and prided themselves on their independence, Turkish fans in the 1960s and 1970s initially forged close ties to the heads of clubs who used them to strengthen their positions. The early Turkish militants were rewarded with funding for their paraphernalia such as flags and banners.

Militant fans of the major Istanbul clubs since then have come to view their loyalty to their club as universal much like their counterparts in North Africa. The Turkish definition of support transcended local, political, ethnic and religious identities. "By rejecting the deep schisms that divide the country, the fans' group can be viewed as a new model of a national community," wrote the French scholar Adrien Battini in an analysis of UltrAslan.[87]

A Turkish researcher Itir Erhat, who in a break with tradition was introduced to soccer by her father and other male relatives at a young age, recalls suddenly realizing in her mid-twenties the macho nature of the songs she was chanting. "I caught myself singing the chant 'Suck my cock Fener' to the tune of 'Those Were the Days' during a derby match and making the appropriate hand gesture. That was a moment of epiphany for me: for years, I had been passionately singing about actions I cannot perform as a woman and had completely adopted the hegemonic male discourse to fit in with the men in the family, to fit in with the football stadium environment," she wrote.[88]

Erhat's realization highlighted one source of soccer violence in Muslim societies like Turkey, irrespective of whether the fans define themselves as secular or not. "In Turkey, the stadiums are masculine, hetero-normative spaces. They are seen as fortresses of masculinity.[89] What Andrei Simic[90] calls the machismo syndrome can be exemplified in various ways. Terrorizing the passers-by before or after the games, vandalizing the stadiums, tearing the seats, smashing bathroom mirrors are common practices in Turkey. These actions arise from the desire to prove strength and dominance. After the games the visiting team is given a half-hour head start to clear the area to avoid possible clashes. Fans take pride in calling themselves *delikanlı*, a Turkish expression which means 'crazy-blooded'," she wrote.[91]

The use of sexual innuendo in Turkish fans' chants and slogans sets them apart from their counterparts in most other Muslim countries. It reflects the imposition of Western cultural concepts at the birth of modern Turkey as well as its control of women by stripping them of their sexuality rather than confining them to their homes. "Turkish fans distance themselves from homosexuality and insult the enemy (the rival team, the fans, the referees, sometimes their own players) by attributing to them sexual weakness and, hence, feminizing them. The most common insults are 'sons of whores' and 'fag.' These insults aim at undermining male respectability ... Players and referees are also abused by references to their wives, mothers, sisters or girlfriends," Erhat wrote. Turks further refer to scoring a goal as entering, inserting or penetrating. They often chant about anal rape when a team scores a goal.

The influence of business fed on the fact that from their inception Turkish soccer clubs remained elitist organizations whose management was populated by close-knit, often impenetrable groups. It also benefitted from the fact that support of a soccer team in Turkey, as in the Middle East and North Africa, is as important as religious and ethnic identity. In the same vein of wealthy businessmen taking over major clubs, second and third tier clubs became more dependent on municipal funding. This turned them into tools of support bases for politicians who controlled the municipality. Mayors often became part of a club's management.

Soccer was subjected in the process to commercial interests and vulnerable to political corruption. Turkey's economic and soccer integration with the European Union accelerated the trend. Liberalization led to clubs becoming economic actors in their own right. Galatasaray, with an estimated fan base of twenty million, became the first Turkish club to list on the Istanbul stock exchange and attract foreign investment.[92] Beşiktaş was quick to follow. The move transformed Turkish soccer from a national pastime into an industry with revenues in the hundreds of millions of dollars.

As a result, the management of soccer clubs changed fundamentally. Political bosses, their cronies and businessmen were joined by financial, business development, legal, marketing, merchandising, branding, sponsorship and communications experts in the running of the club. These new executives were tasked with maximizing income, generating new revenue streams, improving cash flow, reducing debt and funding expanded infrastructure, including stadiums. Following the example of

Europe's top leagues, Turkey's expanding privately owned media meant that broadcast rights significantly helped to produce the cash needed to create a super league and acquire increasingly costly international players able to compete at a European and global level.

To integrate soccer economically and socially into Europe and revive the country's moribund economy, the Turkish President Turgut Özal, who assumed office immediately after a period of military rule in the early 1980s and put Turkey firmly on the road towards economic liberalization, loosened the tight grip on the game imposed by the generals. He granted the Turkish Football Federation (TFF) greater political autonomy in a bid to encourage greater competitiveness and created financial muscle so that the national team and clubs would perform in Europe. As a result, soccer increasingly became an indicator of Turkish ambitions to join the European Union. When in 1991, for example, a match between Fenerbahçe and Atlético Madrid was cancelled because of a power failure, Turkish newspapers reported the incident in terms of a national disgrace.

Similarly, Galatasaray's 1993 and Fenerbahçe's 1996 success against Manchester United, the Turkish national team's first appearance in a Euro competition in 1996 and Galatasaray's winning of the Union of European Football Associations' UEFA Cup and European Super Cup in 2000 were seen as evidence of Turkish progress, vitality and growing strength.[93] To some, it also represented a restoration of past Ottoman glory. Galatasaray's two footballing firsts made them the first team from a Muslim nation to excel in European competitions. The Turkish justice minister Hikmet Sami hailed Galatasaray's victory as Turkey's fulfilling of the European Union's Copenhagen criteria.[94] "A winning Turkish sport team ... helps the Turkish authorities ease the erratic process of integration into the European Union and therefore to affirm that Turkey is indeed part of Europe and belongs to part of its organizations," wrote Adrien Battini.[95] The game also served to highlight Turkey's place as a bridge between east and west. "Fenerbahçe is the first place in Asia when you arrive from the European side. Your first step into Asia brings you to Fenerbahçe," said one of the club's cheerleaders.[96]

The economics and politics of twenty-first-century Turkish soccer increasingly mirrored the country's debt-driven economic model.[97] They also reflected social shifts from Istanbul to the Anatolian hinterland stemming from a decade of rule by a democratically elected Islamist government as well as political struggles waged across the Middle East and North Africa as Turkey emerged as a military and economic powerhouse in a region populated by former Ottoman colonies in the throes of political change.

As a result, a 2012 research note issued by the Moscow-based investment house Renaissance Capital concluded that Turkish soccer, estimated to be the world's sixth largest soccer market, and the country's economy faced the same risks. These risks stemmed from increasing deficits—current account for the state, debt for clubs—and rising inflation. "Turkey's declining success in football can be mapped to economics," the Renaissance Capital note observed. The investment house also noted that Turkish soccer clubs, like the Turkish economy, "import almost all their best players from abroad, and exports one or two good players every year."[98]

In doing so clubs incurred high levels of debt to attract star players with top clubs like Fenerbahçe, Beşiktaş and Galatasaray operating as commercial companies that eschewed competitiveness for profit. *Bloomberg News* quoted the Istanbul stock exchange as saying that short-term borrowings of Istanbul club Beşiktaş JK, its Istanbul rival and Turkish champion Galatasaray SK and Black Sea club Trabzonspor FC created "uncertainty over the sustainability" of their finances. The bourse pointed out that shareholders' equity for each was negative. Galatasaray was staring at US$57 million of short-term debt as the result of the expensive acquisition of players like Didier Drogba and the hiring of coach Roberto Mancini. Even so, Galatasaray, with a debt-to-cash ratio of 13:1, compared favourably to Trabzonspor's ratio of 40:1 and Beşiktaş' 24:1, according to data compiled by Bloomberg.[99] "If Turkish soccer isn't reformed, institutionalized and if all goes as it has so far, Turkish soccer is doomed to hit a wall," concluded the soccer economist and journalist Tugrul Aksar.

The acquired stars were often expensive and old has-beens such as former Real Madrid players Roberto Carlos and midfielder José Maria Gutiérrez Hernández (Guti). Their celebrity boosted merchandising, but contributed little if any added value to the team. The focus on sales rather than performance on the pitch produced the same ills many Turkish companies faced: complacency and reduced competitiveness. "Without an increase in competitiveness Turkey is trapped with manic depressive success," warned Renaissance Capital.[100]

Soccer results proved the point. Turkey's top clubs have dominated the country's soccer for decades but failed twice in a row in 2011 and 2012 to win the Turkish league or qualify for the UEFA Champions League. The poor performance of the three major Istanbul clubs mirrored a trend in Turkish economic development as growth shifted and political power expanded from the country's economic capital to booming urban centres in the Anatolian interior. Two of Turkey's more recent most successful teams, Bursaspor and Trabzonspor, hail from the former Ottoman capital of Bursa and Trabzon, two cities that at the same time boasted trade surpluses while Istanbul accounted for 60 per cent of Turkey's trade deficit.

Critics of Erdoğan alleged that the prime minister was attempting to enlist clubs in much the same carrot-and-stick way that he tamed the Turkish media by exploiting financial vulnerabilities, turning Turkey alongside Iran and China into the country with the most journalists behind bars. The impact of Erdoğan's effort to restrict media independence and limit independent critical reporting was evident when television stations initially broadcast soap operas in 2013 instead of images of the mass anti-government protests on Istanbul's Taksim Square in which soccer fans played a prominent role. Soccer may, however, be a tougher nut to crack than the media. Soccer, unlike the media, has militant fans determined to thwart Erdoğan's attempts to use troubled clubs to whip them into line.

That became evident with a nationwide boycott of a government-sponsored electronic ticketing system in Turkey viewed by fans, as a way of identifying them and barring them from stadiums that has so far all but defeated the effort.[101] The government sought to drive a wedge between militant fans and other supporters by arguing that e-ticketing was a way to combat illegal ticket scalping, to increase tax revenues and to ensure that stadiums are safe for families. "The e-ticket system does not only demote the concept of supporters to a customer, but it also files all our private data. The system aims to prevent supporters from organizing and is designed to demolish stadium culture and supporter identity," some 40 soccer fan groups countered in a statement.[102]

Plummeting stadium attendance as a result of the e-ticket boycott has severely affected ticket sales according to soccer club executives and fans. A match in October 2014 in Istanbul's 82,000-seat Atatürk Olympic Stadium between Beşiktaş and Eskişehirspor Club that would normally have been attended by some 20–30,000 spectators drew only 3,000 fans. Ticket sales for Galatasaray matches were at the time down by two thirds with fans gathering in cafes and homes to watch matches they would have attended in the past. The boycott prompted the government to suspend the e-ticketing system for a friendly in November of that year between Turkey and Brazil.[103] As a result, sales spiked with more than 40,000 tickets sold for the match shortly after the suspension.

The boycott was buoyed by a decision by Yıldız Holding, a conservative conglomerate known for its confectionary and biscuit business and close ties to Erdoğan, which is one of Turkey's largest sponsors of soccer, to no longer fund the sport because of violence and tensions associated with it and government efforts to politically control the beautiful game. The company's reference in a letter to the TFF to tensions was not simply a reference to stadium incidents but also to Erdoğan's interference in the match-fixing scandal, his attempts to depoliticize stadiums, and the legal proceedings against Çarşı.[104] "No one wants their information to be collected, even by the state; this is disturbing. Many fan groups have boycotted the practice, which has added to the low attendance numbers. It is impossible to not admire the spectators in the UK or Germany. I am very sad for the country. I went to a game in the UK recently and the atmosphere was great. This is what we cannot find in Turkey. We should not block the joy from the fans," said Yıldız chairman Murat Ülker.[105]

Yıldız has over the last decade invested some $215 million in Turkish soccer with sponsorships of clubs such as Beşiktaş, Bursaspor FC, Fenerbahçe SK, Galatasaray and Trabzonspor FC as well as the Turkish national team.

The company's decision was not simply a setback for Turkish soccer but for Erdoğan personally whose family has had a long association with Yıldız and its owners, the Ülker family, who made their name as successful, religiously conservative entrepreneurs. Yıldız chairman Murat Ülker moreover was a classmate of Prime Minister Ahmet Davutoğlu in Istanbul's prestigious boys' school, Istanbul Erkek Lisesi. Members of Erdoğan's family owned in the past up to 50 per cent of Emniyet Foods, the distributor of Yıldız's Ülker brand, as well as a stake in Ihsan Foods, the distributor of the company's dairy products, and Yenidogan Foods Marketing, its soft drinks distributor.

The government's efforts to garner favour and votes among soccer fans further stalled as a result of lack of funds to push ahead with a $1.55 billion project announced in 2013 to build some 20 stadiums, 1,000 sports halls and 431 sports facilities for education institutions under the auspices of the Turkey's mass housing administration (TOKI). As a result, unfinished stadiums that were supposed to have been inaugurated in advance of the June 2015 parliamentary election dot the Turkish map. Only two of the stadiums, one of which being Galatasaray SK's Türk Telekom Arena in Istanbul, were completed on time. The other is in Mersin, one of six stadiums planned in predominantly Kurdish south-eastern Turkey, the swing region in the election that for the first time brought a pro-Kurdish party into the Turkish parliament, stopping the ruling Justice and Development Party (AKP) from winning an absolute majority for the third time, and pre-empting Recep Tayyip Erdoğan's plan to amass further power by turning his office into an executive presidency.

John Konuk Blasing, the American-Turkish author of the thisisfootballislife blog, reported that the majority of the projects had stalled because of lack of funding or because contractors had gone bankrupt. "In order to make it happen before the elections the government directed construction firms to work fast, promising extra payments after the elections. With money also needed to fund the campaign, however, extra money for the construction projects dried up… Votes are all that could ever be hoped to be won from such a strategy, certainly not real democracy or—evidently—new stadiums," Blasing wrote.[106]

Economic change and innovation did little to take politics and the corruption associated with it out of the game. At the beginning of the second decade of the twenty-first century, the scandal-ridden Turkish sport was playing two simultaneous existential matches: one to eradicate widespread corruption and match-fixing embedded in Turkish soccer since its birth in clandestinity, the other pitting two Islamist teams competing for the hearts and minds of Turkish soccer fans.

Both Erdoğan and Gülen emerged bruised from their struggle for control of Fenerbahçe, Turkish soccer's most valuable political asset. Erdoğan, determined to preserve Fenerbahçe as his unrivalled domain against attempted encroachments by Gülen, compromised on dealing harshly with those allegedly guilty of match-fixing, first and foremost Fenerbahçe chairman Aziz Yıldırım, stocky military contractor. By contrast, Gülen, a man some prominent players consult before deciding to switch clubs, favoured harsh punishment, including relegation, of those involved in the scandal in a bid to reduce Erdoğan's grip on the club.

Gülen was believed to have wanted to see Yıldırım removed to pave the way for someone closer to his movement to take control of the club. Erdoğan, however, was catering to soccer bosses and their corporate backers as well as to the fans themselves in advance of elections in 2014.[107] The elections as well as the push for constitutional change in the run-up to the poll were crucial for Erdoğan who after three terms as prime minister was eying the presidency, a largely ceremonial post that he would like to see endowed with enhanced power. Erdoğan won the election but his ambition to turn his new post into an executive presidency was dashed in June 2015 when the AKP emerged again from parliamentary elections as Turkey's largest party but failed to secure an absolute majority for a third time.

In months of battles in 2012 in parliament and in the TFF, Erdoğan pushed for leniency as Yıldırım and ninety-two others were charged and convicted of match-fixing. Three months after the TFF rejected a proposal backed by the prime minister that would have shielded clubs guilty of match-fixing from being relegated, Erdoğan succeeded in getting the federation to clear Fenerbahçe as a club and fifteen others of charges of involvement in match-fixing. Erdoğan's successful interference prompted the TFF's three top officials, including its vice chairman Göksel Gümüşdağ, a brother-in-law of Erdoğan, to resign. Erdoğan defended the controversial TFF decision on the grounds that punishing institutions rather than individuals would amount to penalizing "millions of fans who set their hearts on these institutions." The decision followed Erdoğan's earlier success in driving through parliament, against the will of President Abdullah Gül, whose positions at times are aligned with those of Gülen, a bill that limited punishment of match-fixing.[108] Erdoğan's effort to shield Fenerbahçe backfired in June 2013 when UEFA banned the club for three years and Beşiktaş for one year from European championships. UEFA's decision was in response to the TFF's refusal to take action against the clubs on its own.

The battle for Fenerbahçe was politically sensitive for Erdoğan given Gülen's following among AKP members, vast network, and influence in key state institutions. Gülen's influence only grew after he left Turkey in 1998 ostensibly for health reasons but more probably to avoid standing trial for a recording in which he allegedly advocated an Islamic regime. He has since used his self-imposed exile as a tool to garner support by projecting himself as a victim. The support of the Gülen movement was crucial in Erdoğan's successful bid to force the country's powerful military to accept civilian supervision. The movement moreover played an important role in the rise of Turkey's appeal across the Middle East, North Africa and sub-Saharan Africa, with its network often paving the way for Turkish diplomacy and business.

Erdoğan, however, increasingly came to see Gülen as much as a liability as an asset. The cleric's inroads into the judiciary and the police meant that critics of his movement, among who were half of the country's military leadership, more often than not found themselves behind bars on charges of involvement in the murky and controversial Ergenekon affair, named after a valley in eastern Turkey that involved the Kemalist, Ultra-nationalist deep state. The conspiracy allegedly aimed to return the generals to power. The affair led to mass arrests. The arrests and the sentencing of dozens of the 275 defendants, including former chief of staff General İlker Başbuğ to life in prison on at times questionable or non-existent evidence, sparked international criticism and portrayed Erdoğan as increasingly arrogant and authoritarian.

Fenerbahçe's animosity toward Gülen spilled into the streets of Istanbul and onto the internet in May 2012 when fans angry at their club's defeat by Galatasaray in the national championship accused the preacher of engineering the match-fixing schedule that led almost two months later to the arrest and sentencing of Yıldırım. Fenerbahçe fans argued that Gülen frequently socialized publicly with Galatasaray coach Fatih Terim and the squad's star striker Hakan Şükür, who went on to become a member of parliament for Erdoğan's AKP before aligning himself with Gülen, who was a witness at the player's wedding. The Gülen movement's recognition of the importance of soccer was also evident in the creation of clubs by companies close to the preacher such as Kombassan Holding AS in the conservative city of Konya which owns Kombassan Konyaspor, whose fans frequently chant: "Play for the imam, play for the mosque."[109] In an act of vengeance, Erdoğan, fresh from a victory in municipal elections in April 2014 ordered a stadium named after Şükür in Istanbul's Sancaktepe district renamed Sancaktepe Municipal Sports Stadium. "It is better to have your name in people's heart than having a picture on a wall," Şükür, who is viewed as one his generation's best players, quipped in response on Twitter.

Fenerbahçe suspicions were fuelled by the fact that in July when police raided homes and offices in fifteen cities, arresting sixty-one people,

Galatasaray was the only dominant club untouched by the operation and the scandal. The arrests followed an eight-month police investigation that included the wiretapping of phones of senior soccer executives, players and agents. Transcripts of the wiretaps and videos of the surveillance were leaked to the press, again involving all major clubs except Galatasaray. Gülen denounced the protests as "orchestrated by circles that seek to destroy Turkey's peaceful atmosphere."

Fenerbahçe executives and fans increasingly drew parallels to the Ergenekon affair. The match-fixing case, like Ergenekon, was heard by a "specially authorized" court with a "specially authorized" prosecutor and some of the same judicial personnel as in the Ergenekon case. The court sentenced Yıldırım to six years in prison. The murkiness of the Ergenekon proceedings was highlighted by its lack of due process and by the unambiguous use of fabricated and planted evidence. Zekeriya Öz, the public prosecutor in the match-fixing case, was celebrated in Gülen's media for his prosecution of Ergenekon and appointed to the Galatasaray board in March 2011.

The *Zaman* columnist described the soccer scandal as a "second biggest breach in the fortress of Ergenekon."[110] He warned that "as they [Gülen's opponents] fail to understand that their resistance is futile, they will be eliminated faster." Support for Galatasaray in the Gülen media accelerated as the court proceedings against Yıldırım and the ninety-two others got underway. *Zaman* reported that Galatasaray's captain Ayman Kaman joined its editors and reporters in their offices to celebrate Galatasaray's winning of the 2012 championship.[111] *Zaman* columnist Ergun Babahan, a fervent Fenerbahçe supporter, was summarily dismissed after tweeting in anger after Galatasaray won the match, "Let the cup go to America!", a reference to Gülen's residency in Pennsylvania.

There is little but circumstantial evidence to support Fenerbahçe's belief that Gülen and Galatasaray conspired against it. Nevertheless, the plot had already thickened in the minds of Fenerbahçe fans a year earlier after the TFF advised UEFA eleven months before the arrest of Yıldırım that it was withdrawing the club from the UEFA Champions League because there were reasons to believe that match-fixing had enabled it to win that year's Turkish championship. The TFF had made its decision even though the prosecutor had yet to announce an indictment and a court had yet to hear the case and pass judgement. Privately, Yıldırım argued that the plot was far broader than just Gülen and Galatasaray and that other major clubs were also complicit. The lack of clarity at the very least puts into focus Turkish soccer's inextricable ties to politics and at times to organized crime, which has had representatives on the boards of major clubs and has in some cases bankrolled smaller clubs.

In supporting opposition to the reduction of penalties for match-fixing, the Gülen movement signalled that it was challenging Erdoğan's grip on his party.

Gülen, however, ultimately overplayed his hand when prosecutors believed to be close to him launched in December 2013 an investigation into alleged graft by ministers and prominent businessmen. Police at the time detained sons of three ministers and the head of a state-owned bank. Accusing Gülen of establishing a parallel state, Erdoğan moved or fired thousands of police officers and judicial personnel believed to be supporters of the cleric. Among those dismissed was Zekeriya Öz, the prosecutor in the match-fixing case.

The open warfare raised questions about whether Gülen was in full control of his movement, which seemed unprepared, lacking an exit strategy. Gülen appeared to implicitly acknowledge that he may not be in control in two phone calls to Fenerbahçe's Yıldırım in 2011. People familiar with the phone calls quoted Gülen as telling Yıldırım: "There is nothing bad in my heart against you. I am not involved in this. There might be people who did wrong against you but I am not aware of this if it was my people." In an inscription in a book Gülen sent to Yıldırım in between the phone calls, the preacher wrote: "To Aziz Bey whom I never had a chance to meet but admire for his activism, righteousness and perseverance. My prayers are with you that your difficult days may pass." Open warfare between Erdoğan and Gülen did not diminish the fact that the mostly secular soccer fans alongside the mass of others protesters who spanned the political gamut had left an indelible mark on Turkey's political landscape. The protests deprived Erdoğan of much of the glow that enveloped his political, diplomatic and economic successes. Erdoğan may have appeared down but he was certainly not out. He has repeatedly demonstrated his survival instincts and ability to turn tight spots into opportunities. He was jailed in the 1990s for reciting an Islamist poem while he was mayor of Istanbul. He built his party on the ruins of its banned predecessor and then defeated secularist legal attempts to outlaw it. Finally, he emerged the winner of a showdown with the all-powerful military that forced it to submit to civilian oversight.

ISLAMISTS FIGHT OVER SOCCER

"Ultimately, Erdoğan is smarter than the Egyptians. He rails and riles but lets people demonstrate. He caters to the rights of the religious and the Kurds to garner votes and ignores the secularists. The fans are largely secular. The Gezi Park demonstrations have shown that one can stand against his government and that rival soccer fans can work together. The demonstrations have put Erdoğan on notice. But that's not all. They also send a message to Gülen," said one soccer fan as Turkey's battle lines were being entrenched.

Erdoğan and his government set the tone over the summer of 2013 in advance of the opening of a new soccer season as well as the academic year. The prime minister and other senior officials announced measures to prevent soccer stadiums and university campuses from becoming major protest venues and issued threatening warnings. While emerging as the international community's starkest critic of the toppling of President Morsi, Erdoğan took a leaf out of the playbook of Al-Sisi and other Arab autocrats who demonized their opponents as terrorists. The government moved to replace private security forces in stadiums and on campuses with police forces; banned the chanting of political slogans during soccer matches; obliged clubs to force spectators to sign a pledge to abide by the ban before attending a game; encouraged the establishment of pro-government soccer fan groups; and cancelled scholarships for students who had participated in anti-government protests. Plain-clothes policemen were ordered to mingle with militant fans during matches while authorities monitored their activities on social media. It also restricted the consumption of alcohol in stadiums.

At the same time, Sports Minister Suat Kılıç threatened that "those who politicize the stadiums will pay the price." He added:

> if some groups try to infiltrate fan groups, they should know that Turkey is not a banana republic. We have fought terrorism for thirty years. We can handle this too. I do not want to be threatening, but you should know that it is not worth risking yourself and your team. Everyone must know that the law will be enforced. I hope that no one will be hurt, but this can happen. I am noting that there will be electronic monitoring in stadiums. Sports prosecutors will watch the games in stadiums, and we are introducing electronic tickets to monitor the seat of every supporter.

The minister had a similar message for students. "They can try Gezi protests in universities. People should not ruin their lives, should not have criminal records."

Kılıç failed to see the irony of his words. Scores of Turkish intellectuals and journalists have police records earned as a result of the country's military coups and Erdoğan's crackdown on the media. Among them is Erdoğan himself, who spent four months in prison for reciting a controversial poem.

Meanwhile Şamil Tayyar, a member of parliament for Erdoğan's ruling party, suggested that the government punish Beşiktaş if its fan disobey the ban on political slogans by seizing its stadium and turning it into a park. The journalist Burak Bekdil quipped that the government could also opt for the rent-a-fan model of the late North Korean dictator Kim Jong-Il. Kim paid Chinese actors to attend North Korean games during the 2010 World Cup in South Africa. "Mr. Kim was right. When you cannot win hearts and minds you can always rent them," Bekdil wrote.

Similarly, the soccer journalist Gülengül Altınsay, writing on the T24 news website, accused the government of introducing martial law in the stadiums. Addressing the government, Altınsay suggested that "while you are at it, why not declare in a state of emergency manifesto which slogans are permissible. If that does not work, you can fill the stands with dummies. You have no choice, this nation uses its wits when it is silenced."

The government's tough language and measures were not having the expected effect. If anything, they appeared to be fuelling protest. With its own stadium being renovated, Beşiktaş is playing, in a twist of irony, its home matches in Kasimpasa' Recep Tayyip Erdoğan Stadium. Çarşı members unleashed a torrent of anti-government slogans in their opening match in the stadium, prompting state-owned and pro-government television channels to mute the sound of the protests. Fans further demonstratively violated the ban by chanting political slogans in the 34th minute of this season's matches. Istanbul licence plates start with the number thirty-four. Fans of Fenerbahçe reminded the government that the battle was not over and may have just begun when they chanted "Everywhere Is Taksim Square! Everywhere Is Resistance!" in their club's first game after the announcement of the ban and demanded Erdoğan's resignation. Supporters of Ankara's Gençlerbirliği SK sought to circumvent the ban by chanting "Political Slogan" during their first match.

4

STRUGGLING FOR NATIONHOOD, BATTLING
FOR CHANGE

"Soccer club Bnei Sakhnin has changed the relationship between Arabs and Jews in the State of Israel."

Israeli President Shimon Peres

Bridging Divides

A devout Israeli Palestinian Muslim, Abbas Suan, achieved for a brief moment in 2005 what politicians in more than a half-century had not: he united Israelis and Palestinians by securing, with a last minute equalizer against Ireland, Israel's first chance in thirty-five years to qualify for a World Cup. The game earned him the nickname The Equalizer and made him briefly an Israeli hero; his cheery face and toothy smile featured in billboard advertisements for the state lottery even though he refused to sing *Hatikva*, Israel's nation anthem, at kick-offs of the Jewish state's national team.

The sense of unity was shortlived. Fans of Beitar Jerusalem, the celebrated bad boy of Israeli soccer and the country's most nationalistic club, saw Bnei Sakhnin, Suan's Israeli Palestinian team and State Cup winners in 2004, as the devil incarnate. Beitar, a reference to the Jews' last standing fortress in the second-century Bar Kochba revolt against the Romans, was established as part of the revisionist Zionist movement with the same name. The movement was founded in 1923 in Latvia by former Ukrainian war reporter Ze'ev Jabotinsky, who also organized Jewish self-defence groups against pogroms in the Ukraine and became a political leader, to imbue its members with a military spirit. That spirit comes to life when fans of Beitar, the only Israeli club to have never hired a Palestinian player, meets their team's Palestinian rivals. Their support during matches reaches fever pitch as they chant racist, anti-Arab songs and denounce the Prophet Mohammed. In response, Beit Sakhnin's Palestinian fans sing Islamic and anti-Israeli chants.

When a week after the Irish qualifier Suan set foot on the pitch in Israel—the only soccer league in the Middle East that features Muslims, Jews and Christians as players, coaches and referees—in a game against Beitar, Jerusalem fans booed him every time he touched the ball. "Suan, you don't represent us," blared a giant banner in Jerusalem's Teddy Kollek stadium. Fans shouted, "We hate all Arabs." Suan, an advocate of Israeli-Palestinian reconciliation, an independent Palestinian state alongside Israel and a solution for Palestinian demands to recover land and homes lost when Israel was founded, took the insults in his stride. "I ignore them," he insisted. "They're not worth my attention. They portray me as an Arab in a Jewish country. They try to put me in one group, but I represent both."[1]

Suan's Bnei Sakhnin, much like Beitar, which counts an estimated one-fifth of all Israeli soccer fans across the country as its supporters, symbolizes the struggle between Israelis and Palestinians as well as internal battles in both communities. Together their stories chart the faultline between Israelis and Palestinians. They also tell the tale of two fan groups who perceive themselves as subversive and opposed to the establishment. Yet their deep-seated animosity towards one another is mutual. More importantly, they are both products of the politicization of sports as well as the role soccer has played in the development of separate national identities in historic Palestine.

The Palestinian sports historian Issam Khalidi documented the battle over rival claims to land and identity waged on the soccer pitch in the decades leading up to the founding of the Jewish state. Muslim, Christian Orthodox and secular sports clubs reinforced national identity and constituted a vehicle to strengthen ties among different Palestinian communities. Similar to the role of the Algerian national team during that country's war of independence, soccer allowed Palestinians to forge relations with other Middle Eastern and African nations. The utility of sports in general, and soccer in particular, was reflected in Palestinian media. In the first four decades of the twentieth century reporting in *Filastin*, a newspaper that appeared twice weekly, "maintained a consistent critique: challenging the authorities' neglect of Arab sport and its support of Jewish sport activities. About 80 per cent of the news in *Filastin*'s sport section was about soccer, the most popular game in Palestine. *Filastin* used its football coverage to deepen national sentiments and helped to maintain the Palestinian national identity ... Sports began to be viewed in the Palestinian community as an important element for raising social consciousness and as an essential component of national culture," Khalidi wrote.[2]

Sports, which as a term in Arabic derives from a word that denotes domestication, amounted in *Filastin*'s view to a national duty, observed the Israeli sports historian Tamir Sorek who analysed the paper's sports reporting in the 1940s. *Filastin* propagated soccer's emphasis on discipline and obedience. "Soccer teaches us to obey the team's manager, and the referee teaches us to adhere to law and justice. Soccer also teaches us how man must obey his conscience, and, furthermore, how he must obey the commands and instructions of God. The crowd also learns to obey the referee and the rules ... Obedience is one of the most important qualities that the soldier in the battlefield must equip himself with. The war will not be fought without obedience, and I request of everyone that they obey whomever they are subordinate to, no matter whether you are players, spectators or referees, and to heed to his every law, decision and limitation," said the newspaper.[3]

In an appeal to the Supreme Muslim Council in 1946 to encourage sports, *Filastin* announced that it was "calling upon you as a soldier active on the sport field for many years ... I would ask you to direct the attention of the preachers in the mosques, and the speech-givers in the houses of God, so that through their speeches they may point the nation to sport, to urge them to care for their bodies, to ensure its cleanliness and activeness, to strengthen its limbs and to behave according to the rules of health, and its health will advance with us ... in the struggle..."[4] In a similar appeal to school principals, it proclaimed: "Remember that history demands of you that you create a new generation for Palestine, one that combines science and sport ... Remember that history urges you to raise an army of well-educated and healthy people, which will defend this country against the demon of colonialism."[5] The newspaper's campaign reflected the views of nationalist leaders at the time. "The youth is to the nation as the heart is to the body ... I see sport as the best means of equipping the nation with the youth it longs for," Gaza mayor Rushdi al-Shawa told the paper in 1945.

By contrast, most Jewish clubs in British-mandated Palestine sought to forge alliances with their British counterparts in a bid to build ties with those who one day would be influential in formulating British policy and cementing Palestine's identity as a Jewish entity. Those ties, they hoped, would also assure Jews of British protection at times of Palestinian violence against their settlement of the land. In the process, soccer became a barometer of British-Jewish relations as the Zionist movement campaigned at times violently for Jewish statehood and against British efforts to restrict Jewish immigration. Relations between opposing players and fans reflected the status of British-Jewish ties. It also served, according to Palestinian historians, as a cover for further illegal Jewish immigration into Palestine in the 1930s as when Maccabi, the centrist Zionist youth movement named after the Maccabees who fought the Seleucid empire and briefly achieved Jewish independence in the second century CE, organized games attended by Jews from across the globe.

The Jewish effort to solidify ties was boosted by Palestine's admission in 1928 to the world soccer body FIFA. The Palestine Football Federation (PFF), despite having been established as an organization that grouped, in the words of Josef Yekutieli, the PFF's founder and initiator of the Maccabean games, teams "regardless of religion and race," projected itself as one of the driving forces of Jewish sports in British-controlled Palestine. Palestine, in its view, was Jewish and British, and Palestinians did not figure in its nationalist calculations. The PFF dubbed the squad it sent in 1930 to Egypt for a friendly, the Land of Israel. The team was made up of six Jewish and nine British players but no Palestinians.[6] Neither were Palestinians included in teams Palestine fielded in qualifiers for the 1934 and 1938 World Cup. When Palestinians revolted in 1936 against Jewish immigration, sports served to further bind Jews and British. "Efforts to dominate athletics, marginalize the Arabs, and cultivate cooperation with the British at any price were the main traits that characterized Zionist involvement in sports," wrote Khalidi in a history of sports in pre-Israel Palestine.[7] The Zionist effort to co-opt sports in its nationalist struggle prompted Palestinians, two years after an earlier revolt against Jewish immigration, to establish their own, short-lived sports governing body, the

Arab Palestine Sports Federation (APSF) in 1931. A second attempt thirteen years later re-established the APSF. It banned its members from any contact with Jews. In doing so, it challenged Zionist claims that their sports body represented Palestine. In the interim, members of sports clubs, in a forerunner of the role of soccer fans in the twenty-first century's popular Arab revolts, increasingly participated in anti-Zionist and anti-British demonstrations, set up food distribution during the 1936 revolt, helped taking care of those wounded or killed in the protests and patrolled beaches to prevent illegal Jewish immigration.

The Zionist effort to forge close relations with the British stumbled when ties with the colonial power frayed in the wake of World War Two as Jews geared up for independence and extreme nationalist groups attacked British forces. Beitar, the right-wing nationalist movement that encompassed Beitar Jerusalem, played an important role in the push for independence. The movement was ultimately banned because of its links to the Jewish underground. Founded by Beitar's Jerusalem branch in 1936, the year of a Palestinian uprising, and supported throughout its history by right-wing Israeli leaders including current Prime Minister Benjamin Netanyahu, Beitar Jerusalem initially drew many of its players and fans from Irgun, an extreme nationalist paramilitary Jewish underground group. Its players and fans were active in various right-wing Jewish underground organizations that waged a violent campaign against the pre-state British mandate authorities. As a result, many of them were exiled to Eritrea in the 1940s. Beitar's initial anthem reflected the club's politics, glorifying a "with blood and sweat, a race will be established by/ for us, brilliant, generous and cruel/fierce." An Israeli journalist wrote: "This was a team with an ideal. Everybody was a member of [the Jewish underground movement Ha'Etzel] with the Menorah [Jewish candelabrum] emblem, which was something of a sacred symbol. The public was aware of the connection between Beitar and Ha'Etzel."[8]

Bnei Sakhnin's history and symbolism is diametrically opposed to that of Beitar. It was founded as a model of coexistence: a majority of Israeli Palestinian players, some Jews and some foreigners. "Bnei Sakhnin is living proof that Jews and Arabs can live together," said Avi Danan,[9] scion of a Moroccan Jewish family that settled in the right-wing Likud party bastion of Beit She'an. Danan played as a defender when Bnei Sakhnin became the first Israeli Palestinian team to win an Israeli State Cup and compete in a European UEFA tournament. It has since sent women runners to represent Israel in international competitions.

Bnei Sakhnin and Suan did wonders for Palestinian pride and self-confidence. Danan's presence in a team lacking in money and facilities like that of his hometown helped find common ground between two urban centres who once barely communicated. It reflected Israeli Palestinians' greater willingness to assert identity within Israel following 1976 Land Day protests against Israeli expropriations in which six Palestinians were killed and confrontations in 1987 during the first Intifada, a Palestinian uprising in the West Bank and Gaza against Israeli occupation. That greater willingness followed a failed attempt a decade earlier to establish independent Israeli Palestinian clubs with their own league. The effort was an initiative by Al Ard, an Israeli Palestinian nationalist group banned by Israel in 1964. It was an attempt to escape the grip of the ruling Israeli labour movement's effort to co-opt Israeli Palestinians with sports and prevent the emergence of a Palestinian national awareness. Israel countered the threat by banning independent sports competitions and arresting the league's organizers. Sabri Jiryis, a Palestinian intellectual and Palestine Liberation Organization (PLO) executive, recalled Israeli authorities sealing off villages to prevent league matches from being played.[10]

Bnei Sakhnin, a town of 25,000 inhabitants nestled in olive and fruit groves that built a memorial to those who died in 1976, stood for Israeli acceptance of the existence of Palestinians within its borders and beyond as a separate national identity rather than as part of a more generic Arab nation. Its story is the tale of the frustrations and aspirations of Israeli Palestinians and the projection of a model of bridging divides and cooperation. It traces its roots to a decision by a majority of Bnei Sakhnin's residents during the war in 1948, when Israel was founded, to stay rather than leave their homes in the futile hope that they would return once Arab armies ultimately prevailed. That history added significance to the fact that Israeli Palestinians staged their first Land Day protests, a reflection of deep-seated resentment at perceived discrimination fuelled by restrictions on construction of new homes, lower municipal budget allocations and past land expropriations, in a town whose residents had opted to become part of rather than flee the Jewish state.

Suan and Danan personified the ability of soccer to enhance social mobility and be a catalyst for communal or national identity for disadvantaged communities like the Palestinians and the Sephardim. On a speaking tour of the United States, Uri Davis, a prominent Jewish anti-

Zionist activist, described Bnei Sakhnin's success on the pitch as "an occasion of great pride and satisfaction ... [that] was not regarded only in professional football terms but gave expression to broader sentiments. First of these was the satisfaction of making it to the top despite many decades of being victimized by the calculated government policies of underdevelopment."[11] A 2005 Gallup study published by the Israeli Football Association (IFA) showed that Bnei Sakhnin had one of Israel's highest percentages of residents as fans who ranked as Israel's most loyal club supporters.[12]

Bnei Sakhnin became the first Palestinian club to win an Israeli championship on the same day in 2004 that Israeli troops launched a five-day military campaign to stop the smuggling of rockets and other weapons into the Gaza Strip. That did not prevent Yasser Arafat and Ariel Sharon from picking up the phone to congratulate the team on its success. For Bnei Sakhnin, the victory constituted a rare success for a minority that was oppressed, disinherited and disadvantaged. It spotlighted the divisions in Israeli and Palestinian society. It also reflected the professionalization and globalization of Israeli soccer and how it reduced the influence of political parties. Soccer's new commercial drive made the quality of a player more important than his religion or ethnicity. As a result, ever more Israeli Palestinians like Suan joined the top ranks of the country's soccer clubs, at times sharpening rather than blurring dividing lines.

Bnei Sakhnin's success, like Suan's equalizer in Ireland, enabled it to build bridges and break down barriers where heads of state, diplomats, businessmen and peace activists had failed. It won the club funding from oil-rich Qatar to build its own stadium, the Arab world's only public direct investment in Israel since the establishment of the Jewish state, and prompted Arabs from countries formally at war with the Jewish state to defy bans on travel to Israel to attend the team's matches. It also attracted US$400,000 from Arcadi Gaydamak, the controversial Russian businessman, who on the day he invested in Bnei Sakhnin also announced his acquisition of the club's nemesis, Beitar Jerusalem.

Beitar fans, like their Palestinian counterparts, understood the meaning of Bnei Sakhnin's success: soccer players had succeeded in defeating Israel, a goal Arab governments had failed to achieve for decades. The Beitar fans marked the victory with a day of mourning as they did six months later when Bnei Sakhnin defeated their club 4–1. In a YouTube video overlaid with a Sephardic song of mourning, Beitar declared that "yesterday was the most painful, humiliating and embarrassing day in the history of our club since it was founded in 1936 ... This day is now inscribed in the history books as a day of mourning."[13]

Beitar fans, who have the worst disciplinary record in Israel's top league, also recognized that the Arafat and Sharon's phone calls constituted a break with past Israeli efforts to prevent soccer from becoming a tool for Palestinian nationalistic expression and a refusal by many exiled Palestinians to accept that those with Israeli citizenship had adopted a dual identity as both Palestinians and Israeli citizens. Their days of mourning were the latest in a string of protests that shocked Israelis. Earlier, they refused to observe a moment of silence for assassinated Prime Minister Yitzhak Rabin, who initiated the first peace negotiations with the Palestinians. Since 2005 the club has faced more than twenty disciplinary hearings and been punished with point deductions, fines and matches behind closed doors because of its fans' racist behaviour.

The rise of Suan and his club, like that of Israeli Palestinian soccer in general, followed a familiar pattern in which much of the history of Palestinian efforts to achieve recognition of nationhood and statehood has mirrored the development of the Jewish national movement. The vision of sports by Max Nordau, a prominent pre-state Zionist thinker, as a tool "to produce a Judaism of muscles again that should lift us up... [and] arouse self-awareness in us"[14] could just as well have been expressed by either an Israeli Palestinian, an executive of Bnei Sakhnin, or Hamas. In a cinematic portrait of Bnei Sakhnin, *We Too Have No Other Land*, a Palestinian teacher positioned the stadium as a venue that could persuade Israelis that Palestinians exist, "that we've got a home and a land. That we were born here. All our families and relatives are here ... They've got to understand that [we are] two peoples in one country."[15] The teacher's plea went to the core of issues that Bnei Sakhnin's chairman and main benefactor, Palestinian building contractor Mazen Ghaneim struggled with. "Our problem is that the Arabs say we are traitors and Israelis think we are Arabs," he said.[16]

Bnei Sakhnin's model of engagement and cooperation is Israel's best known but not its only one. Tamir Sorek tells the story of Israeli Palestinian club Maccabi Kafr-Kana that in the mid-1990s visited Jordan to play against Al Wehdat, a symbol of Palestinian nationalism named after the Palestinian refugee camp in the Jordanian capital where it was founded. The match gained symbolic importance because it pitted two teams projecting a shared identity, but who had long been divided by more than physical borders, against one another. Residents of Al Wehdat included families that had fled Kafr-Kana when the Jewish state was established. Minutes before the start of the match, Al Wehdat's manager pulled Kafr-Kana's manager and sponsor Faysal Khatib aside to request that he not field his three Jewish players, or if he did to ensure that they would not speak Hebrew. Khatib refused, saying his team consisted of players, not Palestinians and Jews, and that all his players spoke Hebrew, not Arabic. The match was postponed and it took Khatib several days to get his way. When the match was finally played, Kafr-Kana won 3–2. Its three goals were scored by its non-Arabic speaking players.[17]

Bnei Sakhnin's embrace of integration of Palestinians into Israel as Palestinians did not stop its fans from violent assertions of their identity and revulsion at Beitar, the bigoted defender of discriminatory government policies. Defeating Beitar constituted for them a battlefield victory. The fans' ire at times targeted ordinary Israeli Jews. Journalist Neri Livneh was stoned after Bnei Sakhnin's meteoric rise was interrupted by a defeat to Israeli opponent Ahi Nazareth, a club that fields both Jewish and Palestinian players: "In response, the Sakhnin fans attacked the cars belonging to the journalists who had come to cover the match, with stones. I was extremely insulted. I didn't know which was preferable—to be stoned because I was a journalist, even after I had become friends with all the players after three meetings with them, or to be stoned because I was a Jew ... I still don't know the answer to the question of what aroused the ire of the Bnei Sakhnin fans."[18]

Soccer has nevertheless enabled Israeli Palestinians to create what Sorek calls an "integrative enclave,"[19] a space that enables integration and an equal exchange in a society that encourages the opposite. Sorek, like his Israeli colleague Amir Ben-Porat, argues that soccer creates a rare opportunity for Palestinians to win acceptance by Israel's Jewish majority. To them the soccer pitch is as much about a quest for identity as it about a quest for equal opportunity.[20] That quest is reflected in the Palestinian press portraying Palestinian-Jewish matches as proof that peaceful coexistence is possible while the Hebrew press sees them as examples of Israeli tolerance.[21] "Soccer is the tool of the underdog. It's the one Israeli sector where Palestinians do not confront a racially defined glass ceiling," remarked an Israeli football executive.[22] That reflects the fact that Israeli Palestinian teams account for 42 per cent of the clubs that are members of the Israeli Football Association even though Palestinians account for only 17 per cent of the Israeli population.[23]

To succeed, however, Israeli Palestinian players are expected to swallow their pride and tolerate racist taunts. "Arabs know that along with technical qualifications they need a strong character to succeed,"[24] said an Israeli journalist in an article on Israeli Palestinians. Rifaat "Jimmy" Turk, Israel's first Palestinian national team player, had the right character traits. "Turk was constantly cursed and was called a terrorist. But he restrained himself, fastened his teeth and did not break down; he did not lose his head," *Yediot Ahronoth* reported.[25]

That is not quite how Turk, who played thirty-four international matches for Israeli teams, was a trailblazer for other Israeli Palestinian players and went on to become deputy mayor of Tel Aviv, would phrase it. He recalls coach Ze'ev Segal telling him when he joined Hapoel Tel Aviv: "There is one important rule. We live in a racist country. They will curse you, they will curse your mother and your sister. They will spit at you. They will try to undercut you, cut your legs from under you. You have to be smart about it and know how to deal with it. You can't allow yourself to be provoked. You have to stay focussed. If you are smart, you'll survive. If you're not smart, you can take everything I told you and throw it out the window."

Experience taught Turk how prescient Segal's advice was. "It happened all the time. Boom! An apple flew my way! Boom! A pear! I was blamed for every terrorist incident in the country," he says. "It was tough. I cannot remember one game in which I was not insulted and attacked. They continuously tried to undermine my confidence and performance. There was not one game in which the spirit of sports dominated. It was as if I was at war, not as if I was playing soccer. Only because of who I am."[26]

Turk prides himself on never having received a red card and scoring his most goals against what he views as Israel's most racist club, Beitar Jerusalem. He vividly paints one instance in 1980 when he was playing against Beitar at the height of a violent campaign by a Jewish underground grouping that targeted elected Palestinian leaders in the West Bank. Beitar fans shouted: "Hey, Arab! Too bad you didn't lose your legs like Bassam Shaka'a," the mayor of Nablus who was crippled for life in one of the bombings.

The insults strengthened Turk's resolve:

> I kept saying to myself: "Oh, God, Oh, God. Let me succeed." I remember that we were in the 80th minute and Beitar was leading 1:0. I was determined to force a draw. I would shut them up that way. The minutes ticked away. I

begged Allah. They just kept cursing me. The 89th minute came and went. In the 90th minute we got a free kick from 30 metres away. Beitar formed a wall of 10 players in front of their goalkeeper. Again, I pleaded: "Please God. Let me shut them up." I was in tears. The crowd went mad. I kicked the ball as hard as I could. It soared and landed in the goal. The game was over. I went crazy. I ran towards the Beitar fans and shouted, "Bassam Shaka'a?" I stood there as they pelted me with tomatoes and oranges, but didn't move an inch. I stood my ground. I was mad, and kept shouting, "Bassam Shaka'a?" They kept throwing things at me. I did not move. I saw an orange fly towards me, I stuck out my chest so that it would hit me. I wasn't afraid. I was standing up to them. They could have thrown bricks at me and I wouldn't have moved. It was the one game in which I let it all go.

Israeli Palestinian clubs like Bnei Sakhnin or Hapoel Taibe, the first Palestinian team to play in Israel's premier league, initially sought to downplay their national identity in favour of their professional one. It was a strategy that worked for a while. But that changed with provocations by hardline fans of Israeli Jewish clubs like Beitar Jerusalem and Bnei-Yehuda Tel Aviv, the emergence of a Palestinian national movement and the fact that Israeli Palestinians were becoming increasingly urban and proletarian. Confrontations between supporters of Jewish and Palestinian teams, according to Ben-Porat, were "bellicose, vociferous and ugly, and eventually turned into a confrontation at the national level—Jews against Arabs."[27] Denouncing Palestinians as terrorists, Beitar fans portrayed Jews as loyal and Palestinians as disloyal citizens. In response, Palestinian fans chanted in an expression of attachment to the land, *biladi, biladi* [my homeland] or, in the interpretation of one Hapoel Taibe supporter: "we are here by right ... we belong here."[28] According to Ben Porat: "When an Arab individual chooses to support an Arab club, he enters a 'battle zone' that is much more than a competition over a position in the league."[29]

Beitar Jerusalem's matches often resemble a Middle Eastern battlefield. Its hardcore fans—lower middle- and working-class Sephardi males of Middle Eastern and North African origin who defined their support as subversive and against the country's Ashkenazi establishment—revelled in their status as the villains of Israeli soccer. Their dislike of Ashkenazi Jews of East European extraction, rooted in resentment against social economic discrimination, rivals their disdain for Palestinians. It dates back to their early years when Beitar supporters accused the predominantly Ashkenazi Labour movement of making it difficult for them to put food on their families' tables. "The Histadrut, the all-powerful trade union confederation that doubled as the government's employment agency, determined who was awarded a job. Right-wing Beitar supporters, who often were not members of the left-wing Histadrut, accused Labour of persecuting them politically and economically," said a former member of Herut, the predecessor of the Likud party that enjoyed support in predominantly lower-class Sephardi neighbourhoods of Jerusalem.[30] It was those neighbourhoods that brought Menachem Begin, Israel's first right-wing prime minister, to office in 1977. A journalist close to Beitar recalled sitting next to Beitar supporters on the stands in Tel Aviv in the 1950s during a match between Maccabi Tel Aviv and his team: "I look at them and what do I see essentially? How are they are dressed? Completely different from the locals in the same stadium ... We're speaking about ten thousand small apartments of the Beitar supporters, deeply insulted by a regime which they considered to be virtually 'foreign', and by an economic and social situation which unites almost all the Mizrachim" or Easterners, the Hebrew reference to Sephardic Jewry.[31]

Initially an underdog with the appeal of an unruly rebel, Beitar emerged from almost thirty years in the doldrums to win the Israeli Cup for the first time in 1976. Its home, the Teddy Kollek Stadium, which boasts Israel's highest attendance rate, was where its passionate fans sought to intimidate their opponents. Its Eastern Stand, where its most militant supporters congregated, became notorious as Israel's most vicious stadium terrace. Beitar basked in being a reflection of the rise of Likud brought to power by the Sephardic vote. It was the club of outsiders who, like Begin, despite his Polish roots was a political outsider in Labour-dominated Israel. It took Begin, the standard bearer of Beitar's ideological roots, almost thirty years to win an election and for the first time in Israel's history deprive Labour of its majority in parliament and claim to the prime ministership. Like Begin, Sephardi immigrants from Arab and Muslim nations were political and economic outsiders in Israeli society. In the wake of Begin's 1977 electoral victory, politicians, military leaders and intellectuals rushed to associate themselves with Beitar, a potent symbol of the new mainstream.

Beitar's triumphs tracked the rise of the Israeli right. They also constituted symbols of defiance as Palestinian resistance to continued Israeli occupation mounted and efforts to achieve an Israeli-Palestinian peace moved forward. Beitar's 1976 success foreshadowed Begin's rise. In 1987 the club won the Israeli championship for the first time. The first Palestinian Intifada erupted that year. Beitar celebrated its heyday and marked its return to its status as the country's bad boy in 1993 as Israel signed its historic Oslo agreement with Arafat's PLO and Hamas suicide bombers terrorized the country. The bombing campaign gave birth to Beitar fans' key slogan, "Death to the Arabs." Increasingly, Beitar fans broke the taboo of portraying the Palestinian-Israeli conflict as a racial, religious and existentialist conflict rather than a national dispute between two peoples.

Just how far Beitar had drifted from the country's projected image of a peace-seeking nation despite its continuous shift to the right was evident when Hapoel Tel Aviv, a team historically associated with the Histadrut movement that was captained by a Palestinian, defeated it in the 2010 championship finals. Hapoel supporters put their disdain for Beitar on full display, chanting "Give Jerusalem to Jordan, there is nothing worthwhile about it." The slogan also reflected the growing divide between Israel's two foremost urban centres: secular, wealthy Tel Aviv versus increasingly religious, conservative and impoverished Jerusalem with its larger than average families, above average unemployment and multiple tensions between orthodox and secular, rich and poor and Israeli and Palestinian.

Beitar's dilemma was compounded by the fact that the club's management and its more moderate fans refused to confront militants among the supporters who were grouped in La Familia, named in honour of the Italian mafia. Many of La Familia's members were also supporters of Kach, the outlawed violent and racist party headed by assassinated Rabbi Meir Kahane. La Familia frequently displays Kach's symbols. The refusal to stand up to the group's blatant racism reflected the ambiguity of a society that long yearned for peace, increasingly grew frustrated at how beyond its grasp it seemed to be and finally concluded that peace was no longer essential to its survival. Many disgusted Beitar fans opted to vote with their feet, abandoning Beitar for less controversial clubs such as Hapoel Katamon Jerusalem, Israel's only fan-owned club that has witnessed a meteoric rise since it was founded in 2006. The failure to confront La Familia entrenched Palestinian perceptions of an Israeli society that is inherently racist. The Israeli Palestinian member of parliament Ahmed Tibi, a supporter of Bnei Sakhnin, laid the blame for La

Familia's excesses at the door of Israeli political and sports leaders. "For years, no one really tried to stop them, not the police, not the club, not the attorney-general and not the Israeli Football Association," he said.

Underlying La Familia's racism is a deep-seated belief that peace with the Arab world is an illusion. It reflects a broad swath of thinking in Israeli society that is not fed by racism but by repeated failures of the Israeli-Palestinian peace process, the split among Palestinians between the Al Fatah movement in West Bank and Islamist Hamas in the Gaza Strip and the rise of Islamist movements across the region. It also feeds on a policy symbolized by the wall separating the West Bank from Israel within its pre-1967 war borders and a landscape in occupied territory that segregates Jewish and Palestinian towns with separate roads for each community and a network of checkpoints. "Peace will never happen. We don't hate Arabs because they are Arabs. We hate them because they are the enemy who wants to kill us. The government projects football as a peacemaker. We don't believe in peace, we believe in war," stated Guy Israeli, one of La Familia's founders. The latter's justification for imposing its will on the club is further rooted in the ideology of the Ultras which sees fans as the true owners of a club. "I choose who represents me," said Israeli, justifying his group's rejection of Palestinian players. "This is my team. I am Beitar."

The perception of being at war is also rooted in the club's origins and has lived on ever since. It predates the emergence of La Familia in 2005. When Moshe Nissim drove a bulldozer in 2002 on the instructions of Israeli security forces to destroy hundreds of Palestinian homes in the Jenin refugee camp on the West Bank in retaliation for the death of twenty-three soldiers in eight days of fighting, he planted a Beitar flag on his Caterpillar D-9. The soldiers were killed in what was dubbed the Battle of Jenin during which Palestinians had booby trapped the camp to prevent Israeli infantry and commandos backed by assault helicopters from entering. Israel charged that Jenin had been a launch pad for attacks on civilians during the ongoing second Palestinian Intifada against the occupation.

Nissim, a disgruntled Jerusalem municipality inspector who had been fired on charges of corruption, told the Israeli newspaper *Yediot Ahronoth*:

> I did not know how to operate the D-9 … They taught me how to drive forward and flatten a surface … I had never demolished a house before. Or even a wall … The moment I drove the bulldozer into the camp my brain flipped

… The despair over my personal circumstances vanished … What remained was anger at what had happened to our guys … I just thought about how I can help these soldiers … Loudspeakers warned the inhabitants to leave before I came. But I do not give anyone a chance. I did not wait … I was giving the blow to crumble as fast as possible. I wanted to get it done as fast as possible so that I could get to the other houses … A lot of people were inside the houses we started to demolish … I didn't see, with my own eyes, people dying under the blade of my D-9, and I didn't see the house fall on the people living in it. But if there were any, I did not care. I am sure people died inside these houses … Every house that came down gave me great pleasure … I built a stadium in the middle of the camp.

Wearing a Beitar pendant on a chain, his car decorated with his club's symbols, and drinking whiskey as he bulldozed for seventy-five hours straight, Nissim became a rare Beitar supporter with the opportunity to put into practice what he and his fellow fans preached.

Nissim's sentiments are reflected in La Familia's chants that often derive from traditional Sephardi religious tunes:

Listen well you Arabs,
We don't reconcile.
The chorus will always be:
May your villages burn.

La Familia at times reinforces its militant projection of the Jewish state with prayer sessions during matches against Israeli Palestinian teams. "My family has lived in Jerusalem for 500 years. We pray not because we are religious but because we are Jewish and have to demonstrate that we are Jewish," Israeli says. Members of his group have joined Jewish settlers in provocatively planting the Israeli flag on hilltops in disputed East Jerusalem.

La Familia's emergence at the height of the second Intifada coincided with the club's acquisition by Arcadi Gaydamak. The marriage between Beitar and Gaydamak initially seemed to be one made in heaven. Both basked in their image as underdogs willing to confront the establishment. However, Gaydamak's election programme projected his Social Justice Party as a platform for disadvantaged minorities, a reference to both Palestinians and Sephardis that did not go down well with Beitar supporters.

With a core of several thousand, La Familia started initially as an online group emerging from the ashes of its predecessor, The Lion's Den. It built on The Lion's Den's aim of preventing Beitar from signing a Palestinian player at a time when all other premier league teams were discovering Arab talent. Despite the fact that they are a minority among the club's hundreds of thousands of supporters, their will has become law. Beitar Jerusalem executives concede that they will not contradict La Familia. Even players at times join the group in their in racist denunciations:

> *This is the Jewish state!*
> *This is Israel, Salim Tuama!*
> *I hate all the Arabs!*
> *I hate you Salim Tuama!*
> *I hate all the Arabs!*

National team and Beitar striker Amit Ben Shushan led several fellow Beitar players in denouncing Tuama, a Palestinian Christian, who played with him in Israel's squad.[32] Summoned in 2009 to a meeting with La Familia after he said he would be happy to have a Palestinian in his team, Beitar captain Aviram Baruchyan apologized saying that he was "sorry for the pain that I caused to the fans and I do understand that I've hurt them. I'm not the one who takes such decisions but if the fans don't want an Arab player, there will be no Arab player in Beitar."

An amateur video published on an Israeli news website in 2011 showed La Familia fans teaching young children how to chant:

> *Arabs are sons of bitches*
> *Death to the Arabs*
> *A Jew has soul, an Arab is a son of a bitch*
> *Son of a bitch, Son of a bitch, Son of a bitch*
> *Mohammed is a gay son of a bitch*
> *I hate Arabs.*[33]

The journalist Neri Livneh describes Beitar as a product of the religious fanaticism and ethnic hatred that over the years had sparked the migration of liberals from Jerusalem to Tel Aviv:

> If we are to judge according to the shouting and cursing that accompany the violent conduct of the Beitar fans, then those who play on the soccer fields are not people but two kinds of gods—our God, the Jewish God who is known as 'Elokim' by those who love Him, as opposed to the Arabs' god, Muhammed. In order for Beitar to win on the field, judging by the contents of their songs and their curses, it is not enough for all the Arabs to die, but Mohammed must also die. Every goal is proof of the existence of the Jews' god and the death of the Muslims' god. From the primitive point of view of those fans, what takes place on the soccer field is a religious war. From that point of view, Beitar is a reflection of everything that is off-putting in Jerusalem and likely

to lead to its destruction—unwarranted hatred and religious zealotry. Even if the extremists among the religious population don't go to the soccer fields on the Sabbath, their interests are taken care of on the field. Also those of the most extreme nationalists. The attitude of the police toward the fans who go on the rampage is likewise similar to its attitude toward the Ultra-Orthodox and the rioters who retaliate after terrorist attacks. They ignore them, either out of fear or perhaps even out of identification with them. It is also possible that it's due to the fact that, to them, all the fans seem to look alike (a frequent excuse on the part of the police for their inability to apprehend Ultra-Orthodox rioters)—the very same expressions of anger, hatred, racism and primitiveness.[34]

Ben-Porat warned that "the football stadium has become an arena for protest: political, ethnic, nationalism, etc ... 'Death to the Arabs' has thus become a common chant in football stadiums ... Many Israelis consider the Israeli Arabs [Palestinians] to be 'Conditional Strangers,' that is temporary citizens ... Contrary to conventional expectations, these fans are not unsophisticated rowdies, but middle-class political-ideological right-wingers, whose rejection of Arab football players on their team is based on a definite conception of Israel as a Jewish [Zionist] state."[35]

Beitar fans with the club's black and yellow scarves and La Familia logo broke new ground in early 2013 by employing language used by the Nazis when they unfurled a banner reading "Beitar Will Be Pure Forever." The protest was in response to the club's acquisition of two non-Arab Muslim players from Chechnya. The transfer constituted Gaydamak's attempt to finally challenge La Familia and succeed where others had failed. An earlier acquisition, Ibrahim Nadallah, a Nigerian Muslim, lasted half a season before leaving. "I don't recommend a Muslim to join Beitar—the extremists won't change," he said. La Familia quotes him frequently. Gaydamak's hiring of the Chechens was as much an effort to boost the club's results as it was a throwing down of the gauntlet for the extremists after two years of failed dialogue with the group. Less than a year after their hiring, the Chechens were gone. So was Gaydamak and Izhak Kornfein, the club's general manager and long-time player, whom the militants blamed for the hiring of the two Muslims. Gaydamak sold Beitar to Israeli businessman Eli Tabib, who was quick to pander to its most fanatical supporters in a bid to calm the situation.

Initially, it had looked as if Gaydamak's challenge would succeed. Thousands of Maccabi Haifa fans stood up, clapped their hands and cheered Chechen striker Zaur Sadayev when, a month after La Familia's controversial protest, he walked on to the pitch to salvage Beitar from yet another defeat. Supporters of Sadeyev's club remained seated in silence. Members of La Familia, many of whom justify their racist stance with having been born in an era of war against the Arabs, argued that accepting non-Arab Muslim players was a first step towards their enemy, Palestinians, joining their team. "It sets a very dangerous precedent," warned Ronnie Resnick, another of the group's founders.

La Familia's adoption of the Nazi notion of racial purity had a devastating effect on Beitar's attendances which dropped to some of the club's worst ever. At times it played in a stadium that can accommodate 30,000 people with only 5,000 present. "I don't want to be treated like a criminal for supporting my team," said one fan embarrassed by La Familia's notoriety. In a reversal of the process where clubs are usually penalized for their fans' behaviour, Beitar asked the IFA to be allowed to play behind closed doors. The request was rejected, with the IFA barring only specific individuals. The fan boycott spotlighted Beitar's dilemma, one that looms large for the future of the Jewish state itself: while Israel has to decide whether continued occupation of the West Bank is worth the price of democracy to maintain the Jewish character of the state, Beitar has to either reinvent itself or ultimately become an entity whose morals and ethics undermine its viability.

The banner and La Familia's subsequent setting fire to the club's unofficial museum sparked public outrage, prompting even President Shimon Peres and Benjamin Netanyahu to express their condemnation. "We cannot countenance such racism. The Jewish people, who suffered from boycotts and ostracism, must be a light unto the nations," urged Netanyahu. If "they're burning buildings now they might just burn people next," added a visibly shocked Jan Talesnikov, Beitar's assistant coach. The public outcry contrasted starkly with the meek public and official response to earlier attacks by La Familia on Palestinian shoppers and workers in the Malha Mall just opposite Jerusalem's Teddy Kollek Stadium and a Jewish musician who denounced their attitudes. The condemnations proved to be little more than empty words.

The left-wing Israeli journalist Gideon Levy cautioned after the attack on the mall that "those who fail to raise their voice now over Malha will get Toulouse in Jerusalem. Sticks today, guns tomorrow," (He was referring to an attack on a Jewish school in the French city of Toulouse a week before the mall incident in which four people, including three children, were killed.) According to Levy:

It's not hard to imagine what would have happened had hundreds of people burst into a mall in Toulouse and beat up Jews who worked there. Israel and the Jewish community would have set up a hue and cry. The president of the republic would have rushed to Toulouse, met with representatives of the Jewish community and expressed his shock and regret. Our prime minister and foreign minister would have competed with each other in expressing shock, and columnists would be fulminating about anti-Semitism raising its ugly head in Europe. Everyone would agree: Jews were beat up (again) simply for being Jewish. It's also not hard to imagine what would have happened had hundreds of Arabs stormed the Jerusalem mall, beating up Jewish workers. Dozens of rioters would have been arrested and tried. But when it comes to Beitar fans, all is forgiven, all is overlooked. No one was arrested, almost no one said anything, and even after it was made public the mall's manager was the only one to apologize to the workers, who were beaten up simply for being Arab.

In opposing the acquisition of the Chechens, La Familia not only employed the imagery of the Holocaust but also implicitly challenged a founding principle of Israeli foreign and defence policy coined by David Ben Gurion: the need to ally Israel with non-Arab Muslim nations to compensate for the historical lack of relations with Arab countries and the more recent volatility in the region in the wake of the Arab revolts. Beitar coach Eli Cohen perverted Ben Gurion's principle when he attempted to defend the acquisition of the Chechens by saying: "I don't understand the fans who don't want to see a Muslim player in Beitar. There are a billion Muslims in the world and we must learn how to live with them. There is a difference between a European Muslim and an Arab Muslim, and the fans here have a problem with Arabs living in the Middle East." The outcry the fans' attitude provoked reflected the outcome of national elections a month earlier and a growing awareness that Israeli policies—controversy over Israel's settlement policy and mounting criticism of the treatment of prisoners, highlighted by the release in 2012 of a hunger striking Palestinian national soccer team player as a result of international pressure—were alienating even its closest allies.

The battles on the Beitar soccer pitch also reflected struggles within Israeli society and particularly in Jerusalem between rival Jewish and Muslim nationalist and religious claims to the city. Dov Waxman warned of an atmosphere of escalating tension between Jews and Palestinians. "Attitudes on both sides have hardened, mutual distrust has intensified, fear has increased, and political opinion has become more militant and uncompromising ... Jews and Palestinians are currently on a collision course, with potentially severe consequences for their continued peaceful co-existence, as well as for stability and democracy in Israel," he wrote.[36]

Increased racism in Israeli soccer is closely linked to the virtual death of the Israeli-Palestinian peace process and the dwindling number of Palestinians and Israelis participating in non-governmental reconciliation efforts. Hope and interest in peace has faded, battle lines have hardened and racist stereotypes are gaining increased currency on both sides of the divide. In response, authorities saw the need to curb mounting violence on and off the pitch as exclusively a law enforcement problem rather than a social and political issue. "The first thing to do is significantly increase the punishments. I have been talking about this for more than twenty years, and that was a time football was much more violent," said Maccabi Haifa Chairman Jacob Shahar.[37] That approach, however, was likely to be less effective in reducing Israeli-Palestinian soccer tension. "The field has become a battleground, involving not only fans but also players, coaches, officials … it is impossible to stay silent," conceded Israeli Culture and Sports Minister Limor Livnat.[38]

The IFA nevertheless allowed what Ben-Porat described as "permissive territory" in which "some deviant behaviours are tolerated (such as using profanities) as long as definite rules are followed (that is, no racist chants)" to get out of hand. It demonstrated its lack of resolve by failing to impose its anti-racism policy with the same determination it was targeting what amounted to hooliganism. Forcing Beitar Jerusalem to drop its ban on Palestinian players, a violation of Israeli equal opportunity laws, and severely penalizing it for its fan behaviour rather than simply rapping the club on its knuckles (while also taking Bnei Sakhnin to task for the behaviour of its fans) would have gone a long way to tackling the issue of mounting racism on the pitch.

It would also have sent an encouraging signal to Israelis and Palestinians at a time when Palestinians were increasingly disinclined to engage with Israelis in the belief that reconciliation efforts were senseless as long as the Israeli-Palestinian peace process is stalemated. An IFA crackdown perceived as an effort to root out racism would have countered Palestinian claims that there was no partner in Israel amidst the violence employed by Israeli security forces against protesters on the West Bank and anti-Palestinian statements by Israeli Ultra-nationalists.

The Israeli Palestinian Maccabi Haifa striker Mohammed Ghadir challenged Beitar and officialdom in late 2011 by publicly offering to join

Beitar.[39] He was following the examples of Tuama, who volunteered in 2008, and Suan three years earlier when he negotiated a deal that fell through after Beitar fans denounced him in their stadium. Ghadir argued that that he and Beitar were a perfect match. "I am well suited to Beitar, and that team would fit me like a glove. I have no qualms about moving to play for them," he said, noting that the Jerusalem club had a large squad, a significant fan base, wide media coverage and that it lacked talented strikers. There was only one hitch: as with Suan and Tuama, Beitar did not want a Palestinian. "Our team and our fans are still not ready for an Arab soccer player," stated Beitar's management.[40] Ghadir's bid was significant. It countered Beitar's argument that it had broken no laws by not having hired Palestinian players because no Palestinian had ever applied for a place in its team.

Haaretz columnist Yoav Borowitz alleged that "this is a mark of Cain for Beitar Jerusalem and its fans, and also for the city of Jerusalem, the state of Israel and its legal system, the IFA and also for the media, which continues to cover this soccer team. Day by day, we reinforce and popularize this loathsome form of racism."[41] IFA chairman Avi Luzon, like Jerusalem mayor Nir Barkat and most Israeli media, remained silent on Beitar's rejection of Ghadir. Said Borowitz: "Could an English or French soccer squad get away without putting a black or Jewish player on the field throughout its history? How would its fans respond to that? Would football associations in such countries countenance such blatantly racist policy?"[42] Borowitz noted that Jerusalem's 280,000 Palestinian residents contributed NIS100,000,000 (approximately US$27 million) in taxpayers' money to the renovation of Jerusalem's stadium. "Yet this contribution does not entitle the city's Arabs to representation, even of the most minimal sort, on Jerusalem's sole team in the nation's top league," Borowitz concluded.[43]

Playing for Nationhood

> *"The imagined community of millions seems more real as a team of eleven named people. The individual, even the one who only cheers, becomes a symbol of his nation himself."*

Eric Hobsbawm

The phones ring incessantly at the Swedish Kurdish soccer club Dalkurd FF. Dalkurd is a hot team for agents and players. In 2009 it signed the Bosnian international Nedim Halilovic and the upcoming

Algerian Swedish star Nadir Benchinaa. More prominent signings are in the works. Started in 2004 as a project to create jobs for Kurdish youth, Dalkurd's meteoric rise has put it on the international soccer map.

Kurdistan, however, does not feature on that map. In fact, Dalkurd is a product of the carve-up of the Ottoman Empire in the early twentieth century that turned Kurds into the world's largest nation without a homeland, scattered across the Middle East and the globe. As a result, Dalkurd is making its mark not in Iraqi Kurdistan, Iran, Turkey or Syria, where Kurds constitute a significant minority, but in Sweden, where it wins league after league. Its players are Kurdish refugees who fled Saddam Hussein's attempt, aided by chemical weapons, to cleanse northern Iraq of its Kurdish identity, the suppression of Kurdish cultural identity in Turkey and religious and ethnic discrimination in Iran. Dalkurd chairman Ramazan Kizil, a Kurdish immigrant from Turkey, was sentenced in 2010 in absentia to ten months in prison in his homeland for giving a speech in his native Kurdish and campaigning on behalf of a pro-Kurdish political party. Kizil's ambition is to take Dalkurd into FIFA's European Championship where he dreams of unfurling the Kurdish alongside the Swedish flag.

In doing so, he would put a dent in Kurdistan's status as a soccer outcast. Kurdish players are international stars and Kurdish clubs dominate the Iraqi league, but the Kurdish flag flies only at the VIVA World Cup, a tournament that operates by a set of standards different from those of FIFA. VIVA competitors are those who hail from a tribal area, an agricultural province, an occupied nation, a semiautonomous region, an ancient city-state, a disenfranchised minority enclave or a nation that doesn't get any acknowledgement from soccer's international governing body. "The goal is ideological," said Luc Misson, a Belgian lawyer and vice president of VIVA organizer New Federation Board. "It's about allowing peoples to project themselves through sport."[44] In VIVA, Iraqi Kurds, who are the closest to statehood that Kurds have ever come in the last century join at various times fellow wannabe nations such as Chechnya; Tibet; Northern Cyprus; Spain's Basque Country and Catalonia; the Sami Tan from Lapland, which stretch across northern Finland, Sweden and Norway; northern Italy's Padania; and Greenland— a country FIFA doesn't recognize in part because it is too cold for grass to grow there.

Soccer is an important vehicle in furthering their national dreams. Like religion, it is a tool for socialization that generates a sense of belonging, representation and recognition. "Sport in general, and football [soccer] in particular, have proven to be significant theatres for the working up and expression of national identity, and its most mobilized form, nationalism," write scholars John Sugden and Alan Tomlinson.[45] "The sport of soccer has played an important role in maintaining Palestinian identity. Through shared symbols, machinations of government and also sports, especially soccer, the Palestinians have forged a national identity that is separate from that of other people in the region ... The game has contributed to greater Palestinian recognition globally ... Appearing on the world stage promotes an image of being as equal and legitimate as any other state ... When the Palestinian team members wear their green or white jerseys, the team reinforces a sense of national identity. The flag is raised, the name 'Palestine' used and the team competes against de jure states," adds Glen Duerr.[46]

Thanks to the support of Arab and Muslim states, Palestine has achieved what VIVA associates strive for: it is FIFA's only member that is not a full-fledged state. The inclusion of Palestine made FIFA one of the first international organizations to recognize Palestinian statehood even though it has yet to be accepted by the United Nations. Officials of the Iraqi Kurdish soccer association express what their political leaders only dare say privately. "FIFA membership amounts to political recognition of our national ambition," observed the Kurdish Football Association President Safeen Kanabi.[47] Iraqi Kurdish President Massoud Barzani, a former guerrilla leader who still commands his own Peshmerga army, understands that in order to be a proper nation Kurdistan has to have a proper soccer team to serve as a battering ram to further claims for political recognition, Kanabi noted.

Iraqi Kurdish government and soccer officials argue that FIFA is opportunistic about the applications of its rules. Palestine is not their only piece of evidence; so is FIFA's structure inherited from the days of colonialism. Britain is not a FIFA member but England, Wales, Scotland and Northern Ireland are and so is Hong Kong alongside China. The British owe their special status to the fact that England, historically soccer's greatest promoter that played the world's first international match against Scotland in 1872, created FIFA's rules. Those rules recognize only one soccer association per country.

A relatively, autonomous entity with a booming economy in a country wracked by sectarian divisions, Iraqi Kurdistan is biding its time although advances in Iraq by the Islamic State, the jihadist group that controls a swath of Iraq and Syria, have heightened prospects for independence. Kurdish soccer benefitted from the violence that enveloped the rest of Iraq. Iraqi soccer players, fearing for their lives from insurgents and criminal gangs, fled north, giving Kurdish clubs their pick. Kurdistan's FC Erbil emerged as Iraq's champion three times in a row and represented Iraq in 2009 in the Asian Champions League.

Building and maintaining an Iraqi Kurdish national team remains a political balancing act. Recruitment of diaspora players is sensitive. Turkish Kurds are off limits. A nation whose Kurdish players and coach helped it reach the semi-finals of both the World Cup and the European Championships in recent years, Turkey fears losing some of its best players and encouraging national aspirations among its estimated fifteen million Kurds who account for one-fifth of the population. "We don't carry or wear our uniforms or anything that identifies us as Kurds when we travel via Turkey because it involves too much risk. The Turks would confiscate them," said Kanabi. Iraq, too, is afraid that the Kurdish team will continue to lure some of its best players despite the fact that without FIFA recognition Kanabi cannot demand that Iraqi Kurds choose between the Iraqi and Kurdish national squads.

In using soccer as a tool to further nation and statehood, Palestinians and Kurds adhere to a tradition established at the time that soccer was introduced in the region by the British. It has since been perfected by Israelis and Algerians. "Sport was ... used as a means of resisting, to different degrees, French and British colonial presence, and of defending the Arab cause in the international arena," writes Mahfoud Amara, singling out the Algerian national team, which traces its roots to the National Liberation Front (FLN) during the war of independence. The FLN formed its pre-independence team in 1958 from Algerian players in France who clandestinely left their colonial motherland to help the group forge closer ties with its socialist supporters. The FLN move came on the heels of the first sport protest involving several Arab nations during the 1956 Olympic Games in Melbourne, which Egypt, Lebanon and Iraq boycotted in protest against that year's invasion of Egypt by British, French and Israeli troops.[48]

A statement by Iraqi Kurdish president Barzani equating sports to politics as a way of achieving recognition adorns the Kurdish state-in-waiting's three major stadiums and virtually all of its sports centres and institutions. "We want to serve our nation and use sports to get everything for our nation. We all believe in what the president said," insisted Kanabi, scion of a legendary supporter of soccer who led anti-regime protests in Kurdish stadiums during Saddam Hussein's rule. Kanabi's KFA co-organized VIVA's 2012 tournament with financial support from the Iraqi Kurdish government. "Like any nation, we want to open the door through football. Take Brazil. People know Brazil first and foremost through football. We want to do the same. We want to have a strong team by the time we have a country. We do our job, politicians do theirs. Inshallah (if God wills), we will have a country and a flag" said Kurdistan national coach Abdullah Mahmoud Muhieddin.[49]

Sitting on the floor of a hotel room in the Kurdish capital of Erbil in June 2012, Sheikh Sidi Tigani, president of the Western Sahara Football Federation explained that the Sahrawi government-in-exile formed by liberation movement Frente Polisario saw soccer as a way of keeping youth away from violence and drugs. It also allowed the guerrilla movement to channel discontent with the fact that thirty-seven years after the territory was occupied by Morocco, Saharans are no closer to a state of their own. According to Sheikh Sidi, "our external objective is primarily to project our identity through sports. Many people don't know our problem or would not be able to find us on a map. Soccer can change that. We had a French woman visit our refugee camps. When she told children that she was from France, they all replied saying 'Zidane'"—a reference to retired star soccer player Zinedine Zidane, a Frenchman of Algerian origin.[50] "We've replaced the gun with a soccer ball," added Western Saharan national sports director Mohammed Bougleida.[51]

Western Sahara's presence at the Kurdistan tournament constituted a victory not only for the African desert region but also for Kurdistan. It allowed Kurdistan to demonstrate its ability and intention to conduct a foreign policy at odds with that of Baghdad by hosting a World Cup for nations that world soccer body FIFA refuses to recognize. The fact that Morocco protested against the inclusion of the disputed Saharan territory to the Kurdish department of foreign relations rather than to the Iraqi foreign ministry, and negotiated a deal with the Kurds under which the Saharans were not allowed to fly their flag during ceremonies and matches, added to Kurdistan's sense of recognition.

* * *

Most soccer-centred soap operas thrive on romantic entanglement and power struggle. Palestine's thirty-episode *The Team*[52] has plenty of that too, but much of its drama reflects the hardship imposed on Palestinian daily life by conflict, occupation and conservative social mores. *The Team* projects through soccer a different perspective on resolving national, political and gender disputes and economic hardship using vignettes based on Palestine's daily reality.

High unemployment among West Bank Palestinians forces players Tony and Hakim to sneak across the Green Line separating Israel from territories conquered in 1967 to find work on the Jewish side of the border. Another player Abu Ayaaed, is on the run from the Israeli military. Fellow player Ahmed is arrested by Israeli soldiers after he is wounded by a rubber bullet during an anti-Israel demonstration. Zeinab, the mother of yet another player, defies tradition by refusing to marry her brother-in-law following her husband's death. She adds insult to injury by enrolling in Bethlehem University and launches a campaign against honour killings after a co-student is killed for bringing shame on the family.

The Team's underlying themes—equitable rule of law, the right of freedom of association, peaceful and creative conflict resolution and the importance of pursuing one's dreams—contrast starkly with Palestinians' harsh reality. Violence is a fact of life. Palestinians fire rockets from Gaza into Israel and Israel retaliates—three top Palestinian soccer players were killed in Israel's attack on Gaza in early 2009.

The political paralysis stymies Palestine's national soccer team and complicates its efforts to make its mark in international competitions. Travel restrictions by Israel and Egypt stopped the Palestinians from competing in 2010 World Cup qualifiers. FIFA forced the Palestinians to forfeit their qualifier to Singapore because they failed to field a full team after Israel denied permits to eighteen players and officials from Gaza. In a twist of irony, Palestine instead made its international debut at the 2010 Homeless World Cup in Brazil with a team from the Palestinian refugee camps in Lebanon. "We are proving to the whole world that the Palestinians have a right to play," said Sameh Zeidani, a member of the Palestinian Sport Office in Lebanon who put the team together.[53] Palestine Football Association president Jibril Rajoub, a 62-year-old tough anti-Israeli activist, former security chief and member of the central committee of Abbas' Al Fatah guerrilla group-turned political party who served seventeen years in Israeli jails for throwing a grenade at

Israeli soldiers when he was seventeen, positions soccer as an important building block in Palestinian president Mahmoud Abbas' stalled effort to achieve United Nations recognition of Palestinian statehood.

Soccer, despite disruptive Israeli policies, has flourished under Rajoub's leadership. Stadiums are being built or refurbished across the West Bank, and the PFA hosted international tournaments in advance of the 2012 London Olympics, held fifty years after the PLO's Black September killed eleven Israelis during the Munich Olympic Games in 1972, and the 2014 World Cup finals. Rajoub worked hard to obtain Israeli consent for an upgraded soccer stadium in Al-Ram, a town between Jerusalem and Ramallah, a stone's throw from the barrier that separates the West Bank from Israel, and FIFA funding for its refurbishment. He then convinced FIFA to allow Palestine to play its first ever match on home ground in 2008 rather than in a neighbouring Arab capital. The crowds in the stadium, named after Palestinian nationalist Faisal al Husseini, shouted, "Football is nobler than war" as Palestine took part in a friendly against Jordan. Controversy was nonetheless the game's DNA, from the name Palestine, which remains controversial in Israeli and Jewish circles, to Rajoub's claim that the game was being played in Jerusalem, an assertion of Palestinians' claims to the city as the capital of their future state.

Supported by Abbas, the PFA has since seen its annual budget balloon from US$870,000 in 2008 to more than US$6 million in 2010, according to PFA finance manager Jihad Qura.[54] The PFA had three full-time employees in 2008, now it has thirty. Five new stadiums have been built and refurbished in the recent years on the West Bank. The most recent was inaugurated in the southern town of Dura on 12 June 2011 with a friendly between the Palestinian and Italian Olympic teams. Thousands watched.

It is a far cry from Palestine's World Cup qualifier against Uzbekistan in 2006, when it fielded a national team cobbled together from players of Palestinian origin from the United States, Kuwait, Lebanon and Chile, a country that boasts Latin America's largest Palestinian community and has had its own soccer team for almost a century, as well as from the West Bank and Gaza. Many of the players had never met before they gathered in a training camp in Egypt thirty days before their make-or-break match. Some players did not speak Arabic, others had no command of English, while some of the South Americans only knew Spanish. For Austrian coach Alfred Riedl it amounted to Babylon. Eleven players from Gaza struggled for weeks to get past Palestinian,

Israeli and Egyptian checkpoints to cross the Gaza-Israel border that was more often than not closed, for no obvious reason. Ultimately only six showed up two weeks late, the other five were refused passage by the Israelis. Playing two years before FIFA lifted its ban on international matches on the West Bank, the Palestinians went into their home game against Uzbekistan in an empty stadium in Qatar. Uzbekistan easily knocked Palestine out with a 3–0 victory.

Writing in his diary the day before an Iraq-Palestine World Cup qualifier in a stadium just a few miles from a military base of the United States, Israel's staunchest ally, Morad Fareed, a New York-based athlete-turned-real estate developer, fantasized about inviting American troops to the match. "I wanted to force us each to see how that might make the Iraqis feel … after all it wasn't my call to make because I didn't have to live with the consequences. But I still believe they would've gladly accepted, and been gladly welcomed, and the uncanny pairing of Palestine v. Iraq in FIFA's 2006 World Cup Qualifier match would have gotten that much more bizarre with 100 Marines cheering in the crowd. That is perhaps one of the innumerable unlikely scenarios that are playing for Palestine. We all would have loved that—all of us."[55]

The initial recruitment of diaspora Palestinians with foreign passports who had a better chance of getting past an Israeli checkpoint and across the Allenby Bridge to Jordan for training sessions and matches came at the expense of gifted local players like Raad Qumsieh.[56] A West Bank player famous for scoring a wonder goal in a game against Kuwait, Qumsieh finally opted for a soccer scholarship in the United States. Qumsieh laughed when asked if he would consider playing for an Israeli team. "Israeli teams don't scout Palestinian players," he said wryly, referring to those who do not carry Israeli passports.[57]

PFA secretary general Abdel Majid Hijjeh argues that "ours is more than just a game. It breaks the siege on Palestinian sports and the Palestinian people."[58] The player Murad Ismail added: "When teams come to play on our land, it's a way of recognizing the Palestinian state. That benefits the Palestinian cause, not just Palestinian sports."[59] Ever the strategist, Rajoub believes that "we can achieve a lot for our cause through sports. The world is changing and we have to push the legitimacy of our national aspirations through sports. I hope sports will help Israel reach the right conclusion. We are 4.2 million people living under Israeli occupation; I hope that I can convince the Israelis that we should open a new page that recognizes the existence of Palestinian people. I don't wish the suffering of the Palestinian people on anyone, including the Israelis. If we are for sport in the world, it has to be fair and just for all. I speak with Shimon Peres, and on this we have some common ground." The Palestinian sports czar was referring to the Israeli president's suggestion that soccer could play a role in solving the Palestinian-Israeli conflict.

The Palestinian effort kicked into high gear in October 2011 with the unveiling of an ambitious ten-year plan backed by the International Olympic Committee (IOC) and the Palestinian Authority to develop sports. The plan drafted by Spanish consultants hired by the IOC calls for a €61 million investment in sports facilities to be funded by donors. With Israel claiming sovereignty over all of Jerusalem, the plan focuses on the West Bank minus East Jerusalem, which lags with a mere thirty-three sporting facilities behind predominantly Jewish West Jerusalem with its 531 venues.

The plan and the Palestinian Authority's emphasis on sports and the presentation of its ten-year plan[60] could not have come at a politically more convenient time for the Palestinian Authority. To be sure, the plan had been long in the making and Palestine has come a long way since Palestinians became the first nation without a state to be admitted to FIFA in 1998. In 2011 Palestine played its first World Cup and Olympic qualifiers on Palestinian soil. Its national women's soccer team is breaking taboos in a traditionally conservative society.

Nonetheless, Abbas' Palestinian Authority has been politically weakened by its inability to force Israel to make the concessions the Palestinians need to achieve peace and by Israel's boost of Hamas with the swap in October 2011 of Israeli Staff Sergeant Gilad Shalit for more than 1,000 Palestinians incarcerated by Israel. In emphasizing sports and identifying with it, the Authority was following in the footsteps of other Middle Eastern leaders who saw soccer, the region's most popular sport, as a tool to polish their tarnished images and distract attention from discontent with government policies. But in contrast to those leaders, they were promoting sports on a far more popular and transparent level and in ways that benefit the public and encourage social development.

"We want this [plan] to be seen as an integrated part of our national development plan, an indispensable component," Palestinian Prime Minister Salam Fayyad told diplomats, describing the sports initiative as "a hopeful enterprise." He said, recalling his recent attendance at a soccer match, that sports provides "a sense of joy, happiness of the people with just being there."[61]

The development plan was designed to project Palestine internationally as a nation and a state, strengthen nation-building and and focus attention on the debilitating effects of Israeli travel restrictions on Palestinian athletes. "For me, sport is a tool to realize the Palestinian people's national aspirations by exposing our cause through sports. I think that the ethics of sports and football is a rational and humanitarian way to convince the international community that we deserve freedom and independence," said Rajoub, who doubles as head of the Palestine Olympic Committee.[62]

Israeli restrictions disrupt the PFA's efforts to build a coherent national team and hamper Rajoub's efforts to create a national league. He has met his Israeli Olympic Committee and soccer association counterparts on several occasion to discuss cooperation in easing the restrictions on athletes as well as the movement of sports materials. They established a hotline to facilitate the movement of athletes stuck at Israeli checkpoints on the West Bank. They also looked at ways of enabling travel between the West Bank and the Hamas-controlled Gaza Strip.

Despite goodwill, the effort produced limited results. Palestinians hoped that the processing in August 2011 of a shipment from FIFA through Tel Aviv's Ben Gurion Airport in less than a week constituted a change in Israeli attitudes. Until then shipments were held up for up to six months, incurring storage and other costs for the Palestinians that exceeded the value of the goods shipped. Four years later, the track record is mixed. There have been only limited improvement in athletes' ability to move around the West Bank or between the Palestinian Authority-controlled region and the Gaza Strip, home to players who constitute the team's core. "The problem is the Israeli committee is not the relevant authority for the movement of people and equipment. We are trying, but I don't want to embarrass anyone," Rajoub explained.

The failure of the Israeli-Palestinian mechanism initially prompted FIFA to establish a committee to mediate between Israelis and Palestinians in an effort to ease the effect of the Israeli occupation. Palestinian soccer officials and players say that meanwhile crossing Israeli checkpoints has become easier. They attribute the relaxation primarily to improved security, with Israel less concerned about the threat of terrorist attacks being launched from the West Bank. In addition, the PFA has created sleeping quarters in the Faisal al Husseini Stadium so that players can get together to train without worrying whether they will be able to return home.

However, frustration with the inability of the Israeli Football Association's inability to influence security authorities and FIFA's failure to find a solution drove the PFA to table a resolution at the world soccer body's congress in Zurich in May 2015 calling for Israel's suspension for alleged obstruction of Palestinian soccer, racism, and support of Israeli policy in the West Bank. Pressure persuaded Rajoub to drop the demand for Israel's suspension in return for the establishment of a committee of the FIFA congress. Rajoub's backtracking was met with widespread Palestinian criticism. The tabling of the resolution and the backroom negotiations constituted a test run for the Palestinian Authorities' strategy to isolate Israel in international organizations in a bid to force to seriously negotiate an end to the Israeli-Palestinian conflict. Palestine joined the International Criminal Court weeks before the FIFA congress.

Palestine's efforts to build a competitive soccer sector that can project their nation on the global map is complicated by the fact that at times the line between players and activists is blurred. The promising national team career of Mahmoud al-Sarsak was cut short when he was detained in 2009 at an Israeli military checkpoint and held indefinitely as an unlawful combatant without ever being charged. Sarsak hails from a family of soccer players. He says he was the last person to cross the border between Gaza and Egypt on the day of his arrest before it was closed after several Egyptian soldiers had been kidnapped. Israeli authorities variously alleged that he was a member of Islamic Jihad, a militant Palestinian group in Gaza from where he hails, and had been involved in violent acts against the Jewish state. Sarsak denied the charges. He was released in 2012 on the ninety-second day of a hunger strike under pressure from FIFA and European soccer body UEFA. The hunger strike was his last resort.

> When I was growing up I looked up to Palestinian players. We didn't have TV so we didn't know anything of any international players. We looked up to them because they were so confident and happy. They made people smile. They brought spirit and life into the destructive places we were living in. That's what I wanted to do. Put smiles onto people's faces in such a hard place to live. But the Israeli killed my dream. I had a choice: hold my head high or allow them to bury me.

Playing soccer also enabled Sarsak to support his family in over-crowded Gaza, an economically crippled region as the result of an Israeli blockade. Similarly, Mohammed Nimr was forced to quit the national team after he spent eighteen months in an Israeli prison between 2007 and 2009. Nimr was again detained in 2012 together with Omar Abu Roweis, a goalkeeper in the Palestinian Olympic team, on charges of having been involved in a shoot-out with Israeli troops.

The perceived easing at the West Bank checkpoints has done little for thirteen of the twenty-five members of the Palestinian national soccer team who hail from Gaza, widely viewed as the squad's core. Goalkeeper Assem Abu Assi thinks of his wife and son in Gaza whenever the Palestinian flag is raised at an international match. Abu Assi has not seen them in four years because of Israel's refusal to grant him a travel permit. Midfielders Maali Kawari and Ismail Al Amur, too, have not been allowed to return for visits to Gaza. "My dream is to just play football with my family watching in the stadium. It has never happened. Happiness is never complete. I'm always only half happy," admitted Abu Assi.[63]

* * *

The flip side of soccer's importance as an assertion of identity is that in some cases, like Egypt, it also serves to reinforce sectarian faultlines as part of the regime's divide-and-rule approach. Hany Ramzy returned to Egypt from the 2012 London Olympics a soccer hero and a model. A Coptic Christian and one-time legendary national soccer team captain in a squad whose former national coach Hassan Shehata established Muslim piety as a criterion for membership equal to skill, Ramzy symbolized what is possible as well as the immense problems Middle Eastern and North African nations have in coming to grips with their ethnic and religious minorities.

Ramzy led his team to the quarterfinals in London against the backdrop of a popular revolt and more than a year of subsequent political volatility and violence. In one incident in October 2011, twenty-eight people, mostly Copts, were killed and 212 injured when security forces and the military attacked demonstrators protesting against the demolition of a church in Upper Egypt.[64] "Egypt's participation in the Olympics could not be more symbolic of the role sports plays as a means to regain national pride and social unity," remarked the journalist Mustafa Abdelhalim in an analysis published by Common Ground[65] that was as much about hope as it was about reality. Abdelhalim argued that "in June 2012 London's Wembley Stadium was the site of a 'faith and football' day that united students from Muslim, Christian and Jewish schools. This event was planned by the Three Faiths Forum (3FF), a UK-based organization dedicated to building relationships between people of all faiths, and the English Football Association, which officially oversees the sport in the country. Egyptians could replicate this example by creating nationwide leagues to promote intergroup and interfaith cooperation. These teams could include anyone who wants to participate in the sport and make Egyptians' shared interest in sports a tool for a more inclusive society."

The crediting of Ramzy with Egypt's winning of the 1998 Africa Cup of Nations championship was indeed as significant as Kurds playing in Iraqi squads, Palestinians in Israel's national team, Berbers in Algerian formations and Azeris in Iranian line-ups. Egypt's national team has, moreover, abandoned its religious discrimination against Copts under its former coach, American Bob Bradley. But getting from formally reversing discrimination to integration is a bumpy road. Ramzy, one of the few if not the only Coptic Egyptian national team players in past decades, is the exception that proves the rule in a country in which the Coptic Church sponsors its own soccer matches. Ramzy owes his success to a significant extent to the fact that he earned prestige by being hired by various European teams, including Neuchâtel Xamax, Werder Bremen and Kaiserslautern. Writing on his website, Copts United, Safwat Freeze Ghali[66] said that "in Egypt, there is a problem that many people don't even consider. This problem relates to not allowing the Copts to play in the national teams of sports, especially soccer which is the most popular game in Egypt. Marginalization of young Copts by the Football Association and the administrations of Egyptian clubs resulted in having no Coptic players in the core teams. Youth teams have very few Copts and they are laid off as soon as they reach certain age and never take the chance to promote."

Arguing that soccer discrimination against Copts encourages discrimination by Muslims and anger and hate among Copts, who account for some 10 per cent of all Egyptians, Ghali spoke out of personal experience. "I suffered from this problem with my son who was born in 1995 and has a great talent in soccer. Many people have said so after they saw him playing. My son then started in a small club, but never took a chance to play. His coach treats him so badly and his colleagues make fun of his Christian name. His coach told him: I won't let you touch the ball (play in the team) and never ask me why! We got fed up and I took him to a bigger club and they liked him very much and promised to recruit him but they never did. Then, I moved him to another club where they liked him too, but when the coach knew his name [a Christian name], he said: We'll see, later!"[67]

Sectarianism Trumps Soccer

"The dark shadow we seem to see in the distance is not really a mountain ahead, but the shadow of the mountain behind—a shadow from the past thrown forward into our future. It is a dark sludge of historical sectarianism."

David Trimble, former First Minister of Northern Ireland

Rival, pot-bellied, physically out-of-shape Lebanese political and militia leaders donned T-shirts and shorts to commemorate the thirty-fifth anniversary of their fifteen-year-long civil war by playing a soccer match. The game's motto, "We are one team," was heavily laced with symbolism and irony. It pitted two squads against one another that had been assembled on the basis of political allegiance and whose members had been for years at each other's jugular. The players were the men responsible for Lebanon's sectarian and ethnic bloodshed, corruption and economic mismanagement. They played as Lebanon once again teetered on the brink of civil strife with a United Nations tribunal pointing fingers at Shiite militia Hezbollah's role in the murder five years earlier of Prime Minister Rafik Hariri. The irony was further underscored by the fact that the match was played in an empty stadium from which spectators had been barred for security reasons.

Rafik Hariri's son, Saad, Lebanon's Western-backed prime minister at the time of the match, led his team to victory over Hezbollah member of parliament Ali Ammar's squad. Sami Gemayal, a divisive figure and sworn enemy of the Shiite militia, scored the two winning goals. Gemayal attributed his team's victory to the Hezbollah squad's weak defensive strategy, a reference to the group's insistence on maintaining a militia to confront Israel. For Hezbollah, scoring political points on the pitch was more important than goals. The match put Hezbollah on a par with Hariri's March 14 movement. Captain Ammar suggested his team had allowed its opponent to win to spare the government embarrassment.

The fleeting sense of unity on the pitch had born little resemblance to Lebanon's harsh political reality. The politicians had included the

Lebanese soccer association in their sectarian carve-up of the country. Clubs were turned into extensions of religious sects. Sectarian antagonism regularly exploded into violence on the pitch. Fans were banned for five years from the terraces after Rafik Hariri, a billionaire businessmen, was killed in a massive car bombing in Beirut.

"Politics entered football and destroyed it," said Lebanese Football Association secretary general Rahif Alameh. It all started, he believed, in 2001 when the government intervened in a murky match-fixing scandal[68] which allowed Lebanon's sectarian leaders to restructure the association in line with their arrangements for the sharing of power between the different Muslim and Christian communities. In doing so, they reinforced the fact that Lebanon's national identity had always been overshadowed by that of its eighteen different sects. The carve-up that fed on continued sectarian tension even after the civil war ended in 1990 made it impossible to use sports, as South Africa had done, to heal wounds or nurture new shared values.

The tension increasingly defined rivalries between clubs dependent on patronage in a country of four million in which ticket receipts and broadcast rights do not account for much. As a result, sports serves to reinforce rather than bridge sectarian divisions. Lebanese increasingly identified clubs as Maronite Christian, Sunni, Shiite, Druze or Armenian and associated them with various political factions even if teams were often religiously mixed. Hariri's assassination in 2005 sparked Lebanon's anti-Syrian Cedar Revolution, forcing Syria to withdraw its forces that had effectively occupied the country for three decades. Lebanese retreated into their sectarian identities in the wake of the assassination. The UN investigation into Hariri's death threatened to deepen the cleavages and again tear Lebanon apart.

Hariri's father sponsored several sports clubs. He bought Nejmeh soccer club, Lebanon's most popular team founded in 1945 as the country's first non-Christian club, which was largely cross-sectarian but had always attracted Shiite support. Hariri initially saw his investments as moneymaking ventures, but later turned them into vehicles for consolidating Sunni Muslim and some Shiite support at political rallies, which he backed up with the awarding of jobs and favours. Similarly, Lebanon's other top league clubs mirror the country's sectarian fracturing. Tripoli SC and Al Ansar are Sunni clubs funded by a prominent Sunni businessmen; Al Ahad is financed by Hezbollah and plays with shirts bearing the symbol of the movement's Al Manar TV station; Chabab el Sahel and Al Mabarra are also Shiite; Homenetmen is part of an Armenian sports movement, while Sagresse and Salam Zgarta are tied to the Maronites. "The politicians have removed the thin veneer that separated soccer from politics. I was all my life a Nejmeh fan, but that's no longer an option because Nejmeh is owned by Hariri," said a Shiite soccer enthusiast as he looked down at the carnage.[69]

"Football was one of the few things that could have helped create a national identity that could compete with sectarian ones," remarked the Lebanese soccer player and academic Karim Makdissi.

That is a lesson that neighbouring Syria, a major behind-the-scenes player in Lebanon that continues to keep the country balancing on the edge of a cliff, understood in the years preceding the 2011 popular uprising against the regime of President Bashar al-Assad. Ironically, pre-revolt Syria was, like Somalia, a rare example of Middle Eastern soccer resisting political interference. Syrian soccer reduced the all-powerful military's grip on the game by professionalizing the sport. The Syrian Football Association (SFA) banned the country's two most decorated teams owned and managed by the military and the police from relying exclusively for recruitment on conscription or exercising their prerogative to snatch players from other clubs. Professionalization forced them to start competing for players on the market. The association's move constituted a brave and rare stand in a country that does not brook dissent. It did wonders for pre-civil war Syrian soccer and made it an example for other leagues in the region.

The military's grip on sports and soccer had been evident. The country's corrupt and match-fixing sports associations and judicial arbiters were run by senior military commanders who neglected Bashar al-Assad's efforts to clean up the game by mandating the judiciary to handle legal disputes. Reformers within the Syrian Football Association were threatened with death and the kidnapping of their children. The management of the country's foremost soccer club, Al Jaish [The Army], maintained the military's chain of command. A general managed the club; a colonel was its technical director. Syria's most crowned club, it won ten titles and countless cups triumphs. It benefitted from the military's dominant role in politics and the economy. The military's prevalence was evident in soldiers patrolling the streets of the capital Damascus even before the uprising. Many in the city made their living from serving the military.

National service was crucial to Al Jaish's success. The moment a talented young player came of age, the army conscripted him to play for Al Jaish. When the league was still amateur, there was no compensation. By sucking up the league's talent they won honours and attracted huge crowds. Al Jaish flew the Syrian flag at home and abroad. Failure to support it was akin to treason. Other clubs grumbled in silence. Professionalization hit Al Jaish hard and deprived it of its unfair advantage. "Al Jaish effectively was the national team. They commanded all the good players. That is what the SFA changed. Now of course, the uprising has destroyed all of that," said a member of the board of the SFA.[70]

All that is history, initially as result of professionalization and since because of the civil war. Pre-war private investment in clubs dramatically changed the map of Syrian soccer as clubs trained and played in improved facilities and players and managers earned more. The SFA's promotion of young players produced promising results. The association identified and developed talent throughout the ranks by beefing up its scouting and training capability and encouraging league teams to field younger players. Syria's Under-17 and Under-20 teams were making their mark in international competitions. Many of their players were spearheading Syria's attempt to qualify for the next World Cup. The efforts offered clubs a more level playing field that Al Karamah SC of Homs, Syria's third largest city, fully exploited. It became the first Syrian club to compete in the Asian Champions League finals and the first team to simultaneously win the Syrian league and cup.

The revolt against Bashar al-Assad—the most protracted and bloodiest in the Middle East and North Africa to date—reversed those advances and returned Syrian soccer to its darkest days. Soccer, never distant from Middle Eastern politics, weaves its own thread through the brutal battle for the future of Syria.

Four months into the revolt, Abdelbasset Saroot, the then 17-year-old curly-haired goalkeeper of the youth teams of both Al Karamah and Syria and singer of revolutionary folk songs, announced in a grainy YouTube video that he was "now wanted by security forces which are trying to arrest me." In the low budget video shot in bare surroundings resembling those issued by suicide bombers in Iraq and Afghanistan, Saroot assured his viewers that he had no intention of ending his life. "I declare with sound mind and of my own volition, that we, the free people of Syria, will not give in until our one and only demand is met: the

185

regime must go," he asserted, denying government claims that he had turned jihadist.

Three attempts on his life later he held up for television cameras empty shells, which he claimed were the "Iranian heavy weapons" with which the regime had attacked protesters. Twelve people died in the attempts on his life, including his brother and some of his closest friends. Their bodies were dumped on a street and crushed by tanks. He has denounced Syrian exile opposition leaders for leading a life of luxury in five-star hotels and obstructing efforts to persuade the international community to intervene. Saroot issued one of his statements lying on a cot covered by a blanket as he recovered from injuries he allegedly suffered in one of the assassination attempts.

"There is something I want to tell everyone. I lost one of my brothers but this is something I shouldn't be saying because we've lost 13,000 people and a lot of people have been detained or have disappeared … They are all like my brothers … It's a big honor for everybody to say: 'We have a martyr in this family,'" Saroot told Al Jazeera.

In another video, Saroot addressed a packed square in Homs. He called on Syrian mothers to prepare their sons for martyrdom in confronting the Assad regime. "The clothes of the heroes are the shrouds of burial, the shrouds of the martyrs that every hero is searching for. I want to send a message to our mothers at home making *Du'a* [a Muslim religious invocation] for us: O mother, my shrouds are new, prepare a funeral procession for me for I have come to you as a martyr in my celebratory clothes, my new home is Jannah [paradise]," he chanted to applause by the crowd. "O mother, prepare a funeral for me and be happy on my behalf and forgive me, O mother. O mother, my shrouds are new, O mother to a martyr. O mother, collect your tears, make me happy by smiling. My testament isn't money or gold, my testament is that you are satisfied with me. Kiss my brother and sister goodbye … O mother, call my people and my children to walk the path of the martyrs."

Saroot prefaced his call with an invocation of Allah designed to appeal to both Muslims and Christians. Calling on the crowd to raise their hands, he said: "I bear witness that there is no God worth worshipping but Allah and I bear witness that Mohammed is His servant and messenger and I bear witness that Jesus was a messenger of Allah. There is no God but Allah." His words were repeated by the cheering crowd.

By referring to Jesus, Saroot sought to make his Muslim terminology more palatable to Syria's Christian minority, which, alongside other minorities, has remained on the sideline of the revolt. Many Christians fear that forcing Assad out of office would pave the way for an Islamic regime that would be less tolerant toward non-Muslims and those ortho-dox Muslims denounce as heretics—a fear the Assad regime has sought to cultivate.

Saroot might have led a somewhat less perilous life had he not joined the rebellion, but probably not a more glamorous one. The government in Damascus has gone to great lengths to use the game as evidence that it remains in control and is functioning normally. Indeed it seemed will-ing to go to any length. Syria's national soccer team flagrantly violated rules in its line-ups. In September 2011 FIFA barred Syria from compet-ing for the 2014 World Cup in Brazil after the national team fielded an ineligible player in a qualifying match against Tajikistan. Lebanon accused Syria two months later of fielding six players in an Under-19 Asian Football Championship qualifier whose ages had been falsified to qualify them for the team.

At the same time, the regime went out of its way to ensure that it would not be embarrassed by defections. It refused to send athletes to the 2011 Arab Games. Saroot was living proof of widespread discomfort and discontent among sportsmen and women. So was national soccer goalkeeper Mosab Balhous, who was long believed to have been killed after he was detained on charges of sheltering armed gangs and possess-ing suspicious amounts of money. Balhous mysteriously reappeared in mid-2012. Ahmed al Sheban, another soccer player, was killed in Homs in unclear circumstances.

Individuals like Saroot stand out in a region in revolt, in which soccer players feted by autocratic leaders and managers appointed by their regimes remained largely on the sidelines of mass anti-government pro-tests. He became part of a small group of players and officials who joined the popular uprisings. Libyan national team players waited four months after the eruption of protests against Qaddafi and joined only after relatives and friends of theirs were killed by pro-government forces. In Bahrain, players joined because as Shiite Muslims they resented dis-crimination by a Sunni majority regime. Elsewhere in Algeria, Egypt, Yemen, Morocco, Tunisia and Syria, players and managers remained largely aloof.

Saroot led the life of a fugitive after the attack on his home. He avoids daylight, travelling only at night. Constantly on the run, he never stops moving and stays at any one place at most a few days. He describes his role as "a big responsibility to lift people's morale. We always try to stay optimistic about the future. The more optimistic we are the more the revolution keeps going. It's worth it. I'm free. I've travelled all over the world to play football. But freedom is not just about me or about traveling. What about everyone else? Freedom is a big word. It's about freedom of speech and freedom of opinion. If you see something wrong being done, freedom is being able to talk about it," he observed in an Al Jazeera interview. He asserted that he knew personally that a majority of athletes slated to represent Syria in London were doing so to shield their family from the repercussions of defection. "They don't want to play for a flag that they have no pride or faith in."

In a column last year in the London-based Arabic daily *Al Quds al Arabi*, writer Elias Khoury described a documentary entitled *Al Waar* [Rocky Terrain] by an anonymous Syrian filmmaker; it portrayed Saroot as a leader of the protests in Homs and a composer of some of its slogans and songs. "His features are Bedouin; he is a thirsty person who is not satisfied with only freedom. It is he who composes for the nocturnal gatherings for a popular festival in the suburbs of Homs where the air bears bullets. The slogans are an appeal by a decapitated nation and the will of a people determined not to bow to anyone," Khoury wrote. The film quotes the chants of protesters crafted by Saroot:

> *Go is the cry of the brave,*
> *A cry of the city with Bedouins,*
> *A cry of all religions,*
> *The cry of Syria and the land it covers:*
> *Let them leave him and his dogs and the destruction they have wrought.*

To Khoury, Saroot is the protagonist whose voice challenges the Assad forces' weaponry. "Our weapon is our voice," Saroot says in his film. Throughout the film a picture of Bashar al-Assad superimposed on that of his father, Hafez al-Assad, constitutes the background with the words, "Assad or nothing," a play on the slogan that accompanied the portrait of Hafez during his rule: "Our leader in eternity and beyond."

If soccer symbolized the resilience of protest in the besieged and battered city of Homs,[71] it also went to the heart of the *shabiha*, the irregular, civilian-clad, armed groups blamed for many of the atrocities committed by forces loyal to the Assad regime. In an account of the history of the *shabiha*, whose designation derives from the Arabic word for ghost, Syrian scholar Mohammad Daghan[72] traces their origins to members of the Assad family as well as to young, impecunious Alawites in northern Syria who saw their escape from poverty and humiliation in smuggling banned luxury goods from Lebanon and involvement in soccer.

Witnesses as well as opposition and human rights groups hold the *shabiha* responsible for a host of early atrocities, including the killing of twenty-one peaceful protesters in Latakia in March 2011,[73] another twenty-one a month later in Homs[74] and scores of demonstrators in May 2011 in Banias, Jableh and Latakia.[75] The *shabiha* are further accused of conducting a scorched earth campaign in northwestern Syria, burning crops, ransacking houses, shooting protesters and raping women.[76] They are also believed to have committed the massacre in May of 2012 in Houla,[77] a region north of Homs in which 108 people, including forty-nine children, were killed and in June in Al Qubair[78] in which seventy-eight people, many of them women and children, died.

While the term *shabiha* has come to mean thugs rather than ghosts in Syria, the associated verb, *shabaha*, describes a goalkeeper, a *shabih*, jumping into the air or going airborne to stop an opponent's shot.[79] The *shabih* in Assad's Syria jumped and saved whether he was the goalkeeper or the smuggler who enabled his clients to jump in status with the goods he provided.

Fawwaz al-Assad, a cousin of Bashar, is widely viewed as the original *shabih*. He started his career as a fervent supporter of the city's Tishreen soccer team before becoming its president. He rose to control the lucrative port of Latakia and its adjacent smuggling route. Daghan recalls Fawwaz driving a demonstrative loop around the Al-Assad stadium in "his big Mercedes" before sitting on a chair to watch a match in a fenced off area reserved for players and coaches. "Always Fawwaz would have a few words with the referee before the game. In one very famous incident Fawwaz took his gun out and let out some shots. The game was between Hutteen and Tishreen and a forward scored an offside goal for Fawwaz's team Tishreen. The referee in that famous incident changed his mind after the gun shot to claim the goal in favor of Fawwaz's team. That made Fawwaz happier and he let out more shots. Fawwaz was a real bully and acted like one," Daghan wrote.

Fawwaz is largely credited with giving the word *shabih* the meaning of thug rather than ghost in Syria. The European Union put Fawwaz and his brother Munzir, who ranks with Fawwaz among the original *shabiha* but remained in the background, on its sanctions list for alleged involvement in "the repression against the civilian population as members of the shabiha."[80]

If Fawwaz inspired fear and disgust, Saroot represented inspiration and resilience. Lulu Shanku, a Syrian national team player, returned to his Swedish premier league team Syrianska disgusted with the corruption in Syrian soccer and the intimidation of players by the Assad regime.[81] In some ways, he may have jumped from the fire into the frying pan, illustrating the importance Arab autocrats attribute to soccer even when it is played beyond the Middle East and North Africa. Power within the Swedish team, made up of Assyrians who fled Syria, Lebanon and Turkey in the 1970s, appears to rest with Ghayath Moro, a pro-Assad former Syrianska board member, who now serves as its unelected head of security. Former club board members and officials asserted that Moro, a mechanic and failed gas station owner, allegedly had close ties to members of Soderatalje's criminal underground including Bülent Özcan Melke Aslanoglu, the fugitive brother of the club's coach Özcan Melkemichel.[82]

Aslanoglu disappeared after the killing, in a struggle for underground power, of the Lebanese-Assyrian Syrianska rival Assyriska goalkeeper Eddie Moussa, widely seen as an act of revenge for the criminal dealings of his brother, Danny.[83] "How much of Syrianska's rise was funded by crime money is the million dollar question," said Eric Niva, one of Sweden's top investigative sports reporters.[84]

Replying to a question posed to Shanku about the fate of Mosab Balhous, Moro claimed that "Mosab disappeared because of one of the gangsters against the regime." Using terminology employed by the regime, the Syrianska official denounced Syrian protesters and rebels as "gangsters" and accused the United States, Israel and Al-Qaeda of waging war against Assad. "It is clear that the people want Assad," Moro said. He asserted that Syrian forces had captured twelve French and some twenty-five Turkish generals who had been supporting the rebellion, but could produce no evidence or reporting to back up his claim.[85]

Supporters of Assad portrayed Syria's clinching of the West Asian soccer championship in late 2012 as a unifying, national achievement against all odds, similar to Iraq's winning of the Asian Cup in 2007 at the peak of that country's sectarian violence. The Syrian success, however, unlike the Iraqi victory, offered Syrians no hope of an end to the bloodshed and greater unity.

"I give this win and this worthy title to the Syrian people. I thank God that we succeeded in bringing happiness to the sad people," said the Syrian striker Omar Al Soma in a televised interview after the match. State-run television used the victory to deny that Damascus was suffering power cuts. "Even football has not escaped the bloodthirsty media, who tried to ruin the joy of our people after the victory by broadcasting false information about a general power cut in Damascus, and about clashes," the television channel remarked. Opponents of Assad asserted that the team's victory had nothing to do with politics. "It is thanks to the 11 players who played and won this victory for all the country. All the players are Syrian. Some are pro-regime, some are anti-regime, and some are neutral," said the satirical Facebook page Shu Ismu? [What is His Name?]

In contrast to Syria, Iraq secured its place in the 2007 Asian Cup final in a dramatic penalty shoot-out with South Korea. Cheering fans in Baghdad paid the price. A suicide bomber and celebratory gunfire killed fifty. The team met to discuss quitting. But after watching a television news report in which a mother emotionally begged the team to win the cup in honour of her son, who had been killed in the bombing, they believed they had only one choice.

Fate would produce a just result, they predicted, and indeed it did. Players felt they were playing for their nation, not a regime. In a soccer fairy tale, the team, dubbed Assood al-Rafidain or the Lions of Mesopotamia, a reference to a cave inscription dating back to a pre-Christian Assyrian ruler, emerged against Saudi Arabia as the winner of the cup. It was its second post-Saddam Hussein triumph after reaching the medal round in the 2004 summer Olympics and the first victory since legendary player Emmanuel Baba Dawud, better known as Ammo Baba [Uncle Father], led the country to secure the Gulf Cup three times in the late 1970s and 1980s. Dawud owed his success as much to his skill, highlighted by a spectacular bicycle kick, as to his refusal to engage with the politics of officials and club owners. He was one of the few who dared to stand up to Uday, Saddam's son, and lived to tell the tale. He was able to do on the back of his popularity that had earned him Saddam's protection. That allowed him to disregard Uday's insistence on determining the national team's line-up and ignore his threats. "I told him to go to hell. I said he knew nothing about football. How did I survive? Because the people loved me."[86]

The multi-ethnic and multi-sect character of the team gave its winning of the Asian Cup added significance. The decisive goal was scored by a

Sunni Muslim after taking a pass from a Kurdish team mate. The team's Shiite goalkeeper contributed his part by ensuring that his Saudi opponents remained goalless. Their teamwork constituted a rare ray of hope for Iraqis. It offered a glimpse of a life beyond conflict in a war-ravaged country devoid of prospects and inclusive institutions. It was a mirage of religious and ethnic harmony. For Iraq's Brazilian coach, Jorvan Vieira, achieving the impossible amounted to madness. "If my contract had been for six and not for two months, they would have had to take me to the hospital for crazy people," he said as he handed in his resignation.[87]

Nothing could have prepared Vieira, a 57-year-old multilingual, Arabic-speaking, Brazilian convert to Islam with a doctorate in sports science, and a twenty-year track record as a coach of clubs and national teams across the Middle East, for the problems he confronted in Iraq. Iraq's troubles in the wake of the US toppling of Saddam were dumped on his doorstep. Vieira had four weeks and a shoestring budget to whip his team into shape and get them to the Asian Cup finals in Southeast Asia. Meanwhile, Iraq teetered on the brink of civil war, jihadists and criminals targeted players and their families as well as fans for kidnapping and assassination; corruption was rampant and lack of funds had left the team deprived of basic needs. To the jihadists, the team that brought rival Sunnis, Shiites and Kurds together was the single remaining symbol of Iraqi national unity. "The players have problems in their lives; they are not normal footballers," Vieira recalled.[88]

Team members refused to set foot on Iraqi soil, training sessions were held in Jordan; the Iraqi soccer association had its de facto offices in an Amman hotel lobby where its controversial president, Hussein Saeed, a leftover of the Saddam era, was beyond the reach of Iraqi authorities who had issued a warrant for his arrest. The government, in a bid to wrest control of soccer from the association, had accused Saeed of having been an accessory to Uday's brutal tactics, a charge he dismissed out of hand. To government critics, the feud between the government and the soccer association was more of the same. Little had changed from the days of Saddam. His successors followed in his footsteps in believing that soccer was too popular and too important to be beyond their purview.

The association hit back at the government where it believed it would hurt most. Its assertion that it was too dangerous to operate out of Baghdad complicated the government's efforts to attract foreign investors despite the sectarian violence. So did the fact that Iraq's national team played its "home" games away, in front of a handful of fans in stadiums in Aleppo, Dubai or Doha. Its players turned out for clubs in Qatar and Saudi Arabia. Those that did go home travelled mostly to relatively safe Iraqi Kurdistan and often did not return for training or matches. "I lost two members of my family. It's difficult when you have no safety. Cars explode all the time. I had to pick up my two guns before going to prac- tise, because I'd been threatened. You can buy guns anywhere in Baghdad. You need them," said Hawar Mulla Mohammad, the team's Kurdish striker, who lost his stepmother four days before the Asian finals.[89] The team's physiotherapist was killed by a suicide bomber on the way to his travel agent to pick up his plane ticket.

Iraqis, separated by ethnic hatred and desperate for something to hold on to, united around their national team as it advanced in the Asian tournament. Kurds yearning for the independence of their autonomous Kurdish region replaced the Kurdish flag with the Iraqi one. The team captain and star centre forward Younis Mahmoud, alternatively nick- named The Butcher or the Desert Fox for his aggressive attack style and uncanny ability to be in the right place at the right time, embodied a new-found sense of national unity even though he refused for security reasons to return to Iraq for the victory celebrations. A Sunni Muslim from the disputed province of Kirkuk, where Arabs, Turkmens and Kurds continuously live on the brink of ethnic and sectarian conflict, Mahmoud, the youngest player ever to play for the Iraqi national team, symbolized a unified Iraq with a tattooed map of the country on his left arm. Scoring more goals than any other player in the Asian tournament, he restored what Saddam had destroyed and the US had failed to pro- vide: a vision of a peaceful future. That utopian vision briefly became reality as Iraqis celebrated the team's victory. Shiite education ministry employee Abdul-Rahman Abdul-Hassan reconnected during the street celebrations with Sunni friends and former soccer team mates he had not seen in two years because sectarian violence had forced them into differ- ent neighbourhoods. "None of our politicians could bring us under this flag like our national football team did. I wish that politicians could take a lesson from our team," said Abdul-Hassan.[90] Not even two car bombs that exploded as Iraqis celebrated dampened the brief moment of joy. Prime Minister Nouri al-Maliki, seeking to capitalize on the team's suc- cess, granted players diplomatic passports and US$10,000 in cash each.

The soccer team's symbolism of national unity did not survive for long even though the beautiful game was the one institution in which Kurds,

Sunnis and Shias focused on a common goal. Barely three months after winning the cup, Vieira's assistant coach and three of his players sought asylum in Australia. Most players were afraid of playing in Baghdad. They never knew when or where the next bomb would go off. Every single member of his squad had lost a friend or family member in the violence, Captain Noor Sabri recalled. A bomb blast as the team played a warm-up before the crucial 2014 World Cup qualifiers killed thirty people in a used car park adjacent to the Baghdad stadium.

As Iraq descended in 2013 yet again into a spiral of sectarian violence, authorities in the volatile province of Diyala, northeast of Baghdad, bulldozed soccer pitches after a series of deadly bombings during games killed or wounded dozens of spectators. The head of the local soccer federation, Salah Kamal, said that more than twenty pitches had been razed, causing the cancellation of several matches and angering youth who had few options for relaxation and leisure: "The solution should have been providing better security at the fields instead of punishing the youth."

Iraqis crowded into cafés to watch their team on huge television screens as Iraq played to qualify for the 2014 World Cup in Brazil. Security checks at the entrances to the coffee shops failed to shield them from the sectarian violence engulfing their country. Up to three cafés a day were being bombed. "It is troublesome. Visiting a café is becoming increasingly risky. I worry each time I go to watch a match. But that won't stop me from going. The team needs our support. We want to see them play in Brazil. That is one of the few things that offer a glimpse of hope that is real," said Mohammed, a Baghdad vendor, after watching Iraq defeat South Korea.

The failure of the Iraqi national team to offer Iraqis something that would allow them to move beyond the deadly cycle of sectarian violence for more than just a brief moment also symbolized the failure of the United States to harness the popularity of soccer in both Iraq and Afghanistan to build inter-communal relations and project itself as more than just an occupying force. US Maj. Gen. Mark Hertling, commander of the 1st Armored Division and Multi-National Division North, savoured the brief moment when Americans and Iraqis forgot their differences in 2008 on a dirt field in northern Iraq. The US Army's 87th Infantry's 1st battalion played the Sons Of Iraq made up of former insurgents in running shoes with goal nets made of thin blue mesh and with only several hundred fans willing to brave the 42°C heat. The Iraqi 9–0 thrashing of the Americans bore a message that US officials naively believed would resound far beyond the pitch: balls can be more powerful than bombs. "You lose a game, but you win a lot of friends," Hertling quipped enthusiastically months after members of the two teams had been trying to kill one another.[91] US soldiers with M-16s and Iraqi security and police forces with AK-47s and pistols patrolled the sidelines, just in case.

The game was intended as a confidence-builder in America's effort to win—if not hearts and minds of their former adversaries—at least a growing sense of solidarity. "This is the sort of thing you see as a turning point. For the mayor and chief of police of Multaka to take the risk to be here—this is history being made," enthused Hertling at halftime as he together with the mayor handed out soccer shirts, shorts and sweatshirts to dozens of Iraqi boys.

Soccer may seem an odd foreign policy tool or military priority. But with at least half the population of Iraq and Afghanistan under the age of eighteen, balls and shoes were to American nation builders as basic to mending the two countries' social fabric as beams and girders are to mending damaged buildings. Before US-led coalition troops entered Baghdad in 2003, Saddam Hussein's men went into neighbourhoods, handing out guns and storing weapons in schools. Because it was too dangerous to take away arms confiscated during and after the invasion of Iraq, American forces blew them up, damaging schools and surrounding homes in the process. Though the Army returned to clear away the debris, distribute balls and help set up teams and leagues in tense towns like Ramadi and Sadr City, unexploded shells remained in fields and playgrounds where children practise.

US Provisional Reconstruction Teams worked in partnership with Spirit of Soccer, a Johnstown, Pennsylvania, NGO which uses soccer to educate youth about the risk of mines in a country of 24 million with an estimated 42 million landmines or two landmines per person. Trained by Spirit of Soccer, Iraqi coaches, including fifteen women, went into neighbourhoods to discuss fair play, avoiding dangers from landmines and other unexploded munitions, sportsmanship, tolerance and the need for non-violent conflict resolution while dribbling and taking penalties. Their interlocutors returned to their communities as coaches and organizers of Youth Soccer and Mine Awareness Festivals.

US military and civilian officials believed that raising awareness about landmines through soccer, reopening soccer stadiums and encouraging people to play free of fear or persecution would win hearts and minds among those scarred by regimes for which soccer was either the enemy or a weapon of terror. To Iraqis, soccer stadiums were as much the focus of deep-seated passion as homes to mass graves discovered by US and Iraqi forces. The US also saw the pitches as important in its competition with Iran for the hearts and minds of ordinary Afghans.

The match in northern Iraq mirrored a game played shortly after the overthrow of the Taliban between the US-led international force and an Afghan team in Kabul's Ghazi Stadium. The match was intended to highlight the change the international force was bringing to the war-ravaged country. Grass had grown where the Taliban once staged public executions, but initially few Afghans dared visit the stadium in the evenings, believing that the souls of the victims still roamed the sprawling grounds. The goalposts, where the black-turbaned Taliban used to force convicts to kneel before executing them or from which they hung the severed arms or legs of thieves for all to see, were given a fresh coat of white paint. New portraits of Afghanistan's leaders, including the late King Zahir Shah, President Hamid Karzai, anti-Taliban hero Ahmad Shah Masood and the country's latest star, Olympic taekwondo bronze medalist Rohallah Nikpai, hung from the empty stands.

Soccer symbolized Afghanistan's choices coming full circle much as it did in Iraq as US forces withdrew a decade after they invaded it. A major Afghan telecommunications company, Roshan Telecom Development Co., and media tycoon Saad Mohsen's Moby Group launched an Afghan Premier League in what David Ignatius of *The Washington Post* juxtaposed as Afghanistan's post-withdrawal options: televised soccer rivalry or armed civil war.[92] The Afghanistan Football Federation (AFF) president Keramuddin Karim argued that "to establish peace and stabilize a country, one must not only focus on training soldiers. Sport is also a strong base for peace, as it embodies values such as unity, integration, pride and prevents racism, drugs and other elements that bring insecurity to the country."

In a letter announcing the league of eight teams, the AFF stated that it would cut "across all ages, socio-economic groups, regions and tribes." In fact, it will cut across regions and ethnic, tribal and religious groups that have in the past been at loggerheads with one another. Abdul Sabor Walizada, a trainer for the project and former national team players, said the AFF hoped that the league would also help stimulate business and build bridges. "After years of civil conflict and war, people will focus on football and the businessmen from each zone will try to have the best players. It will create national unity because if the central zone, for example, has a really good player, the southern zone team will want to buy him. They will not care about his ethnicity. They will not care about his tribe. They will care that he is one of the best players," said Walizada.

The launch of the Premier League came amid fears that the Afghan army would split along ethnic and sectarian lines following an American withdrawal, plunging the country into chaos with the Taliban stepping up its insurgency and various groups that fought each other in the past picking up arms again. Soccer failed in Iraq sustainably to bridge divides between communities. Iraq's 2007 Asian Cup triumph demonstrated that soccer is a tool capable of more than a momentary distraction only if employed in an environment that favours reconciliation. Afghanistan threatens to confirm that rule.

Controlling Soccer is Mastering Politics

"You can't be a real country unless you have a beer and an airline. It helps if you have some kind of a football team, or some nuclear weapons, but at the very least you need a beer."

Frank Zappa

Controlling Iranian soccer is mastering Iranian politics.

"Almost every institution within civil and political society attempts to impose its own agenda on football. The game has become a highly charged area where contending factions carry out a curious war by proxy, since it is not in their interest to declare open hostilities," says Iranian scholar Babak Fozooni.[93]

Soccer's popularity rivals that of religion. It forced the mullahs who swept to power in the 1979 Islamic revolution to drop their initial opposition to the game. Instead, the soccer pitch has become the battleground for rival factions within the regime, opposition to the regime and the struggle for political, ethnic and gender rights.

Iranian spiritual leader Ayatollah Ruhollah Khomeini set the tone when he used soccer in the late 1980s to curb the influence of more conservative clerical forces by catering to popular demands for more non-religious television programming. He did so by responding to written questions from then National Radio and Television head Mohammed Hashemi Rafsanjani, the younger brother of former Iranian parliament speaker and President Ali Akbar Rafsanjani. Rafsanjani asked Iran's spiritual leader to comment on viewers' complaints that broadcasts of soccer matches showed men playing with their body parts uncovered. Khomeini decreed that this was not an issue as long as viewers did not watch the matches with a lustful eye.[94] He also allowed, to the consternation of the conservatives, the airing of films in which women were not totally covered.

Khomeini's ruling opened the door to political tugs of war being fought on the pitch. Soccer has suffered the consequences. The list of its woes reads like the laundry list of complaints of opponents of the regime: the mullahs' ambivalent attitude towards anything Western; the post-revolution nationalization of clubs because of their close links to the shah's regime and the imperial military; Iran's international isolation and economic hardship as a result of its nuclear programme; its harsh gender segregation; eight years of leadership by Holocaust denier Mahmoud Ahmadinejad who frequently interfered to further his political interests; state ownership of all but two of Iran's top clubs; and the control of clubs by members of the Revolutionary Guards, the parallel military force established to protect the regime. As a result, Iran, a potential sporting powerhouse, has lacked effective management, performed poorly and become one of the world's most unattractive destinations for international players and trainers. Football Federation of the Islamic Republic of Iran (FFIRI) president Ali Kafashian complained in 2012 that payments to his group and Iranian referees by the Asian Football Confederation (AFC) had been held up by the exclusion of Iranian banks from the international financial system. "There is no basis whatsoever for the American Government to block our money. We are an NGO and have nothing to do with politics. We have approached the AFC and several other organizations to persuade the Americans to release our money, which we are desperate to have, to no avail," Kafashian said.

Politics on the soccer pitch pre-date Iran's Islamic revolution and influenced post-revolution attitudes towards the game. Clubs were the mullahs' first target. Taj [The Crown], the Shah's hated club founded by an army general, was high on their list. The club was renamed Esteghlal [Independence] Tehran FC. It was viewed with particular suspicion because it had spawned clubs across the country that served to build a popular base for the shah. They would celebrate birthdays of members of the ruling family. State-run television focused on Taj, and highlighted Crown Prince Reza Pahlavi's attendance at matches. To control it, the renamed club was put under the auspices of the state organization for physical education.

Taj's arch rival, Persepolis, a club with left-wing roots, was taken over by the industry ministry. It nonetheless became Iran's most popular team, rallying those opposed to the new regime's authoritarianism. Persepolis was renamed Piruzi [Victory], but Iranians continue to refer to it by its old name. The club cemented its opposition status a year after the revolution by endorsing presidential candidate Masud Rajavi, the leader of the Mujahedeen-e-Khalq, an opposition urban guerrilla movement that waged a deadly campaign against the new Islamic regime in its early days. The Mujahedeen later discredited themselves by forging an alliance with Iraq during the Iran-Iraq war and developing a religious sect-like personality cult.

The mullahs' hesitancy towards soccer was apparent in a pamphlet published a year after the revolution by the Islamic republic's propaganda arm. It argued that monies spent on soccer would be better invested in social and economic development:

> Would it not have been better if instead of spending a lot of money on this sort of entertainment, it were spent on sending some of our nation's young people abroad to acquire skills that our country needs? Would it not have been better if instead of spending this innocent and oppressed nation's blood on such useless pursuits, clinics were built and villages electrified? Would it not have been better if instead of clowning around like the British and Americans in order to 'shine' in international arenas, [the players] shone in the company of the brothers of the Construction Jihad in our villages, where the simplest amenities are lacking? Have all our political, economic and cultural problems been solved that we have turned to sport?[95]

The leaflet appeared as Iran was cracking down on opposition to the war with Iraq, sparked by an Iraqi invasion on the very day that Iran's national team was in Kuwait for an Asian Cup match. The war provided the regime with additional ammunition for its campaign against soccer. The mullahs saw the game as a conduit for decadent Western culture, which Iranian youth imitated. Iranians, however, were unwilling to abandon their beloved football. They set up local competitions in poorer neighbourhoods, the regime's popular power base as it afforded a rare opportunity to relax and be entertained in a country that banned most amusement, rather than an expression of discontent. State media, however, denounced the sport as counter-revolutionary. Senior officials, including then prime minister Mir-Hossein Mousavi, who decades later emerged as a reformer, sought to distract attention from soccer and other spectator sports by promoting participatory sports. Government-sponsored research argued after a soccer riot in 1984 demonstrated the pitch's potential as a safety-valve for discontent that soccer hindered advancement in developing countries and constituted a colonialist plot. The research decried the failure of government efforts to persuade spectators to chant Islamic rather than soccer-related slogans at matches.

Clerical opposition to soccer was motivated in no small part by the game's close association with the military, whom the clerics so distrusted that they created their own military force, the Revolutionary Guards or Pasdaran. The close ties to the military were symbolized by Mohammed Amir Khatami (not to be confused with cleric and later President of Iran, Mohammed Khatami), the national team's captain in the mid-1970s who became a four-star general, commander of the Air Force and the Shah's brother-in-law. Clerical fear of uncontrolled public spaces such as soccer grounds was reinforced by the Mujahedeen-e-Khalq's deadly post-revolution bombing campaign that killed leaders, including several presidents and prime ministers. Control of clubs and pitches became a sine qua non. A key venue, Tehran University's soccer pitch, was converted into grounds for Friday prayers where leaders of the revolution held forth. The clerics' subsequent efforts to cancel leagues and matches, however, served only to spark protests that united arch foes like the rival supporters of Tehran's two foremost clubs, Persepolis and Esteghlal.

Soccer's challenge to Islamist morals such as gender segregation and dress codes resurfaced in the 1990s when celebrations of a victory in an Iranian World Cup qualifier against Australia exploded into mass demonstrations with men and women mixing freely and holding hands. The crowds celebrated both their team's success and the electoral triumph of reformist presidential candidate Mohammed Khatami. As mentioned earlier in this book, women stormed Tehran's Azadi Stadium in protest against their banning from attendance of soccer matches. They publicly discarded their black headscarves, drank alcohol and danced. Celebrations turned into a demonstrative rejection of Iran's strict restrictions on mixing of genders, women's public appearance and the consumption of alcohol. Ali Afshar Jowa, a political analyst and occasional soccer commentator, recalled that "people in Iran partied for three days with the usually brutal government unable to suppress. It revitalized my hopes that Iran could improve. The celebrations connected Iranians, we came together irrespective of our religious, or political convictions. For the first time in twenty years Iranians became a wholehearted community again, and soccer was the uniting tool. I forever cherish that day."[96]

The demonstrations confirmed soccer as a catalyst for potential change. So did a campaign for women's rights to attend sporting events by women tired of dressing up as men to be able to enter a stadium. "Never has a masculine sport like soccer been celebrated with such a feminine defiance," said Shahin Gerami.[97] The street celebrations defeated regime attempts to monopolize the public outbursts by organizing a men-only welcoming ceremony for the national team in Azadi Stadium. "There is no legal basis for women to be banned from soccer stadiums. In Iran, you take one step forward, two steps back," commented the Iranian women's rights activist Asieh Amini.

Protests erupted again three years later as Iran seemed on its way to the 2002 World Cup finals. Across the country, protesters threw stones, shouted "Death to the Mullahs" and demanded the return of the toppled monarchy. The scenes were repeated in 2006 when the Islamic Republic finally made it into the final leg of the tournament. Like in 1998, women celebrated soccer victories in 2002 and 2006 by discarding their veils and mixing with the opposite sex. When Iran's chances to play in the 2002 finals were dashed by losing a crucial qualifier to Bahrain, rumours abounded that the match had been fixed to ensure a defeat so that people would not take to the street. Journalist Nicole Byrne, who attended a match against Ireland in Tehran's Azadi Stadium days after Iran's defeat, reported that "under an enormous mural of the late Ayatollah Khomeini, Iranians ripped out and set fire to seats, tore down banners depicting images of the country's senior mullahs and trashed the windscreens of several hundred cars outside."[98]

The terraces during the 1998 match against the US in the French city of Lyon were a battlefield for proponents and detractors of the Islamic regime. With France home to the Mujahedeen-e-Khalq, the terraces were populated by the group's supporters. Their T-shirts bearing the image of their leader, Maryam Rajavi, the widow of the 1980 presidential candidate, were visible to the world's television cameras. The absence of slogans such as "Death to America" and "Death to Israel" during the match and the subsequent celebrations-turned-demonstrations in Iran positioned Iran's relationship with the great Satan as one of love and hate rather than purely hate. Yet optimism that Iran would change and allow global culture to intrude was shortlived. President Khatami's inability to capitalize on the public mood, improve Iran's standing in the international community and enact change at home dashed hopes for a brighter future.

There was worse to come under Khatami's hardline successor, Mahmoud Ahmadinejad, who drove Iran further into global isolation. Soccer was not immune to the wrecking ball of the new president, who had little empathy for FIFA and its feeble attempts to separate sports and politics. "We will respect FIFA regulations, but FIFA is just an agency and should not be allowed to interfere in the internal affairs of Iran," he quipped after the organization ordered him to allow the Iranian soccer body to hold free and fair elections. Nineteen of the twenty candidates dropped out by the time the elections approved by FIFA were held. Ahmadinejad's candidate, Ali Kafashian, the secretary general of Iran's Olympic Committee, won. Acting on Ahmadinejad's instructions, Kafashian's first decision as Iranian Football Federation president was to dismiss the national team's foreign coach. Iran's European-based stars were curtailed too. Differences between players and the game's political managers exploded in 2009 when several players wore green armbands during a World Cup qualifier in solidarity with the opposition Green Revolution movement. Their sentiment was echoed on the terraces where supporters unfurled banners reading "Free Iran." The players were forced to take the armbands off during the second half of the game and were later penalized. The regime used the Revolutionary Guards and the Basij militia to crack down on the Green Revolution, mass protests against the 2009 elections that many Iranians felt had fraudulently returned Ahmadinejad to a second term in office at the expense of reformist candidates Mousavi and Mehdi Karrubi.

Kafashian failed, however, to deliver what Ahmadinejad needed most: a stellar performance that the president could exploit to improve his increasingly tarnished image. Even worse, soccer grounds were more frequently turning into protest venues on Kafashian's watch. As a result, relations between Ahmadinejad and Kafashian deteriorated. Ahmadinejad went to court when his blatant efforts to nullify Kafashian's re-election failed. Kafashian had narrowly defeated his opponents, a candidate backed by the president and another supported by the Revolutionary Guards. Ahmadinejad's attorney general unsuccessfully argued that Kafashian was banned from holding public office because he was a retired public employee. The court's ruling was part of a double blow to the president. It coincided with a humiliating summons by parliament to defend his track record. It was the first time that the assembly subjected a president to public scrutiny. Yet these setbacks did not thwart

Ahmadinejad from micromanaging Iranian soccer. "Unfortunately, this sport has been afflicted with some very bad issues. I must intervene personally to push aside these destructive issues," he said in defence of his meddling in the soccer federation's affairs.

A 2009 cable from the American "Iran Regional Presence Office" in Dubai disclosed by WikiLeaks[99] described how Ahmadinejad sought with limited success to associate himself with Iran's national team in a bid to curry popular favour. "President Ahmadinejad has worked hard to associate himself with Iran's beloved national team—'Team Melli'—a tactic that backfired in March when he was accused of 'jinxing' the team, which suffered a last-minute defeat to Saudi Arabia just after Ahmadinejad entered the stadium. That event, coupled with an unexpected loss by the national wrestling team with Ahmadinejad in attendance earlier in the year, set off a firestorm of SMS messages and internet jokes holding the President personally responsible for the teams' defeats," read the cable. Similarly, the president's attempt three years earlier to lift the ban on women attending soccer matches in stadiums was defeated in one of his first public disagreements with Supreme Leader Ali Khamenei.

To make matters worse, the commemoration in May 2011 of a famous Iranian soccer player in the Azadi stadium turned into a mass protest against the government of Ahmadinejad.[100] Tens of thousands attended the ceremony for Nasser Hejazi, an internationally acclaimed defender and outspoken critic of the president. In a rare occurrence, some 1,000 women were allowed to attend the ceremony. Mourners chanted "Hejazi, you spoke in the name of the people" in a reference to Hejazi's criticism of the Iranian president's economic policies. Hejazi had taken Ahmadinejad to task for Iran's gaping income differences and budgetary measures which hit the poorest the hardest. The mourners shouted "Goodbye Hejazi, today the brave are mourning" and "Mr Nasser, rise up, your people can't stand it anymore." The anti-government chants prompted authorities to bury Hejazi's body as quickly as possible. Security forces rushed his body from the stadium to Tehran's famous Behsht Zahra cemetery with tens of thousands of mourners following it to its burial place. Mourners in the cemetery shouted "Mubarak, Ben Ali, now it's your turn Khamenei!" putting Khamenei on par with ousted Egyptian and Tunisian presidents, Hosni Mubarak and Zine El Abidine Ben Ali.

Soccer had gained too much of a hold on Iran by the time of Hejazi's death for the government to revert to its opposition to the game in the early days of the revolution. In February 2011, weeks after the toppling of the presidents of Tunisia and Egypt, the FFIRI nevertheless postponed league matches in Tehran in a bid to prevent celebrations of the 32nd anniversary of the Islamic revolution from turning into anti-government protests.

The authorities succeeded in February but failed several months later when environmental and nationalist protests erupted in the stadium of Tabriz, the capital of the predominantly Azeri province of East Azerbaijan and home to Traktor Sazi FC, a flashpoint of Iranian Azerbaijan's identity politics. The club is owned by the state-run Iran Tractor Manufacturing Co. (ITMCO), which in turn is part of the economic empire of Iran's Revolutionary Guards and the Basij, a militia that provided Iran's cannon fodder during the war against Iraq in the 1980s. The protest was particularly sensitive because Azeris are the largest and only Iranian minority that primarily speaks its own language, Azeri Turkish, rather than Persian. Azeris account for an estimated one-quarter of Iran's population, have traditionally been critical of the Islamic republic, and occupy the most industrialized part of the country outside the area around the capital Tehran, which also forms Iran's increasingly tenuous transportation link to Europe.

A prominent Azeri ayatollah, Shariatmadari, emerged early in the revolution as one of the most prominent opponents of Ayatollah Khomeini with his rejection of theocratic rule and call for greater cultural freedoms. Shariatmadari, a soft-spoken man with a friendly smile as opposed to Khomeini's scowl, was ultimately defrocked and forced into internal exile. The protests echoed Azeri boycotts of post-revolution referendums on the establishment of the Islamic Republic of Iran, the institution of the *vilayat-e-faqih* or religious guardianship of the Islamic jurists that solidified the predominant role of the clergy and the first post-revolution presidential and parliamentary elections. Azeris nonetheless occupied prominent positions in revolutionary Iran's political, military and economic power structure. They included the Islamic republic's first prime minister Mehdi Bazargan as well as subsequent prime ministers Mahmud Jam, Ali Soheili, Ebrahim Hakimi and Mir-Hossein Mousavi, who later became a symbol of the opposition; former Revolutionary Guard Corps head Yahya Safavi; and the former president of the Atomic Energy Organization of Iran, Gholam Reza Aghazadeh. The environmental protests were of particular concern because Azeris, unlike other minorities such as the Kurds, had positioned their past protests as contributing to the democratic development of the Islamic republic rather than as efforts to achieve independence.

This time, however, the protests took on a secessionist nature that implicitly questioned acceptance of a Persian-led republic. "As the economy slips, the government becomes more and more worried about separatism. As a result, East Azerbaijan has become increasingly militarized. At times, the entire stadium in Tabriz chants Turkish songs as a protest," said a Baku-based analyst. "Traktor Sazi has taken on the symbolism of embodying the national identity of Azerbaijanis in Iran. They regard the team's victories as a means of peacefully defeating the enemies of Azerbaijan, and this has become a powerful rallying tool of ethno-nationalism in the region," added Farzin Farzad, executive director of the Network of Azerbaijani-Americans from Iran.

Scores were arrested in August 2011 when fans demanded during a match against local rival Shahrdari Tabriz FC that the government take measures to prevent Lake Orumiyeh from drying up. The fans were angry with parliament for voting against the allocation of funds to channel water from the River Araz to raise the level of the salt lake that lies between the provinces of East and West Azerbaijan near the border with Turkey. Parliament suggested instead that Azeris living near the lake be relocated. Thousands of fans chanted "Lake Orumiyeh is dying, the Majlis orders its execution." The Azeri human rights activist Vahid Qaradagli claimerd that the arrests were designed to prevent further protests. He warned that failure to rescue the lake would expose some ten million tons of salt at great risk to the environment and to public health.

The arrests and government failure to address Azeri concerns fuelled more radical demands during a match a month later against Esteghlal. Fans demanded Eastern Azerbaijan's secession from Iran and unification with the post-Soviet republic of Azerbaijan. In an abortive attempt to prevent protests, security forces barred many Traktor Sazi fans from entering the stadium to watch the match against Esteghlal, which the Azeri team won 3–2. Fans were body searched and then had their tickets confiscated. In response, thousands started shouting "Azerbaijan is united" and "Long live united Azerbaijan with its capital in Tabriz." Scores were injured as security forces tried to break up the protest with force. The protests, boosted by the Traktor Sazi defeat of Esteghlal, moved from the stadium to the city and the Sattar Khan cemetery. Cars honking their horns choked traffic as security forces arrested scores of demonstrators.

Three months later, security forces attacked Traktor Sazi supporters during an away match against Persepolis in Tehran's Azadi stadium. Traktor fans took off their shirts in the freezing cold to highlight a lack of aid for victims of an earthquake in the East Azerbaijan town of Varzagan in August in that killed 300 people and injured some 1,400 others. Allahverdi Dehghani, a member of the Iranian parliament from the region, accused the government of seeking to conceal the severity of the damage and failing to rush sufficient supplies to the region. "The top officials of the Iranian government promised to help survivors and build new houses for them in less than two months but as of now they have failed to do this job. The conditions are deteriorating in Varzagan as the winter is coming and people cannot tolerate the cold weather," *Kabir News* stated in its reporting on the Azadi stadium incident.

Moslem Iskandar Filabi, Sports Commission chairman of the controversial exile opposition National Council of Resistance of Iran (NCRI), an arm of the Mujahedeen-e-Khalq, alleged in a statement that the Traktor fans were also protesting against government "clerics and thugs" who had been sent to the stadium to encourage them to enter into temporary marriages in a bid to prevent them from staging a protest. He was referring to legislation passed by parliament authorizing "temporary marriage" as a way of circumventing Islam's ban on extra-marital sex. The law allowed men to have as many sexual partners as they wanted in accordance with Iran's interpretation of Sharia law as long as they qualified as a temporary marriage. Sex outside marriage is punishable in Iran by 100 lashes or, if adulterous, by stoning to death. A temporary marriage can last a few minutes or several years.

Filabi said the fans chanted slogans, mocking and embarrassing the clerics. "It has been 33 years since the mullahs have committed the worst insults and gravest crimes against Iran's athletes and national heroes, and the entire people in general. Dozens of Iran's national heroes have been murdered by this infamous regime, and quake victims in Azerbaijan, Bam and other cities and towns across the country are in the harshest of conditions, with poverty and hardships engulfing the lives of millions of our compatriots. This is while the mullahs are allocating Iran's enormous wealth for the spread of terrorism, obtaining nuclear weapons and supporting criminals such as Bashar Assad and [Iraqi president] Nouri Maliki."

The Azeri protests touched a sensitive nerve. Azeri demands for secession opened the door to both other minorities in Iran demanding greater rights and potential Turkish fanning of the Azeri flames in a bid to force Iran to lessen its support for Bashar al-Assad. They also risked fuelling mounting discontent as a result of harsh international sanctions and Ahmadinejad's mismanagement of the economy. Finally, they raised the spectre of a revival of racism on the pitch. "Wherever Tractor goes, fans of the opposing club chant insulting slogans. They imitate the sound of donkeys, because Azerbaijanis are historically derided as stupid and stubborn. I remember incidents going back to the time that I was a teenager," said an Azeri fan.

The racist abuse on the pitch of Azeris, who rank among Iran's top national players, as well as of other minorities such as Armenians, Jews, Arabs and Afghans, dates back to the Pahlavi dynasty when they were depicted as barbaric and aggressive as opposed to the honourable and dignified Persians. The spread of television in the late 1960s, coupled with the fact that Iran was pitted against Israel in the Tehran Asian Games a year after Israel had occupied Palestinian, Syrian and Egyptian territory in the 1967 Middle East war, made Jews the focal point of racist ire. The Iran-Israel match put on display a widening gap between the government and public opinion. The Shah hoped to distinguish himself from other leaders in the Middle East by hosting Israel at the time that Arabs rejected any contact with it, including in sports.

Iranian public opinion, however, had swung towards the Arabs in the wake of the 1967 war. The slogan "Death to Israel" was introduced for the first time in an Iranian stadium accompanied by balloons featuring a swastika as the predominantly Iranian spectators protested against the Jewish state. Battles erupted between more liberal and more conservative fans that poured into the streets. A crowd attacked a Jewish hospital and poked fun at Moshe Dayan, Israel's one-eyed 1967 military war hero, by setting a one-eyed donkey loose. Rumours circulated that the Jewish businessman Habib Elghanian, who was executed in the first year after the revolution, had encouraged Jews to attend the match so that they could cheer for Israel. The anti-Jewish character of the protest was reminiscent of the 1930s and 1940s when Jewish soccer players were heckled on their way to training.

The long-standing link between Iranian politics and soccer had a direct bearing on whoever ruled Iran. It was equally evident in June 2013 when Iran celebrated the election of Hassan Rouhani as president. Rouhani held out the hope of an easing of international sanctions imposed to force it to be more transparent about its nuclear programme. His election came days before the Islamic republic qualified for the 2014 World Cup in Brazil. The election of Rouhani, a pragmatic cleric with close ties to the country's leaders and a product of more than three decades of Islamic rule, together with the government's tolerance of soccer celebrations, signalled the regime's realization that eight years of Ahmadinejad—with the taunting of the international community, refusal to seriously engage in talks about the nuclear programme, sanctions and increased repression—had pushed Iran to the brink of popular revolt. Hundreds of thousands of men and women dancing on the streets of Tehran and other Iranian cities wore purple, the colour of Rouhani's campaign as well as green, the colour of the 2009 opposition candidates and the protest movement. They linked Iranian success on the soccer pitch to the election of a moderate president. As in the 1990s when Khatami became president and Iran qualified for the World Cup, expectations were running high. "Mousavi, Karrubi, we qualified for the WC [World Cup]," they chanted.

There were signs in the months prior to Rouhani's election that the regime understood that increased repression in the twilight of Ahmadinejad's reign had brought discontent to a head. Public dress codes were tacitly relaxed. Women in the streets of Tehran and Bandar Abbas appeared in public fashionably, albeit conservatively, dressed with scarves that only partially covered their heads and faces to which they had applied make-up. "It's the regime's way of giving people some breathing room," a critic of the regime quipped. The relaxation of the dress code contrasted starkly with a report by United Nations' monitor for human rights in Iran, Ahmad Shaheen, warning of a crackdown intended to deter potential protests in advance of the election. Scores of journalists were arrested and violations of the rights of women and ethnic and religious minorities mounted. So chilling was the effect of the crackdown that Iranian sports journalists refused to meet visiting foreign scholars because they feared being hauled in by the security service.

The crackdown reflected the Ahmadinejad regime's bunker mentality and its sense of vulnerability as it struggled with the impact of the sanctions and the threat of an explosion of discontent that at times was visible on the pitch. In the run-up to the election, the regime's isolation and fear expressed itself in its pervasiveness, fear-inspired penchant for control, a preference among officials for monologue rather than dialogue and a dread of foreigners reminiscent of the former Soviet Union and North Korea. The impact was on full display at an international conference on geopolitics in the Gulf in Bandar Abbas, the southern Iranian city that abuts the strategic Strait of Hormuz through which much of the world's oil and gas flows.

In a break with a culture that prides itself on its diplomatic, artistic and gastronomic sophistication, officials and clerics embarked on diatribes of at times crude propaganda. Speakers continuously played up Iran's role as a regional power, the strategic geography of Shiite Muslims in oil and water-rich parts of the Gulf, the discrimination suffered by Shiites in countries like Saudi Arabia and Bahrain and the alleged subservience to the United States of wealthy Gulf states which blame Iran for stirrings of unrest within their own borders. Foreign ministry officials and think tank figures associated with the ministry used their role as moderators to rudely cut foreign speakers short so that they could embark on a drumbeat of lengthy, highly politicized and ideological speeches. The degree of control became further obvious when several foreign participants who ventured into town on a shopping spree were intercepted by security officials allegedly for their own protection.

That mentality, coupled with Iran's combustible mix of politics and soccer, was a serious problem for Rouhani in the early days of his presidency. Sport was likely to be an indicator of his ability to manoeuvre deftly. "My experience as the national team manager of Iran was that football plays a major role in the political, social and even economic direction that the nation takes and the people who decide the direction of the country are constantly using the game for their political agenda. There are pluses and minuses to it all. The government's financial resources support the game but it becomes politically manipulated. It becomes too dependent on the political system and the money and it starts operating as a political business," said the former Iranian national coach Afshin Ghotbi in an interview with Al Jazeera.

To fulfil his election promises Rouhani was likely to roll back some of the influence Ahmadinejad ceded to the Revolutionary Guards, including in sports, where they had either taken ownership of clubs or dominated their boards. Tehran mayor Mohammad Baker Qalibaf, a former Revolutionary Guards air force commander, prepared for his presidential candidacy by using his municipality and its bank to sponsor clubs. Soccer and politics had become so intertwined that a year before the election a court sentenced three businessmen and a banker linked to Ahmadinejad to death in a US$2.8 billion fraud case involving the acquisition of soccer clubs and steel factories as well as the establishment of a private bank. The case was widely seen as an attack on the president and a taste of what he might expect once he no longer enjoyed the immunity of being in office. Together with the fact that even conservative presidential candidates like former foreign minister Ali Akbar Velayati argued during the election campaign that sports management needed to be shielded from interference by the government and the Guards by returning it to professionals, it made it easier for Rouhani to curb the worst excesses of political interference in soccer.

According to Iranian soccer analyst Niloufar Momeni:

> It has been fourteen years since Iranian football shone with its golden era in the 1998 World Cup finals. The sport is steadily trending downhill with corruption in the transfer market and political interference among the main causes … To this day, club directors and even team managers are appointed by political affiliation rather than management skills. There are few, if any, functional youth systems within the country. Iran's national broadcaster continually finds spurious reasons to avoid broadcasting domestic fixtures, except for those featuring the government-funded Red and Blue teams of Tehran [Esteghlal]. On top of that, corruption in players' transfer contracts is rife; from the league itself to the players and their agents, no party is free from blame and it will take years of healing to reform this broken system.

While Rouhani may not interfere in soccer to the degree that Ahmadinejad did, he has sought to capitalize on Iran's 2014 World Cup qualification and performance in the tournament by alleviating clubs' huge financial problems as a result of the economic decline that has made it difficult for them to attract foreign players. The Iranian soccer federation moved to halt the exodus of Iranian players to the Gulf, with officials warning that a lesser quality of soccer in the Gulf meant that their chances of playing international tournaments would be reduced. "The players are moving to these countries for economic reasons but because proper training regimes are not in place there, the quality of their play is deteriorating," said Esteghlal coach Hamid Ghalenoei.

Ghalenoei spoke as relations deteriorated between Iran and the Gulf. Led by Saudi Arabia, Gulf nations were at odds with Iran because of its support for Bashar al-Assad, its alleged instigation of anti-government protests in Bahrain and Saudi Arabia's oil-rich Eastern Province, fears surrounding the Islamic republic's nuclear programme and Iran's more than three decades-old occupation of disputed islands sixty kilometres off the coast of the UAE and close to key shipping routes in the Strait of Hormuz. The bad blood spilled onto the soccer pitch in the spring of 2012 when the UAE withdrew its ambassador from Tehran and cancelled a friendly against the Islamic republic after Ahmadinejad paid a controversial visit to the islands amid Iranian threats to close the Strait of Hormuz if Israel or the United States attacked its nuclear facilities. Iranian soccer officials announced that they would seek damages, noting that FIFA had ordered Nigeria to pay US$300,000 to the Iranian Football Federation after it cancelled a friendly against the Islamic republic in 2010 on political grounds. The UAE foreign minister Sheikh Abdullah bin Zayed Al Nahayan denounced the visit as a "flagrant violation of the UAE's sovereignty." The Iranian soccer chief Kafashian meanwhile accused the Emirates two months later of imposing an undeclared boycott on the hiring of Iranian players.

The UAE–Iran tit-for-tat coincided with a crackdown on Iran's use of Dubai to imports goods sanctioned by the United Nations and the United States. The UAE had earlier emerged in remarks made by its ambassador to the United States, Yousef al-Otaiba, as the first Gulf state to publicly endorse military force to prevent Iran from becoming a nuclear power. Otaiba described a nuclear-armed Iran as the foremost threat to the UAE, and one that needed to be neutralized at whatever cost. Contrasting the threat against the UAE with the danger a nuclear-armed Iran would pose to the US, Otaiba told *The Atlantic* that a nuclear Iran would "threaten the peace process, it will threaten the balance of power, it will threaten everything else, but it will not threaten you ... Our military ... wakes up, dreams, breathes, eats, sleeps the Iranian threat. It's the only conventional military threat our military plans for, trains for, equips for ... There's no country in the region that is a threat to the UAE [besides] Iran."

The battle between Iran and various Gulf states for the identity of the energy-rich region also spilled onto their soccer pitches in a symbolic contest between the Persian Gulf League and the Arabian Gulf League. The struggle erupted when the UAE renamed its premier league as the Arabian Gulf League. The Iranian Football Federation, whose own top league, the Persian Gulf League, adheres to the Islamic Republic's position in the war of semantics, responded by blocking the transfer of Iranian players to UAE clubs and breaking the contracts of those who had already moved. The blockage followed the declaration by the UAE a year earlier of a boycott of Iranian players in protest against Iran's occupation of the islands and refusal to put its controversial nuclear programme under international supervision. The boycott was, however, never enforced.

The war of word nevertheless stopped Iran's national team captain Javad Nekounam from being sold for US$2 million to UAE club Al Sharjah. "We had to stop him from joining the Emirati league. We will ask the president to allocate funds to compensate Mr. Nekounam for his loss," said Kafashian. Quoted by Fars news agency, Kafashian admitted that another eight or nine players had also been prevented from moving to the UAE. "The Persian Gulf will always be the Persian Gulf. Money is worthless in comparison to the name of my motherland. I received an offer from Al Sharjah three months ago and no one forced me to deny it, but I refused to do so myself. I would never join a team from a league offending the name of the Persian Gulf," Nekounam said on Iranian state television.

Soccer also played a part in the cyber and covert war between Iran and its detractors. In 2011 two fake soccer websites helped the creators of the Stuxnet computer virus to attack computers used in Iran's nuclear programme and to mislead Iranian authorities. The cyber-attack was part of a larger covert campaign involving assassinations of nuclear scientists and mysterious explosions at Iranian nuclear and military facilities. The creators of the virus used two websites, www.mypremierfutbol. com and www.todaysfutbol.com, as fronts to communicate with Stuxnet-infected Iranian computers in a successful bid to make Iranian authorities believe that related traffic originated from soccer fans. John Bumgarner, a retired US Army special-operations veteran and former intelligence officer, who is chief technology officer of the US Cyber Consequences Unit, a non-profit group that studies the impact of cyber threats, claimed that the fake soccer websites created a smoke screen behind which the Stuxnet virus attack could be launched undetected.

5

SHATTERING TABOOS

"Tall, young, and beautiful girls were picked for the team. Just what our country needed ... A women's soccer team. Is this what our country needs? What about Islamic universities? What about Islamic punishments? What about judges? What about rights and duties? What about the fear of Allah? What about implementing the punishments decreed by Allah?"

Libyan imam, Sheikh Salam Jaber

Controversy ranks high in Sahar Al-Hawari's job description. Perseverance and the subtlety of a diplomat are her trademarks. A trailblazer for the right of women to play soccer and only one of a handful of female trainers in the Middle East, Al-Hawari operates in a conservative man's world in which women's soccer is at best controversial and blasphemous at worst.

The outspoken daughter of an international soccer referee, Al-Hawari set out in the early 1990s to build the Arab world's first association women's soccer team and then a regional women's soccer championship. Initially, she trained her players secretly in her parents' villa in Cairo. Al-Hawari recalls that she "kept going for five years in my house. No one accepted us, no club, no nothing. I sponsored the whole thing alone because no one believed in us. Everyone said it's a crazy idea. When I started to show my girls in festivals, every city has a national feast, with my father's contacts—my late father had good contacts. He was well known all over the country and in the Arab region, so I took this reputation, and I worked with it."[1]

213

Defying criticism that she was violating Islamic dress codes for women and tricking them into playing a man's game, she badgered the Egyptian Football Association until it recognized her team.

Al-Hawari looked for players in rural Egypt, where women suffer fewer social restrictions than in the country's major cities. She cajoled and pleaded with conservative family and friends to allow her to pick twenty-five girls aged between fifteen and twenty-two to join her in Cairo. She countered fears that men would be ogling the girls at games by arguing that spectators would focus on their skills, not their bodies. She sold her belongings to fund her team's stay at her home.[2]

Her battle resembles the culture clash in the 2002 comedy film *Bend it like Beckham*, which portrays a Sikh daughter's rebellion against her parents' refusal to allow her to play soccer in Britain. However, there is one difference: in the Middle East this culture clash is a fact of daily life that challenges multiple divides, including that between secularism and religion and the gender roles of men and women. It has defined the soccer stadium as a venue for women to defy role expectations. Members of Al-Hawari's team bucked the trend in more ways than one. As Iranian and conservative women players in Europe and elsewhere demanded the right to cover their heads during matches, Al-Hawari's girls shed their headscarves once in Cairo.

Sports in general and soccer in particular have given women a platform that allows their struggle for greater rights to escape what amounts to a trap set by authoritarian and religious and/or traditional forces: patriarchal security and protection at the price of surrendering all rights, or economic and social rights in exchange for foregoing political and civil rights. While this is particularly true for middle- and upper-class women, it also often applies to lower-class women who find an opportunity to express pent-up frustration in soccer.

Reema Abdullah, the 33-year-old founder, coach and striker of the private women's soccer team Jeddah King's United, is a leader in the campaign to allow women in Saudi Arabia to participate in sports and compete internationally but did not take off her headscarf. Honey Thaljieh, a Palestinian Christian, does not wear one. But they, too, like Al-Hawari, are standard bearers of women's right to sports. "Nobody is saying completely 'no' to us. As long as there are no men around and our clothes are properly Islamic, there should be no problem. When Saudi women get a chance to compete for their country, they will raise the flag so high ... Women can achieve a lot, because we are very talented and we are crazy about sports," said Abdullah.

Ambiguity towards women's sports is historically and culturally rather than religiously rooted. Half a century before Al-Hawari set out to change the course of history, Palestinians struggled with the question as to whether women had a role in the harnessing of sports to further the quest for nationhood. That ambiguity was evident in the writing of a journalist identified only as Nir in the newspaper *Filastin* in 1945. "Oh, educated young woman! Leave that which should not concern you to those men and women stricken with social diseases. Come gather at the broad sports field, come happy and cheerful to nature's bosom, until you can compete with the Western girls in their city and culture, and then you will be able to show everyone your pride in your achievements on the broad and open sports field," wrote Nir in September of that year.

But only two days later he had a change of heart:

Housework = Sport! Mankind has learned from experience that a woman who does housework is of fine health, with plenty of strength and energy. And are you aware, dear reader, of the reason for this? When a woman is looking after her child, when she caresses him in order to put him to sleep, she is continually active from dawn till dusk—and that is undoubtedly a sporting activity. And when she prepares food she is doing sport, which strengthens the muscles in her arms—and when she cleans the floor of her house she is doing her daily sport. Afterwards, she needs to rest, and in this regard she is like every sportsman who plays football, basketball, or any other sport at all ... Furthermore, women feel satisfaction when they succeed in completing the required housework. Oh, Arab sisters, get to your housework. And do not let it exasperate you, but fulfil your duties—that will make the men respect you, and you will thus achieve two important aims: carrying out your daily work, and strengthening your bodies. Onward, young woman—beseech of the pen to write you a glorious page in the history of our new revival.[3]

Religious resistance to women's sports is not restricted to Sunni Muslims, but is shared by some of their Shiite counterparts. "Frankly. Most people do not approve of sportswomen ... experts are of the opinion that sportswomen lose 50% of their femininity, as they have to endure constant and arduous training in order to achieve international standards. Naturally, they grow rough and speak coarsely. They do not even care about men's opinion of them any more ... Women must not play football or rugby. These are not feminine sports," wrote the prominent Shiite scholar Sayyad Reza Pak Nezhad, whose brother was a fighter for the Mujahedin e-Khalq, a group that resisted both the shah and the mullahs but was discredited by its alliance with Iraq against Iran and its personality cult.[4]

To take her dream beyond Egypt, Al-Hawari persuaded FIFA to threaten Arab football associations that do not have a women's team with sanctions. FIFA left the Egyptian association no choice but to back Al-Hawari's push for an Arab Women's Football Championship. Al-Hawari further lobbied the UEA and Bahrain to allow women to create their own soccer team. Members of the UAE team initially kept secret from their families what they were doing in their spare time and often cancelled training when they were unable to sneak away.

Several fought the attitudes of their conservative families to win the right to play. Nayla Ibrahim, a 25-year-old goalkeeper and police officer, was forced to quit the team after her parents were inundated by complaints from friends and relatives. Her parents finally reneged, but refused to attend games for fear they would be seen by society as overly supporting her. Nada Yousef al-Hashimi, a vivacious economy ministry official who took up swimming and track events in school, chaperones the team when she is not luring foreign investment into the country. She engages critics on the team's Facebook page, which includes a lively discussion page about the merits of women's soccer, dozens of team photos and links to YouTube videos.[5]

Nada and two friends have launched a women's league with six teams and eighty-four players who play behind closed doors in Abu Dhabi, the capital of the UAE, alongside the country's national women's team because they had no opportunity to play in an outdoors environment that banned men. "There are some girls that don't mind playing in front of men. But there is a huge percentage of Emirati women who can't play in front of men because of cultural reasons. Those in the community who want to play the sport after university don't have a place to go. It's all open and there isn't really a place for the sport to be developed," Mariam Al Omaira, a public sector employee and founding partner of Irada [Determination] Sports Development Company, told the Emirati newspaper *The National*.

The decision to play behind closed doors followed a warning by players that the league would collapse if women were forced to compete on public pitches accessible to men despite objections by representatives of the advertisement and sponsoring industry. "If you look at the way football is played and the way the Sports Council is promoting women's football, the game has to be brought outside, just like it is played in the rest of the world, and also because we are trying to attract all participants in the UAE. We want to open it up, as it's a league for the UAE, not a league [only] for Abu Dhabi local women," said Eric Gottschalk, CEO of Mediapro Middle East—the league's co-organizer together with Reem Investments, an Abu Dhabi-based fund owned by among others the royal families of Abu Dhabi and Sharjah, with interests in the leisure industry, including a Manchester United soccer school in the UAE.

Across the Middle East, women's teams fight a continuous battle for their existence. "Female athletes in the Middle East face pressures that include family, religion, politics, and culture," observed a recent study entitled "Muslim Female Athletes and the Hijab" by Geoff Harkness, a sociologist at Northwestern University's campus in Qatar, and one of his basketball playing students, Samira Islam.[6] The study based on interviews with female athletes and their coaches found that sports often empowered young women whose role models are successful sportswomen like Fatima Al-Nabhani, an Omani tennis player, and Bahraini sprinter Roqaya Al-Ghasara, who was fully covered when she ran and won at the 2008 Beijing Olympics. "Both women not only serve as role models for aspiring female athletes from the region, but also shatter Western stereotypes," said the study. Eight other female athletes competed in Beijing wearing the hijab in sprinting, rowing, taekwondo and archery.

Kuwait lifted its ban on women's soccer in 2010, a move since denounced by Islamist lawmakers. Their initial focus was the Kuwaiti team's first international appearance in the 2010 Third West Asian Women Soccer Tournament in Abu Dhabi. Parliament deputy Waleed al-Tabtabai was one of a number of deputies who complained that it was illegal and a waste of money. "Football is not meant for women, anyway," Tabtabai remarked. Two years later, the Islamists criticized Kuwait's Gulf University for Science and Technology (GUST) for organizing a regional competition for women. "Women playing football is unacceptable and contrary to human nature and good customs. The government has to step in and drop the tournament," Tabtabai asserted, reiterating his earlier criticism.[7] "Out of commitment to its social role, besides the academic one, GUST seeks to promote female sports in Kuwait and in the Arabian Gulf region through organizing and patronizing such competitions," countered GUST's Chancellor Afaf Al-Rakhis.

She described women's sports as a reflection of the social and cultural advancement of a country.[8]

Popular revolts that have toppled leaders in the region have not necessarily made it easier for women. A request to pose for a photograph for a Bloomberg News story sparked debate within the Libyan women's soccer team even though their government-funded blue tracksuits cover them neck to toe and they wear a hijab to hide their hair. The team considered various options, including posing with their backs to the camera, but ultimately decided that even this would be too risky in a post-revolt society in which conservatives are on the rise.

The issue is not whether players are dressed with sufficient modesty. It is the fact that women playing soccer challenges conservative concepts of a woman's role in society. Theirs is a political struggle for the future of Libya at a time when the powerful militias beyond the government's control who helped topple Qaddafi remain the law of the land. Salim Jaber, the most senior cleric in eastern Libya and head of its mosque oversight body, alleged in a televised sermon that female players had "soiled the honour of their families with the filth of nudity and shamelessness." The Ansar al-Sharia militia demanded that the team not play in a tournament in Germany because it "could lead to unforgiveable things."

Sheikh Salem Jaber denounced the establishment of a Libyan women's team in a Friday prayer sermon in Benghazi. He thundered:

> It came as a surprise to me to hear the news that a sports team was being established at the university. Is it for youth who are failing in their studies? Or is it for outstanding youth? No, it is for neither. Tall, young, and beautiful girls were picked for the team. Just what our country needed ... A woman's soccer team ... Whose daughters are these? Are they the daughters of Jews, of Christians, or of Zoroastrians? Are they the daughters of heretics? Of Communists? It is written in their fathers' ID cards that they are Muslim. But today, these girls are exposing their heads. Is this to be allowed? In a few months' time, they will be exposing their legs. The day they joined [the team], exposing what should be hidden, these girls sold out their honor, and soiled the honor of their families with the filth of nudity and shamelessness.[9]

To avoid repercussions, the Libyan women's team adopts a routine not very different from that in place in more conservative societies in the region or from how things were when women's soccer first attempted to carve out a space for itself. The team changes training venues weekly for security reasons to evade attack by those who call for women to remain out of public sight and have targeted women's soccer. Team members are advised where to go for training at the last minute by phone or text message. They refuse to raise funds for equipment such as boots and opted against participating in the German competition to avoid drawing attention to themselves.

To complicate matters further, the West Asian Football Federation (WAFF), which groups all Middle Eastern soccer associations with the exception of Israel, and is led by Jordanian Prince Ali Bin Al Hussein, launched a campaign in early 2013 to put women's soccer on a par with the men's game.[10] Glaringly absent among the signatories of the thirteen WAFF members was Saudi Arabia, where women's soccer exists at best in a political and legal vacuum, as well as Yemen. The campaign was inaugurated as women were demanding greater rights as part of the regional push for social justice and transparency. The WAFF statement announcing the campaign defined "an athletic woman" as "an empowered woman who further empowers her community."[11] With its campaign, WAFF was seeking to achieve a paradigm shift in an attitude that at its best sees soccer as a hobby for girls to be abandoned as they enter into womanhood and prepare for marriage.

Women's soccer is not just controversial in conservative societies, but even in those with more liberal traditions. Abu Arab, the municipal director of an Israeli Palestinian town whose premier league team, Bnei Sakhnin, is locked in bitter rivalry with Beitar Jerusalem, exemplifies the hurdles women encounter. A formers sports teacher, Abu Arab, nicknamed Abu Banat [Father of Daughters] because he has four daughters and only one son, is the town's godfather of women's soccer and manager of the only Palestinian team in the Israeli women's soccer league. He sees women's soccer as beneficial and empowering within limits. "We use soccer as a good instrument to educate the girls and also I think it's good to improve their status in society in Sakhnin, because the girls and the women now, they are in all the sites and all the branches in the Arab sector or society—everything—and why not in soccer? I think that some of them will be coaches or sports writers, or they will come to the soccer matches of Sakhnin, and pay for a ticket and they will go to support our team," he told anthropologist Kenda Stuart, making no reference to the sport as a professional career for women.[12]

Abu Arab's position as the town's well-connected sports patriarch made conservative acceptance of women playing soccer easier. The sense that his Banat Sakhnin women's team will never be the equivalent of its male cousin is reinforced by the fact that its players—much to the cha-grin of many of them—are not paid. Instead, players are offered funding for higher education that opens prospects for alternative professional careers. The lack of payment reinforces the patriarchal environment in which the team is embedded.

The fact that the women's initial trainer, Ghalib Abu Badr, was known for his religiosity helped reduce conservative and religious resistance. "When their parents knew that Ghalib is teaching them, they knew [their daughters] are in good hands. Also what was important for me with the girls is that before soccer I want good behaviour," Abu Badr said. He recalled that his players had no interaction with men while in training and once scolded a player for wanting to give her email address to a male friend. "I shouted at her, and she told me: 'But we are friends.' I told her: 'You are friends, but not in the training.'" Abu Badr's successor, Brahim Abu Khater, cited "social conditions" as the reason why the women's team trained less frequently than the men's squad. "In sports the number of girls is smaller, and moreover, worldwide girls' soccer is considered to be not so developed … The majority [in Palestinian society] doesn't accept a girl playing soccer. They refer to it as a masculine game," add-ing that "even the Jewish society is not so developed." Several players initially joined the team without informing their families and it took Abu Arab's intervention to secure parental approval. They often saw him as a guardian of tradition.[13]

WAFF's campaign also constituted a rebuttal of opposition to women's soccer among Islamists and more conservative segments of Middle Eastern society. WAFF stressed that women's soccer did not demean cultural and traditional values.[14] With their campaign, Middle Eastern soccer associations backed by representatives of the United Nations, the Union of European Football Associations (UEFA), the Asian Football Confederation (AFC) and the English Football Association put them-selves at the forefront of efforts to secure equality and women's rights. They emphasized the right of women to play soccer irrespective of cul-ture, religion and race; a women's right to opt for soccer as a career rather than only as a sport; and soccer's ability to promote gender equal-ity on and off the pitch.

The associations called further for the appointment of women to the boards of all WAFF member associations, establishment of a WAFF women's committee, creation of Under-16 and Under-19 women's competitions in the Middle East (West Asia) as well as the compulsory rotation of hosting of subsidized WAFF women competitions. With straightforwardness unusual for the region's public diplomacy, the statement singled out Saudi Arabia by explicitly stating that the kingdom would be included in women's tournaments.

Women soccer players indeed confront the toughest obstacles in Saudi Arabia, ruled by one of Islam's most puritanical sects. Physical education classes are banned in state-run girl's schools and the drafting of the country's first ever five-year national sports plan is for men only. Women organize soccer matches and other sports events in a legal nether land but often have to cancel them when hostile members of the clergy get wind of them.

The struggle of Saudi women is one against deeply engrained ultraconservative views that seem frozen in time. Human Rights Watch, in a sweeping condemnation in 2012, accused Saudi rulers of kowtowing to assertions by the country's powerful conservative Muslim clerics that female sports constitute "steps of the devil" that will encourage immorality and reduce women's chances of meeting the requirements for marriage.[15] The group's allegations, contained in a report of the same name, came on the heels of the Kingdom backtracking in 2012 on a plan to build its first stadium especially designed to allow women to attend soccer matches. The planned stadium was supposed to open in 2014.

Saudi clerics condemn women's sports as corrupting and satanic and charge that they spreads decadence. They warn that running and jumping can damage a woman's hymen and ruin her chances of getting married. One group of religious scholars argued that swimming, soccer and basketball were likely to reveal "private parts," which include large areas of the body. The clerics cautioned also that the mixing of the sexes can lead to a fusion of sports and politics and to protests against autocratic regimes. Their statements were designed to bolster efforts by governments in the Gulf to fend off protests sweeping the Middle East and North Africa with salary hikes for public sector employees and significant social investment. The Saudi grand mufti Sheikh Abdulaziz Al-Sheikh, quoted in the Kingdom's *Al Watan* newspaper, warned that the protests that since early 2011 had already toppled the leaders of Egypt, Libya, Tunisia and Yemen and sparked civil war in Syria were sinful: "The schism, instability, the malfunctioning of security and the breakdown of unity that Islamic countries are facing these days is a result of the sins of the public and their transgressions."[16]

Such sins include, according to Wahhabi Imam Abu Abdellah of the As-Sunnah mosque in Kissimee, Florida, who was speaking in a video posted on the internet, the mixing of the sexes at sports events. "In the past it was only men, now it is almost half [in stadiums]. Allah knows what happens afterwards. Either way it is bad. Either people go out, they are sensing and partying and drinking and all that, so that's negative. And if they don't, they go out and they demonstrate and they're angry and they destroy property and they destroy cars and they destroy people's business. Either way its haram [forbidden], things have to be done in moderation. These are the things that are associated with sports that the believers have to be careful with."[17]

"So there is nothing wrong with watching and practising your favourite sport as long as you adhere to the norms. When it comes to the way you dress and the way you behave, where you're going to be, what are you going to be listening to; are you going to be mingling in crowds you are not supposed to be mingling with? All of those things do matter when you are practising or you are watching your favourite sport," the imam said.

To be fair, less conservative clerics have come out in favour of women's sports as well as for fewer restrictions on women. In addition, the newly appointed head of the kingdom's religious vigilantes is believed to favour relaxation of the ban on the mixing of the sexes.

In defiance of crippling restrictions, women in Saudi Arabia like Reem Abdullah have quietly established soccer and other sports teams with the backing of more liberal members of the ruling Al Saud family. The clubs are often extensions of hospitals and health clubs. Abdullah founded King's United in 2006. Her example was followed in other cities, including Riyadh and Dammam. Two years later seven female teams played in the first ever national women's tournament aimed at creating a clandestine and segregated women's league.

Their defiance was strengthened by mounting pressure on the kingdom to lift restrictions on women's sports. The International Olympic Committee (IOC) forced Saudi Arabia under threat of suspension to field its first ever women athletes at a mixed gender international tournament at the 2012 London Olympics. It did so by fielding two expatriate Saudi females. The Saudi concession to the IOC was sudden. It followed a statement a month earlier by interior minister Prince Nayef Bin Abdul that "female sports activity has not existed [in the kingdom] and there is no move thereto in this regard. At present, we are not embracing any female Saudi participation in the Olympics or other international championships."[18]

The two expatriate Saudis the kingdom dispatched to London were the first to represent their country but they were not the first Saudi women to compete in an international tournament. That honour fell to Dalma Rushdi Malhas, an 18-year-old equestrienne, who competed in the 2010 Singapore Youth Olympics without official support and won a bronze medal. "I didn't know whether I was allowed but when I got invited of course I didn't think twice and went at my own expense, I didn't care much about me being there as a representative of Saudi Arabia, because anyone could probably do that. But getting a medal was the key, and that's not easy for anyone, and I wanted that—and only that gives recognition to my country," she said.

The IOC's success was short-lived. A meeting in September 2014 between IOC President Thomas Bach, who has instructed his group to write adherence to human, gender and labour rights into all future Olympic host city contracts, and Saudi Olympic chief Prince Abdullah bin Mosaad bin Abdulaziz produced little progress on the issue of women's sporting rights. Prince Abdullah insisted that the kingdom had failed to field women at the Asian Games earlier that year because it did not have qualified athletes. Mohammed al-Mishal, the secretary-general of Saudi Olympic Committee, promised however to do so at the 2016 Olympics in Rio de Janeiro. But Al-Mishal said that women's participation would be limited to sports endorsed by a literal interpretation of the Qur'an. The Saudi official said the kingdom was training women to compete in equestrian, fencing, shooting, and archery in Olympic contests because these were the disciplines that were "accepted culturally and religiously in Saudi Arabia".

In a rare admission, Al Arabiya, the Dubai-based television network established by the Saudi royalty to counter Al Jazeera, conceded that professional women athletes in the kingdom were "publicly slammed for going against their natural role." Al Arabiya reported that Saudi newspapers denounced women athletes as "shameless" because they cause embarrassment to their families. Women athletes often receive text messages urging them to stay home and tend to their household duties as mothers and wives, according to Al Arabiya, which quoted 17-year-old basketball player Hadeer Sadagah: "If there is no support from the family we cannot get into these types of activities … some people are extremist or extra conservative."

Saudi activists enjoy support from some members of the ruling family. A group of women led by Princess Reema Bandar al-Saud, a granddaughter of the late King Faisal, organized the first Saudi women's expedition to a Mount Everest base camp as part of a fundraising exercise to promote a healthy lifestyle for breast cancer patients. "As a nation we need to focus on preventative measures that include healthy lifestyle, specifically nutrition and fitness and early detection [of women's illnesses]. The inspiration to climb Everest base camp came from the basic idea that a healthy lifestyle and healthy body can fight illness better," remarked the princess, who appears as comfortable in a traditional *abaya* that makes a woman virtually invisible as she is letting her mane of black hair flow for all to see.

A year later, Saudi Arabia's secretive ruling family considered allowing women to attend soccer matches. No Saudi official had suggested that the controversial issue was under discussion but a series of statements and denials suggested that a debate was underway. The debate was part of discussions that had been waged on and off for past two years.

Granting women sporting rights in the kingdom that in most parts of the world would be taken for granted took on added significance with the Saudi Football Federation's bid to host the 2019 Asia Cup. The tournament was ultimately awarded to the UAE. Indications that Saudi Arabia may want to play a bigger role in international sports emerged with the kingdom's fielding of a candidate for the 2013 election of a new head of the Asian Football Confederation (AFC), and the acquisition by Saudi Prince Abdullah bin Mosaad of a 50 per cent stake in third tier English club Sheffield United was the first such purchase by a member of the ruling family and suggested growing Saudi involvement in the sport internationally.

The Saudi Arabian Football Federation (SAFF) president Ahmed Eid Alharbi stepped into the debate by pointing to the economic impact women spectators would have. He stated that the creation of facilities for women would increase capacity at Saudi stadiums by 15 per cent. Alharbi suggested that the Prince Abdullah Al-Faisal Stadium in Jeddah would be the first to accommodate up to 32,000 women followed by the King Abdullah City stadium in the capital in 2014. He later qualified his remarks by saying that the decision to lift the ban on women was not his.

"A decision like this is a sovereign decision. Neither I nor SAFF can make it. Only the political leadership in this country can make that decision."

The ruling family was caught between conservative mores and mounting pressure from women willing to push for change. A picture of Saudi TV host Elham Yousef filming in Riyadh's Prince Faisal Bin Fahd Stadium caused a stir. "This is the first time I have come here. I'm happy but I'd be happier if I and other female journalists covering sports were allowed to cover a live match from inside the stadium," she told Saudi reporters. A Saudi female accompanied by her male guardian appeared in a sports arena in Al-Ihsa of the Eastern Province to watch an equestrian tournament. A group of Saudi women supporters demonstratively travelled to Kuwait to cheer their club, Al Fateh SC of Al Mubaraz in Al Hasa province, after their request to attend matches in the kingdom was rejected.

It was no coincidence that it was the women of Al Fateh who were in the forefront of using soccer as a key platform for enhancing women's rights in a country in which women retain economic rights but are even more restricted than men in their political rights and personal lives. The columnist Abdulateef al Mulhim credited them in *Arab News* with Al Fateh's success in winning the Saudi soccer championship. The victory broke a cycle of poor performances that had depressed a key manager of the club, Al Mulhim wrote. "His mother was the one who encouraged him not to give up and gave him the financial support needed for running the club. Ironically, she even advised him about many of the deals which involved the transfer of the best players to the club … As time passed, people knew of more women from the families in Al Mubaraz city."

Al Fateh's website lists several women from prominent families as honorary members. According to Al Mulhim, "There are other ladies from other families who also were part of the general public relations through the social media means and through their direct support … In other words, many young men and women from the city of Al Mubaraz put their hands together and accomplished a dream for being the best in the Kingdom. Last year, this club was the most admired for its performance and for the information of the readers."

Al Fateh stands out in moving ahead of the government in enhancing women's sports rights. The government's youth welfare council headed by Prince Nawaf bin Faisal, the ultimate arbitrator in sports, declared a month before the women travelled to Kuwait that it was studying whether Saudi businesswomen who support clubs could be allowed to be honorary or ordinary members. "There is no specific system that prevents women from being sports club members in the country. There have never been women members. This means that women are entitled to provide the clubs with moral and financial support as donors," stated council official Ahmed Rosie. For many women, the council's deliberations do not go far enough. "Why do they limit women to donating money instead of allowing them to be decision makers?" asked Saudi businesswoman Hanan Al-Faisal, a supporter of Jeddah's Al Ahly SC.

The push for recognition of women's right to sports coincided with women playing an increasing role in sporadic anti-government protests in Saudi Arabia, a country where discontent still simmers. It also followed a campaign by Saudis demanding a lifting of the ban on women driving. In June 2012 proponents of women's right to drive submitted a petition to King Abdullah with some 600 signatures. Women driving, like women's soccer, has so far been a bridge too far, however. Scores of women who defied the ban in the year preceding the petition were arrested and forced to sign pledges that they would not drive again. The Saudi activist Manal al-Sharif was arrested for nine days in May 2011 after she videotaped herself flouting the ban by getting behind a steering wheel and driving. She was released only after signing a statement promising that she would stop agitating for women's rights.

The clergy, who only allowed men's soccer to be played in the Kingdom in the 1950s, were nevertheless on the defensive and forced to make concessions. They remained silent when the government announced in 2012 that it would allow girls' physical education in private schools as long as they did so in line with Islamic law. Public schools could follow suit, said the Deputy Minister of Education for Women's Affairs, Nora al-Fayez. In a further move, authorities hinted that they may license women's extra-legal soccer clubs. Earlier, they lifted a ban imposed in 2009 under pressure from the clergy on private women's gyms. Women responded to the ban with a protest campaign under the slogan "Let her get fat." The campaign, in a country where sports facilities for women are virtually non-existent, focused on the lengths women have to go to in order to exercise. The all-women Princess Nora Bint Abdul Rahman University is one of the few exceptions and the only institution of higher education that has sports facilities, including a swimming pool, tennis court and exercise area for females. In further concessions women were granted the right to ride motorcycles and bicycles provided they were properly dressed and accompanied by a male relative, allowed to vote and stand for office in municipal elections scheduled for 2015, admitted to King Abdullah's toothless advisory council and permitted to become sales assistants in lingerie shops.

The push for change was boosted in 2012 with the forced resignation of Prince Nawaf, the first Gulf royal to be forced out of office by fan pressure, and the election of Alharbi as president of the SAFF. According to Sabria Jawhar, a close friend of Alharbi:

> Some people see Ahmed as a reformer, but I don't think the label does him justice. I see him as a visionary. He is probably the single most important male ally that Saudi female athletes have to get a women's football team up and running, and competing against international teams. Ahmed recognizes that SAFF is much more than the umbrella group for football leagues, but can be an agent of change in Saudi society. And what I like most about these efforts to change the way the sport is played and perceived by football fans throughout the Kingdom is that the new president does it all under the radar. His habit is to respond to any invitation to visit female universities in Saudi Arabia and help them develop women's football teams.

The rise of Alharbi and the battle for women's rights in a country where officials are expected to pay lip service to the kingdom's puritanical interpretation of Islam at all public and private events, including sports, reflected an emerging power struggle between the clergy and the Al Saud family that could rewrite the contract that gave birth to modern Saudi Arabia. Conservative clerics see the gradual enhancement of women's sporting rights as a signal that the Al Sauds as they approach a generational change in their leadership may no longer want to share power.

Prominent clerics met in the spring of 2013 with King Abdullah to express opposition to the corrupting effects of women's sports at the very moment that Prince Mutaib bin Abdullah, the head of Abdullah's National Guard, publicly warned against mixing religion and politics. His remarks echoed a similar warning several years earlier by Prince Turki Al-Faisal, a former intelligence chief, who at the time was ambassador to Britain. Prince Mutaib's comments sparked an immediate response. "Whoever says there is no relationship between religion and politics worships two gods, one in the heavens and one on earth," tweeted prominent Salafi Sheikh Abdul-Aziz Al-Tarifi, the kingdom's grand mufti amid mounting signs of a possible confrontation. A potential conflict had been brewing ever since Abdullah, in 2009, demanded the resignation of Sheikh al-Satri after he opposed the monarch's pet project, the US$30 billion co-ed King Abdullah University of Science and Technology (KAUST).

Conservative attitudes in Saudi Arabia and elsewhere in the Muslim world are rooted in traditionalism rather than religion. Palestine's national women soccer team includes fourteen Christians and only four Muslims but a majority of the team has similar tales to tell about the obstacles they needed to overcome and the initial resistance they met from their families.

The team comes last in FIFA's ranking. But Klodi Salameh, a 21-year-old business administration student who spent her first thirteen years in Chile, and her fellow team members are happy that they are playing at all. Israeli movement restrictions, no money, civil strife and no full-size pitches hold them back. West Bank team members train on a concrete court on the grounds of Bethlehem University. A grass pitch fifteen kilometres away is inaccessible thanks to the ring of Israeli checkpoints that surrounds Bethlehem. Gaza players, unable to leave the Strip, train separately.

But for once, conflict with Israel is not these Palestinians' biggest problem. Their team is most threatened by creeping social conservatism, fuelled by Islamist Hamas' control of the Gaza Strip and frustration with the government of President Mahmoud Abbas. Socially conservative Muslim and Christian families feared a public backlash against their daughters playing a rough and aggressive man's sport, wearing shorts and risking injury that could reduce their marriage prospects.

"Some women don't wait for their husbands or fiancés. They believe that they can change things. I am one of those women as are the other members of the team," asserted Honey Thaljieh, the team's founder, first captain, Palestine's first female player and a role model, who like other members of the team played soccer as a kid on neighbourhood streets.[19] Soccer was her way of making a difference and changing Palestinian society. The proof is in the pudding. Headscarved women, young and old, fill the stands in Ramallah's stadium, waving Palestinian flags and shouting in support of their team under a poster picture of Yasser Arafat, the late Palestinian leader.

"Traditionally, the notion is that Palestinian women should be in the kitchen and the care of their husbands. We rejected this. Soccer is our way of letting off steam," said fellow player Marian Bandak. Ironically, Niveen Kolaib, a headscarved Muslim sociology student who wears leggings under her shorts, is the player who encountered the least initial resistance from her parents. "They encouraged and supported me," she said. "If we can defy occupation, we can play soccer."

Four of Klodi and Marian's team mates, including Niveen, are Muslim, the majority stem from Christian families. They hail from Ramallah, Bethlehem and Jericho in the West Bank and the Gaza Strip. Recruitment in nationalistic or religious hot spots like Nablus, Jenin, Tulkarem and Hebron is all but impossible. Nevertheless, they travel the breadth of the West Bank training the next generation of women players.

The national women's team faced two challenges when it met world champions Japan in November 2011 on the soccer pitch in Hebron, the West Bank's most conservative town, which, unlike Ramallah, Bethlehem or East Jerusalem, does not count Christians among its residents: a formidable opponent on the pitch and an Islamist movement divided between Hamas, which supported the team, and Hizb ut Tahrir which opposed it.[20]

Hizb ut Tahrir websites described the team as "naked bitches" even though they wore leggings and at least one of the squad's players donned a *hijab*, an Islamic headdress that covers the hair, ears and neck. Hizb ut Tahrir imams denounced the match from the pulpits of their mosques; school principals in Hebron banned their students from attending the match, warning them that they would burn in hell if they went to the stadium. The Palestine Football Association (PFA) was forced to bus in supporters.

Crowds cheered the team as they left the stadium even though they had lost to Japan by a whopping 19–0. The team, which unlike its opponent was made up of university students rather than professionals, recovered in a second match, losing only 4–0 to the world's best women's team. "It was a social revolution. We broke the barrier and taboo when we went to Hebron and Nablus. The whole barrier collapsed," said the PFA president Jibril Rajoub.[21]

It was without doubt the beginning of a social revolution, but one that has yet to play out. Players continue to encounter pressure from their families. Klodi's family wanted her to stop when she got engaged. Her fiancé's support persuaded her parents to allow her to continue. Other players reported similar splits in their families. "Things are changing. It depends on what area of the country. Lifestyles are changing. Three years ago it was unacceptable for girls to walk in the streets with shorts. It was unacceptable to play soccer, run or ride a bicycle in shorts. Now it is ok in Ramallah, Bethlehem and Jerusalem," said Klodi.

Women in Iran have the right to play provided their kits are compliant with Islamic precepts but, like in Saudi Arabia, are also largely barred from attending matches as spectators in all-men stadiums. A decision by the government in 2015 to partially lift the ban by allowing women to attend volleyball, basketball, handball and tennis matches sparked protests from conservatives as well as women rights activists. "We didn't rise up in an Islamic Revolution for the right of women to enter sports stadiums," said Ayatollah Mohammad Ali Alavi Gorgani, a prominent member of the conservative Qom Seminary. The lifting followed pressure by the International Volleyball Federation that refused to award Iran hosting rights as long as women were barred from stadiums and international protests against the jailing of Ghoncheh Ghavami, a 25-year old British-Iranian national, who had tried to smuggle herself into a volleyball match between Iran and Italy. Iranian Vice President for Women and Family Affairs Shahindokht Molaverdi held out the prospect that the partial lifting was the beginning of a process. "If it practically happens a few times, the concerns will be completely removed and it will be proven that allowing women to watch men's sports matches is not problematic," Molaverdi said.

The government nonetheless encourages women's sports as a way of keeping girls from joining the country's mushrooming community of drug addicts. "Soccer is wildly popular in Iran and became a hot button gender issue in 2006 when Ahmadinejad attempted to relax the prohibition against women attending matches, only to be reversed by the Supreme Leader, who sided with clerics concerned about the effect viewing men in shorts could have on women's morality," noted a US consulate in Dubai cable disclosed by WikiLeaks.[22]

Two women highlighted the issue during a World Cup qualifier between Iran and South Korea in 2012 when they smuggled themselves into the stadium dressed as men only to reveal themselves publicly after the match.[23] Fatma Iktasari and Shabnam Kazimi did so in a picture on an Iranian blog that showed them displaying the victory sign. Adding insult to injury in a country that enforces gender segregation, they posed in the picture with male friends and an Iranian flag. A poem accompanying the picture read:

Heroes, warriors
Dream one day of a workshop with the kids in the "freedom" gym
The name "Iran" did not vanish until the moment of victory and yelling

The days of Good Hope to India
My people even a little bit happy, happiness experienced once again
I was glad that we were always on their side.[24]

This act of defiance, like an earlier apparent willingness by the Iranian soccer federation to allow women into a stadium for Asian Football Confederation (AFC) championship matches in the summer of 2012, sparked debate on Iranian social media with many praising the two women's courage. Their protest highlighted the schizophrenic condition of women's soccer in the Islamic republic where women are allowed to play soccer in front of all-women audiences but are banned from entering an all-men stadium as spectators.

The protest was reminiscent of an earlier campaign by women soccer fans to force their way into stadiums by dressing up as men. The campaign was depicted in *Offside*[25] by the filmmaker Jafar Panahi, who is serving a six-year jail sentence for "creating propaganda against the Iranian republic."[26] Panahi, a key figure in Iran's cinematic New Wave movement, was also banned from filmmaking, travel and speaking to the media for a period of twenty years. *Offside* described the fictionalized arrest by police of six young women and girls who smuggled themselves dressed as men into Tehran's stadium to watch Iran's national team play Bahrain. A more recent movie, *Shirin Was a Canary*, recounts the tale of a girl who is expelled from school for her love of soccer.[27]

The campaign waged by a small group of women prompted Ahmadinejad's failed attempt to lift the ban in 2006. It faltered on conservative opposition. Grand Ayatollah Fazel Lankarani argued that "women looking at a man's body even if not for the sake of gratification is inappropriate."[28] He was supported by Grand Ayatollah Naser Makarem Shirazi, who described Ahmadinejad's proposal as "a severe shock to the community."[29]

The president's bid followed a failed attempt a decade earlier to admit women into stadiums during the 1994 Asian Youth Cup. The Iranian Football Federation tested the waters when it allowed 500 women to attend a match between India and Bahrain in a special section of the stadium. The federation reversed its policy three days after the match on the grounds that male fans had been unable to adapt to the presence of women. The reversal failed to put an end to the controversy. The country's physical education authority continued to advocate allowing women into stadiums but favoured barring them from wrestling and swimming competitions. Ultimately, the decision was put to Ayatollah Khamenei, who ruled that a woman was not permitted to see the body of a man to whom she was not related even if that did not involve elements of lust.

Solmaz Sharif, the founder of *Shirzanan*, an on-line Farsi-language women's sports magazine created after she was refused a licence, highlighted in a commentary in *The Huffington Post* the inherent contradictions in Iranian policy evident in the government's opportunistic decision to allow the women's volleyball team to compete in front of mixed gender audience at the 2012 London Olympics.

> Although the Iranian government has permitted some women's teams to participate in international competitions, it greatly restricts their participation in domestic games. For instance, no men are allowed to watch women's games in Iran. This raises a few questions about the intentions of Iranian sporting officials: If it is "Islamic enough" for women to play in front of global audiences, then why they can't play in Iran? And such international participation doesn't meet Islamic requirements, did the Iranian government merely agree with it to avoid international pressure?[30]

The Asian Football Confederation (AFC) dashed hopes for more structural change when shortly after the London Olympics it failed to act on suggestion that it would impose its standards by insisting that women be allowed into the stadium to watch AFC Under-16 Championship matches scheduled to be played in Iran. The AFC Director of National Team competition Shin Mangal told the Shafaqna news agency that "so far as AFC is concerned, there should be no sex discrimination regarding the presence of men and women at stadiums."[31] The AFC stated that it had received assurances from Ali Kafashian that the FFIRI would comply with AFC regulations. The AFC quoted Kafashian as saying at the drawing of the groups for the tournament that the FFIRI is "fully ready to follow all the requirements and instructions from AFC."[32] The Iranian soccer boss repeated his position in remarks to the Iranian reformist newspaper *Sharq*. In an editorial the newspaper commented: "the youth championships could create a great change in Iranian football. They are an excellent opportunity."[33]

Iran's failure to grant women access to the stadiums was not its only battle with international soccer bodies. So was women's dress. FIFA fought the FFIRI for five years before agreeing to allow the Islamic republic's women's team to wear caps covering players' hair in international competitions rather than the *hijab*, which is banned by FIFA for safety and health reasons.

The dispute over the *hijab* led to the disqualification of the Iranian women's national team in June 2011 after they appeared on the pitch in the Jordanian capital Amman for a 2012 London Olympics qualifier against Jordan. The players wore the *hijab* in violation of an agreement with FIFA reached in Singapore two years earlier under which the Iranians agreed to the wearing of a cap that covered hair but not the neck. Three Jordanian players who wore the *hijab* were also barred.

The treatment of the Jordanian players put the spotlight on observant Muslim women whose opportunities to play professional soccer were curtailed by the FIFA ban or who refrained from pursuing a soccer career because of the issue of a headdress. It sparked a campaign[34] spearheaded by FIFA vice president Prince Ali Bin Al Hussein that portrayed the *hijab* as a cultural rather than a religious requirement and persuaded FIFA as well as the International Football Association Board (IFAB), a secretive body that governs the rules of professional soccer, to entertain commercially produced headdresses that would conform to Muslim norms as well as safety and security standards.[35]

The decision constituted a victory for a majority of observant Muslim players with the exception of those in Saudi Arabia, with its history of discouraging women's sports. It also complicated affairs in Iran, which not only obliged players to wear a headdress in violation of the principle of free choice but also forced foreign women's teams visiting the Islamic republic to do so. Berlin's predominantly Turkish BSV Al Dersimspor, the first foreign women's team to play in the Islamic republic after the lifting of a ban on women's soccer in 1998, had to wear headscarves, long-sleeved shirts and full-length trousers specially made for the 2006 game. The team's visit was documented in the 2008 award-winning documentary *Football Under Cover*.[36]

The match against Dersimspor was the first time since the Islamic revolution that the Iranian women's team was allowed to play in an open air stadium and it revealed divisions within the Islamic Republic's elite. The Foreign Ministry opposed the playing of the match while the FFIRI saw it as an opportunity to further women's soccer.[37] Male spectators were banned and loudspeakers warned the 4,000 *chador*-clad female spectators that the game would be called off if the guardians of Islamic morality detected indecent behaviour. Quotations from the Qur'an were broadcast before the game. The female spectators turned the match into a protest chanting "our share of freedom is half the freedom," and "it's our basic right to enter the stadium."[38] Aita Anjali, one of the documentary's directors, was among the husbands of players who were locked out of the stadium. He kept contact with the women's team by mobile phone.[39]

The match highlighted the fact that soccer is enormously popular among Iranian women. They watch matches on television, read about the players in newspapers and call in to chat with them on live radio. Women trek every week together with scores of male fans to the Davudieh training grounds in the foothills of the Alborg Mountains north of Tehran where they watch their favourite players train, get autographs and take photos.[40] Former *Newsweek* correspondent Maziar Bahari filmed Sara, a female soccer enthusiast, who travelled two hours from her home in southern Tehran to see her hero, Hamid Estili. As Estili sat in his BMW, trying to drive past the hordes of fans, Sara gathered her courage, tapped on his car window and gave him a bouquet of red roses.[41]

In a part of the world where soccer is a battlefield against autocracy and for gender rights, Jordan stands out as an example of the economic benefits of women's soccer. On the eve of mass protests in Egypt and days before the toppling of Tunisian President Zine El Abidine Ben Ali in January 2011, Jordanian women joined their male relatives in supporting their national team in the Asian Cup. Women's interest in the fixture was boosted by the team's performance. Businesses in the Jordanian capital reported increased purchases by both men and women of Jordanian flags, T-shirts, shirts with the names of favourite players, music CDs celebrating the Jordanian team and *shmaghs*, the red and white male Jordanian headgear. "Before the start of the Cup, only tourists came to buy T-shirts to have something to remind them of Jordan. Now, all Jordanians are coming to buy team T-shirts," said a shop owner Ahmed Mahassir.

The struggle for the right of women to play soccer in the Middle East and North Africa is not necessarily a battle for a Western interpretation of human rights. Activists like Al-Hawari or Faezeh Hashemi, a former member of Iran's parliament and daughter of former president Ali Akbar Hashemi Rafsanjani, have ensured that their demands remain within the realm of Islamic law. Hashemi advocates clothing that covers everything but the face and hands of female athletes who compete outdoors. She criticizes the "nudity" of women who compete in conventional kit at international tournaments and does not believe women should attend soccer matches until the "moral behaviour" of men at the stadiums can be improved.[42]

Similarly, the battle over women's dress code was not restricted to Middle Eastern teams. Muslim players in European teams paved the road for the lifting of the ban on women's headdress. They were the first to successfully demand the right on cultural rather than religious grounds to cover themselves in matches. Zeinab Al Khatib, a seventeen year-old Danish striker of Palestinian origin, carried their banner. At a time that parliaments in France, Belgium and Spain were imposing restrictions on Muslim women's garb, Al Khatib, backed by the Danish Football Association, overturned FIFA's ban on religious symbols on the pitch. Europe's first covered national soccer player, Al Khatib wore a black scarf tightly wrapped around her head when she unleashed her lightning fast skills and extraordinary heading ability. The Danish association defended the headscarf of its Under-18 national team's most promising forward as a cultural rather than religious commitment and compared it to Brazilian midfielder Ronaldinho Gaucho's headband, which also violates FIFA's insistence that all players be identically dressed.[43]

Social mobility as well as Kurdish identity drove the women of Hakkari Gücü [or Hakkari Power] in one of Turkey's poorest, most conservative, war-torn and remote mountain provinces bordering Iran and Iraq. The team, barely four years old, boasted a string of wins. Various members played on Turkey's national women's youth team. Relatives of the club's players and officials were fighters of the outlawed Kurdistan Workers Party (PKK) whose mountain-top redoubts in northern Iraq were visible from the club's ground on the edge of Hakkari, the capital of the province of the same name.

At times, exchanges of fire between the PKK and Turkish security forces could be heard on the pitch, located in a region that has witnessed some of the worst fighting and solidly voted for the pro-Kurdish Peace and Democracy Party (BDP). Protesters in the city of Hakkari, a desolate town of 60,000 struggling with 40 per cent unemployment and an influx of thousands of refugees from the war, regularly assaulted the Turkish military with stones and Molotov cocktails.

For Hakkari Gücü's players, soccer was both a passion and a tool to assert their identity and compensate for the lack of private and public investment, opportunities and basic infrastructure such as an airport. It is a battle against the odds. The concept of women playing soccer is one that is relatively new in Turkey and revolutionary in a region like Hakkari where honour killings and arranged marriages are not uncommon. Their success on the pitch helped defeat perceptions that soccer was not a sport for women, who should work to help their families make ends meet. Kymet Kurt hails from a family of ten children. Her father was unemployed when she joined Hakkari Gücü at aged fourteen shortly after it was founded. "We played soccer on the street. The club, however, has given me a sense of team spirit and helped improve my social ties. It has also persuaded my father that it will ensure that I don't get stuck in Hakkari," she said.[44]

Turkey's first women's league was disbanded after a decade in 2003 and reconstituted three years later. Corporate sponsorship of the team is virtually non-existent. It relies on the TFF to pay for travel when it plays away games in scrappy kit. Players train on a synthetic turf pitch that relies on street lights instead of floodlights and has one stand that can accommodate a thousand spectators at best.

Hakkari Gücü cannot afford to pay its players. But they transfer their success on the pitch, much like the Palestinian women of Sakhnin in Israel, into scholarships that allow them to get a higher education and offer tickets to Anatolia's boom towns. The club is careful not to project itself as an element of the PKK's soft power. Yet supporters of its rivals see its success as the guerrillas scoring points. A basketball player, athlete-turned soccer referee and computer science graduate who is taking long distance sports management classes, Cemile Timur founded Hakkari Gücü against the will of her family in the belief that it could help boost women's prospects. "I thought that a woman's team would benefit Hakkari," she remarked, echoing a sentiment among women across the region discussed in this book.[45]

6

COMPETING ON THE WORLD STAGE

"Many men go fishing all of their lives without knowing that it is not fish they are after."

Henry David Thoreau

Soccer: An Alternative National Defence Strategy

Winning the 2022 World Cup hosting rights has been a mixed blessing for Qatar. The wealthy Gulf emirate, three years after world soccer body FIFA voted in its favour, found itself subjected to greater scrutiny than it had ever known. It was tougher than it had bargained for. Qatar's suitability as a host was in doubt, the integrity of its bid was in question, its labour system was under attack and controversial court decisions involving expatriates, including international soccer players, had earned it scathing criticism.

The debate seldom strayed far from charges of violations of the rules of the FIFA bidding process. Qatar did itself no favours by refusing to provide the transparency that could have put an end to lingering suspicions. It refused to reveal its budget for the bid and failed to address investment pledges it may have made to soccer associations of FIFA executive committee members, pledges that may have influenced their vote. Instead, Qatar 2022 Supreme Committee secretary general Hassan al-Thawadi insisted, without providing detail, that the bid had been conducted to the "highest ethical and moral standards." He portrayed Qatar as the victim of a campaign in which "baseless accusations were made against our bid. We were presumed guilty before innocent without a shred of evidence being provided." Al-Thawadi added that "amid all the celebrations and joy, we knew that the work was only just beginning. What we did not know or expect was the avalanche of accusations and allegations that we would face in the immediate aftermath of what was a historic day for sport in our country and for the wider region." Committee officials conceded much later that they had made a mistake by failing to engage. They had left the battlefield to their critics and turning the tables in the battle for the moral high ground had become all but impossible.

The questions about the Qatari bid went to the heart of the worst corruption and mismanagement scandal in the history of FIFA. Virtually half of the soccer body's executive committee members had been tainted by allegations of corruption and wrongdoing. The US in 2015 indicted executives of FIFA and two of its regional confederations in the Americas while Switzerland opened an investigation into the awarding of the World Cup to Qatar and the 2018 tournament to Russia. Swiss authorities raided FIFA's headquarters in Zurich and confiscated nine terabytes of data.

Qatar, the first Middle Eastern nation to win World Cup hosting rights, was first and foremost in the firing line: FIFA's executive committee voted in favour of Qatar despite its experts having raised technical issues, including summer temperatures that soar beyond the 40°C mark; an investigation by *The Sunday Times* based on millions of documents retrieved from the servers of the Asian Football Confederation (AFC) that documented vote buying by disgraced former AFC president and FIFA vice president Mohammed Bin Hammam, Qatari national; and FIFA President Sepp Blatter's own implicit admission that a FIFA investigation had been false, if not fixed, when it concluded that Qatar had not engaged in vote swapping with Spain and Portugal, which were bidding jointly for the 2018 Cup.[1] Blatter conceded that there had been a vote swap agreement, but dismissed it because it had produced no advantage for either party.

The incident constituted the only confirmed case of potential wrongdoing by Qatar but said as much about FIFA's concepts of integrity and upholding of rules and regulations as it did about the Gulf state's bid. Qatar's wheeling and dealing may have raised ethical issues, but demonstrated that FIFA's World Cup bid rules contained huge gaps. It also demonstrated that Qatar and FIFA share much in common. Both are accountable to no one but themselves and shy away from transparency. Theirs is a world of secret backroom deals in which one hand washes the other. Their public face is one of compassion and concern that fails to go beyond platitudes.

Qatar and FIFA's shared values were at the core of many suspicions expressed about the bid, including possible incentives offered to national soccer federations represented on the FIFA executive committee as well as the fact that the Gulf state allocated a significantly larger budget to its bid campaign than did its competitors. Doubt also applied to a political deal forged over lunch at the Elysée Palace with former French President Nicolas Sarkozy that led to Michel Platini, head of the Union of European Football Associations (UEFA), the European soccer body, voting in favour of the Qatari bid. Platini's vote helped cement Qatar's advantage. His son has since Qatar Sports Investments as legal counsel, the entity that bought Sarkozy's favourite club, Paris Saint-Germain (PSG) as part of the deal. The deal further involved Qatar's state-owned Al Jazeera television network gaining an opportunity to buy a stake in France's Ligue 1 broadcast rights, and paved the way for further Qatari investment in France. To cement the deal, Sébastien Bazin, the European representative of Colony Capital, the American owners of PSG, which was haemorrhaging an estimated US$25 million a year, attended the lunch. The lunch crowned several months of efforts by Bazin to rekindle Qatari interest in acquiring the financially troubled club. It was Qatar's first taste of the reputational risks involved in world soccer. It nibbled at acquiring PSG in the first decade of the twenty-first century, but its interest evaporated because of the violence of the club's right-wing fans and the fact that two of the club's key stakeholders, Canal Plus, which accounted for much of its revenues, and the City of Paris, which owns Parc des Princes, PSG's stadium, felt queasy about getting into bed with an autocratic ruler.

The deal allowed Al Jazeera to burnish its sports credentials ahead of Qatar's hosting of the World Cup as part of a broader effort to diversify the network at a time when pan-Arab broadcasting was past its heyday, with Middle Eastern and North African viewers shifting to local and thematic channels. Moreover, Al Jazeera's perceived identification with the Muslim Brotherhood cost it viewers in post-revolt nations like Egypt and Tunisia where disillusionment with Islamists took on an anti-Qatari flavour. The deal therefore expanded Al Jazeera's franchise in a country that had no real sports-only channel and added to its ownership of exclusive broadcasting rights in the Middle East for Spain's La Liga, Italy's Serie A, the 2018 Russia and 2022 Qatar World Cups and the launch of beIN in the United States with an English- and a Spanish-language channel designed to cash in on America's growing appetite for soccer and prepare the ground for Al Jazeera America, a separate channel targeting a US audience. "We are going to look at all the opportunities in Europe. We are going to study each market one by one, and if there is room for another channel, then we will go," said Nasser al-Khelaifi, director of Al Jazeera Sports, and also head of PSG.

The three-way deal spotlighted economically troubled France as a prime example of how Qatar leveraged its financial clout and soccer prominence to its commercial and political advantage, with business ventures as well as joint diplomatic initiatives in what amounted to a love affair with France, based on a concerted effort by the French to woo the gas-rich Gulf state that started when Sarkozy was still interior minister. To consolidate the relationship, the French parliament passed a bill in 2009 granting a capital gains tax exemption to Qatari companies on property they own in France. An appendix to the bill stressed the "very strong" and "privileged" relations between France and Qatar, based on "the wish of the Qataris to diversify their alliances and their partnerships so as not to depend exclusively on the United States."

Qatari holdings in France include significant real estate properties such as the seventeenth-century Hôtel Lambert in Paris whose restoration sparked controversy; the equally controversial investment of millions of euros into the promotion of economic activity in France's depressed and neglected suburbs through small and medium-sized enterprises; sponsorship of the Prix de l'Arc de Triomphe, France's most famous horse race; and PSG's €100-million sponsorship deal with Qatar National Bank; as well as investments in major French companies, including Total oil group, construction firm Vinci, Veolia Environment and Louis Vuitton Moët Hennessy (LVMH), the world's largest conglomerate of luxury products and French art.

In an interview with *Al-Monitor*, Qatar's ambassador to France, Mohamed Al Kuwari, explained Qatar's interest in France, saying that "you invest in France, you build partnerships and you go elsewhere, to Africa, to Asia. We are looking for strong partners like Total, Vinci,

Veolia." Moreover, he added, France, like Qatar, charts its own course internationally. It "has an independent policy, plays an important role in the world, diplomatically and politically."

And yet the relationship between Qatar and France goes far deeper. In many ways, Qatar's embrace of sports as a tool of soft power emulates France's post-World War Two efforts to employ soccer and basketball to differentiate itself from other nations and forge a new identity built on principles of democratic republicanism and fair play in a world of European integration, globalization and Cold War.[2]

If most countries bid for mega sporting events as country branding exercises and potential boosts to their economy, for Qatar the cost-benefit analysis was one that went to its core defence and security concerns. Qatar, no matter how many sophisticated weapons it purchases, will never be able to defend itself. The 1990 Iraqi invasion of Kuwait taught it two lessons. For one, big brother Saudi Arabia, unable to ensure its own defence, was an unreliable guarantor that depends on a US defence umbrella. Confidence in the reliability of the United States has, however, been called into question by the US' economic problems, its reluctance to engage militarily post-Iraq and Afghanistan and its likely emergence within a decade as the world's largest oil exporter. Equally importantly, the international coalition that came to Kuwait's aid demonstrated that soft power and embeddedness in the global community at multiple levels earn one friends when in need. For Qatar, the message was clear. It vested its soft power in sports, and particularly soccer, even if it was a late convert to the beautiful game. Qataris first saw British oil workers in the 1940s engage in what they thought was an odd but amusing spectacle. "We had no idea of sports like that ... But we used to enjoy watching the strange spectacle," recalled Ibrahim al-Muhannadi, a government official and member of the Qatar Olympic Committee.

Ivan Sekazza exemplifies the depth of the soft power Qatar is developing through soccer. Ivan's dream was to become a professional soccer player.[3] To him, that was his ticket out of the slums of the Ugandan capital of Kampala. Representatives of Qatar, a country he had never heard of, gave him the chance when they organized a competition to identify Uganda's best young players. Raised by his four brothers after his mother's death, the 13-year-old competed against half a million kids born in 1995 from 800 cities in nine African countries, Paraguay and Vietnam in the biggest talent contest in the history of soccer. Boys from remote villages across Africa travelled to match locations where they slept near the pitch before the game. To them, it was a once-in-a-lifetime opportunity to break out of the cycle of poverty.

Ivan participated in what amounted to an unprecedented search for the next generation of world class soccer talent. It was Qatar's innovative way of tackling its demographic deficit and winning hearts and minds among youth on three of the world's continents. For Qatari emir Sheikh Hamad bin Khalifa Al Thani, the US$15 million a year proposal to adopt the concept of American Idol to soccer put to him by the Spanish professional Josep Colomer, who discovered soccer superstar Lionel Messi when he was Ivan's age, was a perfect way of endearing Qatar to an upcoming soccer-crazy generation and playing a key role in the game's future.

Ivan emerged among his country's best and travelled for the first time in his life by plane to Nairobi to compete with fifty other top East African players. There he was selected as one of twenty-five top players invited to Qatar to compete for three elite training slots in Aspire, Qatar's world-class sports academy. He wore number 10 in the 2009 Football Dreams tournament in Aspire Dome, the academy's sports facility.

Ivan played six matches against some of Europe's best youth teams. The matches were more than just a game to him. He was playing for a future that would allow him to repay his brothers for everything they had done for him. He thought his dream had been shattered when he was replaced midway in his last game against AC Milan. He was sure he had lost his chance to be one of three top players to be accepted by Aspire. But all was not lost. Qatar invited Ivan to join twenty-one other boys who did not qualify for training in Doha to go instead to Aspire's satellite academy in the Senegalese capital of Dakar.

Qatar will always have a place in Ivan's heart. Its ability to wield its soft power has nevertheless proven to be more complex than many Qataris had expected. The sour grapes over its World Cup success stemming from its financial muscle, the arrogance of large nations seeking to delegitimize it on the grounds of it being tiny in population and territory and anti-Arab and anti-Muslim prejudice threw up unexpected obstacles. So did the fact that the winning of the World Cup exposed Qatar to greater international scrutiny than ever before and made it more vulnerable to criticism by rights activists. The silver lining was that the World Cup not only imposed a timeline for completion of Qatar's massive infrastructure projects, but also potentially offered the Gulf nation a framework for inevitable social reforms, particularly in terms of the migrant labour conditions.

Conditions for migrant workers, who account for the majority of Qatar's population and 94 per cent of its work force, topped the agenda of activists. International trade unions and human rights groups threatened a boycott of the World Cup and pressured international infrastructure contractors to adopt global labour standards. In a call entitled "Qatar: Do the Right Thing" on Equal Times, the news website of the International Trade Union Confederation (ITUC), the union told its members: "Don't let your World Cup team play in a shamed stadium. Help us fill the stadium now, and send a message to Qatar that there will be no World Cup in 2022 without workers' rights."

At stake was more than simply capitalist exploitation or what the ITUC termed modern slavery. In the form of the ITUC with 175 million members in 153 countries, Qatar faced a far more formidable critic than it had with human rights groups like Amnesty International and Human Rights Watch, who wield moral power but have no further leverage. The ITUC targeted Qatar where it hurt by pressuring major companies from the US, Britain, France and Brazil that were bidding for contracts worth US$75 billion for World Cup-related projects, including stadiums, rail and subway networks, hotels and a new city that would house 200,000 people, to incorporate workers' rights in their bids. "Under Qatari law, employers have near total control over workers. They alone choose if a worker can change jobs, leave the country or stay in Qatar … Contracts for the new World Cup stadiums and infrastructure will be announced. Millions more workers will be hired from overseas for the road, rail and building infrastructure for the World Cup. We are putting multi-national companies tendering for these contracts on notice to abide by international law and respect workers' rights," warned the ITUC's secretary general Sharan Burrow.

ITUC dismissed Qatar's efforts to improve recruitment procedures as well as working and social conditions because they failed to encompass internationally accepted principles of the right to collective bargaining and the formation of independent trade unions. A further bone of contention was *kafala* or the sponsorship system, under which an employee is beholden to his or her employer.

Ray Jureidini, a sociologist and migration expert at Beirut's Lebanese American University, who advised the Qatar Foundation on establishing standards for the full cycle of a foreign worker's employment in Qatar, including recruitment, deployment, working and living conditions and return to country of origin, noted that abolishing the *kafala* system would amount to a significant overhaul of the Qatari economy. "The kafala system exists as part of an effort by Qataris to retain control of their country. Abolishing the system means opening up a labour market in a country where there is no labour market. The requirement for an exit visa is partly the result of Qatar not having extradition treaties with a lot of countries and wanting to prevent those who break the law from simply skipping the country."[4]

Human Rights Watch documented in a 146-page report, *Building a better World Cup: Protecting Migrant Workers in Qatar Ahead of FIFA 2022*,[5] a host of problems with labour conditions in Qatar, including unpaid wages, illegal salary deductions, crowded and insanitary labour camps and unsafe working conditions. It described "pervasive employer exploitation and abuse of workers in Qatar's construction industry, made possible by an inadequate legal and regulatory framework that grants employers extensive control over workers and prohibits migrant workers from exercising their rights to free association and collective bargaining." The report alleged that the government had failed to enforce laws that on paper were designed to protect worker rights and laid bare problems workers faced when they complained or sought redress. "The government needs to ensure that the cutting-edge, high-tech stadiums it's planning to build for World Cup fans are not built on the backs of abused and exploited workers. Workers building stadiums won't benefit from Qatar's general promise to end the sponsorship system. They need a deadline for this to happen before their work for the FIFA games starts," said Human Rights Watch's Middle East director, Sarah Leah Whitson.

In response, Qatar's 2022 Supreme Committee unveiled a Workers' Charter that offered a set of lofty principles affirming the right of those working on World Cup-related projects "to be treated in a manner that ensures at all times their well-being, health, safety and security" but ceded no rights for workers to organize themselves or bargain collectively. Labour welfare "is a matter of utmost importance for all those involved in the organization of the FIFA World Cup in Qatar 2022. We have always acknowledged that the current state of workers' welfare needs to be improved. From the very beginning, we have pointed to the power of football as a tremendous catalyst for tangibly improving labour conditions in

Qatar and the region at large. From day one, we have been working towards this objective with much care and great dedication to ensure that this is a key legacy of our tournament," claimed the committee.

In tandem, Qatar Foundation, the government's main charity and funder of social, education and research projects, drafted a charter of its own that went significantly beyond the principle enunciated by the Supreme Committee. The foundation said its charter and measures were "based upon a holistic and principled approach that combines Qatari Labour Law and international best practice." The charter enshrines the principle that a worker should not pay for his recruitment—a key issue with vast numbers of labourers indebted for years to corrupt and unethical middlemen who arrange for their employment. To ensure that the foundation was looking to overhaul the recruitment system to cut out the middlemen, options it was considering ranged from setting up its own recruitment system to working with government labour offices in countries supplying labour and or "ethical" employment agencies.

To demonstrate its sincerity—despite not altering legislation—Qatar allowed the Institution of Occupational Safety and Health (IOSH) to open a Doha branch. The UK-based charity, which works with employers and practitioners to improve standards of work-related health and safety, claimed it had developed a five-year plan to improve "road traffic, fire and construction safety" in Qatar. Olumide Adeolu, the head of the new branch, said that he aimed to raise standards of occupational safety and health in line with Qatar's plan to develop a legal framework to ensure a safe workplace: "Our duty is to ensure that workers are adequately protected from accidents at their workplace and also to provide support to safety practitioners, who are charged with the responsibility of ensuring a safe workplace." IOSH would also offer the 2022 organizing committee guidance on construction safety and sports events planning.

As Qatar worked hard to project an impression that it was taking criticism seriously, Nepalese diplomats, whose nationals populate the construction sector, warned that the number of work-related deaths was rising. They pointed out that a lack of independent auditing complicated the tracking of incidents and deaths. "There have been cases where we have suspected that there has been a mutual understanding between the doctor and the company, and the doctor has made a false report saying that they died of cardiac arrest—it is easier for a company to say they died of that," said Harihar Kant Proudel, a second secretary at Nepal's embassy in Doha. He attributed the deaths to the fact that "many workers are going without meals, and without enough water, then they are working in high temperatures all day. The weather here is different from our country. Our nationals are not used to it." His remarks echoed the Human Rights Watch report that pointed to a discrepancy between the number of construction worker deaths reported by foreign embassies and the number acknowledged by the government.

Proudel and Human Rights Watch's assertions added to conclusions of a study in the *Journal of Arabian Studies* that listed late wages, significant debts accrued to pay labour brokers and inconsistent access to healthcare as common problems encountered by foreign workers in Qatar. Funded by Qatar Foundation's Qatar National Research Fund, the study, entitled 'A Portrait of Low-Income Migrants in Contemporary Qatar', stated that 56 per cent of the workers interviewed reported not having received a government-mandated health card needed to access free healthcare.[6]

The ITUC's secretary general alleged that two years after winning the World Cup, and despite international pressure, Qatar had failed to address key issues. "The government of Qatar has had two years to do two things: introduce freedom of association and [address] the kafala system that effectively mounts to 21st century slavery. The government has done nothing. How long are we supposed to wait and listen to the same things? Three years? Five years?" asked Sharan Burrow. She asserted that "hundreds of workers are dying and thousands more are injured in Qatar" as a result of its failure to adhere to international labour standards.

In a break with past practice, Qatar allowed Human Rights Watch executive Jan Egeland to present the group's annual report at a news conference in Doha. "Qatar's rulers asserted in 2010 that the country's successful bid for the World Cup could inspire positive change and leave a huge legacy for the region, but the past two years have seen an absence of reform. If this persists, the tournament threatens to turn Qatar into a crucible of exploitation and misery for the workers who will build it," he stated in criticism rarely voiced in Qatar itself. The Qatari prime minister Sheikh Hamad bin Jassim bin Jaber al-Thani announced in 2011 that his government was "seriously studying" abolishing the sponsorship system. "We are studying the issue very carefully to preserve the rights of citizens and foreign workers," said Sheikh Jaber. The government has yet to say what its study concluded, let along take steps to alter it.

The spectre of more foreign workers pouring into Qatar to complete World Cup-related projects sparked a rare public debate. A series of articles in *The Peninsula*, a Qatari English-language newspaper, portrayed aspects of the lives of migrant workers, including informal self-organized money pools that constitute a rudimentary social security system. The paper noted the lack of entertainment and relaxation opportunities and access to the internet. Qatar University sociologist Kaltham Al-Ghanim pointed out that unskilled foreign workers were not included in the country's National Strategy for Social Security. "Isolating these large sections of our population can make them vulnerable to crime. They can be a challenge to social security," she said. The newspaper warned that the lack of free-time opportunities had sparked the illegal sale of pirated CDs at Doha's Al Ghanim bus station, where workers congregate on Fridays, their day off, because there were no facilities in the Industrial Zone where their camps are located. Qatar's foremost pastime, a visit to the mall or a park, was often off limits because the conservative state restricts the entry of single men. "We welcome the expats, and we want them here. But we will not permit any disrespect to our religion or culture. This is your home, for now. But it is our home forever, and we will not bend to your ways," said Salma, a 25-year-old Qatari.

Yet, even that longstanding attitude is being challenged in a debate fuelled by the fallout of the hosting of the World Cup. In an almost unprecedented vision of a future Qatar, a columnist who used the pen name Jassim bin Sosibo Al Thani to lead people to believe that he was a member of the ruling family, mapped out a society that would be non-racist, non-sexist, Islamic rather than Arab and inclusive in its definition of the country's youth as both Qatari and non-Qatari—a move that if adopted would radically transform Qatar.[7]

Al Thani's vision, published in *Qatar Chronicles*, came as Qatar's new emir, Sheikh Tamim bin Hamad bin Khalifa Al Thani, appeared to be focusing his attention on domestic rather than foreign issues amid griping by Qataris over the country's population explosion, unchecked Westernization inflation and gridlock in a city that is one big construction site.

"Qatar belongs to all its youth; Arabs and non-Arabs, male and female. Every young person who was born here is a citizen of Qatar; a country on the West Asian continent. As a consequence, we are Asians regardless of race, colour, gender or creed ... Our success depends on the country and continent's ability to move in a steady direction, through which we are united with one common purpose as a people together in our diversity. Thus, we propose that young people embrace the diversity that is their birthright, bearing in mind that it is not and must never be a source of division," Al Thani asserted in a break with the notion that birth does not give anyone but Qataris rights and reformulating a national identity that has hitherto focused on the country being Arab.

The columnist, whose identity remains a mystery even after it was revealed that he was writing under an assumed name and was not a member of the ruling family, furthermore propagated a society that would be based on Islamic values, social justice and fundamental human rights rather than—although he did not say so explicitly—an autocratic state in which the emir effectively has absolute power. "This commitment is based on the understanding that our society cannot move forward if today's conditions are still the same as those of yesterday. Consequently, we have to grapple with the enduring insight that Qatar will not succeed merely on the basis of 'stability and continuity.'"

With Sheikh Tamim bin Hamad Al Thani, who succeeded his father as emir in the summer of 2013, moving to apply lessons of the Singapore model by increasingly moving Qataris into positions of responsibility and streamlining Qatar's bureaucracy, Al Thani decried Qatari society's "erosion of values of honesty, loyalty, social solidarity [and] commitment to the responsibilities to which we are charged whether in the private or public sectors. This is manifest in such malaise as corruption, an entitlement culture, below average performance in the work place, low levels of service to the people [customer service] accompanied by demands for more and more rewards." Al Thani claimed that his comments were meant to spark discussion among youth and forge a "consensus in pursuit of building a Qatar that belongs to all who live in it."

Taking up Al Thani's challenge, a long-term Qatari resident and Jordanian national Firas Zirie was quoted by *Doha News*:

> Consider the following anecdote—which applies to me as well as a large number of young expat professionals here: I have spent nearly all of my life in Qatar. I have been through the school and university systems and eventually got a job here, and am trying to get my career on the right track. If one day, I decide to change jobs and am unable to get a No Objection Certificate from my current employer, I would have to leave the country and could not return to work for two years. This seems highly illogical, doesn't it? And while unlikely, reality dictates that it could still happen. That possible future makes

it difficult for people like myself and others in the same boat from feeling stability and security in our lives. That little niggling doubt that it could all come crashing down over a piece of paper, is always there. And it leads to social rifts and resentment.[8]

In emulation of the Singapore model, Zirie, rather than calling for abolition of the controversial *kafala* system, proposed the introduction of a permanent resident status that "would provide flexibility for long-term residents, while reducing fears among Qataris about a dilution of their culture, a concern presented whenever naturalization is discussed."

Yet even naturalization in the wake of the awarding of the World Cup to Qatar is no longer a taboo subject of debate across the smaller Gulf states, which all share a similar demographic dilemma. In a rare public discussion of demography by a Gulf national, Sharjah intellectual and businessmen Sultan Sooud al Qassemi explained in a 2013 *Gulf News* article that "the fear of naturalization is that Emiratis would lose their national identity; we are after all a shrinking minority in our own country. However, UAE national identity has proven to be more resilient and adaptive to the changing environment and times than some may believe."[9]

Noting that the UAE had taken a first step, by granting the offspring of mixed Emirati-non-Emirati nationals the right to citizenship, Al Qassemi pointed out that Saudi Arabia, the one country in which local nationals constitute a majority, albeit a small one, was the only country in the region to have legalized procedures for naturalization. Al Qassemi, however, went a step further in noting that the success of the United States was in no small part due to the contribution of immigrants: "Perhaps it is time to consider a path to citizenship for them that will open the door to entrepreneurs, scientists, academics and other hard-working individuals who have come to support and care for the country as though it was their own."

The cost to Qatar of maintaining an exploitative labour system and building walls between population groups went beyond reputational damage. A study by researchers of Weill Cornell Medical College in Qatar published in *Perspectives on Public Health* concluded that Qatar would be near the top of the United Nation's Human Development Index (HDI) if adjustments were made for the country's large population of migrant workers.[10] That conclusion cut to the core of obstacles to Qatar's soft power strategy to project itself as a cutting edge, twenty-first century, knowledge-based society.

To Qataris, the issue of foreign labour raised fundamental existential questions about the nature, culture and identity of a society that is theirs but in which they constitute at most 15 per cent of the population. Sports was one vehicle that Qatari leaders believed would strengthen national identity, albeit in a situation in which Qataris will always be a minority in their own country. The Doha-based Arab Center for Research & Policy Studies concluded in a report entitled "Foreign Labour and Questions of Identity in the Arabian Gulf" that fears that any degree of integration of foreigners would threaten family-run Qatar's political, cultural and social identity made change unlikely. "The issues touch upon the essence of the question of the transition towards a 'citizenship society' … In the absence of the establishment of a modern state based on the bond of citizenship, justice, the rule of law, and equal opportunity among all components of society, it is extremely difficult to assimilate immigrants … The Gulf countries, due to the delay in the construction of the modern state on the institutional, legal and constitutional levels, have extreme difficulties integrating the population of their home societies—let alone assimilating immigrants."[11]

Yet the desire of many in the region to be citizens rather than subjects constituted a key driver of the popular revolts that have been sweeping North Africa and the Middle East. In the Gulf, this could include generations of Gulf-born descendants of immigrants with no rights, no secure prospects and no real stake in the countries of their birth. As their number continued to increase, educated and prosperous Gulf-born expatriates were beginning to demand equal rights and to caution that they could no longer be bought off with tax-free incomes and benefits. The Gulf-born scion of a wealthy South Asian family, when asked whether he minded that his Gulf-born children would grow up with no rights and no security, responded: "Absolutely, that is no longer acceptable. Gulf societies will have to change by hook or by crook."

With some time to go till the 2022 World Cup, the jury is out as the battle over labour rights unfolds. The outcome is likely to demonstrate the limits of the leverage of both parties and the price they risk paying. The unions could well succeed in reducing, if not stopping, the influx into Qatar of unionized labour but are unlikely to dissuade millions of impoverished unskilled and semi-skilled Asian and African workers from seeking a better life for their loved ones. "What happens to the workers if Qatar loses the World Cup? The ITUC loses its bargaining chip.

Moreover, they are campaigning for taking away the World Cup even before the bids for construction of stadiums have been awarded. Qatar's construction boom will continue with or without the World Cup. Even if they lose those workers, others will come. It's the market's push and pull factor. If the Nepalese don't come, the Bangladeshis will. If the Bangladeshis don't come, the Vietnamese will and if the Vietnamese don't come, the Chinese will," said an independent labour analyst.[12]

Qatar's greater vulnerability to international criticism made it the first Gulf state to ease the restrictions then in place to ensure that foreigners left the country once their employment contracts ended. To provide entertainment and leisure activity, the Qatar Stars League, the country's main league, organized the region's first competition for clubs founded by foreign workers in advance of establishing a league for foreigners that would group thirty-two clubs. Qatar University sociologist Kaltham Al-Ghanim went further. She called on the country's sports clubs to set up branches in the capital's Industrial Zone, where many of foreign workers are housed, "to channel their energy to productive avenues and hunt for sporting talent." She warned that if foreign workers were allowed to "live on the social fringes, the danger is they would take to illegal activities and emerge as a threat to social security." The Qatari moves emulated a programme rolled out by Al Jazeera FC of Abu Dhabi that targeted foreigners by offering them soccer as well as entertainment. The programme, sweetened by a lottery prize of one million dirham (US$272,000) and a Ferrari at its final game of the season, helped the club quadruple match attendance to 20,000, one of the highest figures in the Gulf outside of Saudi Arabia. Other UAE clubs offered to pay fans approximately US$13 to attend matches in a bid to attract nationals to the stadiums. Fans were promised bonuses if they expressed admiration, sang, applauded and cheered throughout the match. Coaches were appointed to help fans who found cheering and singing difficult.

Qatar's efforts to counter criticism and project itself onto the world stage were further overshadowed by a string of controversial court cases and labour disputes.

Similarly, employment-related complaints by two international soccer players, one of whom was barred from leaving Qatar, threatened to overshadow the 2022 World Cup organizing committee's release of its charter of workers' rights. French-Algerian player Zahir Belounis, who was locked into a salary dispute with Al Jaish SC, the club owned by the Qatari military, and barred from leaving the country, and Moroccan international Abdessalam Ouadoo, who left to join AS Nancy-Lorraine, complained about failures to honour their contracts and pay their salaries as well as ill treatment. "This is a crazy story … I cannot move around freely, I cannot work anymore, I'm 33 years old … Who wants a player who has not played for months? Frankly, my career takes a hit," said Belounis. "The Qataris showed me no respect and I can never forgive them for that. I know that money is king but you don't treat a man like that without paying a price," complained Ouadoo, asserting that he had been "treated like a slave." He said he was forced to train in temperatures that went up to 50°C, "just to push me to forget my rights. They did everything to discourage me … The Qataris think they can do everything because they think money can buy anything: buildings, jazz, beautiful cars and men … Human rights are not respected. Human beings are not respected. The workers are not respected. A country that does not respect all these things should not organize the World Cup 2022."[13]

The reputational risks posed by labour conditions, lack of human rights and criticism of Gulf legal systems loomed large as wealthy nations like Qatar, Saudi Arabia, the United Arab Emirates and Bahrain competed for the hosting of mega sporting events; this was something that ruling families and businessmen investing in European and US soccer clubs were to discover. By 2015, Qatar's engagement policy was losing credibility as the Gulf state failed to match words with deeds by implementing its lofty promises.

Human Rights Watch meanwhile alleged that the UAE was using its 2010 acquisition of Manchester City—and its subsequent commitment to create a new club that would compete in the US Major League Soccer—to launder its image. The former English Football Association chairman Lord Triesman called for making a country's human rights record one of the criteria for establishing whether a state entity or member of a ruling family passed the "fit and proper person test" for ownership of an English Premier League club. The charges threatened to undermine the effort by Gulf states to endear themselves to a global public in a manner that would ensure empathy and support in times of need.

The Human Rights Watch allegation was part of a condemnation by major human rights groups and prominent activists of a mass trial in the UAE of ninety-four people, of whom sixty-nine were sentenced to lengthy prison sentences. They asserted that the trial had been unfair and

COMPETING ON THE WORLD STAGE

had violated due process because defendants had been denied legal assistance while being held incommunicado. They further cited allegations of torture, and the lack of a right to appeal. In its response, the UAE justice ministry implicitly did not rule out the possibility of torture. It argued that alleged victims should have reported abuse to the police. The defendants, who included lawyers, teachers and academics, were accused of being members of the Muslim Brotherhood.

Human Rights Watch researcher Nicholas McGeehan described the UAE as "a black hole" for basic human rights. "In this situation, a Premier League club [Manchester City] is being used as a branding vehicle to promote and effectively launder the reputation of a country perpetrating serial human rights abuses. That should be of concern to football supporters as well as human rights organizations." The paper further quoted Human Rights Watch's view that Abu Dhabi's purchase of Manchester City enabled it to "construct a public relations image of a progressive, dynamic Gulf state, which deflects attention from what is really going on in the country."[14]

The sense of soccer serving to launder reputations loomed large as the list of big bucks Middle Eastern acquisitions and sponsorships expanded, even if Gulf buyers at times signalled their refusal to buy at any price and discovered that money cannot buy everything. Qatar had failed to secure what would have been the prize catch, Manchester United, because of a discrepancy of several hundred million dollars between the asking price and the Gulf state's bid. Its attempt to acquire AS Roma also foundered. An offer by Qatar's sovereign wealth fund, the Qatar Investment Fund, to purchase the media agency that controls the broadcasting rights to world soccer body FIFA's World Cup lost out to a London-based private equity firm, Bridgepoint Capital. Dubai International Capital's efforts to gain control of Liverpool FC failed too.

The Emirates kicked off the Middle East buying spree with Emirates Airlines' fifteen-year sponsorship deal with Arsenal FC in 2004 valued at US$160 million. This led to the renaming of the Premier League club's ground as Emirates Stadium and its subsequent takeover of Manchester City but was ultimately overshadowed by Qatar's World Cup bid and a more strategic approach to sports. The Arsenal agreement was at the time the largest ever British sponsorship deal. Other Emirates European sponsorships followed including AC Milan, Real Madrid, Paris Saint-Germain, Hamburger SV and Olympiakos FC as well as FIFA. Emirates stood out in one other respect: it proved among the sponsors of FIFA to be the most vocal in its criticism of the soccer body's handling of its mushrooming corruption scandal.

Fans enthusiastically greeted Manchester City at the team's first post-acquisition match by wearing Arab headdress and waving British bank-notes with the picture of the queen replaced by a Gulf sheikh. Its new owner, Sheikh Mansour bin Zayed, had given them every reason to cel-ebrate. Within twenty-four hours of the takeover he put US$160 million on the table for player acquisition and clinched Real Madrid's Brazilian forward Robinho for a British record of US$52 million, just as he seemed destined for Chelsea. A stream of high-profile acquisitions followed. The club's performance improved radically, culminating in 2011 when Manchester City won its first FA Cup in forty-two years and qualified for the first time for the UEFA Champions League. Manchester City has since concluded a controversial, ten-year, US$640 million sponsorship deal with Abu Dhabi airline Etihad.

The acquisition of Manchester City, followed in 2011 by that of Spanish La Liga soccer club Getafe CF by Dubai-based company Royal Emirates Group owned by Sheikh Butti Bin Suhail Al Maktoum, a mem-ber of Dubai's ruling family, for an estimated US$100 million, and of financially troubled second division German soccer club TSV 1860 Munich by a 34-year-old Abu Dhabi-based Jordanian businessman, Hasan Abdullah Ismaik, were exceptions to the rule of the UAE's sports strategy. Unlike Qatar, the UAE seemed more narrowly focused on the commercial aspects of sports with sponsorships, the hosting of interna-tional tournaments and finance. Brasher than Dubai and Abu Dhabi, certainly after the financial crisis in Dubai in 2008 that left the emirate laden with debt, Qatar has emerged as the Middle East's buyer par excel-lence with a willingness to invest in everything and anything associated with sports, and with more associated assets to leverage such as its Al Jazeera television network.

In an illustration of the UAE's focus on finance, Dubai's United Investment Bank launched the region's first alternative investment soccer fund, modelled on similar controversial European vehicles that encoun-tered opposition from fans in Turkey, Spain and Portugal. The Royal Football Fund aimed to hedge bets in player markets by acquiring the economic rights of young players in Latin America, Africa and Europe. An estimated 20 per cent of the fund was to be invested in listed soccer clubs and television rights for friendly games and tournaments.

With at least five of the twenty richest clubs in Europe enjoying sponsorship by a Gulf entity, UAE and Qatari deals with the two most prominent clubs in their investment portfolios, Manchester City and Paris Saint-Germain, drew negative publicity when UEFA announced that it was investigating whether they had violated its fair value rule. The inquiry involved PSG's annual US$200 million with the Qatar Tourism Authority and Manchester City's US$640 million arrangement with Etihad.

UEFA's fair value rule is designed to prevent owners from circumventing its Financial Fair Play rules by injecting cash into their clubs using entities under their control. The inquiry was sparked by the fact that the distinction between ownership of the two clubs and the sponsoring entities was blurred at best. "We have a regulation which speaks about fair value of deals and the fact that a related party cannot just inject money into a club directly or indirectly," said the UEFA secretary general Gianni Infantino.

The criticism of the UAE took on particular significance as Middle Eastern investors adopted a new strategy in the acquisition of foreign soccer clubs. After initial high-profile investments like Manchester City and PSG, investors moved to buy low and sell high with a series of acquisitions of second- and third-tier European soccer clubs.

Saudi Prince Abdullah bin Mosaad bin Abdulaziz Al Saud, the billionaire former president of Saudi Arabia's most successful club, Al Hilal, and founder and chairman of the publicly-listed Saudi Paper Manufacturing Group, the largest paper tissue manufacturer in the Middle East, bought a 50 per cent stake in Sheffield United with the aim of helping the club graduate from the third division to England's Premier League. "This is the best way to make profit if the club rises to League One and then the premiership," remarked the prince, the first member of the Saudi ruling family to invest in a foreign soccer team.

Prince Abdullah's statement echoed earlier remarks by Bahraini investors, who in late 2012 bought the famous English second-tier club Leeds United for US$82.5 million, and Kuwait's Al-Hasawi family which acquired Nottingham Forest. Bahrain-based Gulf Finance House (GFH) Capital was the first Islamic finance institution to acquire a European soccer club. "Sport is one area where there haven't been many Islamic investments—certainly not to the degree of a full takeover by an Islamic investment firm—but we saw a huge opportunity there ... Ultimately, we're a bank and we're here to make money for investors ... Leeds is one of the very few clubs in the Championship that has a real possibility of becoming a self-sustaining investment, and we really want to get the club into that position," stated David Haigh, deputy CEO of GFH Capital.

Within a year of acquiring the club, GFH Capital had sold more than half of its holding to other Middle Eastern investors. "I see Leeds as a sleeping giant and the more I am involved, the more I appreciate that. There were many clubs available for sale in the Championship, but Leeds have a different reputation and because of this potential that we were attracted," said Salah Nooruddin, a Bahrain-based businessman, who became chairman of the club after buying a 3.3 per cent stake from GFH Capital.

GFH's acquisition of Leeds initially raised questions because of the group's mixed financial track record and negative experiences with other clubs such as Portsmouth FC, Swiss Super League club Servette FC, Austria's Admira Wacker and Spain's Malaga CF. These suffered from problems sometimes aggravated by acquisitions by Middle Eastern commoners or lesser members of ruling families whose takeovers proved to be whimsical rather than strategic. GHF's close ties to the minority Sunni Muslim ruling family in Bahrain, who in 2011 with Saudi help crushed a popular uprising by the island's majority Shia Muslim population, raised the spectre of the Leeds acquisition being partially intended to shore up the island's tarnished image.

The acquisition was Bahrain's second exposure to the risks involved in using sports to project itself. Its hosting of Formula 1 races turned into a public relations disaster two years in a row with international media focusing on widespread anti-government protests rather than the high-powered car race. Bahrain emerged not as an island state that had put a squashed popular uprising behind it, but as a nation wracked by continued strife to which the government responded with extreme force.

Israel, a nation that despite mounting international criticism of its continued occupation of Palestinian land, still enjoys a reservoir of international empathy, proved more successful in fending off efforts to take the shine off its hosting of FIFA's Under-21 finals in 2013. "Football is an effective vehicle for Israel to rehabilitate its image with the international community. A large sporting event is an ideal opportunity for Israel to present itself as a normal country," Tamir Sorek, a University of Florida expert on Israeli soccer told UAE newspaper *The National*. However more than sixty prominent European players, allegedly including Chelsea's Eden Hazard, Arsenal's Abou Diaby and PSG's Jérémy Ménez, warned that holding the U-21 competition in Israel would be "seen as a reward for actions that are contrary to sporting values." The players went on to say in a statement that "we, as European football players, express our solidarity with the people of Gaza who are living under siege and denied basic human dignity and freedom."

Qatar, Bahrain, Saudi Arabia and Israel learnt the hard way that mega sporting events have costs as well as benefits. They potentially allow countries to showcase themselves, polish or improve their image, serve as tools to enhance soft power and create commercial, economic and political opportunity. But mega events empower activists, spotlight their demands amid intense media focus and give them the moral high ground if a country fails to respond adequately to criticism. The lesson learnt from experiences in the Middle East is that mega events give leverage not only to countries and governments but also to their detractors.

The responses of Qatar, Bahrain, Saudi Arabia and Israel failed to give them the upper hand in the public relations battle with activists who highlighted their failure to adhere to international standards of human, labour and/or gender rights. Worse still, the public relations battles reinforced the negative perceptions they were trying to reverse. Their failure strengthened calls for such rights to become key criteria in the awarding of future mega events. The IOC, in a foretaste of things to come, cited labour conditions as one reason for its rejection of Qatar's bid for the 2020 Olympics. It also rendered the separation of sports and politics a fiction and focused attention on the need to develop systems that acknowledge the relationship, but eliminate conflict of interest and ensure that it is not abused for partisan political interests on an individual, national, regional and international scale.

The Middle Eastern acquisition by the same token did succeed in forging some cultural bridges. Fans have been willing to accept cultural compromises stemming from association with Muslim entities and investors such as Sheikh Abdullah Ben Nasser Al Thani's replacement of bookmaker William Hill PLC with United Nations culture agency UNESCO as Malaga's shirt sponsor—because gambling is banned under Islamic law—and Royal Emirates' plans to set up a pavilion about Arab culture at Getafe's stadium. Real Madrid's decision to remove a Christian cross from its official logo in what it described as the cost of doing business in a globalized world sparked some ire, particularly among anti-Muslim right-wingers. The removal came as Real Madrid embarked on the construction of a US$1 billion sport tourist resort in the UAE that was halted because of lack of funding.

Little changed in Qatar's commitment to sports as a key foreign, defence and security policy tool with the rise of 33-year-old Sheikh Tamim as emir. Sheikh Tamim took over the reins of power from his father Sheikh Hamad in a rare voluntary handover in a region in which rulers hang on until death often despite deterioration of their physical and/or mental health. Sheikh Tamim nibbled at best at the fringe of his father's bold policies while maintaining his focus on domestic issues and sports, manifested in his chairmanship of the Supreme Education Council and the Qatar Olympic Committee and his introduction of Qatar National Sports Day, a popular annual event. Filling Sheikh Hamad's shoes was, however, no mean feat. The former emir had put his tiny country on the world map, changed the Middle East and North Africa's media landscape with the creation of the Al Jazeera television network, offered the Gulf an alternative vision of leadership by stepping aside to make place for a younger generation and turned Qatar into a nation with the world's highest income per capita of the population.

In contrast to Sheikh Hamad, Sheikh Tamim appeared to be more sensitive to criticism by conservative segments of Qatari society of the cost of the former emir's policy. They griped about the huge expenditure involved in a foreign policy that put Qatar at the forefront of regional demands for greater freedom and change but also earned it significant antipathy; unfulfilled promises of change at home that would give Qataris a greater say in where their country was going; a stark increase in foreign labour to complete ambitious infrastructure projects many of which were World Cup-related and exposed Qatar for the first time to real pressure for social change; more liberal catering to Western expatriates by allowing the controlled sale of alcohol and pork; and potential tacit concessions Qatar may have to make to non-Muslim soccer fans during the World Cup, including expanded areas where consumption of alcohol would be allowed, public rowdiness, un-Islamic dress codes largely unseen in the Gulf state and the presence of homosexuality.

Conservative and liberal criticism was unlikely to provoke a popular revolt like it did elsewhere in the region, something US President Barack Obama acknowledged when he was caught off camera by CBS News praising Sheikh Hamad as "a big booster of democracy all throughout

the Middle East," although "he himself is not reforming significantly."
Obama suggested that Qataris with a per capita annual income of
$145,000 felt little urge to embrace reform. "Sheikh Tamim will not rock
the boat. He is well-versed and immersed in Qatari vision and policy. He
understands the importance to Qatar of its sports strategy and all that it
entails. At most, he will be more publicly embracing of traditionalism in
what remains at the bottom line a conservative society," quipped one
Qatari with an inside track.

Nonetheless, Qatar's ruling elite was sufficiently concerned to look at
addressing potential sparks of discontent. One discussion looked at the
possible transfer of ownership of soccer clubs from prominent Qataris,
including members of the ruling family, to publicly held companies in
the realization that Qataris often refused to attend matches because they
had no desire to support "the sheikh's club." The discussion paralleled a
similar one in Saudi Arabia. Fan apathy and empty stadiums in the
smaller Gulf states where local nationals account for at most some 40 per
cent of the population—in the UAE that number drops to 10 per cent,
in Qatar to just over 20 per cent and in Kuwait to approximately 40 per
cent—was in part the result of a small numbers of local fans and a reluctance to attract non-national supporters out of fear that their bonding
with a local club could encourage them to develop a sense of entitlement
and demand more rights. In Saudi Arabia, meanwhile, poor attendances
had more to do with lagging performance, decaying infrastructure and a
growing resentment with random and spurious interference by club owners. The drop in gate receipts did not signal reduced passion for the
game, itself a cause for clerical concern.

Saudi soccer officials envisioned privatizing clubs and using the proceeds to improve infrastructure and restructure the league along the lines
of the English Premier League. The new league would be able to
increase revenues from broadcast rights—a commercial undertaking
which is still in its infancy in the Middle East and North Africa and has
so far benefitted state-owned broadcasters like Al Jazeera and Abu Dhabi
Television with deeper pockets than their private sector competitors. "We
are not only trying to make money, the aim of what we are trying to do
is raise the level of sports in Saudi and in order to do so I think you need
to have healthy club financials so they can afford to bring the best
coaches, the best foreign players. And when you raise the level of Saudi
clubs, you raise the level of the national team," said Prince Abdullah,

who heads the Saudi committee in charge of the restructuring of soccer, in an interview with the *Wall Street Journal*.[15]

As Gulf rulers sought to prevent discontent from boiling over, Sheikh Tamim enhanced his popularity through his close relationship with local tribes, his upholding of Islamic morals exemplified by his refusal to serve alcohol in luxury hotels he owns and his easy accessibility to the public that had earned King Abdullah unrivalled credibility in Saudi Arabia in comparison to most other members of the Al-Saud family. His decision to replace English with Arabic as the main language of instruction at Qatar University curried favour with nationalists and conservatives as did the suggestion that he was empathetic to unprecedented on-line campaigns by Qatari activists against the state-owned telecommunications company and Qatar Airways in protest against their employment and pricing strategies and the airlines' sale of alcohol and pork to foreigners at a shop in Doha—even though he did not reverse those policies. "I never thought the day would come that I have to ask the waiter in a restaurant in Qatar what kind of meat is in their burgers," said a Qatari on Twitter. "Ppl don't get it. Its not about the pork—its about us feeling more & more like a minority—in our own country," tweeted another Qatari.

Critics, including members of the royal family, had questioned Sheikh Hamad's authority to authorize the sale of alcohol and pork. Hassan Al Sayed, a professor of constitutional law and former dean of the College of Law at Qatar University, charged that there was no Qatari law that allowed for the sale of alcohol and that, if anything, several laws, including the constitution, criminalized it. Even "if there is any decision coming for example from the Emir or any department here, this is not okay and this is against the law," stated Al Sayed. He added that for Qatar to legally allow the sale and consumption of alcohol it must change its constitution, which in Article 1 stipulates that "Islam is the State's religion and the Islamic Sharia is the main source of its legislations." Al Sayed argued that the legal ban applies also to free zones the government announced it would create for fans attending the 2022 World Cup. The criticism led to a ban on serving alcohol in restaurants on man-made Pearl Island, a place largely frequented by expatriates. The ban extended beyond public venues to the kitchen, where one resident blogger, Jenifer Fenton, said it could also not be used in cooking. Business at restaurants dropped as much as 50 per cent as a result of the ban. In further moves to maintain conservative mores, a Qatari civic group organized a campaign in malls and other public spaces with posters and flyers to ensure that expatriate women dressed modestly in public in line with Islamic tradition.

Preservation of tradition was one way many Qataris hoped to prevent loss of national identity. If sport was for Qatari leaders a tool in forging national identity and projecting their country internationally, banning alcohol was the equivalent for more conservative and nationalist forces. "I don't see a reason to have alcohol. It impacts very negatively on locals. Locals are not happy with it," commented the Qatari writer Abdul Aziz Al Mahmoud. Conservative Qataris worry that an increasing number of their compatriots, often dressed in full-length robes, the Gulf's national dress, drink publicly in hotels and bars. "It is a taboo in Qatar to see somebody wearing the national dress and drinking," said Hassan Al Ibrahim, a Qatari pundit. Much of the criticism of Sheikh Hamad was quietly supported by Saudi Arabia, the region's behemoth, whose relationship with the emir was troubled. The Saudis never forgave him for seizing power in 1995 in a bloodless coup that toppled his father.

To many Qataris, hosting the World Cup entailed the prospect of change. Qatari blogger Khalifa Saleh Al Haroon wrote:

> It's the fact that it will be bring further development and change that gets me more excited though. Qatar will be under the world's spotlight and will be scrutinized. With people paying attention, things have to change (or most likely will). Remember that road in westbay in front of City Center that was under construction for 6 months and was finished in a week before the UN came over for a meet up? Perhaps this is the kick that Qatar needs to improve quality and get things done faster ... Think about it! New laws which'll open up so many doors and make things more transparent. Expats will most probably no longer need an exit permit, the Human Rights Authority will be given more funds and responsibilities, there'll be more construction in anticipation for the games which'll hopefully provide more accommodation than there is demand (that's good because it means we'll have a market adjustment and commodities will hopefully drop to their true value), plus it'll bring a huge amount of businesses interested in opening up within Qatar. (Fingers crossed that everyone gets in on that action though and it's not just the same group of people running everything). Unlike the Olympics which is hosted in one city, the World Cup is country wide, that means that Qatar will have to develop and focus on other areas of Qatar. This means more variety, more choice and hopefully a more dispersed population that will reduce congestion.[16]

How Sheikh Tamim deals with demands for social change resulting from the World Cup and Qatar's broader soft power strategy will have an impact far beyond its borders. Recent events have already put Qatar at loggerheads with Saudi Arabia, which worries about just how far Qatar may go. Qatar's willingness to engage with its critics has magnified the fact that, alongside the kingdom, it is the world's only state that adheres to Wahhabism, an austere interpretation of Islam. Qatari conservatism is, however, everything but a mirror image of Saudi Arabia's stark way of life with its powerful, conservative clergy, absolute gender segregation and refusal to accommodate alternative lifestyles or religious practices. Qatar's adaptation of Wahhabism, coupled with its lack of an indigenous clergy and long-standing relationship with Islamist groups, including the Muslim Brotherhood, the region's only organized opposition force, has complicated its relationship with Saudi Arabia and the UAE. Liberalizing social restrictions and improving conditions for foreign labour risked strengthening demands for change in the Kingdom itself.

Qatar's ambitious soft power strategy, however, faces two regional challengers: Saudi Arabia, which could see it as a threat that needs to be contained, and Turkey.

Turkey ranks number 18 on the list of the world's largest economies ahead of Saudi Arabia at number 20, the United Arab Emirates at 30 and Qatar at 51 even though many Gulf states have a nominally higher GDP. Turkey has campaigned for two decades to host the Olympic Games and could have won the 2020 tournament had its image not been tarnished by mass anti-government protests and fears that the civil war in Syria could spill across Turkey's 900-kilometre long border with that troubled country.

To be sure, it has not been smooth sailing for Turkey. Its premier soccer teams have been wracked by a major match-fixing scandal that was exacerbated by a power struggle among Islamists and a financial crisis as a result of overspending. Prime Minister Recep Tayyip Erdoğan makes no bones about Turkey's strategy in which sports plays an important role. "The whole world must know that Turkey has big ambitions, based on national will and a strong State," he told Turkish diplomats almost a decade ago.[17]

(West) Asian Soccer: A Cesspool of Government Interference, Struggles for Power, Corruption and Greed

> *"The real president of our country is FIFA. FIFA comes to our country, sets up a state within a state, and leaves."*

> Brazilian protestor

Asian soccer reformists had high hopes that Mohammed Bin Hammam's demise in 2012 would allow them to unravel a network of government interference, power struggles, corruption, greed and vested interests that undermined governance, transparency and accountability in their continent's beautiful game.

Yet, several years later, little has changed with Bin Hammam's banning for life from involvement in soccer and the election of a new Asian Football Confederation (AFC) president who is unblemished in terms of corruption but stands accused of failing to stand up for the rights of soccer players who were dismissed from Bahrain's national team, arrested and allegedly tortured for participating in peaceful pro-democracy demonstrations.

The Bin Hammam affair was not only at the centre of the worst scandal in Asian and global soccer but was also at the core of the most serious challenge to the credibility of good governance in world soccer body FIFA, that mushroomed with the US indictments in 2015 and an investigation in Switzerland into what has become the most controversial awarding of a World Cup in the history of the game. A 64-year-old Qatari national, Bin Hammam had a finger in all pies as the first Arab president of the AFC as well as an executive committee member of FIFA and a major player in Qatari soccer. He was key to FIFA president Sepp Blatter's long-standing, close relationship with former Qatari emir Sheikh Hamad bin Khalifa al-Thani.

The affair, coupled with the failed efforts to reform the governance of Asian soccer and the controversy surrounding Qatar's successful bid to host the 2022 World Cup, serves as a prism of everything that is wrong in the global governance of the game: the cosy, intimate relationship between politics and soccer in which soccer executives, certainly a majority of those in the Middle East and West Asia, serve the interests of their political masters; the role soccer federations play in enhancing the power base of autocratic leaders; the principle of money talks, whether corporate or public funds or the funds of states run like family enterprises; the power of a tiny state like Kuwait to shape the soccer politics of a vast continent like Asia that is home to the world's most populous states; and the emphasis on the personal interests of nation's top soccer executives at the expense of those of the sport.

The affair puts to bed the fiction of a separation of sports and politics. It raises the question whether the time has not come to recognize the intrinsic relationship between the two and to develop a code of conduct or charter that would govern the relationship between politics and sports. That is nowhere more needed than in the Middle East or West Asia where few associations, if any, are independent of government and ruler interests. That has allowed FIFA to employ the fictitious distinction between sports and politics in order to cosy up to autocratic regimes and in effect endorse their manipulation of soccer for their own purposes: witness not only Blatter's relationship with Qatar but also with autocrats like Tunisia's Zine El Abidine Ben Ali, whose son was a FIFA executive committee member, and Al Saadi Al Qaddafi, the failed soccer playing son of Moammar Qaddafi, who was long viewed as one of Blatter's closest allies in Africa.

An analysis of the composition of the AFC's executive committee and the boards of many of its national associations, who include thirteen Middle Eastern federations which account for 28 per cent of the Asian group's forty-six member associations, tells the story.

Six of the AFC executive committee's twenty-one members in the period from 2011 to 2015 hailed from the Middle East. They include its president, Sheikh Salman, a member of a minority Sunni ruling family that in its brutal suppression of a 2011 popular revolt arrested scores of sports officials and athletes among whom national soccer team players who were tortured; Prince Ali Bin Al Hussein, a half-brother of Jordan's King Abdullah who as a reformer was a thorn in Sheikh Salman and embattled, outgoing FIFA president Sepp Blatter's side; the United Arab Emirates' Yousuf Yaqoob Yousuf Al Serkal who maintains close ties to his country's ruling elite; Sayyid Khalid Hamed Al Busaidi, a member of Oman's ruling family; and Hafez Al Medlej, a member of the board of Saudi Arabia's tightly controlled soccer association who made his career in the Kingdom's state-run media.

That number has risen to seven in the executive committee elected in April 2015 that includes Sheikh Salman as well as Mohammed Khalfan Al Romaithi, deputy commander-in-chief of the Abu Dhabi police, a force tainted by multiple allegations of human rights abuses; and representatives of Kuwait, Lebanon, and Saudi Arabia and the head of Islamic Republic of Iran Football Federation (IRIFF), whose premier league teams are largely government-controlled.

The close ties between sport and politics, particularly in the Middle East, is also reflected in the composition of the boards of the region's national soccer associations and many of its major clubs. Almost half of the West Asian Football Federation's members are headed by members of ruling families or commoners closely associated with them, including Saudi Arabia, Kuwait, Oman, Bahrain, Qatar and Jordan as well as people with close government ties as in Iran and Syria.

The Middle East's incestuous political ties to sport are also evident in the Olympic Council of Asia (OAC) that is headed by Sheikh Ahmed Al-Fahad Al-Ahmed Al-Sabah, a prominent member of Kuwait's ruling family and former oil minister, member of the IOC, and head of the Association of National Olympic Committees (ANOC), who recently suffered a humiliating political defeat at home and is mulling running for the FIFA presidency. Sheikh Ahmed is widely viewed as one of world sport's most powerful movers and shakers who played a key role tainted by allegations of vote buying in Salman's AFC election in 2013.

In a recently published memoir, former AFC general secretary Peter Velappan put his finger on the problem. "Football enjoyed complete patronage from the royal families and the sheikhs," Velappan said.[18]

The failed effort by reformists including the soccer associations of Jordan, Singapore, Japan, South Korea, Australia and Guam to use the Bin Hammam affair to break the vicious circle of corruption and lack of transparency has effectively served to highlight Asian and world soccer's inability to reform itself. A series of primarily cosmetic changes in response to the crisis did little to tackle the fundamental structures responsible for the lack of good governance, transparency and account-ability. The failure stands in stark contrast to the far-reaching reforms introduced by the IOC after its 2004 corruption scandals in the wake of the Salt Lake City Olympics. It is the inevitable outcome of a system in which global, regional and national association heads and their executive committees are accountable to no one but themselves.

The allegations against Bin Hammam raised questions about his involvement in Qatar's World Cup bid despite Qatari denials that he had anything to do with it. The Qatari denials did little to explain why the highest Qatari soccer official in world soccer, who enjoyed the backing of Qatari emir Sheikh Hamad bin Khalifa Al Thani, would not have been involved in the bid at least until Bin Hammam announced that he would challenge FIFA president Blatter in the group's 2011 presidential elec-tion. In fact, documents disclosed by reporters of the *Sunday Times* sug-gested that Bin Hammam was intimately involved with the bids and paid off a large number of soccer executives across the globe to ensure that Qatar would win the World Cup bid.[19] Qatari officials suggested privately that Qatar and Bin Hammam's interests began to diverge with the announcement of his presidential bid that many felt posed a real threat to Blatter's tenure. Bin Hammam began to distance himself from the Qatari bid in the final months before the FIFA vote because a simultaneous Qatari winning of World Cup hosting rights and the FIFA presidency could have been too much for world soccer to stomach, they said. Bin Hammam's close ties to the Qatari sports establishment as well as to other soccer associations like that of the UAE were, however, evident with the hiring by Qatar Stars League and the UAE Football Association of AFC personnel who had been dismissed because of their ties to Bin Hammam. Those hired were identified in an independent auditor's report that severely criticized Bin Hammam's financial and commercial management of the AFC. Bin Hammam, moreover, has privately suggested that his presidential bid was intended to safeguard the awarding of the World Cup to Qatar after trust between Qatar and Blatter had broken down as a result of remarks by the FIFA president that he may be susceptible to acting on criticism of the decision.

Ironically, Bin Hammam, the highest official ever to have been banned for life, was both an integral cog in the system and the odd man out. A self-made millionaire who benefitted from a government-dominated economy flush with oil and gas dollars, Bin Hammam, unlike many others, was in soccer not just for the personal glory but also because he was genuinely passionate about the sport. Friend and foe agree that he genuinely cared and was generous to his associates. His downfall was his ambition and his failure to grasp that accepted business practices in the Gulf often violate international business and accounting standards. He ran the AFC much like he would have run his business in Doha. To be fair, the AFC and FIFA's way of doing business was not that different from the backslapping, backhanded practices of the Gulf.

Moreover, critics of Bin Hammam as well as of Singapore-based World Sports Group, the company he contracted as the AFC's marketing arm, concede—the controversies notwithstanding—that both have also contributed to the strengthening of the AFC and of soccer in the region. Yet their predictions that Asia, including the Middle East and North Africa, represents the sport's future have yet to materialize. Even if the region's soccer organizations were able to clean up their act and rein in unbridled political interference, Asia would still come—with the exception of a few like Egypt's Al Ahly SC and Tehran's Persepolis—a distant second in any popularity contest with European leagues and tournaments.

Bin Hammam's naiveté nevertheless may well have been what sparked his demise. It was evident not only in how he managed the AFC but also in the way he ran his 2011 FIFA presidential campaign against the wishes of both Blatter and the Qatari emir and conducted crucial commercial negotiations on behalf of the Asian soccer body. Blatter saw Bin Hammam's candidacy as a formidable threat. The Qatari had financial muscle in a world in which votes were for sale and he was privy to Blatter's secrets. For years he had been both Blatter and Qatar's bagman and the FIFA president's link to the Qatari emir.[20] Bin Hammam's troubles began when he handed out envelopes each containing US$40,000 to twenty-five officials of the Caribbean Football Union (CFU) gathered for the Qatari's campaign meeting in the Grand Hyatt Hotel in Trinidad's Port of Spain. Each of the CFU officials had a vote in the presidential election. Bin Hammam has repeatedly denied that he was bribing potential voters, asserted that Blatter knew in advance that he was offering the CFU delegates compensation for their expenses and accused the FIFA president of deliberately setting him up so that he could run for re-election unopposed.

Bin Hammam's strategy with the CFU fits a way of doing business in FIFA that Blatter, flush with Qatari funds, had long adopted. The German sports reporter Thomas Kistner described being an eyewitness to the handing out of envelopes filled with cash, arranged by Bin Hammam, during Blatter's first election campaign in 1998. "Thick envelopes were handed out in the Meridien hotel where the African delegation was staying in the night before the election which took months to prepare. The next day Blatter takes the lead with 118:20 votes. It is clear to everyone that votes were bought en masse. The writer of this book was present when the evening after the election the chairman of the African soccer federation, Cameroon national Issa Hayatou, and five or six representatives of African national associations apologize to [FIFA Vice President Lennart] Johansson for the scandalous behaviour of their colleagues. One African even forgot to take the envelope with cash. A FIFA employee found the money. Blatter rejects all allegations," wrote Kistner, acknowledging that neither Blatter nor Bin Hammam had been in the Africans' hotel when the cash was distributed. "But what does that say? Can these kind of monies only be distributed personally?"[21]

Jack Warner, the disgraced FIFA vice-president, who resigned in 2011 from the soccer body's executive committee to avoid investigation of his role in the Bin Hammam affair, and who has since been indicted in the United States on corruption charges, alleged in a boisterous, bitter letter to the *Trinidad Guardian* that "we took him [Blatter] on a worldwide crusade through Africa and Asia begging for support for him, and he won! That was the first time I met the present deputy chairman of FIFA ethics committee, Petrus Damaseb, at the time the president of the Namibia FA. I will tell the world what gift Bin Hammam gave to him which was not a bribe then as he has ruled today. With Bin Hammam's private plane, we did the same for Blatter again in 2002 when he faced Issa Hayatou, in a most brutal election, and he won—a second time ... All the real 'gifts' that Blatter gave to secure his two elections will turn stomachs inside out. The conspiracy to protect the FIFA's throne for [UEFA president] Michel Platini by getting rid of the Muslim Bin Hammam and the interruption of the successes of Jack Warner will be uncovered for all to see," Warner said,[22] referring to the fact that Damaseb chaired the ethics committee that initially banned Bin Hammam in 2011 and wanted to investigate Warner. Warner's credibility lies in the fact that he benefitted from, and was part and parcel of, FIFA's dubious business practices. He was forced to resign as Trinidad and Tobago's security minister after the ethics panel of the Confederation of North, Central American and Caribbean Association Football (CONCACAF) accused him of fraudulently enriching himself.

Farah Addo, the late head of the Somali Football Federation, who was deleted from the 1998 delegates' list to the FIFA Congress because of his refusal to be part of Qatari-backed efforts to influence the presidential election, described Bin Hammam as "the financial brain behind Blatter's election campaign. Mr. Bin Hammam arranged via the Gulf region travel to Paris for all [African] association representatives as well as their wives and children. He gave them free airline tickets and cash," Addo reported. In advance of the 2002 FIFA Congress in which Blatter stood for re-election, Addo, who by then was head of the Council for East and Central Africa Football Associations (CECAFA), warned that "unfortunately Blatter and Bin Hammam are using the FIFA Goal development project as a tool to blackmail poor national associations by only allocating aid funds to their clients and countries that have FIFA executive committee members." Bin Hammam, a member of FIFA's financial committee, administered Goal on behalf of FIFA. African media reported in advance of the 2002 election that Qaddafi's son Al Saadi was paying some twenty federations US$200,000 each.[23]

Ultimately, FIFA was unable to make the Caribbean bribery allegation stick. FIFA did however, succeed in forcing Bin Hammam to withdraw from the the group's 2011 presidential race. Bin Hammam's success in appealing against FIFA's decision in the Lausanne, Switzerland-based Court of Arbitration of Sports (CAS) to suspend him days before the election and initially ban him for life allowed his opponents, with Blatter in the lead as well as reformists in Asian soccer, to tackle him on his management of the AFC. Bin Hammam's CAS success proved to be a Pyrrhic victory. The court refused to give him a clean bill of health. It left little doubt that the judges believed that the Qatari was more likely than not guilty of the charges brought against him.

Yet it overturned FIFA's punishment of Bin Hammam on the grounds that the soccer body's investigation had been shoddy. The ruling painted a troubling picture of the status of good governance, accountability and transparency as well as of ethical and moral standards in world soccer FIFA's evidence did not meet the court's standard of "comfortable satisfaction," it said. It portrayed FIFA's ban as having been based on flimsy evidence, inconclusive investigations and witnesses whose credibility was in question. It further suggested that rather than strengthening its evidence, FIFA had unsuccessfully sought to delay the court's decision by introducing evidence not directly related to its case, including an independent auditor's report critical of Bin Hammam's financial management of the AFC.

The court's criticism of FIFA raised questions about the integrity of FIFA's judicial and disciplinary proceedings at a time that the soccer body was embroiled in the worst web of corruption scandals in its 108-year history. What emerged was an image of the world soccer body, as well as of Bin Hammam, in which all parties were tainted. It is an image reinforced by the fact that at least eleven of FIFA's twenty-four executive committee members had been implicated in corruption charges in the preceding three years.

Bin Hammam was initially suspended on the basis of a report by US lawyer John P. Collins on the payments to the CFU that had been privately commissioned by FIFA executive committee member Chuck Blazer, who was later forced out because of US legal proceedings involving his management of North and Central American and Caribbean soccer. Blazer was one of those revealed as a defendant in the 2015 indictments of FIFA officials and executives of soccer bodies and sports marketing companies in the Americas. The Lausanne court asserted that FIFA had failed to establish that monies paid to CFU members came from Bin Hammam or that they were intended to buy votes. It noted that the CFU operated secret accounts and that the report "did not sufficiently investigate the existence of CFU accounts to check whether the CFU had ever had enough funds to provide the cash gifts, or whether there had been cash withdrawals from these accounts."

The court rejected a subsequent report by the Freeh Group, owned by former FBI director Louis Freeh, as consisting of little more than circumstantial evidence. It further questioned the credibility of key FIFA witnesses, including FIFA executive committee member Warner and former CFU general secretary Angenie Kanhai. It concluded that the banning of Bin Hammam without the testimony of Warner was based on "extremely limited sources."

The ruling concluded that "Mr. Warner appears to be prone to an economy with the truth. He has made numerous statements as to events that are contradicted by other persons, and his own actions are marked by manifest and frequent inconsistency." The ruling was referring to Warner both confirming and denying that cash had been distributed at the CFU gathering despite the court being in possession of a video confirming the disbursements. "The majority of the Panel [the court] concludes that Mr. Warner is an unreliable witness, and anything he has said in relation to matters before the panel is to be treated with caution."

Similarly, Kanhai, who handled a suitcase containing the monies distributed, offered contradicting statements.[24] She initially testified that she insisted that she was not advised who the benefactor of the monies or who had arranged the funds, but later changed her statement to say that Warner had advised her that Bin Hammam was the source. The ruling noted that Kanhai altered her version of events two days before she left the CFU to work for FIFA.

Blatter fared little better in the ruling, having first declared in advance of the Caribbean meeting that he was not advised by Warner about the source only to declare a day later in writing that the former soccer official had told him that Bin Hammam intended to hand out monies.

The internal audit of AFC finances that FIFA unsuccessfully attempted to introduce into the CAS proceedings was commissioned in a bid by reformists to get their stymied campaign for change within the AFC back on track as much as it was to give FIFA and the AFC a stick with which to beat Bin Hammam in anticipation of his winning his CAS appeal. The commissioning of PricewaterhouseCoopers (PwC) to conduct the audit in early 2012 came after months of stalled efforts to reform the group and dismantle Bin Hammam's legacy which concentrated power in the hands of the AFC president.

Plans to rewrite the AFC's statutes, which were changed after Bin Hammam took office in 2002, were drafted during an AFC executive committee in July 2012 during which Bin Hammam was suspended as president pending the outcome of the FIFA procedure. These were quickly sidelined by his many supporters within the group. Bin Hammam had drafted the statutes to ensure that they empowered him rather than the executive committee. The statutes virtually strip the office of the secretary general of any authority. They allowed Bin Hammam to install in all of the AFC's departments a person loyal to him whose authority superseded that of the department head. "The secretary general was reduced to a nobody. The standing committees were weakened, they discussed nothing," observed one source.

Peter Velappan, who as secretary general of the AFC from 1979 to 2007 introduced Bin Hammam to the Asian confederation, said that the Qatari further disempowered AFC committees by reducing their scheduled meetings from three hours to ninety minutes and by banning the posing of spontaneous questions. Bin Hammam insisted that questions be presented and cleared by him prior to meetings. Day-long executive committee meetings were also shortened to ninety minutes. Velappan described Bin Hammam as the "architect of bribery and corruption first in the AFC and then in FIFA" and claimed that the two organizations were characterized by "a culture of corruption."[25] He said he had supported Bin Hammam in 2002 in line with a general feeling within the organization that its new leader should for the first time be a non-Malaysian national. "The problem was that he never understood Asia. Asia is multicultural. He was never at ease with anyone. Communications was a big problem because his English was not proficient. His strength was money, not his leadership and not his skills."

Bin Hammam's grip on the AFC even after his suspension and the strength of the opposition to reform by vested interests that benefitted from the Qatari's management style was evident in the inability of Zhang

Jilong, who succeeded Bin Hammam as acting president, to implement the AFC executive committee's recommendations. In an uncharacteristic outburst, Zhang warned in a letter to AFC members dated 17 October 2012 that the AFC was at a crossroads.

> We have a simple choice to make in the face of the distractions being thrown in our direction. We can do the work such as amending our controlling statutes to put in place comprehensive by-laws and regulations which actually create a system of governance that leads to transparency and accountability. Or, we can ignore the truth and go back to business like it was before while pretending that it is acceptable for one man to assume control of this Football Confederation and run it like it was his own private business. I believe, I understand and know the direction we must take to get where we want to be—and I believe right now we must stay the course and see the legal process that has been started through to its end. I never asked to become the Acting President or to take on these incredibly difficult problems and responsibilities. But I will not run away from this work either and I ask for your help and support.

Zhang accused Bin Hammam and his lawyer, Eugene Gulland, of adopting "intimidatory tactics" in the battle to defeat charges of bribery, corruption and financial mismanagement, a charge Gulland denied.[26] He said the two men's "plan is to intimidate and create technical legal issues and objections in the hope that the more serious allegations of secret commissions, bribery, corruption and other wrong-doings are never exposed to the light of day."[27] The acting AFC chairman, who served as head of the AFC Finance Committee under Bin Hammam, rejected charges by Bin Hammam that the AFC's investigation of its suspended president was riddled with conflicts of interest or that he had at any time benefitted personally from the disgraced official's support.

"Mr. Bin Hammam and Mr. Gulland do not want the Asian Football Confederation to consider the evidence that now exists and for which Mr. Bin Hammam must answer. The immediate task I believe is that we must all agree to allow our independent Judicial Bodies to hear the evidence and decide the case against Mr. Bin Hammam. We can then take the next steps in our journey of re-building the Asian Football Confederation. Accordingly, AFC is investigating whether there are sufficient legal grounds to file an ethics violation against Mr. Gulland to stop improper legal defence tactics intended only to interfere with the independent functions of the AFC Judicial Bodies," stated Zhang.

In an email to this writer, Gulland asserted that "a group of AFC officials working with FIFA" was "trying to seize control of the AFC." As part of that scheme, Gulland claimed that the officials and FIFA were "trying to take over the disciplinary decision-making machinery in order to make sure that Mr. Bin Hammam cannot return to AFC. They have threatened to bring disciplinary charges against anyone in Asian football who communicated with Mr. Bin Hammam to oppose their tactics." Bin Hammam had advised the AFC officials whose actions were "in violation of the law and AFC statutes" that he would take "legal measures to protect his rights if the officials persist in this conduct."

The PwC report alleged that Bin Hammam had used an AFC sundry account as his personal account. Few, including Bin Hammam's enemies, believe that the Qatari used the account for personal enrichment. Rather multiple payments from the account to associates and family as well as for personal expenses would likely equal the amounts Bin Hammam advanced to the AFC to cover its cash shortfalls. Friend and foe suggest that in a totalling of sums, the balance between Bin Hammam's advances and withdrawals would be zero. The problem was that Bin Hammam's way of managing the AFC's payment of its debt to him violated every standard of international accounting. Bin Hammam countered the PwC report by furnished FIFA investigators with his own independent expert's report from London accountants Smith and Williamson into the AFC sundry account that included a line-by-line explanation of all expenditure.

More serious were the questions PwC raised about Bin Hammam's negotiation of a US$1 billion master rights agreement (MRA) with Singapore-based World Sport Group (WSG), a US$300 million contract with the Qatar-owned Al Jazeera television network and payments of US$14 million to Bin Hammam by entities belonging to Saudi billionaire businessman Sheikh Saleh Kamel, who has a 10 per cent stake in WSG through yet another of his companies, International Sports Events (ISE). Qatar, too, has an indirect stake in WSG by being a shareholder of WSG majority shareholder Lagardere Unlimited. PwC reported that in February 2008 Bin Hammam had received US$12 million from Al Baraka Investment and Development Co, believed to be owned by Kamel. "We understand that the Al Baraka Group may have been a 20% beneficial owner of the WSG group with which the AFC signed a $1 billion master rights agreement in June 2009 negotiated by Mr. Bin Hammam," stated the report.

Kamel's ties to Bin Hammam and Blatter go back years. Blatter borrowed Kamel's Gulfstream jet in 2002 to visit southern and East Africa as part of his FIFA election campaign at a time that the Saudi controlled 20 per cent of the 2006 World Cup broadcast rights through his 20 per cent stake in Swiss sports rights company Infront. Kamel was at the time being scrutinized by US authorities because of his apparent links to the Muslim Brotherhood through Swiss-based Egyptian financier Youssef Nada, who was taken off the United Nations terrorism list in 2010. Kamel's affairs were also probably being looked at as a result of frequent confusion of US law enforcement officials over Arabic names. The name of Kamel's holding company, Dallah al Baraka, resembled that of an informal Somali money transfer network that had been proscribed by the US Treasury on suspicion of allowing Al-Qaida operatives to wire funds across the globe. Another WSG shareholder, Japanese advertising and public relations company Dentsu, was a shareholder in FIFA marketing partner International Sports Leisure (ISL) that collapsed in 2001 in a cash-for-contract scandal revealed by BBC *Panorama* and British investigative journalist Andrew Jennings. Dentsu and Infront are both shareholders of Match AG, which controls the sale of World Cup tickets.

PwC said that "it is highly unusual for funds (especially in the amounts detailed here) that appear to be for the benefit of Mr. Hammam personally, to be deposited to an organization's bank account. In view of the recent allegations that have surrounded Mr. Hammam, it is our view that there is significant risk that ... the AFC may have been used as a vehicle to launder funds and that the funds have been credited to the former President for an improper purpose (Money Laundering risk)" or that "the AFC may have been used as a vehicle to launder the receipt and payment of bribes."

The WSG Chairman and CEO Seamus O'Brien doubles as head of the New York Cosmos in a partnership with Sela Sport, a Saudi company represented by Hussein Mohsin Al Harthy, according to well-placed sources who assert that Al Harthy is Kamel's brother-in-law. The 2012 *Directory of Islamic Financial Institutions* published by Routledge lists Al Harthy, who sits on the board of a number of companies of Kamel's Dallah Al Baraka group, as a founder, together with the Saudi billionaire, of the Al Baraka Islamic Investment Bank BSC in Bahrain.

PwC questioned the fact that the contract as well as the agreement with Al Jazeera had been awarded without being putting out to tender or financial due diligence. Sources close to AFC stated that the contract awarded WSG all the benefits while ensuring that AFC retained the potential liabilities. PwC pointed out that the contract failed to give AFC a right to audit WSG's services or costs. "In comparison with similar-type agreements for other sports, it appears that the current MRA may be considerably undervalued," the PwC report concluded.

The PwC report further suggested that there may have been cases of AFC money laundering, tax evasion, bribery and busting of US sanctions against Iran and North Korea under Bin Hammam's leadership.

PwC advised the AFC to seek legal advice to ascertain whether the report's discoveries constituted criminal and/or civil breaches by Bin Hammam and others and whether the facts in the audit constituted sufficient evidence for a formal criminal complaint. The report also recommended that AFC obtain legal counsel on whether the WSG shareholder payments warranted "further work to determine if there is a relationship between the awarding of contracts to WSF (World Sports Football, a WSG subsidiary) and (Qatari broadcaster) Al Jazeera and the significant payments made to Mr. Bin Hammam." PwC also suggested that the AFC seek legal advice as to whether there were sufficient grounds to renegotiate or cancel WSG's MRA.

Sources close to the AFC revealed that the soccer body had been advised to conclude a service provider rather than a master rights agreement with WSG. They explained that a service provider agreement would have granted the AFC greater control of its rights and how they are exploited and would have enabled it to continuously supervise the quality of services provided by WSG. It would also have guaranteed that the AFC rather than WSG would have been the contracting party with broadcasters and sponsors and would have insulated the soccer body from any risk should WSG ever default. They pointed out that most international sports bodies had already graduated from master rights agreements to service provider arrangements.

The power the agreement granted WSG was apparent in the way the company was able to influence the AFC's conducting of its affairs. In November 2012 the AFC fired its marketing director Satoshi Saito, who was seconded for two years to the group by the Japanese Football Association (JFA), one of Bin Hammam and WSG's staunchest critics. Sources reported that Saito was advised his contract would not be extended and that he no longer had to come to the office. Saito, the sources added, had long been barred from meetings with WSG on the grounds that "the company holds all plenipotentiary rights to AFC's marketing rights." Some sources futher suggested that the fact that Saito was likely to be replaced by a lower level manager rather than a director strengthened WSG's grip, but was also motivated by the soccer body's budgetary shortfalls.

The AFC was moreover advised by WSG that it needed to authorize whatever its editors put on the soccer body's website. "We own the rights," sources close to the AFC quoted company officials as saying. "WSG felt that they were paying AFC salaries, that any money that went to the AFC was their money. It wasn't. Their job was to raise money for the AFC. Their claim was based on the fact that they had turned the AFC into what it is today and therefore owned the property," said one source.

WSG, which has repeatedly refused this writer's requests for interviews and comments, guarded its secrets jealously. It started legal proceedings in the summer of 2012 in a bid to force me to disclose my sources and silence reporting about its relationship with the AFC and Bin Hammam. In a landmark decision in February 2013, a Singapore court granted the author the right to appeal against an earlier court order that he disclose his sources. The court dismissed WSG's application to strike out his appeal.

In a 28 August 2012 letter WSG Group Legal Counsel Stephanie McManus implicitly admitted the accuracy of this writer's reporting by acknowledging that his sources "must have a very deep knowledge of the matters referred to in your Article." McManus went on to give WSG's first response to the allegations in the PwC report, stating that "PWC are incorrect and misconceived in suggesting that the MRA was undervalued. They have neither considered the terms of the contract correctly, the market, nor the circumstances in which it was negotiated."

WSG's legal action and its refusal to comment publicly on the PwC report appear to stem from concerns that the terms of or circumstances under which its US$1 billion agreement with the AFC was negotiated may become known beyond a very small circle of people. Not all members of the executive committee, the AFC's highest management body, have seen the agreement and those that have were only allowed to view it on the premises of the Asian soccer body, according to sources close to the AFC. These sources were of the opinion that the restrictive handling of the WSG contract contrasted with the way marketing agreements concluded by European soccer body UEFA and other international sports associations are dealt with. UEFA grants its managerial staff and executives access to the group's contracts irrespective of where they may be at any given moment.

The AFC reformers' inability to overcome resistance to change and the rolling back of Bin Hammam's influence persuaded them in November 2012 to hand over the group's investigation of its suspended president to independent FIFA ethics investigator Michael J. Garcia. Garcia and FIFA dropped the case of alleged bribery in the Caribbean in favour of sanctioning Bin Hammam for his alleged mismanagement of the AFC.

The reformers engineered the handover days before they suffered a major defeat in a make-or-break AFC executive committee meeting that stalled moves to reorganize the group's governance structure and investigate Bin Hammam and WSG's controversial marketing rights agreement. The committee's chairman, Pakistani government minister and Pakistan Football Federation (PFF) president Makhdoum Syed Faisal Saleh Hayat, moreover thwarted an attempt to establish an AFC ethics task force to deal with issues of governance and mismanagement by demanding that he be appointed head of the force rather than Moya Dodd, a respected Australian lawyer and member of the AFC executive committee. The executive committee also deferred a proposal for an independent valuation of the WSG contract. "The PwC report was effectively buried," commented one source close to the AFC.

Sources claimed that opponents of change were aided by Zhang's reluctance to take a firm stand in the committee meeting. "Zhang sat on the fence. He allowed Makhdoum's group to reign," said one. They asserted that Bin Hammam's supporters benefitted from the fact that Zhang and others who now are critical of the Qatari are hampered by their past association with him. According to one observer, "Zhang is doing his best but Bin Hammam has made clever use of history—Zhang was head of the finance committee under Bin Hammam. Zhang is a little bit scared and can't be too aggressive. He knows... the ground under him is not rock solid."[28]

Barely a month after taking charge of the Bin Hammam investigation FIFA renewed its ban for life of the Qatari because of "repeated violations" of the FIFA Code of Ethics and conflicts of interest during his AFC presidency. The ban came days after Bin Hammam, under pressure from the Qatari emir, submitted his resignation to FIFA, effectively dropping his effort to clear his name.

Bin Hammam's resignation and subsequent banning paved the way for AFC elections of a president who would complete the Qatari's term.

Bin Hammam nonetheless retains influence, as witnessed in the election campaign involving four candidates, three of which were his associates, and the ultimate winner, Bahraini Football Association head Sheikh Salman Bin Ebrahim Al Khalifa. The campaign, marred by allegations of interference and controversy over the candidates' track records and Salman's election victory, not only appeared to bury hopes of reform but raised a whole new series of questions about soccer's association with politics and the moral and ethical obligations of executives towards their players. AFC general secretary Dato' Alex Soosay in a letter to the group's forty-six member associations on the eve of the election asked them to remember their "ethical obligations" when casting their vote. The letter warned against "offering and accepting gifts and benefits; bribery; and conflicts of interests." Soosay went on to note that "it is the duty and obligation of the Confederation to prevent the introduction of improper methods and practices which might jeopardize the integrity of, or give rise to, the abuse of football..."[29]

Salman's AFC victory with the backing of the powerful Kuwaiti-led Olympic Council of Asia (OCA), as well as his defeat of a Qatari candidate for Bin Hammam's FIFA executive committee seat, was bittersweet. It came four years after Bin Hammam had narrowly defeated him. Nevertheless, Bin Hammam's shadow hung over the campaign. FIFA at the request of the OCA, whose head Sheikh Ahmad Fahad Al-Sabah, a 50-year old jetsetting former government minister and member of the Kuwaiti royal family, is close to Blatter, warned AFC members days before the election against consorting with Bin Hammam. It accused Bin Hammam of campaigning on behalf of UAE soccer association president Yousef Al Serkal, who for his part repeatedly denounced the OCA for interfering in the election. The electoral results mirrored the balance of power in the Gulf where Bahrain and Kuwait are much more closely aligned with Saudi Arabia than Qatar, which has been charting a course of its own in foreign policy and projection of soft power.

It also put the spotlight on the inordinate influence of tiny Kuwait in the world of soccer and sports. Sheikh Ahmed was believed to have persuaded Chinese authorities to ensure that Zhang Jilong dropped plans to compete in the election of Bin Hammam's successor. He also was a behind-the-scenes kingmaker in the election of Thomas Bach as president of the IOC in the summer of 2013. Sheikh Ahmed has steadily built his power base. An IOC member since 1992, he heads the

Association of National Olympic Committees, a consortium of 205 national Olympic committees across five continent that has US$438 million to spend in the years before the 2016 Olympic Games in Brazil. He became one of the youngest IOC members ever when aged twenty-nine he succeeded his father, Fahad al-Ahmed al-Jaber al-Sabah, who died in 1990 defending the Kuwaiti ruler's palace against invading Iraqi forces. Sheikh Ahmad, whom US ambassador Richard LeBaron referred to disparagingly in a Wikileaks cable,[30] attended Kuwait's military academy, served as head of Kuwait's national security commission and was chairman of OPEC. He cuts a striking figure with long black curly hair, dressed in a leather jacket and sunglasses as he puffs on a cigarette. Critics charged that Sheikh Ahmad had aggressively campaigned to replace Mexico's Mario Vázquez Raña as head of the national committees' association. In his resignation letter, Raña wrote that "it is said, quite forcefully, that the sheikh, to ensure support for their ambitious plans and to have the necessary votes, gave 50,000 'compelling reasons' to some leaders."[31] Sheikh Salman in 2015 manipulated the election of Asian representatives to the FIFA executive committee to ensure that Sheikh Ahmad won a seat that would allow him to run for the FIFA presidency at a later stage.[32]

Controversy swirling around Sheikh Ahmad added to the problems of Salman's presidency. The Bahraini official has been dogged by allegations that his office identified athletes, including players for the Bahrain nation soccer team, who were arrested for their participation two years ago in anti-government protests, tortured and charged. Salman, a member of the Bahraini royal family, has refused to denounce the alleged abuses of human rights or to discuss the allegations against him. He has said that there was no reason to apologize to the players because it was an issue for politicians, not his soccer federation. Salman has stopped short of parroting statements by the government that protesters demanding greater freedom and rights were encouraged by Iran, a view described as delusional by a Bahrain expert in the corridors of a conference in Manama aimed at winning sympathy in Washington for Bahrain's position. Bahrain has accused the US State Department of "fuelling terror and terrorists" by alleging that "the most serious human rights problems [in Bahrain] included citizens' inability to change their government peacefully; arrest and detention of protesters on vague charges, in some cases leading to their torture in detention." The State

Department criticized Bahrain's "lack of due process in trials of political and human rights activists, medical personnel, teachers, and students, with some resulting in harsh sentences." It claimed that "discrimination on the basis of gender, religion, nationality, and sect persisted, especially against the Shia population."

Bahraini human rights groups campaigned against Salman's candidacy. Two of the detained players, brothers Mohammed and Alaa Hubail, accused Sheikh Salman of abandoning them. They claimed they had received no apology or compensation from the Bahrain Football Association for the months of alleged mistreatment. "We are his responsibility and people like him should solve the problem, not ignore it. I have a lot of anger. I really miss playing in my team and for Bahrain," Mohammed Hubail told the Associated Press. A third player, Sayed Mohamed Adnan, also speaking to Associated Press, said that "some people sadly want to end my career because of their belief that I am for this and against that. I love Bahrain. Playing in the national team of my country is a great honour. I would love to do it any time. I would do it without hesitation."

In a letter to AFC members, Americans for Democracy and Human Rights in Bahrain (ADHRB) pointed out that:

> in the two years since the uprising began, life has been anything but normal for Bahrain's football players. The actions taken against Bahrain's football players by the Bahrain Football Association, led by Sheikh Al-Khalifa, are hardly credible, are devoid of integrity, and fail to respect the personal rights of the players. As leader of the organization that led such abuses, Sheikh Al-Khalifa bears responsibility for what was done to these players. Yet, in response to recent questions about the arrest, detention, and abuse of Bahrain's football players, Sheikh Al-Khalifa abdicated any personal responsibility for the abuse. Sheikh Al-Khalifa's actions and attitude evidence a clear incompatibility with the AFC Code of Ethics.

Salman's handling of the media holds out little promise that he may be an agent of change. On Twitter the Dubai-based Associated Press sports reporter Mike Casey described Sheikh Salman's notion of transparency when he was asked at a rare press conference about the arrest of the players. "My response is let's talk about football and leave the political side to the other people who deal with that. We hear reports a lot from all sides and I am here to talk about the elections. I don't want to talk about these matters because the moment you talk about it, it opens the door. Since I have been in charge of football here in Bahrain, we always leave religious and political matters and views outside to try to focus on the game," Salman replied. Minutes later, Casey tweeted: "Told to leave #SheikSalman's presser over stories I've written in past, not a good first step for openness." Shortly after that he tweeted: "Organizers at #Sheik Salman's presser allow me to remain after I refuse to leave, welcome them to call security."

At least one other reporter was barred from attending the news conference because of critical reporting on Bahrain.

Sheikh Salman's problems didn't end there. A video tape leaked in 2015 just weeks before the announcement of the US and Swiss legal proceedings forced the suspension and ultimate resignation of AFC general secretary Dato' Alex Soosay on charges of having attempted to obstruct the PwC audit. The AFC studiously avoided linking Soosay's departure to the audit, falsely suggesting instead that it had to do with an unspecified FIFA inquiry. Nonetheless, Soosay's resignation coupled with the legal proceedings threatened to thwart Sheikh Salman's effort to bury the audit and centralize power within the AFC.

Sheikh Salman's manipulations and the FIFA scandal, if anything, put the issue of not only financial but also political corruption in Asian, including Middle Eastern, and global soccer governance center stage. That was evident in revelations about government and corporate deals made to secure Germany's hosting of the 2006 World Cup. Revelations in German weekly *Die Zeit* disclosed that a deal between the German and Saudi governments coupled with investments by German corporates in South Korea and Thailand ensured that Germany won its 2006 hosting rights by one vote in 2000. *Die Zeit* reported that the government of then Chancellor Gerhard Schroeder complied with a request from the German Football Association to lift at short notice an embargo on weapon sales to Saudi Arabia and supply it with anti-tank rocket launchers, in a bid to ensure that then Saudi member of the FIFA executive committee would vote for Germany rather than Morocco.[33]

"Germany's actions may well have been legal but they did not quite meet the definition of the spirit of sports. All of this has been known for more than ten years. The German public however prefers to believe in the fairy tale: corruption is a problem of others like, for example, Trinidad or Vanuatu," the newspaper quipped.

EPILOGUE

More than 90,000 soccer fans in a Tunisian stadium cheered CS Hammam-Lif toward a desperately needed victory in the autumn of 2013. Their support echoed across the empty stadium from forty giant speakers. Watching the match on television at home, the fans used a phone app to tap commands such as shout, clap and blow horns if they wanted the sound of South Africa's vuvuzela, the trumpet-like horn that became a sensation and a trend during the 2010 World Cup.

The app had been developed by the club and the Tunisian franchise of a global public relations agency to circumvent an on and off, but mostly on, ban on spectators attending soccer matches since anti-government protests against President Zine El Abidine Ben Ali erupted in December 2010. The ban, like that in Egypt and at times in other Middle Eastern and North African nations in the throes of popular protests, was designed to preempt violence and to prevent stadiums from becoming anti-government rallying points.

The ban highlighted the importance to rulers and ruled of soccer as a pillar of support for the regime, an important tool to distract public attention and a platform for anti-government protest dating back to the game's introduction to the region by the British in the late nineteenth and early twentieth centuries. The game's increasing popularity made it—unlike other forms of dissent such as underground music—difficult to simply repress. The soccer pitch emerged as a result as one of the region's few contested public spaces; a battlefield for political, social, economic, national, ethnic and sectarian rights as well as for power.

It also reinforced the culture of soccer fans as an indicator of underlying social and political trends and of the public's mood, not only for independent analysts but also for intelligence agencies. A US intelligence official, who spent decades in the Middle East and North Africa, told Quartz that Central Intelligence Agency (CIA) officers routinely attend matches to glean clues as to where a country is heading. Often, the official said, an autocratic regime would cover up burgeoning dissent by blaming it on hooliganism. The CIA person on the ground would mention that, too, in the cable back to headquarters: "They would take note of it all, and put it in context. As soon as the prince shows up, everyone starts booing. That sort of thing."[1]

Politics was written into the DNA of soccer from day one. A vast number of clubs in North Africa and the Levant were founded with some sort of political association. Some were anti-colonial, others pro-monarchy. Yet others projected national or ethnic identity or were associated with a political ideology. In the Gulf, soccer clubs were the playgrounds of sheikhs and members of ruling families. Many of the clubs have long moved beyond the politics associated with their birth, yet the perception of their original identity lives on.

In the waning years of autocracy in countries like Egypt and Tunisia, militant, highly organized and increasingly politicized soccer fans honed their street battle skills in years of confrontation with security forces. The security personnel they confronted in the stadiums were often the same brutal and corrupt men who made daily life even more difficult in the poorer, populous neighbourhoods of cities like Cairo. By the time revolts erupted in late 2010 and 2011 across the Middle East and North Africa as well as in Turkey in 2013, fearless soccer fans were the group with the incentive—deep-seated animosity towards the police and security forces—and the organization, logistics and wherewithal to stiffen popular resolve and confront regimes in their attempts to suppress the rising groundswell of protest.

Some analysts argue that the protesters on Cairo's Tahrir Square would not have been able to force President Hosni Mubarak to resign after thirty years in office if the fans had not been there to man the outer perimeter and fend off attacks by security forces and government-sponsored thugs. Whether true or not, there is no doubt that soccer fans played a key role in several of the region's revolts.

With the Middle East and North Africa embroiled in what is likely to be a decade or more of often messy and at times ugly and bloody political transition, soccer fans together with workers, university students,

Islamists and jihadists are likely to remain at the centre of the struggle for change. Egyptian-general-turned president Abdel Fattah Al-Sisi, in a bid to prevent soccer pitches from re-emerging as battlefield, has kept stadiums closed to the public and promulgated a drastic anti-protest law. In 2015, an Egyptian court banned Ultras as terrorists. Yet the struggle against autocracy erupts almost daily on campus and in popular neighbourhoods with clashes between students protesting against the overthrow of Morsi and security forces. Militant soccer fans play a key role in those protests.

If the soccer pitch was reemerging in post-revolt countries as a battlefield for control of public space and greater freedom, it was a potential catalyst for change in energy-rich Gulf states. Qatar's successful 2010 bid to host the 2022 World Cup was a double-edged sword that propelled its most existential problem and that of other smaller Gulf states to the top of the agenda: the viability of societies in which the citizenry constitutes a small minority of a population that is in majority foreigners, with no rights or prospects beyond the fulfillment of their labour contracts. In the wake of pressure on Qatar as well as FIFA by international trade unions and human rights groups to significantly improve onerous working and living conditions of migrant labour involved in up-coming World Cup-related infrastructure, other Gulf states found themselves in the firing line. Abu Dhabi's efforts to shed its image of a feudal desert fiefdom involved building world-class museums in association with Guggenheim, the Louvre and the British Museum; this, and luxury hotels and a campus for New York University on its Saadiyat [Happiness] Island, focused activist attention. Dubai was likely to be next in line after its winning bid to host the 2020 World Expo that was expected to generate US$7 billion in construction projects.

Abu Dhabi and Dubai, the two most important of the seven emirates that make up the United Arab Emirates, are not just active in the arts and education—on which there are far more restrictions on academic freedom than in Qatar. They are also busy in the field of sports. FIFA has organized several tournaments in Abu Dhabi in recent years while the International Cricket Council (ICC) moved its headquarters in 2005 from London to Dubai. The UAE would like to see other international sports associations follow suit. The UAE has also been awarded the right to host the 2019 Asian Cup.

Nevertheless, in the competition among Gulf states for who tops the list of worst workers' conditions the UAE compared unfavourably with

Qatar not only when it came to academic freedoms. Besides cracking down on research institutions and activists and barring critical research-ers, including Qataris, from entering the country, the UAE also had the dubious distinction of being the world's only government to hire an army of at least 800 Africans and Latin Americans parked outside the capital for the eventuality of major labour unrest or a popular revolt—an indi-cation of how far it is willing to go to keep the ruling family in power.[2]

While Qatar has acknowledged the need for change and problems with implementation and enforcement of existing workers' rights, Abu Dhabi has sought to project itself as a workers' paradise. "The UAE has built the world's greatest labor camp, complete with manicured cricket grounds, a chess center, a multilingual library with works by Ayn Rand and Barack Obama, the UAE's first multi-denominational prayer hall, film screening rooms, tug-of-war competitions, a coffee shop and land-scaped grounds. Regular government press releases show groups of smil-ing dignitaries who have come to admire the Saadiyat Construction Village, while promotional videos show smiling workers playing cricket in spotless whites," remarked a piece in the *The Observer* newspaper, which also noted that a majority of workers on Saadiyat lived in what can only be described as appalling conditions.[3]

The message was clear: Gulf states had long got away with sub-stand-ard living and working conditions because the international community, including sports associations, at best paid lip service to globally accepted standards and their own professed values and because Gulf states prom-ised change and reformed labour laws and regulations but failed to put their money where their mouth is. Qatar's engagement with the trade unions and human rights groups bought it time and some degree of the benefit of the doubt. The proof, however, would be in the pudding.

For Qatar, the UAE and other smaller Gulf states meeting demands that they live up to international labour standards is no mean task. Their soft power approach that builds on sports, arts and commercial invest-ment has focused attention on the dark side of their oil wealth-fuelled defence, security, development and modernization policies. Labour reforms go to one key factor that makes them unique: the hosting of migrant and expatriate communities that outnumber locals by a factor of up to ten to one. Many locals fear that any change, anything that could potentially give a foreigner a stake in the country, including a revision or abolition of the *kafala* or sponsorship system, would endanger their grip on society and threaten their culture.

The World Cup-related pressure forced the issue into the open and broke the taboo on its discussion in public.

With the emir moving to apply lessons of the Singapore model by increasingly moving Qataris into positions of responsibility and streamlining Qatar's bureaucracy, making it more efficient and responsive to people's needs, Al Thani decried Qatari society's "erosion of values of honesty, loyalty, social solidarity (and) commitment to the responsibilities to which we are charged whether in the private or public sectors. This is manifest in such malaise as corruption, an entitlement culture, below average performance in the work place, low levels of service to the people (customer service) accompanied by demands for more and more rewards."

The centrality of the soccer pitch as a battlefield in much of the Middle East and North Africa and the World Cup as a potential agent of social and political change in the Gulf are two sides of the same coin. "Soccer may not determine our future," said a North African Ultra, "but it will certainly help shape it."

NOTES

INTRODUCTION

1. Shaun Lopez, "On Race, Sports and Identity: Picking Up the Ball in Middle East Studies", *International Journal of Middle East Studies*, Vol. 41, 2009, pp. 359–361.
2. Ibid.
3. Paul Aarts and Francesco Cavatorta, "Debating Civil Society Dynamics in Syrian and Iran" in Paul Aarts and Francesco Cavatorta (eds), *Civil Society in Syria and Iran: Activism in Authoritarian Contexts*, Boulder CO: Lynne Rienner, 2012.
4. Gary Whannel, *Culture, Politics and Sport: Blowing the Whistle, Revisited*, London: Routledge, 2008, p. 237.
5. John Sugden, "Critical Left Realism and Sport Interventions in Divided Societies", *International Review for the Sociology of Sport*, (45) 3, 2010, pp. 258–72.
6. Eduardo P. Archetti and Amilcar G. Romero, "Death and Violence in Argentinian Football" in Richard Giulianotti, Norman Bonney and Mike Hepworth (eds), *Football, Violence and Social Identity*, Abingdon, Routledge, 1991.
7. In an incomplete summary, John Bale, Adam Brown, Paul Dietschy, David Head, Pierre Lanfranchi, Richard Giulianotti, John Williams, Matthias Marschik, Doris Sottopietra, Les Black and J. William Baker have published on Europe. Alan Chong, Jana Valencic, Dave Russell, Wray Vamplew, Claudentr Boli, Yves Gastaut, Stephane Mourlane, J. M. Bradley, Daniel Burdsey, Robert Chappell, Peter Byrne, Timothy J. L. Chandler, Chas Critcher, Mike Cronin, Patrick Murphy, John Williams, Norbert Elias, Eric Dunning, G.P.T. Finn, John Goulstone, George G. Graham, Simon Inglis, Charles Korr, Herbert F. Moorhouse and Steven Tischler have written about Britain; Peter J. Beck, Bernd M. Beyer, Roland Binz, Juergen Bitter, Alexander Brand, Arne Niemann, Rene Wiese, Jutta Braun, Franz-Josef Brueggemeire, Juerg Steiner,

Ulrich Borsdorf, Christopher Young, Diethelm Knauf, Ian Watson, Christoph Dieckmann, Felix Linnemann, Erik Eggert, Christiane Eisenberg, Guenter Gebauer, Markus Hesselmnn, Robert Ide, Alan Tomlinson, Christopher Young about Germany; Marianne Amar, Pierre Arnaud, Jean Camy, Loic Ravenel, Didier Reey, Alfred Wahl, Jean-Marc Silvain, Noureddine Seoudi about France. Latin America has been tackled by Joseph L. Arbena, Jorge Barraza, Ernesto Escobar Bavio, Richard Giulianotti, Tony Mason, Pablo Alabarces, Maria Graciela Rodriguez, Fernando Alonso, Eduardo P. Archetti, Christiane Eisenberg, Amilcar Romero, Osvalod Bayer, Jimmy Burns, Beto Devoto, Roberto Fontanarosa, Julio Frydenberg, Alex Bellos, Waldenyr Caldas, Gastón Julián Gil, N. Larsen, Victor F. Lupo, Florian Mildenberger, Ulrich Pradmann, Peter Fuchs, Hejo Heussen, Klaus Humann, Pablo A. Ramirez, Cesar Gordon, Ronaldo Helal, Mario Filho, Alain Fontain, Leite Lopes, Jose Sergio and Anonio J. Guzman; Africa by Paul Darby, Bernadette Deville-Danthu, Michael Fanizadeh, Markus Peter, Ulf Engel, Peter Koerner, Patrick E. Igbinovia, Boyar Ly, Peter C. Alegi, Terence Monnington, Ossie Stuart, Kurt Wachter, R. Clignet, M. Stark, Andre Ntonfo, Bea Vidacs, I.O. Akindurtire, Philip Vasili, Robert Archer, Antoine Buillon, Belinda Bozzoli, Grant Javie, Irene Reid, G. A. Gabe, Ken Bediako, L. Fair, Phyllis M. Martin, N. A. Scott and Patrice Yengo; and Asia by Ben Weinberg, Ossie Stuart, P. Dimeo, J. Mill, Boria Majumdar, James A. Mangan, Fan Hong, Wolfgang Manzenreiter, John Horne, Jonathan Birchall, Derke Bleakley, Bill Murray, Sebastian Moffett, Haruo Nogowa, Maeda Hiroko, Jun Takahshi, Suzuki Kazane, Yoshio Takahashi, Paul Dimeo, Novy Kapadia, Tony Mason, Alex McKay, Dutta Ray, B. B. Pendleton, Ian Andrews, John Nauright, R. Hay, W. F. Mandle, and Mohit Prasad.

8. Steven J. Jackson, "Sport and Corporate Diplomacy", 1 July 2013, JPI PeaceNet, http://jpi.or.kr/board/board.html?mode=read&board_id=En Other&uid=4975

9. Hisham Sharabi, *Neopatriarchy: A Theory of Distorted Change in Arab Society*, Oxford: Oxford University Press, 1992.

10. Michel Foucault, *Discipline and Punish: The Birth of the Prison*, New York: Vintage, 1995.

11. Beth Baron, *Egypt as a Woman: Nationalism, Gender and Politics*, Berkeley: University of California Press, p. 145.

12. Stadiums in Barcelona and Bilbao provided a rare public venue in which Catalans and Basques could speak their native language in a country in which all local languages but Spanish were banned. Fans sported the colours of their teams, which approximated to the colours of their banned national flags. Matches against Franco-backed Real Madrid were rare opportunities to jeer at his regime. See, for example, Duncan Shaw, "The Politics of 'Futbol'", *History Today*, 35(8), 1985.

13. Dag Tuastad, "From Football Riot to Revolution: The Political Role of Football in the Arab World", *Soccer & Society*, (13) 5–6, 2012.

14. Adel Iskandar, *Egypt in Flux: Essays on an Unfinished Revolution*, Cairo: The American University in Cairo Press, 2013, pp. 18–19.

15. Y. Fates, *Sport et Tiers-Monde*, Paris: Pratiques Corporelles, 1994, p. 51.

16. Mohamed Gamal Besheer, *Kitab al-Ultras* (The Ultras Book), Cairo: Dar Diwan, 2011.

17. Said Chikhi, "The Worker, the Prince and the Fact of Life: The Mirage of Modernity in Algeria", in Ali El-Kenz (ed.), *Algeria: The Challenge of Modernity*, London, 1991, p. 220.

18. Ceyda Nurtsch, "Interview with Ezzedine Choukri Fishere, The Arab Revolution Is a Cultural Revolution", Qantara.de, 21 Feb. 2013, http://en.qantara.de/wcsite.php?wc_c=20712&wc_id=22899

19. The Ultras trace their roots to comparable groups called *torcida organizadas* in Brazil in 1939. Their colours and supporters inspired the formation of the first such European group in 1950 among supporters of Croatian club Hadjuk Split. Barely a year, later Ultras groups began mushrooming in Italy, the country that has become most identified with Ultras culture involving choreographic displays, signature banners and symbols, giant flags, drums, flares, smoke guns and fireworks, as well as increased levels of violence.

20. Sidney G. Tarrow, *Power in Movement: Social Movements and Contentious Politics*, Cambridge: Cambridge University Press, 1994.

21. Brian Whitaker, *What's Really Wrong with the Middle East*, London: Saqi Books, 2009; James M. Dorsey, The Turbulent World of Middle East Soccer, http://mideastsoccer.blogspot.com

22. Robert D. Benford and Scott A. Hunt described social movements as dramas involving clashes in which the protagonists seek to influence perception of power in societal institutions; "Dramaturgy and Social Movements: The Social Construction and Communication of Power", *Sociological Inquiry*, 62(1), 1992, pp. 36–55.

23. John D. McCarthy and Mayer N. Zald, "The Enduring Vitality of the Resource Mobilization Theory of Social Movements" in Jonathan H. Turner (ed.), *Handbook of Sociological Theory*, New York: Springer, 2001, pp. 533–65; Ted Robert Gurr, *Why Men Rebel* (Fortieth Anniversary Edition), Boulder, CO: Paradigm Publishers, 2011; Clifford Bob, *The Marketing of Rebellion: Insurgents, Media and International Activism*, Cambridge: Cambridge University Press, 2005; and Sidney G. Tarrow, *Power in Movement: Social Movements and Contentious Politics* (Revised and Updated Third Edition), New York: Cambridge University Press, 2011, all argued that social movements sustain protests when grievances prompt individuals to take action at such a time as they are able to marshal sufficient material and symbolic resources, including the res-

onance of diagnostic and prescriptive frames, changes in political opportunity structures, and the international context.

24. Charles Tilly, "Does Modernization Breed Revolution?" *Comparative Politics*, 5(3), April 1973.

25. Sadek Al-Azm, "Arab Nationalism, Islamism and the Arab Uprising", lecture, London School of Economics and Political Science, London, 30 Nov. 2011,http://blogs.lse.ac.uk/mec/2011/12/07/arab-nationalism-islamism-and-the-arab-uprising/

26. George Orwell, "Such, Such Were the Joys", *Partisan Review*, London, Sept.-Oct. 1952.

27. Heidi Blake and Jonathan Calvert, *The Ugly Game, The Qatari Plot to Buy the World Cup*, London: Simon & Schuster, 2015.

28. Human Rights Watch, "Migrant Workers' Rights on Saadiyat Island in the United Arab Emirates", Feb. 2015, https://www.hrw.org/reports/2015/02/10/migrant-workers-rights-saadiyat-island-united-arab-emirates-0

1. BEARING THE SCARS OF BATTLE

1. Dingxin Zhao, "Ecologies of Social Movements: Student Mobilization during the 1989 Pro-democracy Movement in Beijing", *American Journal of Sociology*, 103, 1998, pp. 1493–529; William Sewell Jr, "Space in Contentious Politics", in Ronald Aminzade, Jack Goldstone, Doug McAdam, Elizabeth Perry, William Sewell Jr, Sidney Tarrow, and Charles Tilly, *Silence and Voice in the Study of Contentious Politics*, Cambridge: Cambridge University Press, 2001.

2. Pablo Albarces, "Post-modern Times: Identities and Violence in Argentine Football", in Gary Armstrong and Richard Giulianotti (eds), *Football, Culture and Identities*, London: Palgrave Macmillan, 1999, pp. 77–85.

3. Dingxin Zhao, "Ecologies of Social Movements".

4. William Sewell Jr, "Space in Contentious Politics".

5. Ibid.

6. Richard A. Berk, "A Gaming Approach to Crowd Behavior", *American Sociological Review*, 39, 1974, pp. 355–73; Max Heinrich, *The Spiral of Conflict: Berkeley, 1964*, New York: Columbia University Press, 1971; and John Lofland, "The Youth Ghetto" in Edward Laumann, Paul M. Siegel, and Robert W. Hodge (eds), *The Logic of Social Hierarchies*, Chicago: Marrham, 1970, pp. 756–78.

7. Samuel D. Kassow, *Students, Professors, and the State in Tsarist Russia*, Berkeley: University of California Press, 1989.

8. Tse-tsung Chow, *The May Fourth Movement: Intellectual Revolution in Modern China*, Stanford CA: Stanford University Press, 1967; Jeffrey N. Wasserstrom, *Student Protests in Twentieth-Century China: The View from Shanghai*, Stanford CA: Stanford University Press, 1991.

9. "Ruled by the Game", *Al-Ahram Weekly*, 11–17 March 2004, http://weekly.ahram.org.eg/2004/681/sp11.htm

10. Ikhwanweb, "Khater slams Arabs for not showing zeal for Aqsa as they do with football", 23 Nov. 2009, http://www.ikhwanweb.com/article.php?id=21828&ref=search.php

11. John F. Burns. 'Soccer Players Describe Torture by Hussein's Son," *The New York Times*, 16 May 2003, https://www.nytimes.com/international/worldspecial.06TORT.html

12. James M. Dorsey, "Syria's Latakia stadium joins long list of region's politically abused soccer pitches", The Turbulent World of Middle East Soccer,18 Aug. 2011, http://mideastsoccer.blogspot.sg/2011/08/syrias-latakia-stadium-joins-long-list.html

13. Ibid, and 'Saddam's Son Tortured Defeated Footballers', *The Telegraph*, 5 Nov. 2000, http://www.telegraph.co.uk/news/worldnews/middleeast/iraq/1373322/Saddams-son-tortured-defeated-footballers.html

14. www.doneberly.com

15. "MBE for getting Iraq back in play", *The Scotsman*, 4 Dec. 2004, http://www.scotsman.com/news/mbe-for-getting-iraq-back-in-play-1-1049706

16. Muammar Gaddafi, *The Green Book*, London: Martin Brian & O'Keeffe, 1976, p. 32.

17. US Embassy, Tripoli, "Black Sheep Made Good? Saadi Al-qadhafi's Export Free Zone In Western Libya", 3 March 2009, *Wikileaks*, http://www.cablegatesearch.net/cable.php?id=09TRIPOLI198&q=ill-behaved%20saadi

18. James M. Dorsey, "Libyan rebels investigate Qaddafi son for murder of soccer player", 15 Oct. 2011, The Turbulent World of Middle East Soccer, http://mideastsoccer.blogspot.com/2011/10/libyan-rebels-investigate-qaddafi-son.html

19. Ibid.

20. Report from Amnesty International to the Government of the Syrian Arab Republic, Nov. 1983, *Amnesty International*, p. 23.

21. Nour Malas, "In Syria, It's Rebel against Rebel", *The Wall Street Journal*, 31 May 2013.

22. James M. Dorsey, "Refurbished Kabul stadium retains memories of Taliban abuse", The Turbulent World of Middle East Soccer, 17 Dec. 2011, http://mideastsoccer.blogspot.sg/2011/12/refurbished-kabul-stadium-retains.html

23. Ibid.

24. Ibid.

25. Pascal Boniface, *Géopolitique du football*, Brussels: Éditions Complexe, 2008, pp. 15–19.

26. Interview with Egyptian soccer analyst Hani Mokhtar, 5 Jan. 2011.

27. "Amr Zaki cites Israeli and Algerian presence at Portsmouth as reason for

shun", *Daily Mail*, 23 Nov. 2009, http://www.dailymail.co.uk/sport/football/article-1230101/Zaki-cites-Israeli-presence-Fratton-Park-reason-shun.html

28. James M. Dorsey, "Soccer vs. Islam: Football and Militant Islam Compete For Hearts and Minds", (InCoherent), 29 July 2010, http://incoherenci.blogspot.com/2010/07/soccer-vs-islam-football-and-militant.html

29. African Manager, "Slim Chiboub a pollué le sport en Tunisie, selon Tarak Dhiab", 28 Nov. 2012, http://www.africanmanager.com/145012.html?pmv_nid=1

30. Mohamed El-Sayed, *Al-Ahram Weekly*, 2004, http://weekly.ahram.org.eg/2004/2010/sc82.htm

31. Interview with Ahmed Eid Saad Alharbi, 30 June 2012.

2. THE BATTLE FOR GREATER FREEDOM

1. Allen Guttmann, *Games and Empires: Modern Sports and Cultural Imperialism*, New York: Columbia University Press, 1995, p. 2.

2. Mohamed El-Sayed, "Love at First Sight", *Al-Ahram Weekly*, 2004, http://weekly.ahram.org.eg/2004/2010/sc82.htm

3. Christoph Bromberger, "Football as world-view and ritual", *French Cultural Studies*, 6, 1995, pp. 293–311.

4. Dingxin Zhao, "Ecologies of Social Movements," p. 1495.

5. Ibid.

6. Ibid, p. 1498.

7. Dennis D. McCarthy, "Constraints and Opportunities of Adopting, Adapting and Inventing" in Doug McAdam, John D. McCarty and Mayer N. Zald (eds), *Comparative Perspectives on Social Movements: Political Opportunities, Mobilizing Structures, and Cultural Framings*, Cambridge: Cambridge University Press, 1996, pp. 152–184; Tarrow, Power in Movement.

8. James M. Dorsey, "Soccer is at the root of high Egyptian divorce rate", The Turbulent World of Middle East Soccer, 1 July 2011, http://mideastsoccer.blogspot.com/2011/07/soccer-is-at-root-of-high-egyptian.html

9. Gamal Al-Ghitani, *The Mahfouz Dialogs*, Cairo: American University in Cairo Press, 2008.

10. Alan Cameron, *Circus Factions: Blues and Greens at Rome and Byzantium*, Oxford: Oxford University Press, 1976, pp. 225–226.

11. Ibid.

12. Ibid.

13. Hisham Sharabi, *Neopatriarchy*, p. 7.

14. Salam Mouusa, "My Nasser", 28 Sept. 2013, *salamamousa*, http://salama-moussa.com/2013/09/28/my-nasser/

15. Hosni Mubarak, "Hosni Mubarak's Speech to the Egyptian People: 'I Will Not … Accept To Hear Foreign Dictations'" (Transcript), *The Washington Post*, 2011, http://washingtonpost.com/wp-dyn/content/article/2011/02/10/AR2011021005290.html

16. Jack Shenker, Peter Beaumont and Harriet Sherwood,"Egypt protesters react angrily to Mubarak's televised address", *The Guardian*, 2 Feb. 2011, http://www.guardian.co.uk/world/2011/feb/02/egypt-protesters-mubarak-address

17. Allen Guttmann, *Games and Empires*, p. 69.

18. *The Times*, 21 June 1996.

19. Wilson Chacko Jacobs, *Working Out Egypt: Effendi Masculinity and Subject Formation in Colonial Modernity, 1870–1940*, Durham NC: Duke University Press, 2011, p. 86.

20. Yoav Di-Capua, "Sports, Society and Revolution; Egypt in the Early Nasserite Period", in Elie Podeh and Onn Winckler (eds), *Rethinking Nasserism: Revolution and Historical Memory in Modern Egypt*, Gainesville, FL: University Press of Florida, 2004, p. 148.

21. Shiva Balaghi, "Football and Film in the Islamic Republic of Iran", *Middle East Research and Information Project (MERIP), MER229, Vol 33*, winter 2003.

22. Wilson Chacko Jacobs, *Working Out Egypt*, pp. 85–87.

23. Shaun Lopez, "Football as National Allegory: Al-Ahram and the Olympics in 1920s Egypt", *History Compass*, 2009, 7(1), pp. 282–305.

24. Ibid.

25. Wilson Chacko Jacobs, *Working Out Egypt*, p. 47.

26. Ibid, p. 286.

27. Interview with the author 10 July 1980.

28. NDP News, 1999, www.ndp.org/AR/News/ViewNewsDetails.aspx?NewsID-72785

29. The Governor of Aden, *Visit of Egyptian Football Team to Aden*, 1 Oct. 1963, British Library archive.

30. *Al-Ahram*, 27 July 1953.

31. *Al-Abtal*, 1 Jan. 1953 quoted in Yoav Di-Capua, "Sports, Society and Revolution".

32. William H. Martin and Sandra Mason, "The Development of Leisure in Iran: The Experience of the Twentieth Century", *Middle Eastern Studies*, 42(2), 2006.

33. Zina Sawaf, "Youth and the Revolution in Egypt: What Kinship Tells Us", *Contemporary Arab Affairs*, 6(1), 2013, pp. 1–16.

34. James M. Dorsey, "Egyptian Striker Zidan Highlights Post-Revolt Transition Problems by Calling Mubarak Father", The Turbulent World of Middle East Soccer, 23 Feb. 2012, http://mideastsoccer.blogspot.sg/2012/02/egyptian-striker-zidan-highlights-post.html

35. James M. Dorsey, "Egyptian Team's Tarnished Image Rides on Soccer Match against South Africa", 22 March 2011, http://mideastsoccer.blogspot.com/2011/03/egyptian-teams-tarnished-image-rides-on.html

36. James M. Dorsey, "Chairman of Zamalek Resigns Amid Criticism of Financial Management", 7 March 2011, http://mideastsoccer.blogspot.com/2011/03/chairman-of-zamalek-resigns-amid.html

37. Ian Taylor, "Soccer Consciousness and Soccer Hooliganism" in Stanley Cohen (ed.), *Images of Deviance*, Harmondsworth: Penguin, 1971.

38. James M. Dorsey, "Ultra Violence, How Egypt's Soccer Mobs are Threatening the Revolution", *Foreign Policy*, 1 Feb. 2012, http://www.foreignpolicy.com/articles/2012/02/01/Ultra_violence

39. Ibid.

40. Ibid.

41. Ibid.

42. Hatem Maher, "Egypt Icon Abou-Treika Incurs Ahli Wrath, Wins Over Fans", *Al-Ahram Weekly Online*, 8 Sept. 2012, http://english.ahram.org.eg/NewsContent/6/51/52323/Sports/Egyptian-Football/Egypt-icon-Abou Treika-incurs-Ahli-wrath,-wins-over.aspx

43. Nathan J. Brown, "Egypt's Ambiguous Transition", *Carnegie Endowment for International Peace*, 6 Sept. 2012, http://carnegieendowment.org/2012/09/06/egypt-s-ambiguous-transition/drsi#

44. Hammed Shahidian, *Women in Iran: Emerging Voices in the Women's Movement*, Westport, CT: Greenwood Press, 2002.

45. *The Economist*, "Football Hooligans They Aren't", 3 Nov. 2001.

46. *Der Spiegel*, "Iranian Protesters Skirt Censors at Soccer Games", 10 Nov. 2011, http://www.spiegel.de/international/world/a-stage-for-resistance-iranian-protesters-skirt-censors-at-soccer-games-a-790065.html

47. Balaghi, "Football and Film in the Islamic Republic of Iran".

48. Ibid.

49. Maziar Bahari, "Football, Iranian Style", 2001, http://www.idfa.nl/industry/tags/project.aspx?id=9FF08BE0–1E4B-4DEC-B04F-350253483EFB

50. La Rédaction, "Finale de la Coupe d'Algérie et 1er mai: Le message du président Bouteflika", Algerie1, 30 April 2013, http://www.algerie1.com/actualite/finale-de-la-coupe-dalgerie-et-1er-mai-le-message-du-president-bouteflika

51. Kerim Kebir and Paul Schemm, "Algeria soccer death seen as part of wider ills, Associated Press, 31 Aug. 2014, https://sports.yahoo.com/news/algeria-soccer-death-seen-part-103619076-spt.html

52. BBC, "World Football—WSWF: The Tragic Death of Albert Ebosse", 29 Aug. 2014, https://wehearus.com/podcasts/episode/109464

53. US Embassy in Jordan, "Jordanian Soccer Game Halted Amidst Anti-Regime

Chants, Hooliganism Towards Palestinians", *Wikileaks Update*, 7 Dec. 2010, http://wikileaksupdates.blogspot.sg/2010/12/jordanian-soccer-game-halted-amidst.html

54. Dag Tuastad, "Al-Wihdat: The Pride of the Palestinians in Jordan", 22 May 2010, *Middle East Institute*, http://www.mei.edu/content/al-wihdat-pride-palestinians-jordan

55. James M. Dorsey, "Rare Attack on Jordanian Queen Heightens Soccer Tensions", The Turbulent World of Middle East Soccer, 7 Feb. 2011, http://mideastsoccer.blogspot.sg/2011/02/rare-attack-on-jordanian-queen.html

56. Tim Lister, "Jordanian tribal figures criticize queen, demand reform," *CNN*, 7 Feb. 2011, http://edition.cnn.com/2011/WORLD/meast/02/06/jordan.monarchy/, Laurent Zecchini, "Bedouin tribes accuse Jordan's Queen Rania of corruption," *The Guardian*, 15 Feb. 2011, http://www.theguardian.com/world/2011/feb/15/bedouin-accuse-jordan-queen-corruption/, BBC News, "Jordan tribes criticise Queen Rania's 'political role'," 8 Feb. 2011, http://www.bbc.com/news/world-middle-east-12400274

57. Tom Little, "Syria's Kurds Undecided Over Future", BBC News, 17 March 2012, http://www.bbc.co.uk/news/world-middle-east-17357590

58. James Montague, "Football: The Slow March to Equality", *The Guardian*, 9 Jan. 2008, http://www.theguardian.com/football/2008/jan/09/womens-football

59. David Goldblatt, "The Power and the Passion, Episode 2: The Secret Policeman's Football—Al Ahly v Zamalek", BBC News, 14 June 2010.

60. Ian Taylor, "Class, Violence and Sport: The Case of Soccer Hooliganism in Britain", in Hart Cantelon and Richard Gruneau (eds), *Sport, Culture and the Modern State*, Toronto: University of Toronto Press, 1982.

61. John Clarke, "Football and Working Class Fans: Tradition and Change" in R. Inghan (ed.), *Football Hooliganism: The Wider Context*, London: Inter-Action Imprint, 1978.

62. Richard Giulanotti, "Social Identity and Public Order" in Richard Giulaniotti, Norman Bonney and Mike Hepworth (eds) *Football, Violence and Social identity*, Abingdon: Routledge, 1999, p. 15.

63. Gabriel Kuhn, *Soccer vs. The State: Tackling Football and Radical Politics*, Oakland, CA: PM Press, 2011.

64. Interview with the author, 1 April 2011.

65. Interview with the author, 2 April 2011.

66. Nadine Semin, "Civil Society in a New Egypt: A Force for Democratization?" Unpublished Master's Thesis, University of Amsterdam, 26 Sept. 2011.

67. Untitled cable from US embassy in Cairo, 30 July 2009, disclosed by Wikileaks, http://www.cablegatesearch.net/cable.php?id=09CAIRO1468

68. Karim Yahya, لماذا يثور المصريون؟ ('Why did Egyptians revolt?'), *Al-Ahram*, 9 Sept. 2011.

69. Alessandro Dal Lago and Rocco De Biasi, "Italian Football Fans: Culture and Organization" in Richard Giulaniotti, Norman Bonney and Mike Hepworth (eds), *Football, Violence and Social Identity*, Abingdon: Routledge, 1999, p. 81.

70. James M. Dorsey, "Football Pitches: A Battleground for North Africa's Future", The Turbulent World of Middle East Soccer, 24 March 2011, http://mideastsoccer.blogspot.sg/2011/03/football-pitches-battleground-for-north.html

71. James M. Dorsey, "Soccer Fans Key to Imminent Cairo Street Battle", The Turbulent World of Middle East Soccer, 3 Feb. 2011, http://mideastsoccer. blogspot.com/2011/02/soccer-fans-key-to-imminent-cairo.html

72. James M. Dorsey, "Egyptian soccer riots set to spread from Port Said to Cairo", The Turbulent World of Middle East Soccer, 25 March 2012, http://mideastsoccer.blogspot.co.uk/2012/03/egyptian-soccer-riots-set-to-spread.html

73. "The Power and the Passion", BBC News, 14 June 2010.

74. Alessandro Dal Lago and Rocco De Biasi, "Italian Football Fans: Culture and Organization", p. 79.

75. Interview with the author, 23 April 2012.

76. Jason Cowley, "More than a game", *Financial Times*, 25 Aug. 2012, http://www.ft.com/cms/s/2/1ab95bda-eab9-11e1-ba49-00144feab49a.html

77. Janet Lever, "Soccer: Opium of the Brazilian People", *Trans-action*, Dec. 1969.

78. Gary Armstrong and Rosemary Harris, "Football Hooligans: Theory and Evidence", *Sociological Review*, 39 (3), 1991.

79. Ibid, pp. 85–86.

80. Alessandro Dal Lago and Rocco De Biasi, "Italian Football Fans: Culture and Organization", pp. 81–82.

81. Hossam el-Hamalawy, quoted in Nadia Idle and Alex Nunnis (eds), *Tweets from Tahrir: Egypt's Revolution as it Unfolded, In the Words of the People Who Made It*, New York: OR Books, 2011, p. 126.

82. Gigi Ibrahim, quoted in Nadia Idle and Alex Nunnis (eds), *Tweets from Tahrir*, 2011, pp. 114–122.

83. Mosa'ab Elshamy, quoted in ibid.

84. Amr Gharbeia, quoted in ibid.

85. Mosa'ab Elshamy, quoted in ibid.

86. Gerry P. T. Finn, "Football Violence: a Societal Psychological Perspective" in Richard Giulaniotti, Norman Bonney and Mike Hepworth (eds), *Football, Violence and Social identity*, Abingdon: Routledge, 2013, p. 101.

87. Gary Armstrong and Malcolm Young, "Fanatical Football Chanting: Creating and Controlling the Carnival in Football Culture" in Gerry P. T. Finn and

Richard Giulaniotti (eds), *Local Contests, Global Visions*, New York: Frank Cass Publishers, 1999, p. 83.

88. J. Pratt and M. Salter, "Football hooliganism", *Leisure Studies*, 3(2), 1984, pp. 201–230.

89. Alessandro Dal Lago and Rocco De Biasi, "Italian Football Fans: Culture and Organization", p. 81.

90. James M. Dorsey, "Soccer Fans Emerge as Driver in Egyptian Protests", 30 Jan. 2011, http://mideastsoccer.blogspot.com/2011/01/soccer-fans-emerge-as-driver-in.html

91. Interview with the author, 1 April 2011.

92. Ibid.

93. Nagat Ali, "The Friday of Rage: The March to Tahrir Square", *The Brooklyn Rail*, Oct. 2012, http://www.brooklynrail.org/2012/10/express/the-friday-of-rage-the-march-to-tahrir-square

94. Nora Shalaby, quoted in Nadia Idle and Alex Nunnis (eds), op. cit., p. 44.

95. Amr El Beleidy, quoted in Nadia Idle and Alex Nunnis (eds), op. cit., p. 116.

96. http://www.youtube.com/watch?v=kWr6MypZ-JU

97. Salwa Ismail, *Political Life in Cairo's New Quarters: Encountering the Everyday State*, Minneapolis MN: University of Minnesota Press, 2006, p. 165.

98. John Chalcraft, "The Arab Uprisings: Mass Protest, Border Crossing and History from Below", Lecture at the London School of Economics and Political Science, 10 Nov. 2011.

99. "US embassy cables: Police brutality in Egypt", *The Guardian*, 28 Jan. 2011, http://www.theguardian.com/world/us-embassy-cables-documents/187359/print

100. http://www.youtube.com/watch?v=Z4-kDd4sqeE

101. Charles Tilly, "Does Modernization Breed Revolution?"

102. Ibid.

103. John Chalcraft, "The Arab Uprisings".

104. Sadik Al-Azm, *The Mental Taboo: Salman Rushdie and the Truth Within Literature*, London: Riad El-Rayess Books, 1982.

105. Yasin Al-Hafiz, *Azma Al-Tanwir*, Damascus: Dar El-Ahal, 1997, p. 34.

106. Interview with the author, 23 Nov. 2011

107. Sadik Al-Azm, "Arab Nationalism, Islamism and the Arab Uprising", Lecture at the London School of Economics and Political Science, 30 Nov. 2011, http://blogs.lse.ac.uk/mec/2011/12/07/arab-nationalism-islamism-and-the-arab-uprising/

108. Eduardo P. Archetti and Amilcar G. Romero, "Death and Violence in Argentinian Football," in Richard Giulaniotti, Norman Bonney and Mike Hepworth (eds), *Football, Violence and Social identity*, Abingdon: Routledge, 2013, pp. 49–68, p. 48.

109. Ibid, p. 54.

110. Ibid, p. 65.

111. James M. Dorsey. "Zamalek Ultras Disrupt African Soccer Match in Stunning Display of Nihilism", The Turbulent World of Middle East Soccer, 3 April 2011, http://mideastsoccer.blogspot.sg/2011/04/zamalek-Ultras-disrupt-african-soccer.html

112. Ibid.

113. Charles Tilly, "Social Movements and (All Sorts of) Other Political Interactions—Local, National and International—Including Identies: Divagations From a Common Path, Beginning with British Struggles over Catholic Emancipation, 1780–1829, and Ending with Contemporary Nationalism", Theory and Society, 27, 1998.

114. Moustafa El Chiati, "When a Game of Football is Ruined by the Game of Politics," KingFut, 14 March 2012, http://www.kingfut.com/2012/03/14/when-a-game-of-football-is-ruined-by-the-game-of-politics/

115. James M. Dorsey, "Egyptian soccer riots set to spread from Port Said to Cairo," The Turbulent World of Middle East Soccer, 25 March 2012, http://mideastsoccer.blogspot.sg/2012/03/egyptian-soccer-riots-set-to-spread.html

116. "Egyptian soccer riots set to spread from Port Said to Cairo", 25 March 2012, http://mideastsoccer.blogspot.co.uk/2012/03/egyptian-soccer-riots-set-to-spread.html

117. Mohamed Elshahed, "Urbanizing the Counter-Revolution", Jadaliyya, 17 Dec. 2011, http://www.jadaliyya.com/pages/index/3581/urbanizing-the-counter-revolution

118. James M. Dorsey, "Port Said boosts youth and soccer demands for civilian rule in Egypt", 4 Feb. 2012, http://mideastsoccer.blogspot.com/2012/02/port-said-blows-boosts-youth-and-soccer.html

119. Leila Zaki Chakravarti, "Performing masculinity: the football Ultras in post-revolutionary Egypt", Open Democracy, 8 March 2013, http://www.opendemocracy.net/5050/leila-zaki-chakravarti/performing-masculinity-football-Ultras-in-post-revolutionary-egypt

120. Wael Eskander, "Clashing with the Ultras: A Firsthand Account", Jadaliyya, 15 Feb. 2013, http://www.jadaliyya.com/pages/index/10204/clashing-with-the-Ultras_a-firsthand-account

121. Some 25,000 garment and textile workers engaged in strike action in Dec. 2006 against poor working conditions in Al Mahalla al-Kubra and did so again in Sept. 2007 and April 2008. The strikes led employees of the real estate tax collection authority to establish Egypt's first independent union. Economic decline following the toppling of Mubarak coupled with attempts by the Supreme Council of the Armed Forces (SCAF) to ban strikes fuelled

trade union activism, culminating in many unions joining the calls for Morsi's resignation in 2013. Workers organized their own anti-Morsi demonstrations in the days leading up to 30 June when one of the largest crowds in Egyptian history gathered on Cairo's Tahrir Square to give the military licence to intervene.

122. Nancey A. Youssef and Amina Ismail, "Prosecutors allege police role in deadly Egypt soccer riot", *McClatchy Newspapers*, 1 Feb. 2013, http://www.mcclatchydc.com/2013/02/01/181750/prosecutors-allege-police-role.html

123. Egyptian Initiative for Personal Rights (EIPR), "State crimes remained unpunished: the Interior Ministry is above the law and the Public Prosecution is missing in action", 22 Jan. 2013, http://eipr.org/en/report/2013/01/22/1602

124. Ibid.

125. Mohamed Elshahed, "Urbanizing the Counter-Revolution".

126. Hazem Kandil, *Soldiers, Spies, and Statesmen: Egypt's Road to Revolt*, London: Verso, 2012, p. 30.

127. Ibid.

128. Interview with the author, 17 Aug. 2013.

129. Interview with the author, 29 March 2015.

130. Interview with the author, 29 March 2015.

131. Interviews with family members, Ultras and sources close to the Ultras, 28, 29, 30 and 31 March, 2015.

132. Yara Bayoumy, Stephen Kalin and Ahmed Tolba, "Sixteen injured in fire at Cairo convention center," Reuters, 4 March 2015, http://www.reuters.com/article/2015/03/04/us-egypt-fire-idUSKBN0M015R20150304

133. Interviews with family members, Ultras and sources close to the Ultras, 28 and 29 March, 2015.

134. Interview with the author, 31 March 2015.

135. Interview with the author, 28 March 2015.

136. Inas Mazhar, "Ultra-violent," *Al-Ahram Weekly*, 26 Sept. 2013, http://weekly.ahram.org.eg/News/4236/17/Ultra-violent.aspx

137. Interviews with the author 28, 29, 30 and 31 March, 2015.

138. Interview with the author, 6 June 2014.

139. Heba Saleh and Erika Solomon, "Egypt's Muslim Brotherhood youth push for confrontational tactics," Financial Times, 10 June 2015, http://www.ft.com/cms/s/0/256f5718–0ab0–11e5-a8e8–00144feabdc0.html

140. Mahmoud Ghozlan, "بمناسبة مرور سبعة وثمانين عاما على تأسيس الجماعة دعوتنا باقية وثورتنا مستمرة" Nafizat Misr, 22 May 2015, http://www.egyptwindow.net/Article_Details.aspx?Kind=5&News_ID=80417

141. Hazem Said, "بين دعشنة الإخوان .. وعسكرة الثورة .. من وحي التعليقات على المقالة الأخيرة" Nafizat Misr, 27 May 2015, http://www.egyptwindow.net/Article_Details.aspx?Kind=5&News_ID=80777

142. https://www.facebook.com/Nahdawy.un12?fref=ts

143. Jadaliyya, "New Texts Out Now: Abdullah Al-Arian, Answering the Call: Popular Islamic Activism in Sadat's Egypt", 1 Oct. 2014, http://www.jadaliyya.com/pages/index/19390/new-texts-out-now_abdullah-al-arian-answering-the-

144. Robert Kagan and Michele Dunne, "Obama embraces the Nixon Doctrine in Egypt," The Washington Post, 3 April 2015, http://www.washingtonpost.com/opinions/obama-embraces-the-nixon-doctrine-in-egypt/2015/04/03/597b3be0-d986-11e4-ba28-f2a685dc7f89_story.html

145. Interview with the author, 31 March 2015.

146. Yezid Sayigh, "Missed Opportunity: The Politics of Police Reform in Egypt and Tunisia", Carnegie Middle East Center, March 2015, http://carnegieendowment.org/files/CMEC49_Brief-Yezid-Egypt_Tunisia.pdf

147. James M. Dorsey, "Ultra Violence—How Egypt's soccer mobs are threatening the revolution," Foreign Policy, 2 Feb. 2012, http://foreignpolicy.com/2012/02/02ultra-violence/

148. Interview with the author, 31 March 2015.

3. ISLAMISTS FIGHT OVER SOCCER

1. Parts of this chapter are included in a forthcoming article in Studies in Conflict and Terrorism

2. Lori Ssebulime, Kampala Eyewitness, 10 July 2010, http://bit.ly/awd53a

3. Adam Robinson, Bin Laden: The Inside Story of the Rise and Fall of the Most Notorious Terrorist in History, New York: Arcade Publishing, 2011.

4. Ibid, Kindle edition, Loc 4027.

5. Alleged Statements from Noordin M. Top, 2009, International Center for Political Violence and Terrorism.

6. US Defence Department, Transcript of Usama Bin Laden Video Tape, 13 Dec. 2001, http://web.archive.org/web/20060623051212/http://www.defenselink.mil/news/Dec2001/d20011213ubl.pdf

7. Ibid.

8. Hierotheos Vlachos, "The 'god' of soccer and Jesus Prayer", The Orthodox Christian Channel—OCC247, 28 Oct. 2010, http://philotimo-leventia.blogspot.com/2010/10/god-of-soccer-rev-metropolitan-of.html

9. Rick Broadbent, "Kaka's outpouring of faith scores massive hit," Irish Independent, 25 May 2007, http://www.independent.ie/sport/soccer/kakas-outpouring-of-faith-scores-massive-hit-26442798.html

10. Sheikh Hamoud al Tuwayjari, "Al Idah wa'l tabayyin lama waqa fihi al akthariyun min musabihat al mushrikin", http://ia600209.us.archive.org/1/items/muchrikintwijri/muchrikin_twijri.pdf

11. Sheikh Abdulaziz bin Abdullah ibn Baz, Sheikh Abdul Razak Afifi, Sheikh

Abdullah bin Ghudayan and Sheikh Abdullah bin Qu'ud, Fatwas no 2857 (8 Rabi al Awal 1400/Jan. 26, 1980), no 3323 (9 Dhul Hijja 1400/Oct. 18, 1980) and no 4967 (20 Ramadan 1402/Oct. 8, 1982), Standing Committee for Islamic Ruling and Research in Saudi Arabia, Riyadh.

12. Abdul Halim Uways, "Mushkilat ash-sha'ab fi daw al-Islam", p. 89.

13. Shukri Ali al-Tawil, "Al-Qimar wa anawahu fi daw ash-shari'at al islamiya", Master's Thesis, University of Jordan, 31 Aug. 1988, pp. 144–148.

14. Sheikh Abdul Aziz as Salman, "Al asilah wal ajwibah fi al fiqhiya", http:// www.islamspirit.com/islamspirit_program_034.php. Salman lists balls along-side film, radio and the shaving of beards as evils that corrupt morality and provoke dissension. He warns that "what is called football prompts people to discard prayer, waste time, employ foul language such as curses and slan-der, expose the 'awrah (the part of the male body between the navel and the knees) and forget the memory of Allah. There is no doubt that soccer is pro-hibited if it provokes these things, including in mature, intelligent people."

15. Ahmad Shalabi, *Al Hayat al ijtimiyyah fi takfir al Islam*, Cairo: University of Cairo, 1982, p. 235.

16. Shaykh Mashhoor bin Hasan Al Salman, Kurrat ul-Qadam, *Bayna 'lMasaa-lih wa'l Mafaasid ash-Sharii'yyah*, Beirut: Dar Ibn Hazam, 1998, pp. 1–41.

17. Badr al-Din Mohammed ibn Ali Al-Bali, "Mukhtaser al fatwa al misriya", LMisriya li Sheikh al-Islam Ahmed ibn Abdelhakim Ibn Abdelsalam Ibn Tamiyyah, Cairo: Maktab al Madani, 1980 Arab World Publishing House.

18. Salman, "Al asilah wal ajwibah fi al fiqhiya", http://www.islamspirit.com/ islamspirit_program_034.php

19. Ibid.

20. Sheikh Mashhoor Bin Hasan Aal Salman, "Mistakes regarding Friday Salat", 2006, http://www.salafitalk.net/st/uploads/Ch6.pdf

21. Ibid.

22. Ibid.

23. The General Presidency of Scholarly Research and Ifta, Fatwas of the Permanent Committee, Group 1, Volume 13: Transactions 1, Part No. 13; Page No. 63, Fatwa no. 16502, http://alifta.com/Search/ResultDetails.asp x?lang=en&view=result&fatwaNum=&FatwaNumID=&ID=4603&search Scope=7&SearchScopeLevels1=&SearchScopeLevels2=&highLight=1&Se archType=exact&SearchMoesar=false&bookID=&LeftVal=0&RightVal= 0&simple=&SearchCriteria=allwords&PagePath=&siteSection=1&searchk eyword=102111111116098097108108#firstKeyWordFound

24. Ibid. Fatwas of the Permanent Committee, Group 1, Volume 15: Transactions 3, Fatwa no. 332, http://alifta.com/Search/ResultDetails.aspx?lang=en&v iew=result&fatwaNum=&FatwaNumID=&ID=5605&searchScope=7&Se archScopeLevels1=&SearchScopeLevels2=&highLight=1&SearchType=e

xact&SearchMoesar=false&bookID=&LeftVal=0&RightVal=0&simple=&SearchCriteria=allwords&PagePath=&siteSection=1&searchkeyword=102111111116098097108108#firstKeyWordFound

25. Ibid. Fatwas of the Permanent Committee, Group 1, Volume 15: Transactions 3, Fatwa no. 18951, http://alifta.com/Search/ResultDetails.aspx?lang=en&view=result&fatwaNum=&FatwaNumID=&ID=5637&searchScope=7&SearchScopeLevels1=&SearchScopeLevels2=&highLight=1&SearchType=exact&SearchMoesar=false&bookID=&LeftVal=0&RightVal=0&simple=&SearchCriteria=allwords&PagePath=&siteSection=1&searchkeyword=102111111116098097108108#firstKeyWordFound

26. Habib Trabelsi, "Islamists denounce 'opium of football'", *Mail & Guardian*, 24 June 2006, http://mg.co.za/article/2006-06-24-islamists-denounce-opium-of-football

27. Ibid. Terdman

28. Hamid bin Abdallah al-Ali, ؟.... اسألك لاعالم, 25 June 2006, http://h-alali.net/z_open.php?id=fb9ed57c-eadb-1029-a62a-0010dc91cf69; http://wincoast.com/forum/archive/index.php/t-34956.html

29. Yaakov Lappin, "Jihadist site: Soccer is against Islam," *Ynetnews*, 21 June 2006, http://www.ynetnews.com/articles/0,7340,L-3265595,00.html

30. Moshe Terdman, "The Ball is Not Always Round: The Attitude to Soccer between Jihadi-Radical and Moderate Muslims", *Prism Papers on Islamist Social Affairs, Global Research in International Affairs (GLORIA) Center, Herzliya, Number 1*, Dec. 2006.

31. Moshe Terdman, "The Ball is Not Always Round". http://www.tajdeed.org.uk/forums/showthread.php?s=28a75f0fc6667bc7962b22201e0cdf7f&threadid=42893

32. Ibid.

33. The ruling was published in *Al Watan*, 26 Aug. 2005-http://www.hajr.biz/forum, but has since been taken down. Details can be found on http://www.memri.org/report/en/0/0/0/0/0/0/1494.htm

34. Moshe Terdman, "The Ball is not always Round".

35. Sheikh Abu Ishaaq Al Huweni, "The Ruling of Watching Football Games In Islam", 29 Dec. 2009, http://www.youtube.com/watch?v=TOE-tGmAI18. This account was subsequently blocked on YouTube

36. *Al Watan*, 26 Aug. 2005.

37. Ibid.

38. Al Arabiya, "Mecca Mayor Announces Launch of 60 Football Fields", 13 May 2013, http://english.alarabiya.net/en/sports/2013/05/07/Mecca-mayor-announces-launch-of-60-football-fields-.html

39. Bahari, "Football, Iranian Style".

40. H. E. Chehabi, "The Politics of Football in Iran", *Soccer & Society*, 7:2–3, 2006, pp. 233–61.

41. Babak Fozzoni, "Religion, Politics and Class: Conflict and Contestation in the Development of Football in Iran", *Soccer & Society*, 5:3, 2004, pp. 356–70.

42. Muhammad Wasim, *Dreams and Nightmares, Perils of Sports Terrorism*, Karachi: Royal Book Company, 2013, p. 48.

43. Interview with the author, 15 Nov. 2010.

44. Interview with the author, 12 Nov. 2010.

45. Interview with the author, 15 Nov. 2010.

46. BBC News, "Somali Militants Threaten World Cup TV Viewers", 14 June 2010, http://www.bbc.co.uk/news/10307512

47. Kunle Solja and Gbolahan Dada, "Islamists murder football fans for watching World Cup", *Free Republic*, 14 June 2010, http://www.freerepublic.com/focus/f-bloggers/2537585/posts

48. Sudarsan Raghavan, "In Somalia, Soccer Can be Deadly Under the Watch of Islamic Militia," *The Seattle Times*, 12 July 2010, http://www.seattletimes.com/nation-world/in-somalia-soccer-can-be-deadly-under-the-watch-of-islamic-militia/

49. Khaled al-Berry, *Life is More Beautiful than Paradise: A Jihadist's Story*, Cairo: American University of Cairo Press, 1999, Kindle edition, Loc 115.

50. Scott Atran, *Talking to the Enemy: Faith, Brotherhood and the (Un)making of Terrorists*, New York: Ecco, 2010.

51. Khaled al-Berry, *Life is More Beautiful than Paradise*, Loc 503.

52. Noor Huda Ismail, "Football recruitment tool for terrorism," *Jakarta Post*, 5 June 2006, http://www.thejakartapost.com/news/2006/06/05/football-recruitment-tool-terrorism.html

53. James M. Dorsey, "Dismal Saudi Performance in Asian Cup Sparks Debate", The Turbulent World of Middle East Soccer, 21 Jan. 2011, http://mideastsoccer.blogspot.com/2011/01/dismal-saudi-performance-in-asian-cup.html

54. Amir Ben Porat, "Cui Bono? Arabs, Football and State", *Soccer & Society*, 2014.

55. Asef Bayat, 'Islamism and the Politics of Fun," *Public Culture*, 19:3 (2007), pp. 433–459, http://publicculture.org/articles/view/19/3/islamism-and-the-politics-of-fun

56. Osama Diab, "Egyptian Football's Pious Turn", *The Guardian*, 29 Jan. 2010, http://www.google.com.pe/url?sa=t&rct=j&q=diab+Egyptian+Football%E2%80%99s+Pious+Turn&source=web&cd=1&cad=rja&ved=0CBkQFjAA&url=http%3A%2F%2Fwww.guardian.co.uk%2Fcommentisfree%2Fbelief%2F2010%2Fjan%2F29%2Fegypt-football-religion&ei=_2RxUPHLG8XLrQeltYHwBQ&usg=AFQjCNEDZV_UwYQvFVDwPm0ZN28liwVBow

57. Interview with the author, 17 Nov. 2010.

58. *Al Watan*, 26 Aug. 2005.

59. Nasser Al-Bahri, *Dans l'ombre de Ben Laden*. Paris: Michel Lafon, 2010.

60. Peter L. Bergen, *The Longest War: The Enduring Conflict Between America and Al-Qaeda*, New York: Free Press, 2011, p. 11.

61. Steve Coll, *The Bin Ladens: An Arabian Family in the American Century*, New York: Penguin Press, 2011, pp. 145–46.

62. Michael Scheuer, *Osama Bin Laden*, New York: Oxford University Press, 2011, p. 110.

63. Steve Coll, "Young Osama", *The New Yorker*, Vol. 81, Issue 40, 12 Dec. 2005.

64. Interviews by the author with Israeli officials.

65. Parts of this chapter were first published in James M. Dorsey and Leonard C. Sebastian, "The Politics of Indonesian and Turkish Soccer: a Comparative Analysis", *Soccer & Society*, Vol. 14, Iss. 5, 2013.

66. https://www.youtube.com/watch?v=tmN8OMhcd-U&feature=player_embedded

67. Jenny White, *Muslim Nationalism and the New Turks*, Princeton NJ: Princeton University Press, 2012, p. 187.

68. *Today's Zaman*, "Arınç differs from Erdoğan on three-child advice for families", 30 June 2013, http://www.todayszaman.com/national_arinc-differs-from-erdogan-on-three-child-advice-for-families_319633.html

69. Human Rights Watch, "Closing Ranks Against Accountability, Barriers to Tackling Police Violence in Turkey", 2008, http://www.hrw.org/sites/default/files/reports/turkey1208web.pdf

70. US State Department Bureau of Democracy, Human Rights and Labor, Country Reports on Human Rights Practices for 2012, US Department of State, Dec. 2012, http://www.state.gov/j/drl/rls/hrrpt/humanrightsreport/index.htm?year=2012&dlid=204348#wrapper

71. Anna Leach, "Another trans woman murdered in Antalya, Turkey", *Gay Star News*, 29 Oct. 2012, http://www.gaystarnews.com/article/another-trans-woman-murdered-antalya-turkey291012

72. Eric S. Edelman, "Turkish P. M. Erdoğan goes to Washington: How strong a leader in the face of strong challenges?", Wikileaks, 20 Jan. 2004, http://www.cablegatesearch.net/cable.php?id=04ANKARA348&q=erdogan

73. Eric S. Edelman, "Erdoğan and AK Party after two years in power: Trying to get a grip on themselves, on Turkey, on Europe", *Wikileaks*, 30 Dec. 2004, http://www.cablegatesearch.net/cable.php?id=04ANKARA7211&q=erdogan

74. Elif Babül, "Gezi Resistance, Police Violence, and Turkey's Accession to the European Union", *Jadaliyya*, 7 Oct. 2013, http://www.jadaliyya.com/pages/index/14469/gezi-resistance-police-violence-and-turkey%E2%80%99s-acces

75. "Turkish government to raise crackdown on football disorder, violence", *Hurriyet Daily News*, 18 June 2013, http://www.hurriyetdailynews.com/turkish-government-to-raise-crackdown-on-football-disorder-violence.aspx?pageID=238&nID=48980&NewsCatID=362

76. Office of Anti-Terrorism, Terörle Mücadele Dairese Başkanligi Kamu Spotu (Office of Anti-Terrorism Public Spot), 15 Aug. 2013, http://alkislarlayasiyorum.com/icerik/140883/terorle-mucadele-dairesi-baskanligi-kamu-spotu

77. Aydinlik, "Istanbul Bar Strongly Condemns Prosecutors of Çarşı Trial," 8 Dec. 2014, http://www.aydinlikdaily.com/Detail/Istanbul-Bar-Strongly-Condemns-Prosecutors-Of-%C3%87ar%C5%9F%C4%B1-Trial/4491

78. Eoin Brennan, "When United went to Istanbul in 1993", 20 Nov. 2012, *Newstalk* 106–108 FM, http://www.newstalk.ie/when-united-went-to-istanbul

79. Guiness World Records, http://www.guinnessworldrecords.com/records-1/loudest-crowd-roar-at-a-sports-stadium/

80. Al Jazeera World, "The Passion and the Penalty", 6 Nov. 2012.

81. Cem Emrence, "From Elite Circles to Power Networks: Turkish Soccer Clubs in a Global Age, 1903–2005", *Soccer & Society*, 11:3 (2010), pp. 242–252.

82. Ibid.

83. Yigit Akin, "Not Just A Game: The Kayseri vs. Sivas Football Disaster", Soccer & Society, 5:2 (2004), pp. 219–232.

84. Sevenc Tunc, *Putting The City On The Map, A Social History of Football in Trabzon to 1967*, Saarbrücken: Lambert Academic Publishing, 2010.

85. US Embassy Ankara, "Trabzon: A City Passed By", *Wikileaks*, http://www.cablegatesearch.net/cable.php?id=05ANKARA4276&q=and%20soccer%20turkey

86. Emrence, "From Elite Circles to Power Networks."

87. Adrien Battini, "Reshaping the national bounds through fandom: the UltrAslan of Galatasaray", *Soccer & Society* (2012), DOI:10.1080/14660970.2012.730771

88. Itir Erhat, "Ladies of Beşiktaş: A dismantling of male hegemony at Inönü Stadium", *International Review of Sociology of Sport*, 2013, 48: pp. 83–98.

89. Tanıl Bora, "Erkeklik ve Futbol: Beslik Yeme Kaygisi", *Kaos GL, 32*, pp. 16–17.

90. Andrei Simic, "Management of the male image in Yugoslavia", *Anthropological Quarterly*, 43: pp. 89–101.

91. Erhat, "Ladies of Beşiktaş."

92. James M. Dorsey, "Galatasaray Plans To Seek Listing For Some Assets", *The Wall Street Journal*, 14 Nov. 2000.

93. David Goldblatt, *The Ball is Round: A Global History of Soccer*, New York: Riverhead Books, 2006, pp. 759–60.

94. Kerim Balci, "Galatasaray enters the EU in Copenhagen", *Hurriyet Daily*

News, 19 May 2000, http://www.hurriyetdailynews.com/default.aspx?pageid=438&n=galatasaray-enters-the-eu-in-copenhagen-2000–05–19

95. Battini, "Reshaping the national bounds through fandom."
96. Al Jazeera World, "The Passion and the Penalty."
97. James M. Dorsey, "Debt fuels Turkish soccer but threatens country's economic growth", The Turbulent World of Middle East Soccer, 1 Jan. 2012, http://mideastsoccer.blogspot.co.uk/2012/01/debt-fuels-turkish-soccer-but-threatens.html
98. Ibid.
99. Ercan Ersoy and Taylan Bilgic, "Debt Dwarfing Manchester United Shows Turkish Soccer Rot", Bloomberg News, 7 Oct. 2013, http://www.businessweek.com/printer/articles/606032?type=bloomberg
100. Ibid.
101. http://z6.invisionfree.com/UltrasTifosi/index.php?showtopic=30688&st=33
102. Anadolu Agency, "Court halts controversial football e-ticketing plan," 8 May 2014, http://www.hurriyetdailynews.com/court-halts-controversial-football-e-ticketing-plan.aspx?pageID=238&nID=66193&NewsCatID=362
103. Ibid.
104. *Today's Zaman,* "Ülker withdraws from football sponsorship in response to Passolig system," 14 Jan. 2015, http://www.todayszaman.com/anasayfa_ulker-withdraws-from-football-sponsorship-in-response-to-passolig-system_369780.html
105. Internethaber, "Murat Ülker'in Milli Takım kararı şok etti," 14 Jan. 2015, http://www.internethaber.com/murat-ulkerin-milli-takim-karari-sok-etti-756454h.htm
106. John Konuk Blasing, "Half Built Stadiums and Promises Left Unkept: Turkey's Political Landscape Seen Through Stadiums," *Thisisfootballislife.com,* 12 June 2015, https://thisisfootballislife.wordpress.com/2015/06/12/half-built-stadiums-and-promises-left-unkept-turkeys-political-landscape-seen-through-stadiums/
107. James M. Dorsey, "Islamist power politics threaten clean-up of Turkish soccer", The Turbulent World of Middle East Soccer, 11 May 2012, http://mideastsoccer.blogspot.co.uk/2012/05/islamist-power-politics-threaten-clean.html
108. Ibid.
109. Anon I, "AKP-Fethullah clash and the Fenerbahçe issue," TurkeyEmergency, 12 Dec. 2011, http://www.turkeyemergency.com/2011/match-fixing-Fenerbahçe-akp-fethullah/
110. Huseyn Gulerce, "Second Breach in Ergenekon's Fortress", *Today's Zaman,* 14 July 2011, http://www.todayszaman.com/columnistDetail_getNewsById.action?newsId=250459

111. "Galatasaray captain Ayhan joins title celebrations at Zaman", *Today's Zaman*, 15 May 2012, http://www.todayszaman.com/newsDetail_getNews-ById.action?newsId=280422

4. STRUGGLING FOR NATIONHOOD, BATTLING FOR CHANGE

1. James M. Dorsey, "Israeli MP drafts legislation obliging players to recognize Israel as a Jewish state", The Turbulent World of Middle East Soccer, Nov. 7, 2011, http://mideastsoccer.blogspot.com/2011/11/israeli-mp-drafts-legislation-obliging.html
2. Issam Khalidi, "Coverage of sports news in Filastin, 1911–1948", *Soccer and Society*, 2012, 13:5–6, pp. 764–776.
3. Tamir Sorek, "The Sports Column as a Site of Palestinian Nationalism in the 1940s", *Israel Affairs*, 13:3, 2007, pp. 605–616.
4. Ibid.
5. Ibid.
6. Haggai Harif and Yair Galily, "Sport and politics in Palestine, 1918–48: Football as a Mirror Reflecting the Relations between Jews and Britons", *Soccer & Society*, 4:1, 2003: pp. 41–56.
7. Issam Khalidi, "The Zionist movement and sports in Palestine", The Electronic Intifada, 27 April 2009, http://electronicintifada.net/content/zionist-movement-and-sports-palestine/8198
8. Amir Ben-Porat. "Oh Beitar Jerusalem: The Burning Bush Protest", *International Journal of the History of Sport*, 18:4, 2001: pp. 123–139; Turkey Emergency, AKP-Fethullah clash and the Fenerbahçe issue, 12 Dec. 2011, http://www.turkeyemergency.com/2011/match-fixing-Fenerbahçe-akp-fethullah/
9. Daphna Baram, "We prove that Jews and Arabs can live together", *The Guardian*, 15 Sept. 2004, http://www.guardian.co.uk/world/2004/sep/15/football.israelandthepalestinians
10. Interview with the author, 13 Sept. 1979.
11. David Finkle, "Israel's Struggle Within: An Interview with Uri Davis", *Against the Current*, 16 Sept. 2004, http://www.solidarity-us.org/node/1127
12. Israel Football Association, "Survey Published on Israel's Status Quo as Viewed by Fans", 23 Jan. 2005, http://football.org.il/Archive/Articles/Pages/oArticle253.aspx
13. http://www.youtube.com/watch?v=1mbsOxYsVJo
14. Max Nordau, "Muscular Judiasm", *Political Documents 1*, 1937, pp. 170–178.
15. Gerald Kessel and Pierre Clochenadle, *We Too Have No Other Land*, 2007, http://www.imdb.com/title/tt1948651/
16. Finkle, "Israel's Struggle Within."

17. Tamir Sorek, "Arab Football in Israel as an 'Integrative Enclave'", *Ethnic and Racial Studies* 26(3), 2003, pp. 422–450.
18. Neri Livneh, "Beitar's Fans are Impossible to Support", *Haaretz*, 31 March 2012, http://www.haaretz.com/opinion/beitar-s-fans-are-impossible-to-support-1.421846
19. Tamir Sorek, *Arab Soccer in a Jewish State: The Integrative Enclave*, Cambridge, Cambridge University Press, 2007.
20. Amir Ben-Porat, "Biladi, Biladi: Ethnic and Nationalistic Conflict in the Soccer Stadium in Israel", *Soccer & Society*, 2: 1, 2001, pp. 19–38.
21. Sorek, "Arab Football in Israel as an 'Integrative Enclave'".
22. Interview with the author, 30 Oct. 2011.
23. Sorek, *Arab Soccer in the Jewish State*.
24. O. Morano, "The Arab League". Tel Aviv Local Newspaper, 11 July 2002, p. 60.
25. M. Rapaport, and Y. Yehoshua, Y. "I am a Palestinian", *Yediot Ahronoth*, 14 March 2003, p. 20.
26. Interview with the author, 1 March 2013.
27. Ben Porat, "Biladi, Biladi".
28. Ben Porat, "Biladi, Biladi".
29. Ben Porat, "Cui Bono? Arabs, Football and State".
30. Interview with the author, 13 April 1979.
31. Ben-Porat, "Oh Beitar Jerusalem".
32. Ben Mittleman, "Israeli team player: I hate all Arabs", *Mako*, 27 May 2009, http://www.mako.co.il/Sports-football-il/israeli-league/Article-12c0ece09c58121004.htm&sCh=3d385dd2dd5d4110&pId=978777604
33. Walla, "Beitar Jerusalem: How Fans Teach Children to Chant Against Arabs", 21 June 2011, http://news.walla.co.il/?w=/157/1833989
34. Livneh, "Beitar's Fans are Impossible to Support".
35. Amir Ben Porat, "Death to the Arabs: the right-wing fan's fear", *Soccer & Society*, 2008, 9:1, pp. 1–13.
36. Dov Waxman, "A Dangerous Divide: The Deterioration of Jewish-Palestinian Relations in Israel", *The Middle East Journal* 66(1) 2012: pp. 11–29.
37. James M. Dorsey, "Mounting Israeli soccer violence reflects fading hope in Palestinian peace", The Turbulent World of Middle East Soccer, 20 April 2012, http://mideastsoccer.blogspot.sg/2012/04/mounting-israeli-soccer-violence.html
38. Ibid.
39. James M. Dorsey, "Striker Mohammed Ghadir puts Israeli anti-racism to the test", The Turbulent World of Middle East Soccer, 22 Dec. 2011, http://mideastsoccer.blogspot.sg/2011/12/striker-mohammed-ghadir-puts-israeli.html
40. Ibid.

41. Yoav Borowitz, "Kick racism out of Beitar Jerusalem soccer team", Haaretz, 18 Dec. 2011, http://www.haaretz.com/print-edition/opinion/kick-racism-out-of-beitar-jerusalem-soccer-team-1.402046
42. Ibid.
43. Ibid.
44. Interview with the author, 1 Dec. 2010.
45. John Sugden and Alan Tomlinson, *FIFA and the Contest for World Football: Who Rules the Peoples' Game?* Cambridge, Polity Press, 1994, p. 8.
46. Glen M. E Duerr, "Playing for identity and independence: the issue of Palestinian statehood and the role of FIFA", *Soccer and Society*, 13(5–6), 2012, pp. 653–666.
47. Interview with the author, 12 June 2012.
48. Mahfoud Amara, *Sport, Politics and Society in the Arab World*, New York: Palgrave, 2011, p. 155.
49. Interview with the author, 11 June 2012.
50. Interview with the author, 11 June 2012.
51. Interview with the author, 11 June 2012.
52. http://www.sfcg.org/programmes/cgp/the-team-palestine.html
53. Interview with the author, 12 Dec. 2010.
54. Ibid.
55. Moraad Fareed, "Diary entries written during the road to the 2006 Mundial—from the diary of Morad Fareed, Palestinian national team member", *Soccer & Society*, 13:5–6, 2013, pp. 834–844.
56. David Keyes, "Culture of Soccer, Player Focus: Raad Qumsieh", *Culture of Soccer*, 12 Dec. 2007, http://cultureofsoccer.com/2007/12/01/player-focus-raad-qumsieh/
57. Ibid.
58. James M. Dorsey, "Palestine: Playing for nationhood", The Turbulent World of Middle East Soccer, 18 June 2011, http://mideastsoccer.blogspot.com/2011/03/playing-for-statehood.html
59. Ibid.
60. Pep Escoda and Isidre Rigau, "Olympic Solidarity Special Program for Developing Sport in Palestine Structure Plan", 4 March 2011, unpublished.
61. James M. Dorsey, "Palestine unveils sports plan in effort to further state- and nationhood", The Turbulent World of Middle East Soccer, 29 Oct. 2011, http://mideastsoccer.blogspot.sg/2011/10/palestine-unveils-sports-plan-in-effort.html
62. Ibid.
63. Ibid.
64. Jadaliyya, "The Maspero Massacre: What Really Happened" (Video), 11 Nov. 2011, http://www.jadaliyya.com/p. s/index/3103/the-maspero-massacre_what-really-happened-(video)

65. Mustafa Abdelhalim, "Can football unite Muslims and Christians in Egypt?", Common Ground News Service, 14 Aug. 2012, http://www.commonground-news.org/article.php?id=31871&lan=en&sp=0

66. Safwat Freeze Ghali, "Copts and soccer, Copts United", Copts United, 23 May 2012, http://www.coptsunited.com/Details.php?I=600&A=5519

67. Ibid.

68. Interview with the author, 22 March 2013.

69. James Montague, "People are afraid, but I have supported this team for 40 years", The Guardian, 21 Dec. 2007, http://www.guardian.co.uk/football/2007/dec/21/sport.comment2

70. Interview with the author, 3 March 2013.

71. James M. Dorsey, "Syrian soccer star symbolizes games importance in protests", 23 May 2012, http://mideastsoccer.blogspot.sg/2012/05/syrian-studies-association-newsletter.html

72. Mohammed Daghan, "The Original Shabiha", Syria Comment, 17 Aug. 2012, http://www.joshualandis.com/blog the-original-shabiha-by-mohammad-d/

73. Adrian Blomfield, "Syria: feared militia kills up to 21 people as protests continue", Daily Telegraph, 21 March 2011, http://www.telegraph.co.uk/news/worldnews/middleeast/syria/8409870/Syria-feared-militia-kills-up-to-21-people-as-protests-continue.html

74. Khaled Yacoub Oweis, "Syria's President ends state of emergency", Reuters, 21 April 2011, http://www.reuters.com/article/2011/04/21/us-syria-idUSTRE72N2MC20110421

75. Ahed Al Hendi, "The Structure of Syria's Repression", Foreign Affairs, 3 May 2011 http://www.foreignaffairs.com/articles/67823/ahed-al-hendi/the-structure-of-syrias-repression

76. Gul Tuysuz, "Syrian men promise to marry women who were raped", The Washington Post, 21 June 2011, http://articles.washingtonpost.com/2011–06-20/world/35233997_1_syrian-president-bashar-al-assad-syria-in-recent-months-jisr-al-shugour

77. Stephanie Nebehay, "Most Houla victims killed in summary execution", UN, Reuters, 29 May 2012.

78. Peter Kellier, "Ghosts of Syria: diehard militias who kill in the name of Assad", The Guardian, 1 June 2012, http://www.guardian.co.uk/world/2012/may/31/ghosts-syria-regime-shabiha-militias

79. Daghan, "The Original Shabiha".

80. BBC News, "Syria unrest: Who are the shabiha?", 29 May 2012, http://www.bbc.co.uk/news/world-middle-east-14482968

81. Interview with the author, 12 May 2012.

82. Interviews with the author, 12 and 16 May 2012.

83. Ibid.

84. Interview with the author, 15 May 2011.

85. Interview with the author, 16 May 2011.

86. Simon Freeman, *Baghdad FC: Iraq's Football Story*, London: John Murray, 2005, p. 99.

87. James Montague. "Iraq's latest kicking has little to do with war", *The Guardian*, 1 Oct. 2008, http://www.guardian.co.uk/sport/blog/2008/oct/01/iraq. football

88. Ibid.

89. James Montague, "How the Lions of Mesopotamia brought a sense of unity to Iraq", *The Guardian*, 12 June 2009, http://www.guardian.co.uk/football/blog/2009/jun/12/iraq-confederations-cup-lions-mesopotamia

90. Tony Karon, "Soccer in Iraq Helps Ease Tensions", *Time*, 25 July 2007, http://www.time.com/time/world/article/0,8599,1647039,00.html

91. Mike Tharp, "Iraqis defeated U.S. troops in a soccer match. More importantly, the game symbolized a turning point in the war," McClatchy News Service, 23 June 2008, http://www.google.com.pe/url?sa=t&rct=j&q=thar p+Iraqis+defeated+U.S.+troops+in+a+soccer+match&source=web&cd= 3&cad=rja&ved=0CCYQFjAC&url=http%3A%2F%2Fwww.mcclatchydc. com%2F2008%2F06%2F22%2F41848%2Firaqis-drubbing-of-us-troops-shows.html&ei=p5pxUJj_BI2zrAeZnIGoBw&usg=AFQjCNHKB0I3_ b2Qfqe3SqdNmuoIAa4zhA

92. David Ignatius, "In Afghanistan, soccer or civil war?" *The Washington Post*, 4 Aug. 2012, http://www.washingtonpost.com/opinions/david-ignatius-in-afghanistan-soccer-or-civil-war/2012/08/03/21ac9dba-dcec-11e1-af1d-753c613ff6d8_story.html

93. Babak Fozooni, "Religion, Politics and Class: Conflict and Contestation in the Development of Football in Iran", *Soccer & Society*, Volume 5, Issue 3, 2004, pp. 356–70.

94. Maziar Behrooz, "Factionalism in Iran under Khomeini", *Middle Eastern Studies*, 27(4), 1991, pp. 597–614.

95. Chehabi, "The Politics of Football in Iran".

96. Interview with the author, 25 Oct. 2010.

97. Shahin Gerami, "Mullahs, Martyrs and Men: Conceptualizing Masculinity in the Islamic Republic of Iran", *Men and Masculinities*, 5(3), 2003: pp. 257–74.

98. Nicole Byrne, "My journey to Iran with Ireland's fearless sisters", *The Observer*, 18 Nov. 2001, http://www.guardian.co.uk/football/2001/nov/18/sport. world

99. "Iran's First Fan: Dissatisfaction with Ahadinejad May Extend from the Soccer Pitch to the Ballot Box", http://wikileaksupdates.blogspot.com/2010/12/irans-first-fan-dissatisfaction-with.html, 7 Dec. 2010.

100. James M. Dorsey, "Soccer match sparks nationalist protests in northwest Iran", The Turbulent World of Middle East Soccer, 16 Sept. 2011, http:// mideastsoccer.blogspot.sg/2011/09/soccer-match-sparks-nationalist.html

5. SHATTERING TABOOS

1. Monika Mueller-Kroll, Monika, "Soccer Pioneer Builds Her Own Revolution In Egypt", National Public Radio, 24 May 2012, http://www.npr.org/2012/05/23/153512361/soccer-pioneer-builds-her-own-revolution-in-egypt?ft=1&f=

2. Donn Risolo, *Soccer Stories: Anecdotes, Oddities, Lore, and Amazing Feats*, Lincoln NE, University of Nebraska Press, 2010.

3. Sorek, "The Sports Column".

4. Quoted by Fozooni, who cited a publication by the Seminary of Qom's Office for Islamic Propagation.

5. James M. Dorsey, "Women's Soccer Teams in Saudi Arabia and UAE Encouraged to be Champions", Al Arabiya, 22 July 2011, http://www.google.com.pe/url?sa=t&rct=j&q=dorsey+Women%E2%80%99s+soccer+teams+in+Saudi+Arabia+and+UAE+encouraged+to+be+champions%2C+Al+Arabiya&source=web&cd=1&cad=rja&ved=0CBkQFjAA&url=httpp%3A%2F%2Fenglish.alarabiya.net%2Farticles%2F2011%2F07%2F22%2F158760.html&ei=65xxUNvwI8fMrQfKzIHACA&usg=AFQjCNEVFrTpw_wpylyr_J5eTvHIFLvrBQ b

6. Geoff Harkness and Samira Islam, "Muslim Female Athletes and the Hijab", *Contexts*, 2011 10, p. 64.

7. Habib Toumi, "Kuwaiti MP Calls for Women's Football Tournament Cancellation", *Gulf News*, 10 July 2010.

8. *Al Watan Daily*, 4 March 2012.

9. "Libyan Cleric Outraged Over Establishment Of Women's Soccer Team, Says Country Needs Sharia Law Lashings Instead…" *Weasel Zippers*, 3 July 2013, http://weaselzippers.us/2013/07/03/libyan-cleric-outraged-over-establishment-of-womens-soccer-team-says-country-needs-sharia-law-lashings-instead/

10. James M. Dorsey, "Middle East Soccer Associations Campaign for Women's Right to Play", The Turbulent World of Middle East Soccer, 14 Jan. 2013, http://mideastsoccer.blogspot.co.uk/2013/01/middle-east-soccer-associations.html

11. Ibid.

12. Kenda Stewart, "A hobby or hobbling? Playing Palestinian women's soccer in Israel", *Soccer & Society*, 13(5–6), 2012, pp. 739–763.

13. Ibid.

14. Ibid.

15. Human Rights Watch, "Steps of the Devil", 15 Feb. 2012.

16. *Al Watan*, 5 May 2012.

17. Video mailed to the author.

18. James M. Dorsey, "Saudi Arabia to Allow Women to Compete in London Olympics", The Turbulent World of Middle East Soccer, 26 June 2012, http://mideastsoccer.blogspot.co.uk/2012/06/saudi-arabia-to-allow-women-to-compete.html

19. Interview with author, 18 March 2013.

20. James M. Dorsey, "Prominent Soccer Executives and Players Seek Compromise on the Hijab", The Turbulent World of Middle East Soccer, 26 Oct. 2011, http://mideastsoccer.blogspot.sg/2011/10/prominent-soccer-executives-and-players.html

21. Ibid.

22. Iran Regional Presence Office Dubai, "Window On Iran", 20 May 2009, http://www.cablegatesearch.net/cable.php?id=09RPODUBAI218&q= soccer

23. James M. Dorsey, "World Cup qualifier: A battle for Iranian women's rights", The Turbulent World of Middle East Soccer, 19 Oct. 2012, http://mideast-soccer.blogspot.co.uk/2012/10/world-cup-qualifier-battle-for-iranian.html

24. Ibid.

25. http://www.imdb.com/title/tt0499537/

26. Amnesty International, "Filmmaker Sentenced to Six Years in Prison", http://www.amnestyusa.org/our-work/cases/iran-jafar-panahi

27. http://www.fcf.ir/en/index.php?option=com_content&view=article&id= 104:shirin-was-a-canary&catid=34:movie&Itemid=56

28. BBC Persian Service, لاب‌توف یاههاکش‌زرو رد نانز روضح اب ی‌بهذم عجارم تفلاخم (Religious opposotion to women in stadiums)", 26 April 2006, http://www.bbc.co.uk/persian/iran/story/2006/04/060426_mf_footbal.shtml

29. Ibid.

30. Solmaz Sharif, "Iran's Female Olympians Face Extra Hurdles", *The Huffington Post*, 9 Aug. 2012, http://www.huffingtonpost.ca/solmaz-sharif/olympics 2012_b_1756992.html?just_reloaded=1

31. Dorsey, 19 Oct. 2012.

32. Ibid.

33. Ibid.

34. James M. Dorsey, "Prominent Soccer Executives and Players Seek Compromise on the Hijab", The Turbulent World of Middle East Soccer, 26 Oct. 2011, http://mideastsoccer.blogspot.sg/2011/10/prominent-soccer-executives-and-players.html

35. James M. Dorsey, "Muslim Players Win Hijab Battle in Their Struggle for Women's Rights", The Turbulent World of Middle East Soccer, 4 March

2012, http://mideastsoccer.blogspot.sg/2012/03/muslim-players-win-hijab-battle-in.html

36. David Assmann and Ayat Najafi, "Football Under Cover", 2008, http://football-under-cover.de

37. Ibid.

38. Ibid.

39. John Turnbull, "Iran: 'As if one were under water'", *The Global Game*, 29 Sept. 2007. http://www.theglobalgame.com/blog/?p=275

40. Balaghi, "Football and Film in the Islamic Republic of Iran".

41. Ibid.

42. Jere Longman, "A quiet revolution in Iran: Beneath coat and scarf women discover the right to play", *The New York Times*, 26 May 1998, http://www.google.com.pe/url?sa=t&rct=j&q=longman+A+quiet+revolution+in+Iran&source=web&cd=1&cad=rja&ved=0CBkQFjAA&url=http%3A%2F%2Fwww.nytimes.com%2F1998%2F05%2F26%2Fsports%2Finternational-sports-quiet-revolution-iran-beneath-coat-scarf-women-discover.html%3Fpagewanted%3Dall%26src%3Dpm&ei=NqBxUL6EOcXmrAeA-4DQDA&usg=AFQjCNHmF_-1E0f8dX-q35GeWxeQay0zfQ

43. Interviews with the author, 28 May 2012.

44. Interview with the author, 3 June 2008.

45. Interview with the author, 3 June 2008.

6. COMPETING ON THE WORLD STAGE

1. James M. Dorsey, "Qatar in Firing Line as Fifa's Political Football", *The National*, 23 Feb. 2011, http://www.thenational.ae/thenationalconversation/industry-insights/economics/qatar-in-firing-line-as-fifas-political-football?pageCount=0

2. Lindsay Sarah Krasnoff, *The Making of Les Bleus, Sport in France, 1958–2010*, Lanham: Lexington Books, 2013, p. 2.

3. Christoph Biermann, "Football's Biggest Talent Contest: Qatar Scouts for Tomorrow's Soccer Superstars", *Der Spiegel*, 27 Feb. 2009, http://www.spiegel.de/international/world/football-s-biggest-talent-contest-qatar-scouts-for-tomorrow-s-soccer-superstars-a-610357.html

4. Interview with the author, 2 Oct. 2013.

5. Human Rights Watch, "Building a Better World Cup, Protecting Migrant Workers in Qatar Ahead of FIFA 2022," 12 June 2012, http://www.hrw.org/reports/2012/06/12/building-better-world-cup-0

6. Andrew Gardner, Silvia Pessoa, Abdoulaye Diop, Kaltham Al-Ghanim, Kien Le Trung, and Laura Harkness, "A Portrait of Low-Income Migrants in Contemporary Qatar", *Journal of Arabian Studies*, 3:1, 2013.

7. Jassim bin Sosibo Al Thani, "A National Day Message for the Youth of Qatar",

Qatar Chronicle, 13 Dec. 2013, http://www.qatarchronicle.com/happenings/45425/a-national-day-message-for-the-youth-of-qatar-by-jassim-bin-sosibo-al-thani/?utm_source=feedburner&utm_medium=email&utm_campaign=Feed%3A+QatarChronicle+%28Qatar+Chronicle%29

8. Firas Zirie, "Opinion: Qatar should consider permanent resident status provision," Doha News, 14 Dec. 2013, http://dohanews.co/opinion-qatar-should-consider-permanent-resident-status-provision/?utm_source=feedburner&utm_medium=email&utm_campaign=Feed%3A+DohaNews+%28Doha+News%29

9. Sultan Sooud al Qassemi, "Citizenship to expats presents challenges," Gulf News, 29 Sept. 2013, http://gulfnews.com/opinions/columnists/citizenship-to-expats-presents-challenges-1.1237072

10. Ravinder Mamtani, Albert B. Lowenfels, Sohaila Cheema, and Javaid Sheikh, "Impact of Migrant Workers on the Human Development Index", Perspectives in Public Health, 5 June 2013, http://rsh.sagepub.com/content/early/2013/06/05/1757913913491350.full

11. Baqer Alnajjar, "Foreign Labor and Questions of Identity in the Arabian Gulf", Arab Center for Research & Policy Studies, 18 Aug. 2013, http://english.dohainstitute.org/release/3010e20a-1bc3–4807–8f42-f7131151c3d0

12. Interview with the author, 17 April 2013.

13. World Service World Football, "Bad times for Qatar," BBC, 26 April 2013, http://wehearus.com/podcasts/episode/80067

14. David Conn, "Abu Dhabi accused of 'using Manchester City to launder image'", *The Guardian*, 30 July 2013, http://www.theguardian.com/football/2013/jul/30/manchester-city-human-rights-accusations

15. Rory Jones, "Gulf Aims to Get Back on Stream", *The Wall Street Journal*, 13 May 2013, http://online.wsj.com/article/SB10001424127887324266904578456741356678544.html?mod=googlenews_wsj

16. Khalifa Saleh Al Haroon, "Why Qatar needs the World Cup!" 5 Oct. 2010, Mr Q A Qatari's View, http://blog.iloveqatar.net/2010/10/why-we-need-the-world-cup/

17. Belgin Akaltan, "Mixed Feelings on Istanbul 2020," Hurriyet Daily News, 14 Sept. 2013, http://www.hurriyetdailynews.com/mixed-feelings-on-istanbul-2020.aspx?pageID=238&nid=54401

18. Peter Velappan, *The Fascinating Story of the Blesssed Life of Peter Velappan s/o Palaniappan*, Kuala Lumpur: Peter Velappan s/o Palaniappan, 2013.

19. Heidi Blake and Jonathan Calvert, *The Ugly Game: The Qatari Plot to Buy the World Cup*, London: Simon & Schuster UK, 2015.

20. Blake and Calvert, *The Ugly Game*;/Thomas Kistner, Fifa-Mafia: Die schmutzigen Geschäfte mit dem Weltfußball, Berlin: Knauer, 2012, Kindle Edition.

21. Kistner, *FIFA Mafia*, p. 92.

22. Jack Warner, "Jack Warner Responds to London Telegraph Video: Ingratitude Worse than Witchcraft", *Trinidad Guardian*, 18 Oct. 2011, http://www.guardian.co.tt/news/2011/10/18/jack-warner-responds-london-telegraph-video-ingratitude-worse-witchcraft

23. *Libya Watanunna*, April 2002, http://www.libya-watanona.com/news/news0402/0402nwsc.htm

24. Court of Arbitration of Sport, "Arbitral Award Delivered by the Court of Arbitration of Sport, CAS 2011/A/2625 Mohamed Bin Hammam v. FIFA"

25. James M. Dorsey, "Asian Football Federation moves to dismantle Bin Hammam's legacy," The Turbulent World of Middle East Soccer, 2 Aug. 2011, http://mideastsoccer.blogspot.dk/2011/08/asian-football-federation-moves-to.html

26. Matthew Grayson, "Newsdesk—Jilong Rejects Bin Hammam's Tactics; Valcke Tells Brazil to Pick Up Pace," World Football Insider, 17 Oct. 2012, http://worldfootballinsider.com/Story.aspx?id=35396

27. Ibid.

28. Interviews with AFC sources and sources close to Jilong, Sept./Oct. 2012.

29. Andrew Warshaw, "Exclusive: Leaked letter warns AFC members against accepting bribes", Inside World Football, 16 Sept. 2013, http://www.insideworldfootball.com/world-football/asia/12375-exclusive-leaked-letter-warns-afc-members-against-accepting-bribes?highlight=WyJkYXRvJyIsImFsZXXgiLCJzb29zYXkiLCJkYXRvJyBhbGV4IiwiZGF0bycgYWxleCBzb29zYXkiLCJhbGV4IHNvb3NheSJd

30. Richard LeBaron, "Succession Struggle: Jabers vs. Salems with Parliament Stuck in the Middle," 22 Jan. 2006, US diplomatic cable disclosed by Wikileaks, http://www.wikileaks.org/plusd/cables/06KUWAIT200_a.html

31. Mary Pilon, "Kuwaiti Sheikh's Influence in Olympic World Grows," *The New York Times*, 5 Sept. 2013, http://www.nytimes.com/2013/09/06/sports/olympics/kuwaiti-sheiks-influence-in-olympic-world-grows.html?_r=0

32. James M. Dorsey, "AFC Power Struggle Reflects Sorry State of Soccer Governance," The Turbulent World of Middle East Soccer, 10 June 2014, http://mideastsoccer.blogspot.dk/2014/06/afc-power-struggle-reflects-sorry-state.html

33. Oliver Fritsch, "Die verkauften WM-Turniere," *Die Zeit*, 4 June 2015, http://www.zeit.de/sport/2015-06/chuck-blazer-fifa-fussball-weltmeisterschaft-2022

EPILOGUE

1. Josh Meyer, "To locate the next Arab Spring revolution, look to the soccer stands", Quartz, 22 May 2013, http://qz.com/87105/to-locate-the-next-arab-spring-revolution-look-to-the-soccer-stands/

2. Mark Mazzetti, "Secret Desert Force Set Up by Blackwater's Founder", *The New York Times*, 14 May 2011, http://www.nytimes.com/2011/05/15/world/middleeast/15prince.html?pagewanted=all&_r=0

3. Glenn Carrick and David Batty, "In Abu Dhabi, they call it Happiness Island. But for the migrant workers, it is a place of misery," *The Observer*, 22 Dec. 2013, http://www.theguardian.com/world/2013/dec/22/abu-dhabi-happiness-island-misery

INDEX

Aarts, Paul, 2
abaya, 224
Abbas, Mahmoud, 174, 175, 177, 228
Abbasaga Park, Istanbul, 130
Abdel-Razek, Mahmoud, 35
Abdelhalim, Mustafa, 180–1
Abdi Aros, Mohamed, 105
Abdi Salaam Mohamed Ali, 107
Abdin, Cairo, 65, 67
Abdirahman Mohamed Ali, 107
Abdul-Hassan, Abdul-Rahman, 193
Abdulghani Sayeed, 104
Abdulhamit II, Caliph of the Ottoman Empire, 123, 133
Abdulkader Dheer Hussein, 106–7
Abdulkader Yahye Sheik Ali, 107
Abdullah bin Abdulaziz Al Saud, King of Saudi Arabia, 21, 226, 227, 260
Abdullah, Reema, 214–15, 222
Abdullah, Tal'at, 76
al-Abikan, Abdel Muhsin, 101
abortion, 118
Abou-Treika, Mohamed, 35, 70
Absuge, Hassan Yusuf, 107
al-Abtal, 33
Abu Abdellah, 222
Abu Arab, 219–20

Abu Assi, Assem, 180
Abu Badr, Ghalib, 220
Abu Dhabi, United Arab Emirates, 216–17, 251, 253, 254, 264, 285, 286
Abu Dhabi Television, 259
Abu Ghaith, Suleiman, 95
Abu Ghraib prison, Baghdad, 100
Abu Khater, Brahim, 220
Abu Roweis, Omar, 180
AC Milan, 242, 253
Adanaspor, 135
Addo, Farah, 268
Aden, Colony of (1937–1963), 33
Adeolu, Olumide, 245
Admira Wacker, 256
Adnan, Sayed Mohamed, 280
Adonis, 64, 65
Afghan Premier League, 196–7
Afghanistan, 7, 17–18, 94, 99, 102, 103, 107, 109, 111, 185, 194, 195, 196–7, 241
   1979–89 Soviet War, 111
   1999 execution of Zarmeena in Ghazi Stadium, 18
   2000 Pakistani team arrested in Kandahar for wearing shorts, 102
   2001 US-led invasion, 17, 194,

195, 196–7; ISAF–Afghan football match at Ghazi Stadium, 196

2008 Rohallah Nikpai wins bronze medal at Beijing Olympics, 196

2012 establishment of Afghan Premier League, 196–7

Afghanistan Football Federation (AFF), 196

Afgoye, Somalia, 105

Afifi, Abdul Razak, 97

Africa Cup of Nations, 8, 18, 28, 34, 41, 48, 181

1998 Burkina Faso, 181

2010 Angola, 8, 34

2013 South Africa, 41

African Union (AU), 103

Agence France Presse, 17

Aghazadeh, Gholam Reza, 204

al-Ahad SC, 114, 183

al-Ahly Benghazi SC, 15–16

al-Ahly Cairo SC, 4, 27, 31–5, 47–8, 54, 55–6, 60, 63, 65, 69–80, 84, 86, 87, 91, 107, 267

al-Ahly Jeddah SC, 226

al-Ahly Tripoli SC, 15

Ahmad Shah Masood, 196

al-Ahmad, Ali, 22

Ahmadinejad, Mahmoud, 33, 198, 202–3, 207, 208, 209, 210, 211, 230, 231

al-Ahram, 12, 31–2, 87

Air Defence Stadium, Cairo, 20, 85

Ajram, Nancy, 20

AK-47s, 86, 103, 195

al-Akhdar SC, 16

Akhund, Maulvi Hameed, 102

AKP (Adalet ve Kalkınma Partisi), 118, 120, 122, 142, 143

Aksar, Tugrul, 139

Alawites, 189

Alborg Mountains, Iran, 234

alcohol, 94, 117, 118, 120, 147, 200, 258, 260

Aleppo, Syria, 193

Alevis, 117

Alexandria, Egypt, 86

Alf Maskan, Cairo, 91

Algeria, 2, 5, 6, 7, 18–19, 30, 37, 39–42, 94, 110, 170, 172, 181, 187, 251

1954–62 War of Independence, 19, 30

1958 players leave France to form national team, 30, 172

1998 jihadi terrorists target World Cup matches, 94–5

2001 Djamel Beghal arrested for plot against US embassy in Paris, 112

2007 protests in Bou Saada and Oran, 42

2009 violent clashes between Algerian and Egyptian fans, 18–19

2011 soccer matches suspended after protests, 42

2012 MC Saida fans stab USM players, 41; fans demonstrate ahead of championship; express disdain for Bouteflika, 39–40; brawl at African Cup qualifier against Libya, 41; violence at JSS–USM match, 41; Bachir Tartag recalled from retirement to head DSI, 42

2014 elections; soccer matches suspended, 42; Bachir Tartag replaced by Ali Bendaoud as DSI chief, 42; Albert Ebossé Bodjongo killed by rock thrown onto pitch, 41

Algeria Cup, 40
Algiers, Algeria, 39, 41
Alharbi, Ahmed Eid, 224, 227
Ali Ali, 16
Ali, Ehab, 70
al-Ali, Hamid bin Abdallah, 99
Ali, Nagat, 60
All Cops are Bastards (ACAB), 48
Allenby Bridge, West Bank-Jordan, 176
Altınsay, Gülengül, 149
Amer, Abdelhakim, 32
Amer, Mansour, 76
American Idol, 242
Americans for Democracy and Human Rights in Bahrain (ADHRB), 280
Amini, Asieh, 201
Amman, Jordan, 4, 31, 43, 192
Ammar, Ali, 182
Ammo Baba, 191
Amnesty International, 17, 243
al-Amur, Ismail, 180
anarchism, 48, 57, 68, 73, 123, 131
Anatolia, 120, 121, 134, 135, 138, 140, 236
Anjali, Aita, 234
Ankara, Turkey, 118, 127, 134–5, 148
Ansar al-Sharia, 218
al-Ansar SC, 183
Answering the Call, Popular Islamic Activism in Sadat's Egypt, (al-Arian), 89
Antalya, Turkey, 121
Anti-Terrorism Office, Turkey, 126
'Anything but Bullets', 87
apartheid, 3
al-Aqabawi, Ahmed, 19
al-Aqsa Mosque, Jerusalem, 12, 95–6
Arab Games, 187
Arab League, 53

Arab News, 225
Arab Palestine Sports Federation (APSF), 153
Arab Women's Football Championship, 216
Arabian Gulf League, 211
al-Arabiya, 223
Arafat, Yasser, 43, 46, 114, 155, 156, 161, 228
Arc de Triomphe, Paris, 1, 240
archery, 217, 223
Archetti, Eduardo P., 66
al-Ard, 154
Argentina, 49, 69, 106
al-Arian, Abdullah, 89
Arınç, Bülent, 118
Arkan, 49, 50
Armenians, 38, 121, 131, 183, 184, 207
arms smuggling, 86
Armstrong, Gary, 56, 59
Arsenal FC, 94, 253, 257
Arslan, Mücahit, 122
AS Nancy-Lorraine, 252
AS Roma, 253
Asbar, Ali Ahmad Said, 64, 65
Ashkenazi Jews, 159
Asian Champions League, 172, 185, 187
Asian Cup, 8, 23, 102, 190–3, 197, 199, 207, 224, 234, 285
    1968 Iran, 207
    2007 Indonesia, Malaysia, Thailand, Vietnam, 8, 190–3, 197
    2011 Qatar, 234
    2019 United Arab Emirates, 224, 285
Asian Football Confederation (AFC), 4, 198, 224, 231–2, 238, 263–7, 269–78, 280–1
Asian Games, 223
Asian Youth Cup, 231

Aspire, 242
al-Assad, Bashar, 17, 47, 117–18,
    184, 187, 188, 189, 190, 191, 206,
    207, 210
al-Assad, Fawwaz, 189
al-Assad, Hafez, 47, 188
al-Assad, Munzir, 190
Associated Press, 41, 280
Association of National Olympic
    Committees (ANOC), 265, 279
Assood al-Rafidain, 191
Assyrians, 190, 191
Atatürk, Mustafa Kemal, 118, 121,
    123, 130, 144
Atatürk Olympic Stadium, Istanbul,
    140–1
Atlantic, The, 211
Atlético Madrid, 138
Atomic Energy Organization of
    Iran, 204
Australia, 4, 21, 37, 95, 105, 194,
    200, 265, 277
Austria, 256
authoritarianism, 5, 12, 29, 47, 75,
    82, 121–2, 199
autocracy, 2, 4, 5, 6, 7, 9, 11, 12, 17,
    18, 21, 25, 28, 31, 34–5, 37, 50,
    53–4, 64, 67, 81–2, 90, 109, 133,
    147, 190, 234, 239, 248, 263, 264,
    284–5
Avenue Habib Bourguiba, Tunis, 53
ayran, 117
Azadi Stadium, Tehran, 38, 39,
    200–1, 203, 206
Azeem, Hamdi Abdul, 27–8
Azerbaijan, 38, 204–7
Azeris, 7, 38, 181, 204–7
al-Azhar University, 19
al-Azm, Sadik, 7, 65

Baath Party

of Iraq 12–13
of Syria, 47, 64
Babahan, Ergun, 145
Babül, Elif, 124
Bach, Thomas, 223, 278
Bad Blue Boys, 51
Baghdad, Iraq, 13, 173, 191–5
Bağış, Egemen, 122
Bahari, Mazar, 101
Bahari, Maziar, 234
Bahrain, 3, 4, 38, 43, 116, 187, 209,
    210, 216, 217, 231, 252, 255–6,
    257, 263, 264, 265, 274, 278–81
    2001 defeat of Iran in World Cup
        qualifier, 38
    2008 Roqaya al-Ghasara makes
        semi-finals in Olympic sprint-
        ing, 217
    2011 Shia uprising, 256, 263, 264,
        279
    2012 Grand Prix; protests erupt,
        3, 256; acquisition of Leeds
        United, 255–6
    2013 Grand Prix; protests erupt,
        3, 256; Salman Bin Ibrahim
        Khalifa elected AFC president,
        4, 264, 265, 278
Bahraini Football Association, 280,
    278
baksheesh, 83
Baku, Azerbaijan, 205
Balaghi, Shiva, 31, 39
Balhous, Mosab, 187, 190
baltageyya, 66, 91
Bam, Iran, 206
Banat Sakhnin, 219–20
Bandak, Marian, 228–9
Bandar Abbas, Iran, 208, 209
Bangladesh, 253
Baniyas, Syria, 17, 189
banners, 7, 34, 39, 49, 54, 57, 58,
    68, 132, 136, 165, 166

Bar Kochba revolt (132–6 AD), 149
al-Baraka Investment and Development Co, 273
al-Baraka Islamic Investment Bank BSC, 274
Barbarossa, Hayreddin, 130
Barkat, Nir, 169
Barltrop, Keith, 96
Barmak, Sedigh, 17
barras bravas, 69
Baruchyan, Aviram, 164
Barzani, Massoud, 47, 171, 172
Başbuğ, İlker, 144
Basij militia, 202, 204
basketball, 217, 221, 230, 236, 241
Basque Country, 170
Battini, Adrien, 136, 138
Battle of Mogadishu (1993), 103–4
Battle of the Camels (2011), 60, 70–1
Battle of the Dakhliya (2011), 66
Bayat, Asef, 109
al-Baydah, Libya, 15–16
Bazargan, Mehdi, 204
Bazin, Sébastien, 239
beards, 94
Bechar, Algeria, 41
Beckham, David, 96
Bedouin, 6, 46, 90–1
Beghal, Djamel, 112
Begin, Menachem, 160–1
Behsht Zahra cemetery, Tehran, 203
Beijing, China
    1989 Tiananmen Square protests, 11–12, 26, 28
    2008 Olympics, 196, 217
beIN, 240
Beirut, Lebanon, 243
Beit She'an, Israel, 153
Beitar Jerusalem, 31, 149–50, 153, 155–69, 219

Beitar movement, 149, 153
'Beitar Will Be Pure Forever', 165
Bekdil, Burak, 148
el-Beleidy, Amr, 61
Belgium, 170, 235
Belgrade, Serbia, 50–1
Belhadj, Nadir, 19
Belounis, Zahir, 251–2
Belushi, John, 124
Ben Ali, Leila, 46
Ben Ali, Zine El Abidine, 6, 20, 26, 29, 46, 53, 54, 58, 59, 203, 264, 283
Ben Bella, Ahmed, 39
Ben Gurion, David, 167
Ben Gurion Airport, Tel Aviv, 178
Ben Porat, Amir, 157, 159, 165, 168
Ben Shushan, Amit, 164
Bencherif, Hamza, 41
Benchinaa, Nadir, 170
Bend it like Beckham, 214
Bendaoud, Ali, 42
Benghazi, Libya, 1, 15, 218
Benjedid, Chadli, 39
Berbers, 7, 42, 181
Berlin, Germany, 233
Berlusconi, Silvio, 16
al-Berry, Khaled, 107–8
Beshir, Mohamed Gamal, 48–9
Beşiktaş JK, 36, 115, 124, 125, 126, 127–32, 133, 134, 137, 139, 140, 141, 148
Bethlehem, West Bank, 174, 228, 229
bicycle kicks, 191
Bin al-Hussein, Ali, 219, 233, 264
Bin Faisal, Nawaf, 21
Bin Ghudayan, Abdullah, 97
Bin Hammam, Mohammed, 238, 263–78
Bin Laden, Osama, 94, 107, 108, 110–11, 114

Bin Qu'ud, Abdullah, 97
Binsraiti, Khalifa, 15
Birkirkara FC, 16
Black Bloc, 73, 75, 76, 84
Black Hawk Down, 104
Black Sea, 121, 131, 134, 135, 139
Black September (1970), 44
Black September Organization, 4, 175
Black Stockings, 132
Blasing, John Konuk, 142
Blatter, Joseph 'Sepp', 238, 263, 264, 265, 266, 267, 268, 269, 270, 273, 278
Blazer, Chuck, 269
Bloomberg News, 139, 218
Bloomfield Stadium, Jerusalem, 95
Bnei Sakhnin, 149–50, 153–7, 159, 168, 219–20, 236
Bnei Yehuda Tel Aviv, 159
Bodjongo, Albert Ebossé, 41
Borowitz, Yoav, 169
Borussia Dortmund, 112, 127
Bosnia Herzegovina, 49, 169
Bosporus, 117, 118, 130
Bou Saada, Algeria, 42
Boudarene, Mahmoud, 41
Bougleida, Mohammed, 173
Bouteflika, Abdelaziz, 18, 39–40, 42
Bradley, Robert 'Bob', 181
Brazil, 26, 38, 56, 96, 141, 173, 174, 192, 235, 243, 254, 262, 279
breast cancer, 224
bribery, 15, 62, 63, 83, 267–78
Bridgepoint Capital, 253
British Broadcasting Corporation (BBC), 41, 274
British Museum, London, 285
Bromberger, Christoph, 25
Brown, Nathan J., 35
Brunei, 4

BSV Al Dersimspor, 233
Building a better World Cup, 244
built environment, 11–12, 25–7, 53, 81
Bulduk, Hikmet, 122
Bumgarner, John, 212
Buneyste, Mahmoud Ali, 107
Burrow, Sharan, 243, 246
Bursa, Turkey, 140
Bursaspor FC, 135, 140, 141
al-Busaidi, Sayyid Khalid Hamed, 264
Bush, George Walker, 47, 108
Byrne, Nicole, 201
Byzantine Empire (c. 330–1453), 29

Cairo, Egypt, 1, 4, 6–7, 20, 26, 30, 31, 32, 35, 50–69, 70, 72, 73–5, 78, 81, 85, 86, 87, 88, 91, 115, 116, 213, 214, 267, 284
Cairo International Stadium, 68, 70, 91
Cairo Stock Exchange, 73
Cairo University, 60
Cairobserver, 81
California, United States, 39
Caliphate, 102, 118
camels, 60, 70–1
Cameroon, 41, 267
Canal Plus, 239
Caribbean Football Union (CFU), 267, 269–70, 277
Carlos, Roberto, 139
Çarşı, 36, 115–16, 124–7, 129–32, 141, 148
Casey, Mike, 280–1
Catalonia, 170
Catholic Agency to Support Evangelisation, 96
Cavatorta, Francesco, 2
CBS News, 258

Cedar Revolution (2005), 183
Celik, Ömer, 122
Cemaat (the Community), 119
censorship, 117, 140
Central Intelligence Agency (CIA), 284
Central Security Force (CSF), 58
Chabab el Sahel SC, 184
chador, 233
Chakravarti, Leila Zaki, 75
Chalcraft, John, 62, 64
chants, 7, 11, 16, 21–2, 25, 34, 38, 39, 42, 45, 47, 48, 49, 59, 61, 62, 63, 73, 75, 78, 84, 87, 114, 124–6, 128, 129–31, 136–7, 144, 147, 148, 150, 161, 163, 164, 165, 200, 206, 207
Chechnya, 165–7, 170
Chelsea FC, 254, 257
Chemical Ali (Ali Hassan Abd al-Majid), 115
chemical weapons, 115, 170
Chiboub, Slim, 20
Chikhi, Said, 5
Chile, 175, 228
China, 11–12, 26, 28, 117, 140, 148, 171, 251, 278
choreography, 7, 49, 50, 57
Christianity, 93–4, 96, 106, 150, 164, 180–1, 183, 186–7, 191, 214, 218, 228, 229, 257
Çiller, Tansu, 120
citizenship society, 250
civil society, 3, 5, 63–4
Clark, Mark, 14
Clarke, John, 48
class, 34, 43, 48, 54, 55, 76, 77, 128, 165
von Clausewitz, Carl, 31
Clericus Cup, 96
Club Africain Tunis, 49

Coalition Provisional Authority (CPA), 13–14
cocaine, 112
Cohen, Eli, 167
Cold War, 241
Collins, John P., 269
Colomer, Josep, 242
colonialism, 4, 20, 28, 30–3, 74, 100, 132, 152–3, 171, 172, 200, 283
Colony Capital, 239
Common Ground, 180–1
communism, 123, 134, 218
Conditional Strangers, 165
Confederation of African Football (CAF), 32, 54, 68
Confederation of North, Central American and Caribbean Association Football (CONCACAF), 268, 270
Congo, Democratic Republic of, 54–5
Conquest 1453, 119
conservatism, 2, 28, 37–8, 55, 90, 91, 94, 108–10, 112, 117, 119, 122, 123, 132, 141, 144, 197–8, 207, 214, 216, 218–36, 247, 258, 260–2
Constantinople, Ottoman Empire, 119
contraception, 118
Coptic Christianity, 180–1
Copts United, 181
corporate diplomacy, 3
corruption, 3, 8, 32, 40, 46, 48, 52, 53, 62, 63, 77, 78, 83, 122, 132, 134, 137, 141–6, 162, 182, 192, 209–10, 238–9, 254, 262–81, 287
Council for East and Central Africa Football Associations (CECAFA), 268
Court of Arbitration of Sports (CAS), 269–71

Cowley, Jason, 56
cricket, 25, 108, 285, 286
criminal gangs, 13–14, 62–3, 69, 82, 146, 161–2, 172, 190
criminalisation of fans, protesters, 9, 36, 64, 66, 76, 85, 119, 126, 147
Croatia, 49, 50–1
Crusaders, 95, 99, 100
CS Hammam-Lif, 283
Cuba, 100
culture of impunity, 62
cyber-warfare, 212
Cyprus, 170

Daei, Ali, 39
Daghan, Mohammad, 189
Dakar, Senegal, 242
Dakhliya (Ministry of Interior), 11, 53, 59, 63, 65, 66–9, 72, 73, 84
Dal Lago, Alessandro, 53, 55, 57, 59
Dalkurd FF, 169–70
Dallah al-Baraka, 274
dam of autocracy, 82
Damascus, Syria, 1, 47, 184, 187, 191
Damascus University, 47
Damaseb, Petrus, 268
Dammam, Saudi Arabia, 222
Danan, Avi, 153–4
Danish Football Association, 235
Dar es Salaam, Tanzania, 95
Davis, Uri, 154–5
Davudieh training grounds, Alborg Mountains, 234
Davutoğlu, Ahmet, 122, 141
Dawud, Emmanuel Baba, 191
Dayan, Moshe, 207
De Biasi, Rocco, 53, 55, 57, 59
'Death to America', 201
'Death to Israel', 201, 207
'Death to the Arabs', 161, 164, 165

'Death to the Mullahs', 38, 201
deep state, 72, 144
Dehghani, Allahverdi, 206
Deir-ez-Zor, Syria, 47
delikanlı, 136
democracy, 9, 13, 14, 32, 41, 53, 57, 58, 65, 66, 81, 82, 91, 116, 119, 124, 126, 138, 142, 168, 258
Democratic Republic of Congo, 54–5
Dentsu, 274
Dera'a, Syria, 17
al-Dersimspor, BSV, 233
Dessouki, Ali al-Din Hilal, 52
Dev-Sol, 131
Dhiab, Tarak, 20
Diaby, Abou, 257
Dinamo Zagreb, 50–1
Dink, Hrant, 121
Directorate for Internal Security (DSI), 42
Directory of Islamic Financial Institutions
Direttivo, 57
divorce, 2, 27–8
Diyala, Iraq, 194
Djezzy, 19
Dodd, Moya, 277
Doha News, 248–9
Doha, Qatar, 193, 242, 245, 246, 247, 260, 266
Dolmabahce Palace, Istanbul, 130
donkeys, 15, 71, 207
dramaturgical model, 7
driving, 226
Drogba, Didier, 128, 132, 139
drugs, drug trafficking, 69, 112, 173, 196
Druze, 183
Du'a, 186
Dubai, United Arab Emirates, 193, 203, 211, 223, 230, 253, 254

Dubai International Capital, 253
Duerr, Glen, 171
Dummar, Damascus, 47
Dunne, Michele, 90
Dura, West Bank, 175
Dutschke, Rudi, 120

earthquakes, 206
East Azerbaijan Province, Iran, 38, 204–7
East Jerusalem, 12, 113, 163, 177, 229
Eastern Province, Saudi Arabia, 22, 210, 225
Eberly, Donald, 13
ecology of built environment, 11–12, 25–7, 53, 81
economic liberalization, 40, 78, 138
Edelman, Eric Steven, 121–2
education, 48, 63, 65, 68, 69, 87, 89, 94, 117, 119–20, 133
Egeland, Jan, 246
Egypt, 1, 2, 4, 5, 6–7, 9, 11, 18–20, 26–30, 31–6, 42, 46, 47–91, 99, 107, 109–10, 113, 115, 116, 126, 147, 152, 172, 174, 175–6, 179, 180–2, 187, 203, 207, 213–14, 216, 221, 234, 239, 267, 274, 284–5
  1882 soccer introduced by British troops, 20
  1907 foundation of Al Ahly SC, 4, 31
  1919 Revolution, 4, 31, 74
  1922 Unilateral Declaration of Independence, 4
  1930 friendly against Palestine's Land of Israel team, 152
  1952 Revolution, 32, 47
  1956 Suez Crisis; Melbourne Olympics boycott, 4, 172
  1957 establishment of Africa Cup of Nations, 32
  1963 national team barred from Aden, 33
  1967 Six Day War, 6, 89, 207
  1977 Anwar Sadat chides students during television interview, 29
  1981 assassination of Anwar Sadat, 107
  1998 victory in Africa Cup of Nations, 181
  1999 assassination attempt on Mubarak in Port Said, 76
  2006 labour strikes, 78
  2007 formation of Ultras after Zamalek–Al Hilal match, 49
  2009 Mubarak enflames nationalism after loss of World Cup qualifier, 18–19
  2011 Revolution, 2, 4, 6–7, 9, 26, 29–30, 34–6, 46, 49, 50, 53, 57–65, 68, 70–2, 74, 85, 88, 90, 115, 116, 187, 203, 221, 234, 239, 284; Moshagheb leads pitch invasion at Zamalek–Espérance Sportive match, 68, 85; protests banned; demonstrators ordered to leave Tahrir, 65; police and Ultras clash in Abdin, 65, 67, 73; Ultras attack Israeli and Saudi embassies, 72; Maspero Massacre, 180; Battle of the Dakhliya, 65–7, 72, 73
  2012 Port Said riot, 34–5, 36, 69–80, 83, 84, 87, 91; Morsi elected President, 36, 64, 69, 71, 81, 83; Abou-Treika sides with Ultras, 35; London Olympics, 180–1
  2013 Port Said trial verdicts; protests erupt, 73–80, 84; Bassem

Youssef charged with disturbing public peace, 78; anti-Morsi protests; Raba'a al-Adawiya Square sit-in, 81–3, 88, 116; coup d'état; al-Sisi comes to power, 20, 36, 67, 76, 81, 83–5, 90, 147, 285; crackdown on Muslim Brotherhood, 64, 67, 83–4, 147; pro-Morsi protests, 76, 83, 84

2015 Moshagheb attempts to escalate protests in Matareya, 87; stampede at Air Defence Stadium, 85, 91; Moshagheb arrested, 86; Port Said trial death sentences reduced, 74, 84; Mortada Mansour withdraws charges against UWK, 85–6; Ultras banned as terrorists, 285

Egypt Air, 19

Egyptian Football Association (EFA), 32, 70, 74, 214

Egyptian Initiative for Personal Rights (EIPR), 80

al-Elaimy, Ziad, 71

Elawady, Tarek M., 86

electronic ticketing, 140–1, 147

Elghanian, Habib, 207

Elpis, 132

Elshahed, Mohamed, 72, 81

Elshamy, Mosa'ab, 58

Elysée Palace, Paris, 239

Emirates Airlines, 253

Emirates Stadium, London, 253

Emniyet Foods, 141

Emrence, Cem, 133

England (national team), 94, 171

English Football Association, 181, 220, 254

English Premier League, 19, 22, 96, 252–3, 255, 259

ENPPI (Engineering for the Petroleum and Process Industries Sporting Club), 35

environmentalism, 117, 123, 126, 131, 204

Equal Times, 243

equestrianism, 223, 225

Erbakan, Necmettin, 120

Erbil, Kurdistan, 172, 173

Erdoğan, Emine, 122

Erdoğan, Recep Tayyip, 2, 36–7, 114–29, 135, 140, 141, 142–8, 262

Erg, 17

Ergenekon, 144, 145

Erhat, Itir, 136–7

Eritrea, 117, 153

Erten, Bagis, 116

Eskander, Wael, 75

Eskişehirspor, 140–1

Espérance Sportive de Tunis, 49, 54, 68, 84

Essam, Ramy, 78

Esteghlal SC, 31, 55, 198, 200, 205, 210

Estili, Hamid, 39, 234

Ethiopia, 103–4

Ethiopian Village restaurant, Kampala, 93

Etihad, 254, 255

European Champions League, 135

European Super Cup, 138

European Union (EU), 124, 137, 138, 189–90

Eurosport, 116

Evren, Kemal, 134–5

extra-marital sex, 206

fabricated urban crises, 72

Facebook, 18, 21, 35, 75, 83, 88, 191, 216

al-Fahim, Sulaiman, 19
Faisal I, King of Syria and Iraq, 44
Faisal al Husseini Stadium, al-Ram, 179
Faisal bin Abdulaziz al-Saud, King of Saudi Arabia, 224
al-Faisal, Hanan, 226
al-Faisali SC, 31, 43–6
Faith-Based and Community Initiatives, 13
La Familia, 161–7
fan-player relations, 34–6
Faraj, Ali, 19
Fareed, Morad, 176
Farzad, Farzin, 205
al-Fatah, 114, 162, 174
al-Fateh SC, 225
al-Fatwa SC, 47
fatwas, 98–102
Fawkes, Guy, 115
al-Fayez, Nora, 226
Fayyad, Salam, 177
FC Erbil, 172
Federal Bureau of Investigation (FBI), 270
Fédération Internationale de Football Association (FIFA), 3, 8, 30, 93, 104, 152, 170, 171, 173, 174–9, 187, 211, 216, 232, 233, 235, 237–9, 244, 253–4, 256–7, 262–81
    1928 admission of Mandatory Palestine, 152
    1957 establishment of Africa Cup of Nations, 32
    1958 Algerian FLN team banned, 30
    1998 admission of Palestine, 171; presidential election, 267 Farah Addo deleted from delegates' list, 268
    2002 presidential election, 268–9, 273–4
    2010 Qatar awarded 2022 World Cup, 3, 8, 237–52, 263, 265–6, 285, 287; Nigeria fined for cancelling Iran match, 211
    2011 Iranian women's team disqualified from Olympic qualifier for wearing hijab, 233; presidential election, 265, 267, 268, 269; resignation of Jack Warner, 268; Bin Hammam suspended; banned for life, 268, 269–71
    2012 Bin Hammam's ban annulled by CAS, 269, 271; Bin Hammam banned for life, 263, 265, 277
    2013 Israel hosts Under-21 finals, 256–7
    2014 Syria barred from World Cup, 187
    2015 corruption case, 3, 8, 238–9, 254, 263, 268, 281; PFA resolution calling for suspension of Israel, 179
fencing, 223
Fenerbahçe SK, 115, 119, 127, 128, 129, 131–2, 133, 134, 138, 139, 141, 142, 143–6, 148
Fenton, Jenifer, 260
Ferguson, Alex, 128
fez, 118
fighting culture, 57
Filabi, Moslem Iskandar, 206
Filastin, 151, 215
Financial Fair Play, 255
Finland, 170
Finn, Gerry P. T., 59
fiqh, 97
fireworks, 7, 20, 48, 54, 66, 68

flares, 7, 48, 49, 54, 60, 68
FLN (Front de Libération Nationale), 18, 30, 172
Florida, United States, 222, 256
Fondu, Ahmed, 51, 60
Football Dreams tournament, 242
Football Federation of the Islamic Republic of Iran (FFIRI), 198, 202, 204, 211, 231, 232, 264
Football Under Cover, 233
foreign agents, 64, 66
foreign workers, 3, 8, 243–51, 258, 262, 285–6
Formula One, 3, 256
Fortuna Düsseldorf, 112
Foucault, Michel, 4
Fozooni, Babak, 197
France, 4, 11, 19, 25, 30, 94–5, 112, 121, 166–7, 173, 200, 201, 235, 239–41, 243, 251
  1789–99 Revolution, 11
  1954–62 Algerian War, 19, 30
  1956 Suez Crisis, 4, 172
  1958 Algerian players leave to form national team, 30, 172
  1998 World Cup, 13, 37, 39, 94–5, 200, 201
  2001 al-Qaeda plot against US embassy in Paris, 112
  2009 Qatari companies granted capital gains tax exemption, 240
  2010 national team discord at World Cup, 8; Sarkozy makes Qatar World Cup bid deal, 239
  2012 attack on Ozar Hatorah school in Toulouse, 166–7; Qatari acquisition of PSG, 255
Franco, Francisco, 4–5
Freedom and Justice Party (FJP), 72
Freeh Group, 270

Frente Polisario, 173
fulul, 66

Galatasaray SK, 115, 127, 128, 129, 131–2, 133, 134, 137, 138, 139, 141, 142, 144–5
Galatasaray Lyceum, Istanbul, 128, 133
Gallup, 155
gambling, 94
Garcia, Michael J., 277
Garrone, Riccardo, 17
gas masks, 115, 130
Gaucci, Luciano, 16
Gaucho, Ronaldinho, 235
Gaydamak, Arcadi, 155, 163, 165
Gaza, Palestine, 58, 94, 110, 112, 113–14, 154, 155, 162, 174, 178, 179–80, 228–9, 257
Gaza Dialogue and Tolerance Cup, 113–14
Gemayal, Sami, 182
Genç Party, 136
Gençlerbirliği SK, 148
gender rights, segregation, 3, 4, 5, 7, 21, 94, 118, 120, 198, 200–1, 203, 208, 213–36, 262, 280
General Presidency of Scholarly Research and Ifta, 98–9
Gerami, Shahin, 201
German Football Association, 281
Germany, 4, 39, 94, 105, 112, 120, 141, 181, 219, 233, 254, 281
  2006 World Cup, 99, 100, 103, 149, 175–6, 274
Getafe CF, 254, 257
Gezi Park, Istanbul, 115, 116, 121, 123, 125, 126, 127, 128, 129, 130, 131–2, 140, 146, 147, 148
Ghadir, Mohammed, 168–9
Ghafar, Adel Abdel, 56

Ghalenoei, Hamid, 210
Ghali, Safwat Freeze, 181–2
Ghaneim, Mazen, 156
al-Ghanim bus station, Doha, 247
al-Ghanim, Kaltham, 247, 251
Gharbeia, Amr, 58
al-Ghasara, Roqaya, 217
Ghavami, Ghoncheh, 230
Ghazi Stadium, Kabul, 17–18, 196
al-Ghitani, Gamal, 28
Ghotbi, Afshin, 209
Ghozlan, Mahmoud, 88
Ghrib, Omar, 40
globalisation, 241, 257
Gönül, Mehmet Vecdi, 122
Gorgani, Mohammad Ali Alavi, 230
Gottschalk, Eric, 217
graffiti, 49, 50, 53
Grand Hyatt Hotel, Port of Spain, 267
Greek Orthodox Church, 96
Green Book, 14
Green Eagles, 70, 74, 75, 77, 79
Green Line, 162, 174
Green Movement, 4, 202, 208
Greenland, 170
Greenpeace, 131
grievance model, 7
grunt schools, 37
Guam, 265
Guantánamo Bay detention facility, Cuba, 100
Guevara, Ernesto 'Che', 131
Guggenheim, New York, 285
Guinness Book of Records, 128
Gül, Abdullah, 122, 143
Gülen, Fethullah, 37, 119–21, 123, 124, 142–7
Güler, Muammer, 125–6
Gülerce, Hüseyin, 120
Gulf Cup, 191

Gulf Finance House (GFH) Capital, 255
Gulf Institute, 22
Gulf University for Science and Technology (GUST), 217
Gulland, Eugene, 272–3
Gümüşdağ, Göksel, 143
Gutiérrez Hernández, José Maria, 139
gyms, 226

Ha'Etzel, 153
Haaretz, 169
Haddad, Ali, 40
hadith, 101, 111
Hafez, Mona el-Sayyed, 27
al-Hafiz, Yasin, 64, 65
Hagia Sophia, Istanbul, 29
Haifa, Israel, 165, 168
Haigh, David, 256
Hakimi, Ebrahim, 204
Hakkari Gücü, 235–6
Halil Pasha Artillery Barracks, Istanbul, 123
Halilovic, Nedim, 169
Hama massacre (1982), 17
Hamad bin Khalifa, Emir of Qatar, 242, 258–61, 263, 265
el-Hamalawy, Hossam, 58
Hamas, 94, 110, 112–14, 156, 161, 162, 228
Hamburger SV, 253
Hamed, Ahmed-Rahim, 12
Hammam-Lif CS, 283
handball, 230
Haniyeh, Ismail, 94, 110, 114
Hapoel Katamon Jerusalem, 161
Hapoel Taibe, 159
Hapoel Tel Aviv, 158, 161
al-Harbi, Ahmed Eid Saad, 21
Hariri, Rafik, 182–4

Hariri, Saad, 182
al-Harithi, Dayf Allah, 100, 110
Harkness, Geoff, 217
al-Haroon, Khalifa Saleh, 261
Harris, Rosemary, 56
al-Harthy, Hussein Mohsin, 274
al-Hasa Province, Saudi Arabia, 225
al-Hasawi family, 255
Hashemi, Faezeh, 234
Hashemite monarchy, 43–5
al-Hashimi, Nada Yousef, 216
Hassan II, King of Morocco, 20
Hassan, Hashim, 13
Hassan, Muhamed, 60
Hatikva, 149
Hawar Mulla Mohammad, 193
al-Hawari, Sahar, 213–15, 234
Hayat, Makhdoum Syed Faisal
    Saleh, 277
Hayatou, Issa, 54–5, 267, 268
Hazard, Eden, 257
Hebron, West Bank, 112–13, 229
Heikal, Mohammed, 32
Hejazi, Nasser, 203
Hertha Berlin FC, 39
Hertling, Mark, 194–5
Herut, 160
Hezbollah, 114, 182, 183
hijab, 217, 218, 229, 232–3
Hijjeh, Abdel Majid, 176
al-Hilal SC (Omdurman), 49
al-Hilal SC (Riyadh), 21–2
Histadrut, 160, 161
hit-and-run tactics, 57
Hizb ut Tahrir, 229
Hizbul Islam, 105
hogra, 41
Holocaust, 167, 198
Homeless World Cup, 174
homemade explosive devices, 66
Homenetmen SC

homosexuality, 94, 121, 130, 137,
    258
Homs, Syria, 185, 187, 188, 189
Honduras, 19
Hong Kong, 171
honour killings, 174
horse racing, 240
Hoş, Mustafa, 119
Hôtel Lambert, Paris, 240
Houla, Syria, 189
Hubail, Mohammed and Alaa, 280
Huffington Post, The, >232
Human Rights Watch, 121, 221,
    243, 244, 246, 252
human rights, 3, 8, 48, 62, 63, 79,
    116, 121, 122, 124, 189, 205, 208,
    221, 223, 234, 243–53, 256–7,
    261, 264, 279–80, 286
humiliation of rivals, 56, 59, 67, 68,
    72
Hummus, 79, 80
Hunter Brigades, 123
Hussein bin Al Abdullah, Crown
    Prince of Jordan, 45
Hussein ibn Ali, 133
Hussein, Saddam, 7, 12, 21, 47, 115,
    170, 191, 192, 193, 195
Hussein, Uday, 12–13, 191, 192
al-Husseini, Faisal, 175
Hutteen SC, 189
al-Huweni, Abu Ishaaq, 101
Hyde Park, London, 130

Ibn Baz, Abdulaziz bin Abduallah,
    97
Ibn Taymiyyah, Taqi ad-Din Ah-
    mad, 97
Ibrahim, Gigi, 58
al-Ibrahim, Hassan, 261
Ibrahim, Hassan, 55, 58
Ibrahim, Nayla, 216

Ignatius, David, 196
al-Ihsa, Saudi Arabia, 225
Ihsan Foods, 141
Iktasari, Fatma, 230
Imam Hatip Liseleri schools, 117
Imogene FC, 132
improvised explosive devices (IEDs), 90
India, 231
Indonesia, 95, 108
Industrial Zone, Doha, 247, 251
Infantino, Gianni, 255
Infront, 274
İnönü Stadium, Istanbul, 115, 124, 125, 127
Institution of Occupational Safety and Health (IOSH), 245
integrative enclaves, 157
Interior Ministry, Egypt, 11, 53, 59, 63, 65, 66–9, 72, 73, 84
International Cricket Council (ICC), 285
International Criminal Court (ICC), 179
International Football Association Board (IFAB), 100, 233
International Olympic Committee (IOC), 3, 177, 222–3, 257, 265, 278–9
International Sports Events (ISE), 273
International Sports Leisure (ISL), 274
International Trade Union Confederation (ITUC), 243, 246, 250
International Volleyball Federation, 230
Internet, 46, 49, 58, 61, 63, 69, 73, 75, 79, 81, 83, 88, 101, 117, 118, 142, 144, 147, 148, 185, 191, 212, 216, 231, 260, 280–1

Interpol, 14
Irada Sports Development Company, 216
Iran, 4, 7, 20, 31, 32, 33, 37–9, 55, 94, 98, 101–2, 109, 117, 140, 170, 186, 197–212, 215–16, 230–4, 235, 264, 265, 267, 275, 279
   1926 construction of first soccer pitch, 32
   1968 hosting of Asian Cup; anti-Israel protests, 207
   1979 Islamic Revolution, 37, 98, 102, 197–9, 204, 230
   1980 presidential election; outbreak of Iran-Iraq War, 199, 201, 216
   1981 protests against crackdown on soccer, 55
   1984 government research concludes soccer to be 'colonialist plot', 200
   1994 Asian Youth Cup; women allowed into stadiums, 231
   1997 Khatami elected President, 37, 39; Talebi appointed national team's coach, 39; national team qualifies for World Cup; protests erupt, 37, 200
   1998 ban on women's soccer lifted, 233; al-Qaeda plot to attack World Cup match, 94–5; defeat of US in World Cup, 39, 94, 201
   2001 loss of World Cup qualifier to Bahrain; protests erupt, 38, 201
   2005 Ahmadinejad elected president, 202
   2006 World Cup; protests erupt, 99, 201; BSV Al Dersimspor play national women's team,

233; Ahmadinejad attempts to relax prohibition on female sports attendance, 230, 231

2009 Ahmadinejad re-elected; Green Movement protests, 202, 208; national team wear green armbands at World Cup qualifier, 4, 202

2010 Nigeria cancels friendly match, 211; Jafar Panahi imprisoned, 231

2011 FFIRI postpones league matches, 204; death of Nasser Hejazi; protests erupt, 203; East Azerbaijan protests, 204–6; security forces attack Traktor Sazi supporters at Azadi Stadium, 206; women's team disqualified from Olympic qualifier for wearing hijab, 233; Stuxnet computer virus outbreak, 212

2012 Ahmadinejad visits disputed Hormuz islands, 211; Ali Kafashian complains about hold up of AFC payments, 198; businessmen linked to Ahmadinejad sentenced to death, 210; Fatma Iktasari and Shabnam Kazimi sneak into World Cup qualifier, 230; female athletes perform in front of mixed audiences at London Olympics, 232

2013 Hassan Rouhani elected president, 207–8; qualification for World Cup, 208

2014 Ghoncheh Ghavami arrested for attending volleyball match, 230

2015 partial lifting of ban on female stadium attendance, 230

Iran Tractor Manufacturing Co. (ITMCO), 204

Iranian Revolutionary Guard Corps, 20, 198, 200, 202, 204, 209–10

Iraq, 4, 7, 8, 9, 12–14, 17, 21, 44, 47, 95, 99, 100, 115, 170, 171–3, 176, 185, 190–7, 199, 235, 241, 279

1956 Melbourne Olympics boycott, 4, 172

1980 outbreak of Iran-Iraq War, 199

1986 World Cup; players heads shaved, 13; al-Anfal campaign begins, 115, 170

1990 invasion of Kuwait, 241, 279

1993 players permitted to play for foreign teams, 13

1997 national team tortured after losing World Cup qualifier, 13

2003 US invasion; de-Baathification program, 13, 17, 192, 193, 194–6; Abu Ghraib prisoner abuse scandal, 100; Saudi national team players join jihad, 100, 110

2004 Athens Olympics, 191

2007 Asian Cup victory, 8, 190–3, 197

2008 US 87th Infantry plays Sons Of Iraq, 194–5

2009 FC Erbil represent country in Asian Champions League, 172

2010 Saudi military officer arrested for World Cup terror plot, 95

2012 bombing near Baghdad Stadium, 194

2013 bombings of football matches and cafés, 194

Iraqi National Olympic Committee (INOC), 13

al-Iraqi, Abu Yahya, 106
Ireland, 149, 155, 201
Irgun, 153
Irhal, 78
Işıklar, Mehmet, 127
Iskandar, Adel, 5
Iskanderiya, Rami, 86
Islam, 5, 6, 12, 21, 22, 33, 43, 63,
   68, 78, 96–114, 117–21, 133, 144,
   150, 151, 181, 182–4, 186, 192,
   193, 197–200, 204, 206, 208, 209,
   213–36, 247–8, 258, 260–2, 285
   fatwas, 98–102
   fiqh, 97
   hadith, 101, 111
   jihadism, 5, 9, 17, 18, 90–1,
      93–113, 118, 186, 192, 285
   pan-Islamism, 102
   Qur'an, 101, 110, 111, 133, 233
   Salafism, 78, 94, 99, 100, 109
   Sharia'a law, 63, 75, 94, 101, 102,
      105, 111, 117, 118, 123, 206,
      213, 234, 258, 260–1
   Shia Islam, 21, 22, 102, 182,
      183–4, 192, 193, 194, 209,
      215–16, 256, 280
   Sufism, 118
   Sunni Islam, 117–18, 122, 183,
      192, 194, 215, 256
   Wahhabism, 22, 101, 222, 262
Islam, Samira, 217
Islamic Courts Union, 103
Islamic Jihad, 114, 179
Islamic Movement (Israel), 96, 109
Islamic Republic of Iran Football
   Federation (IRIFF), 198, 202, 204,
   211, 231, 232, 264
Islamic State (IS), 17, 86, 91, 172
Islamism, 5, 6, 9, 12, 13, 17–18,
   19, 39–40, 52, 73, 82, 83, 88–91,
   94–114, 117–21, 131, 133, 138,

142, 146, 172, 197–200, 204, 217,
   220, 228, 239, 262, 285
Ismaik, Hasan Abdullah, 254
Ismail, Salwa, 62
Israel, 4, 7, 12, 18, 19, 31, 44, 72,
   74, 96, 99, 100, 109, 110, 112–14,
   149–69, 172, 174–80, 181, 190,
   207, 211, 219–20, 228, 236,
   256–7
   1948 Arab–Israeli War, 43, 154
   1956 Suez Crisis, 4
   1964 al-Ard group banned, 154
   1967 Six Day War; annexation
      of East Jerusalem, 6, 12, 162,
      174, 207
   1974 tensions at Tehran Asian
      Cup, 207
   1972 Munich massacre, 4, 95, 175
   1976 Land Day protests, 154;
      Beitar wins State Cup, 160–1
   1977 Menachem Begin elected
      prime minister, 160–1
   1982 Lebanon War, 18
   1987 Beitar wins championship,
      161; First Palestinian Intifada
      begins, 154, 161
   1990 assassination of Meir Kah-
      ane, 161
   1993 Oslo agreement, 161
   1995 assassination of Yitzhak
      Rabin, 156
   2000 Second Palestinian Intifada
      begins, 113
   2002 security forces arrest Muhsin
      Qawasmeh, 113; construction
      of West Bank barrier begins,
      162; bulldozing of homes in
      Jenin refugee camp, 162–3
   2003 Hamas suicide attacks; secu-
      rity forces assassinate Abdullah
      Qawasmeh, 112–13

2004 terrorist plot against Bloomfield Stadium, Jerusalem, 95;
military campaign in Gaza,
155; Bnei Sakhnin win State
Cup, 149, 153, 155

2005 defeat of Ireland in World
Cup qualifier, 149; emergence
of La Familia, 162, 163; Arcadi Gaydamak invests in Bnei
Sakhnin; acquires Beitar, 155,
163

2006 foundation of Hapoel
Katamon Jerusalem, 161; Suan
offers to join Beitar, 169

2007 Mohammed Nimr imprisoned, 180

2008 Tuama offers to join Beitar,
169

2009 ground invasion of Gaza,
174; Mahmoud al-Sarsak
detained at checkpoint, 179;
legislative elections, 44

2010 Hapoel Tel Aviv defeat Beitar in championship finals, 161

2011 Ultras attack embassy in
Egypt, 72; Mohammed Ghadir
offers to join Beitar, 168–9; exchange of Palestinian prisoners
for Gilad Shalit, 177

2012 La Familia attack Malha
Mall in Jerusalem, 166–7; Mahmoud al-Sarsak released from
prison after hunger strike, 167,
179; Mohammed Nimr and
Omar Abu Roweis detained,
180

2013 Gaydamak signs Chechen
players to Beitar; La Familia
set fire to club museum, 165–7;
Gaydamak sells Beitar to Eli
Tabib, 165; hosting of FIFA
Under-21 finals, 256–7

2015 PFA tables resolution calling
for suspension of Israel from
FIFA, 179

Israeli Football Association (IFA),
109, 155, 157, 162, 166, 168, 169,
178, 179

Israeli Olympic Committee, 178

Istanbul, Turkey, 36, 49, 114–17,
120, 125–42, 144, 146, 148

Istanbul Bar Association, 126

Istanbul Erkek Lisesi, 141

Istanbul Stock Exchange, 137, 139

Istanbulspor, 135

Italy, 16–17, 49, 51, 53, 55, 57, 59,
161, 170, 175, 230, 240, 253

al-Ittihad SC, 21–2

Ivory Coast, 128

Izmir, Turkey, 132

Izzedin al-Qassem Brigade, 113

Jaber, Salam, 213, 218

Jableh, Syria, 189

Jabotinsky, Ze'ev, 150

Jackson, Steven J., 3

Jadaliyya, 89

al-Jaish SC (Qatar), 251–2

al-Jaish SC (Syria), 20, 184–5

Jakarta, Indonesia, 95

Jam, Mahmud, 204

Japan, 265, 274, 275

Japanese Football Association (JFA),
275

Jawhar, Sabria, 227

al-Jazeera, 132, 186, 188, 209, 223,
239–40, 254, 258, 259, 273, 274,
275

al-Jazeera FC, 251

Jeddah, Saudi Arabia, 21, 110, 111,
214, 222, 224, 226

Jeddah King's United, 214, 222

Jenin, West Bank, 162, 229

Jennings, Andrew, 274

Jericho, West Bank, 229

Jerusalem, 12, 31, 95–6, 113, 149–50, 153, 155–69, 175, 177, 229

Jesus, 186

jet set lifestyle, 34

Jeunesse Sportive de la Saoura (JSS), 41

al-Jihad SC, 46

jihadism, 5, 9, 17, 18, 90–1, 93–113, 118, 186, 192, 285

Jiryis, Sabri, 154

Johansson, Lennart, 267

Johnstown, Pennsylvania, 195

Jordan, 2, 31, 42, 43–7, 96–8, 156–7, 192, 219, 233, 234, 248, 254, 264, 265

1946 Independence, 43

1948 Arab–Israeli War, 43; annexation of West Bank, 44

1970 expulsion of PLO from country, 43, 44

1986 Wehdat shut down after supporters chant against monarchy, 45

1998 Mashhoor Bin Hasan Al Salman publishes treatise on soccer, 96–8

2008 friendly match against Palestine in West Bank, 175

2009 Faisali supporters chant anti-Palestinian slogans; denigrate monarchy, 45

2010 general election, 44; violence at Wehdat–Faisali match, 43; Tareq Khouri receives jail sentence in absentia, 44

2011 security forces attack protesters in Amman, 45–6; women's team members barred from Olympic qualifier for wearing hijab, 233; national team reach quarter finals of Asian Cup, 234

2013 premiere of *Neither East nor West*, 46

José de Jesus, Manuel, 70

Journal of Arabian Studies, 246

journalists
incarceration of, 117, 140, 148
violence against, 107, 157

Jowa, Ali Afshar, 200

JS Kabylie (JSK), 41

Judaism, 99, 100, 101, 114, 132, 149–69, 181, 198, 207, 218, 220

Jureidini, Ray, 243

Justice and Development Party (AKP), 118, 120, 122, 142, 143

'Justice or Death', 75

Justinian I, Byzantine Emperor, 29

Juventus FC, 16

Kabir News, 206

kabo, 51

Kabul, Afghanistan, 17–18, 196

Kach, 161

Kadikoy FRC, 132

kafala, 243–4, 249, 286

Kafashian, Ali, 198, 202, 211, 212, 232

Kafi, Ali, 39

Kafr-Kana, Israel, 157

Kaftan, Eylam, 132

Kagan, Robert, 90

Kahane, Meir, 161

Kaiserslautern, 181

Kaka, Ricardo, 96

Kamal, Salah, 194

Kaman, Ayman, 145

Kamel Nuseirat, 46

Kamel, Saleh, 273–4

Kampala, Uganda, 93–4, 241

Kanabi, Safeen, 171, 172
Kandahar, Afghanistan, 102
Kandil, Hazem, 82
Kanhai, Angenie, 270
al-Karamah SC, 185
Karim, Keramuddin, 196
Karrubi, Mehdi, 202, 208
Karzai, Hamid, 196
Kasimpasa, Istanbul, 148
Kasr el Nil Bridge, Cairo, 58
'Kassaman' (We Pledge), 30
Kawari, Maali, 180
Kayseri, Turkey, 134
Kazakhstan, 13
Kazarlan, Hassan, 86
Kazimi, Shabnam, 230
Keegan, Kevin, 13
Kemalism, 123, 144
Kemalist Republican People's Party
    (CHP), 130
Kenya, 95, 103
Khalidi, Issam, 150–1, 152
al-Khalifa, Salman Bin Ibrahim, 4,
    264, 265, 278–81
Khamenei, Ali, 203, 230, 232
Kharsina settlement, West Bank, 113
Khatami, Mohammed, 37–8, 200,
    201
Khatami, Mohammed Amir, 200
Khater, Hassan, 12
Khatib, Faysal, 157
al-Khatib, Zeinab, 235
al-Khelaifi, Nasser, 240
Khomeini, Ruhollah, 197–8, 201,
    204
Khouri, Tareq, 44
Khoury, Elias, 188
Khuzestan, 38
Kim Jong-Il, 148
King Abdullah City, Riyadh, 224
King Abdullah University of Science
    and Technology (KAUST), 228

King Fahd International Stadium,
    Riyadh, 22
Kirkuk, Iraq, 193
Kiryat Arba settlement, West Bank,
    113
Kissimee, Florida, 222
Kistner, Thomas, 267
Kitab al-Ultras (Beshir), 48–9
Kizil, Ramazan, 170
Kılıç, Suat, 147–8
Kohan, Mayeli, 38
Kolaib, Niveen, 228–9
Kombassan Konyaspor, 135, 144
Konya, Turkey, 135, 144
Kornfein, Izhak, 165
Kosovo, 49
Kurdish Football Association, 171
Kurdistan Workers' Party (PKK),
    123, 235
Kurds, Kurdistan, 7, 30, 47, 123,
    142, 147, 169–73, 181, 192, 193,
    205, 235–6
Kurt, Kymet, 236
Kurtulus metro station, Ankara, 118
Kuwait, 99, 175, 176, 199, 217, 225,
    241, 255, 259, 263, 264, 265, 278,
    279
al-Kuwari, Mohamed, 240–1
Kyadondo Rugby Club, Kampala,
    93

Labour Day, 131
labour rights, 3, 6, 8, 54, 62, 77, 123,
    154, 159, 223, 243–52, 257, 258,
    262, 285–6
Lagardere Unlimited, 273
laïcité, 121
Lake Orumiyeh, Iran, 205
Lalas, Alexi, 94
Land Day protests (1976), 154
Land of Israel, 152

Lankarani, Fazel, 231
Lapland, 170
Latakia, Syria, 17, 189
Latvia, 149
Lausanne, Switzerland, 269–70
Lebanese American University,
  Beirut, 243
Lebanese Football Association, 183
Lebanon, 4, 7, 17, 20, 44, 114, 172,
  174, 175, 182–4, 187, 189, 190,
  243, 264
  1956 Melbourne Olympics boy-
    cott, 4, 172
  1970 arrival of PLO in exile from
    Jordan, 44
  2005 assassination of Rafik
    Hariri, 182–4; Cedar Revolu-
    tion, 183–4
  2007 conflict with Fatah al-Islam
    at Nahr al-Bared camp, 17
LeBaron, Richard, 279
Leeds United FC, 128, 255–6
left-wing, 115, 128, 131–2, 166
Lerman, Eran, 112
Levy, Gideon, 166–7
LGBT (Lesbian Gay Bisexual Trans-
  gender) community, 121, 130,
  137, 258
liberalism, 6, 38, 55, 77, 90, 116,
  119, 121, 123, 207, 258
Libya, 1, 6, 14–17, 19, 21, 29, 33,
  34, 41, 187, 213, 218, 221, 264,
  269
  2000 destruction of Al Ahly
    Benghazi headquarters after
    anti-government protests,
    15–16; Al Saadi Qaddafi signs
    with Birkirkara, 16
  2002 Al Saadi Qaddafi bribes
    FIFA federations, 269
  2003 Al Saadi Qaddafi resigns

from Juventus board; signs with
  Perugia, 16
  2005 murder of Bashir al-Ryani,
    14–15; Al Saadi Qaddafi signs
    with Sampdoria, 17
  2011 Revolution, 14, 15, 16, 29,
    187, 218, 221
  2012 brawl at African Cup quali-
    fier against Algeria, 41
  2015 Al Saadi Qaddafi tried for
    murder of al-Ryani, 14
Libyan Football Federation, 14, 15
Lieberman, Avigdor, 44
Likud, 153, 160
lingerie, 227
Lion's Den, The, 163–4
Lions of Mesopotamia, 191
Liverpool FC, 253
Livnat, Limor, 168
Livneh, Neri, 157, 164
London, England, 96, 108, 130, 188,
  253, 273, 285
  2012 Olympics, 4, 175, 180–1,
    188, 222–3, 232, 233
Lopez, Shaun, 2, 31
Los Angeles Times, 15, 16
Louis Vuitton Moët Hennessy
  (LVMH), 240
Louvre, Paris, 285
Luzon, Avi, 169
Lyon, France, 201

M-16s, 195
al-Mabarra SC, 184
Maccabi, 152
Maccabi Haifa, 165, 168
Maccabi Kafr-Kana, 156–7
Maccabi Tel Aviv, 160
Madrid bombings (2004), 110
mafia, 161
Mahad Mohamed, 102–6

al-Mahalla al-Kubra, Egypt, 78
Mahfouz, Naguib, 28
Mahmoud, Abdul Aziz, 261
Mahmoud, Younis, 193
Makdissi, Karim, 184
Makram, Omar, 53
Maksimir Stadium, Zagreb, 50
al-Maktoum, Butti Bin Suhail, 254
Malaga CF, 256, 257
Malaysia, 95, 271
Malha Mall, Jerusalem, 166
Malhas, Dalma Rushdi, 223
Mali, 102
al-Maliki, Nouri, 193, 206
Malta, 16
Manama, Bahrain, 279
al-Manar, 114, 184
Manchester City FC, 252–5
Manchester United FC, 95, 128, 217
Mancini, Roberto, 139
Mandela, Nelson, 3
al-Mando, 80
Mangal, Shin, 232
mansaf, 46
Mansour, Mortada, 85–6
marginalization, 11
Markaryan, Alen, 131
Marmara Sea, 118
Maronite Christianity, 183, 184
marriage, 2, 27–8, 206
Marriott hotel, Jakarta, 95
Marseille, France, 94
Marx, Karl, 105
Marxism, 64
masculinity, 7, 136–7
Mashhur, Mustafa, 89
Maspero Massacre (2011), 180
al-Masry SC, 69–80, 84
master rights agreements (MRAs),
    273, 275, 276
Matareya, Cairo, 87

Match AG, 274
match-fixing, 132, 134, 141–6
MC Saida, 41
McGeehan, Nicholas, 253
McManus, Stephanie, 276
Mecca, Saudi Arabia, 101
Mediapro Middle East, 217
Mediene, Mohamed 'Tewfik', 42
al-Medlej, Hafez, 264
Melbourne
    1956 Olympics, 4, 172
    Cricket Ground (MCG), 95
Melke Aslanoglu, Bülent Özcan, 190
Melkemichel, Özcan, 190
Ménez, Jérémy, 257
Menorah, 153
Meral, Adem, 126
Meridja, Algeria, 41
meritocracy, 5
Mersin, Turkey, 142
Mesbah, Chafiq, 41
Messi, Lionel, 242
Mexico, 1, 13, 279
middle-class, 34, 43, 54, 128, 165
Milan AC, 242, 253
military, 1–3, 11, 20, 31, 32, 34,
    36–7, 39, 41–2, 44, 46, 47, 51, 62,
    64–7, 69, 71, 72, 74, 76, 80–6, 88,
    90–1, 120, 184–5
    de-politicization, 82
    ownership of stadiums and teams,
        20, 184–5, 251
Milosevic, Slobodan, 49
Mine Awareness Festival, 195
minorities, 6, 7, 38, 42, 90–1, 117,
    121, 131, 181, 183–4, 186–7, 193,
    204–7
al-Mishal, Mohammed, 223
Misson, Luc, 170
MKE Ankaragücü, 135
mobile mosques, 109

Moby Group, 196
Moda FC, 132
modernity, 32, 37, 119, 123, 133
Mogadishu, Somalia, 18, 103, 104, 105, 106, 107
Mohamed, Um, 27
Mohammed, Prophet of Islam, 33, 43, 78, 94, 101, 110, 120, 150, 164, 186
Mohammed VI, King of Morocco, 50
Mohammad Reza Pahlavi, Shah of Iran, 31, 33, 198, 200, 207
Mohammed Adel Mohammed, 79, 80
Mohammed Mahmoud Street, Cairo, 66, 67, 72
Mohsen, Saad, 196
Moktar, Abdallah, 30
Molaverdi, Shahindokht, 230
Molotov cocktails, 61, 62, 66, 80, 128, 235
Momeni, Niloufar, 210
Monitor, 240
Moro, Ghayath, 190
Morocco, 20, 49, 50, 51, 153, 173, 187, 281
Morsi, Mohammed, 20, 36, 64, 66, 67, 69, 71, 75–85, 88, 89, 90, 116, 126, 147, 285
Moscow, Russia, 139
Moshagheb, Said, 68, 84–7
mosques, 12, 22, 47, 60, 62, 68, 96, 99, 108–9, 110, 112–13, 144, 217, 222
Motagi, Khalid, 48
Motorola, 135
Mouloudia Club d'Alger (MCA), 40
Mount Everest, 224
Mousavi, Mir-Hossein, 199, 202, 204, 208

Moussa, Eddie, 190
Moussa, Salam, 29
Mubarak, Hosni, 2, 4, 7, 9, 18–20, 29–30, 31, 34, 35, 36, 46, 51, 52, 53, 56, 57, 60–74, 76, 77, 78, 81, 82, 83, 84, 85, 115, 203, 284
al-Mubaraz, Saudi Arabia, 225
Mugamma, Cairo, 53
al-Muhannadi, Ibrahim, 241
Muhieddin, Abdullah Mahmoud, 173
Muhsin Ertugrul Theatre, Istanbul, 131
Mujahedeen-e-Khalq, 199, 200, 201, 206, 216
Mukhabarat, 86
al-Mukhtalaf, 32
Mulhim, Abdulateef, 225
Multaka, Iraq, 195
mulukhiyeh, 46
Munich 1972 Olympics, 4, 95, 175
Murat Ülker, 141
al-Murshidi, Majed, 22
Murtaja, Abdulmohsen Kamel, 33
music, proscription of, 94
Muslim Brotherhood, 9, 12, 17, 19, 64, 65, 66, 67, 72, 74–85, 87–91, 116, 120, 126, 147, 239, 253, 274
'Muslim Female Athletes and the Hijab' (Harkness), 217
Mutlu, Hüseyin Avnni, 130
Muwallad, Fahd, 22

al-Nabhani, Fatima, 217
Nablus, West Bank, 158, 229
Nabulsi, Suleiman, 44
Nada, Youssef, 274
Nadallah, Ibrahim, 165
Nafpatkos, Greece, 96
Naguib, Mohammed, 33
al-Nahas, Mahmoud, 76

al-Nahyan, Abdullah bin Zayed, 211
al-Nahyan, Mansour bin Zayed, 254
Nairobi, Kenya, 95
al-Najdi, Abdullah, 101
Namibia, 268
Nancy-Lorraine AS, 252
Napoleon I, Emperor of the French, 53
Nasrallah, Hassan, 114
Nasrawi Revolution, 21
al-Nasser FC, 21
Nasser, Gamal Abdel, 6, 29, 32–3, 82, 89
Nateq Nuri, Ali Akbar, 38
National Council of Resistance of Iran (NCRI), 206
National Democratic Party, 53, 76
national identity, 171, 250, 261
National Liberation Front (FLN), 18, 30, 172
National Museum, Cairo, 53, 58
National Strategy for Social Security, 247
National, The, 216, 256
nationalism, 4, 18–19, 30–3, 55, 64, 74, 84, 117, 122, 123, 128, 131, 133, 136, 144, 152, 153, 154, 156, 159, 167, 170–3, 204, 260–1
Nayef Bin Abdulaziz al-Saud, Crown Prince of Saudi Arabia, 222
Nazareth, Ahi, 157
Nazism, 165, 166, 167, 198, 207
Negohot settlement, West Bank, 113
Neither East nor West, 46
Nejmeh SC, 183–4
Nekounam, Javad, 212
neo-patriarchy, 4, 6, 7, 29, 34, 35, 37, 40, 82
Nepal, 245–6, 251
nepotism, 5, 40, 76, 78, 135

Neruda, Pablo, 37
Netanyahu, Benjamin, 153, 166
Netherlands, 93, 112
Network of Azerbaijani-Americans from Iran, 205
Neuchâtel Xamax, 181
New Federation Board, 170
New York Cosmos, 274
New York University, 285
Newsweek, 234
Nezhad, Sayyad Reza Pak, 215–16
Niger, 14
Nigeria, 9, 106, 165, 211
Nikpai, Rohallah, 196
Nimr, Mohammed 180
Nissim, Moshe, 162–3
Niva, Eric, 190
Nokia, 135
noms de guerre, 51
Noor Huda Ismail, 108
Noordin Mohammed Top, 95
Nooruddin, Salah, 256
Nordau, Max, 156
North Korea, 148, 209, 275
Northern Cyprus, 170
Northern Ireland, 171, 182
Northwestern University, 217
Norway, 170
Nottingham Forest FC, 255
NTVSpor, 116
nuclear power, weapons, 131, 198, 206, 208, 210, 211–12
Nur, Said Mohamed, 107
Nursî, Bediüzzaman Said, 119

O'Brien, Seamus, 274
Obama, Barack, 258–9, 286
Observer, The, 286
Offside, 231
'Oh Council, You Son of a Bitch' (Essam), 78

'Oh Nesting Crow', 63
oil, 17, 40, 209, 210, 241, 265
Olympiakos FC, 253
Olympic Council of Asia (OCA), 265, 278
Olympic Games, 1, 3, 4, 13, 38, 95, 107, 172, 175, 177, 178, 180–1, 188, 191, 196, 202, 222–3, 241, 257, 258, 261, 262, 265, 278–9
  1956 Melbourne Summer Olympics, 4, 172
  1972 Munich Summer Olympics, 4, 95, 175
  2002 Salt Lake City Winter Olympics, 265
  2004 Athens Summer Olympics, 191
  2008 Beijing Summer Olympics, 196, 217
  2010 Singapore Youth Olympics, 223
  2012 London Summer Olympics, 4, 175, 180–1, 188, 222–3, 232, 233
  2016 Rio de Janeiro Summer Olympics, 223, 279
  2020 Tokyo Summer Olympics, 257, 262
al-Omaira, Mariam, 216
Oman, 217, 264, 265
Optik Baskan, 127
Oran, Algeria, 42
Orange CAF Champions League, 54, 68
Orascom Telecom, 19
Orwell, George, 7
Oslo agreement (1993), 161
Osman, Yusuf Ali, 107
al-Otaiba, Yousef, 211
Ottoman Empire (1299–1923), 117, 118–19, 120, 123, 126, 130, 132–3, 134, 138, 139, 140

Ouadoo, Abdessalam, 252
Outside Left, 131–2
ownership, 11, 26, 53
Öz, Zekeriya, 145, 146
Ozak, Faruk Nafiz, 135
Özal, Turgut, 119, 135, 138
Özel, Soli, 120

Padania, 170
Pahlavi dynasty (1925–79), 31–3, 102, 198–200, 207
Pakistan, 102, 277
Palestine, Palestinians, 4, 7, 12, 17, 18, 30, 31, 43–7, 58, 94, 95, 96, 99, 100, 109, 110, 112–14, 149–69, 171, 172, 174–80, 181, 207, 214–15, 219–20, 228, 234, 236, 256–7
  1928 admission of Mandatory team into FIFA, 152
  1930 Land of Israel team play friendly against Egypt, 152
  1931 foundation of Arab Palestine Sports Federation (APSF), 153
  1936 Arab revolt, 152–3; foundation of Beitar Jerusalem, 153
  1948 Arab–Israeli War, 43, 44, 154; Jordanian annexation of West Bank, 44
  1967 Six Day War; Israeli annexation of East Jerusalem, 6, 12, 162, 174, 207
  1970 Black September; expulsion of PLO from Jordan, 43, 44
  1972 Black September Munich massacre, 4, 95, 175
  1976 Land Day protests, 154
  1982 Sabra and Shatila massacre, 18
  1987 First Intifada begins, 154, 161

1988 recognition of PLO by US, 43

1993 Oslo agreement, 161

1998 admission into FIFA, 171

2000 Second Intifada begins, 113

2002 Israeli security forces arrest Muhsin Qawasmeh, 113; construction of West Bank barrier begins, 162; bulldozing of homes in Jenin refugee camp, 162–3

2003 Hamas suicide attacks in Israel; assassination of Abdullah Qawasmeh, 112–13

2004 Israeli military campaign in Gaza, 155

2006 World Cup qualifier against Uzbekistan and Iraq, 175–6

2007 Lebanon conflict, 17; Hamas takeover of Gaza, 114; World Cup qualifier cancelled due to travel restrictions, 174; Mohammed Nimr imprisoned by Israel, 180

2008 hosting of friendly match against Jordan, 175

2009 Israeli ground invasion of Gaza, 174; Mahmoud al-Sarsak detained at Israeli checkpoint, 179; Gaza Dialogue and Tolerance Cup, 113–14

2010 national team competes in Homeless World Cup, 174

2011 IOC/Palestinian Authority launch development plan, 177; World Cup and Olympic qualifiers, 175, 177; women's team play Japan in Hebron, 229; Gilad Shalit exchanged for prisoners, 177

2012 Mahmoud al-Sarsak released from prison after hunger strike, 167, 179; Mohammed Nimr and Omar Abu Roweis detained by Israel, 180

2015 accession to ICC; PFA tables resolution calling for suspension of Israel from FIFA, 179

Palestine Football Association (PFA), 174–80, 229

Palestine Football Federation (PFF), 152

Palestine Liberation Organization (PLO), 43, 44, 154, 161, 175

Palestine Olympic Committee, 178

Palestine, 4, 7, 17

Palestinian Authority, 177–9

Palestinian Sport Office, Lebanon, 174

pan-Arabism, 33

pan-Islamism, 102

Panahi, Jafar, 231

Panorama, 274

Paraguay, 241

Parc des Princes, Paris, 239

Paris, France, 95, 112, 239, 240

Paris Saint-Germain (PSG), 239, 240, 253, 255, 257

Partizan Belgrade, 51

Pasdaran, 200

patriarchalism, 3, 4, 6, 7, 29, 34, 35, 37, 40, 82

Pattani, Thailand, 112

Peace and Democracy Party (BDP), 235

Pearl Island, Qatar, 260

Peninsula, The, 247

Pennsylvania, United States, 93, 119, 145, 195

pepper spray, 115, 116, 129

Peres, Shimon, 149, 166, 177

Persepolis SC, 31, 55, 199, 200, 267

Persian Gulf, 209–12
Persian Gulf League, 211–12
Perspectives on Public Health, 249
Perugia AC, 16
Peshmerga, 171
Petraeus, David, 13
PKK (Partiya Karkerên Kurdistanê), 123, 235
Platini, Michel, 239, 268
police, *see under* security forces, police
pork, 258, 260
Port of Spain, Trinidad, 267
Port Said, Egypt, 34–5, 36, 69–80, 83, 84, 87, 91
Porto Sokhna, Egypt, 76
Portrait of Low-Income Migrants in Contemporary Qatar, A, 246
Portsmouth FC, 19, 256
Portugal, 238, 254
PricewaterhouseCoopers (PwC), 271, 273–7, 281
Prince Abdullah Al-Faisal Stadium, Jeddah, 224
Prince Faisal Bin Fahd Stadium, Riyadh, 225
Princess Nora Bint Abdul Rahman University, 226
Prix de l'Arc de Triomphe, 240
propaganda, 1, 14, 18–20, 28, 31, 209
Prostitution Cup, 99
Proudel, Harihar Kant, 245–6
Provisional Reconstruction Teams, 195
punishment of players, 11, 12–13, 21, 102

Qaddafi, Al Saadi, 14–17, 33, 264
Qaddafi, Moammar, 1, 14, 16, 19, 21, 29, 33, 34, 218, 264
al-Qaeda, 94–6, 107, 108, 110–11, 114, 190, 274

Qalibaf, Mohammad Baker, 209
al-Qamishli, Deir-ez-Zor, 47
Qaradagli, Vahid, 205
al-Qarni, Muhammad, 22
Qasr al-'Ayni Street, Cairo, 62
Qasr al-Nil bil-Jazira, 32
al-Qassemi, Sultan Sooud, 249
Qatar, 2, 3, 4, 8, 9, 155, 176, 193, 217, 237–55, 257–78, 285–7
    1995 Hamad bin Khalifa seizes power in bloodless coup, 261
    2002 Bin Hammam elected president of AFC, 271
    2009 companies granted capital gains tax exemption in France, 240; Aspire Football Dreams tournament, 242
    2010 awarded 2022 World Cup, 3, 8, 9, 237–52, 253, 258, 260, 261, 263, 265–6, 285, 287; bid for Manchester United, 253
    2011 bid to host 2020 Olympic Games, 257; Bin Hammam campaigns for FIFA presidency, 265, 267; Bin Hammam suspended from FIFA; banned for life, 268, 269–71
    2012 Bin Hammam's FIFA ban annulled, 269, 271; female athletes fielded at London Olympics, 4; acquisition of PSG, 255; alcohol banned on Pearl Island, 260; Bin Hammam banned for life by FIFA, 263, 265, 277
    2013 Tamim bin Hamad becomes Emir, 248, 258
    2015 FIFA corruption case, 3, 8, 238–9, 254, 263, 268, 281
Qatar Airways, 260
Qatar Chronicles, 247
Qatar Foundation, 243, 245, 246

Qatar Investment Fund, 253
Qatar National Bank, 240
Qatar National Sports Day, 258
Qatar Olympic Committee, 241, 258
Qatar Sports Investments, 239
Qatar Stars League, 251, 266
Qatar Tourism Authority, 255
Qatar University, 247, 251, 260
'Qatar: Do the Right Thing', 243
Qawasmeh clan, 112–13
'al-Qissas aw al-Damm', 75
Qom Seminary, 230
Quartz, 284
al-Qubair, Syria, 189
al-Quds al Arabi, 188
Qumsieh, Raad, 176
Qur'an, 101, 110, 111, 133, 233
Qura, Jihad, 175

Raba'a al-Adawiya Square, Cairo, 81, 88
Rabin, Yitzhak, 156
racism, 3, 21–2, 128, 150, 156, 158, 161–9, 179, 196, 207
radicalisation, 54, 85, 90, 108–14
Rafsanjani, Ali Akbar Hashemi, 197, 234
Rafsanjani, Mohammed Hashemi, 197
Rahif Alameh, 183
Rajavi, Maryam, 201
Rajavi, Masud, 199, 201
Rajnatovic, Zeljniko, 49, 50
Rajoub, Jibril, 174–5, 178, 229
al-Rakhis, Afaf, 217
al-Ram, West Bank, 175
Ramadi, Iraq, 195
Ramallah, West Bank, 175, 228, 229
Rammali, Hussein, 14
Ramzy, Hany, 180–1

Rand, Ayn, 286
Rania, Queen consort of Jordan, 45, 46
Raqqa, Syria, 17, 86
Real Madrid, 139, 253, 254, 257–8
Recep Tayyip Erdoğan Stadium, Kasimpasa, 126, 148
Red Star Belgrade, 50–1
Refah Party, 120
reformism, 35–6, 38–9, 42, 45–6, 53–4, 67, 71–3, 77, 79, 82, 83, 90, 123, 199, 200, 202, 227, 232, 243, 246, 259, 263
Renaissance Capital, 139
rent-a-fan, 148
Resnick, Ronnie, 166
'Retribution or Blood', 75
Revolutionary People's Liberation Party-Front, 131
Reyhanlı, Turkey, 117
Reza Khan Pahlavi, Shah of Iran, 32, 102, 198
Riedl, Alfred, 175
right-wing, 51, 128, 136, 153, 160, 165
Rio de Janeiro, Brazil, 223
Ritz Carlton hotel, Jakarta, 95
River Araz, 205
Riyadh, Saudi Arabia, 4, 21, 222, 224–5
Robinho (Robson de Souza), 254
Rockefeller family, 135
Rocky Terrain, 188
Roma AS, 253
al-Romaithi, Mohammed Khalfan, 264
Roman Empire (27 BC–476 AD), 28–9, 149
Romero, Amilcar G., 66
Roshan Telecom Development Co., 196

Rosie, Ahmed, 226
Rouhani, Hassan, 207–10
Routledge, 274
rowing, 217
Royal Emirates Group, 254, 257
Royal Football Fund, 254
rubber bullets, 60
rule of law, 124, 126, 174, 250
Russia, 12, 49, 111, 139, 155, 238
al-Ryani, Bashir, 14–15

Saadiyat Island, Abu Dhabi, 285, 286
al-Sabah, Ahmed al-Fahad al-Ahmed, 278–9, 265
al-Sabah, Fahad al-Ahmed al-Jaber, 279
Sabra and Shatila massacre (1982), 18
Sabri, Noor, 194
Sadagah, Hadeer, 223
Sadat, Anwar, 29, 82, 107
Sadat metro station, Cairo, 60
Sadayev, Zaur, 165
Sadr City, Baghdad, 195
Saeed, Hussein, 192
Safavi, Yahya, 204
safety-valve, soccer as, 2, 5, 200
Sagresse SC, 184
al-Sahli, Saud, 22
Sahrawi, 173
Said, Hazem, 88
Saito, Satoshi, 275–6
Salafism, 78, 94, 99, 100, 109
Salam Zgarta SC, 184
Salameh, Klodi, 228–9
Saleh, Ali Abdullah, 18, 33
Salem, Abdelaziz, 32
Salem, Mahmoud, 48
Salheen, Yusuf, 88
al-Salman, Abdul Aziz as, 97

al-Salman, Mashhoor Bin Hasan, 96–8, 102
Salt Lake City, Utah, 265
El Salvador, 19
Sami Tan, 170
Sami, Hikmet, 138
Sampdoria U.C., 17
Samsun, Turkey, 121
Sana'a, Yemen, 18
al-Sananiri, Kamal, 89
Sancaktepe Municipal Sports Stadium, 144
Sandmonkey, 48
Sandys, Duncan, 33
São Paulo, Brazil, 56
Sarkozy, Nicolas, 239, 240
Saroot, Abdelbasset, 185–8, 190
al-Sarsak, Mahmoud, 167, 179–80
Sarwat Pasha, Abdel Khaliq, 31, 56
al-Satri, Abu Bakr, 227–8
Sattar Khan cemetery, Tabriz, 205
al-Saud, Abdullah bin Mosaad bin Abdulaziz, 223, 224, 255, 260
al-Saud, Mutaib bin Abdullah bin Abdulaziz, 227
al-Saud, Nawaf bin Faisal bin Fahd bin Abdulaziz, 225, 227
al-Saud, Nayef Bin Abdulaziz, 222
al-Saud, Reema Bandar, 224
al-Saud, Turki bin Faisal, 21, 227
Saudi Arabia, 2, 4, 18, 19, 21–3, 72, 95, 96, 97–102, 103, 108–9, 110, 191–2, 193, 209, 210, 214–15, 219, 221–8, 241, 249, 251–2, 255–7, 259–62, 264, 265, 273, 274, 278, 281
    2000 Germany lifts weapons embargo for World Cup vote, 281
    2002 Abdullah al-Najdi issues fatwa against soccer, 101
    2003 national team players join Iraqi jihad, 100, 110

2005 fatwa against soccer issued, 100

2006 World Cup, 99, 100; foundation of Jeddah King's United, 214, 222

2007 loss to Iraq in Asian Cup, 191–2

2009 ban on women's gyms, 226; King Abdullah demands resignation of Sheikh al-Satri, 227–8

2010 military officer arrested in Iraq for World Cup terror plot, 95; mobile mosques used during World Cup, 109; Dalma Rushdi Malhas competes at Singapore Youth Olympics, 223

2011 Manal al-Sharif arrested for driving, 226; Ultras attack embassy in Egypt, 72

2012 female athletes fielded at London Olympics, 4, 222–3; Nawaf bin Faisal resigns from Football Association, 21; Human Rights Watch condemns government policy on women's sports, 221; Alharbi elected head of SAFF, 227

2013 clerics meet with King Abdullah to discuss women's sports, 227; Hilal SC racism scandal, 21–2; Prince Abdullah bin Mosaad buys stake in Sheffield United, 224, 255; fielding of candidate for AFC; bid to host 2019 Asian Cup, 224

2014 government promises progress on women's sports at IOC meeting, 223

2015 municipal elections, 227

Saudi Arabian Football Federation (SAFF), 21, 224, 227

Saudi Gazette, 22

Saudi Paper Manufacturing Group, 255

Saved Sect, 93, 100

Sawat, Majid, 100, 110

sayaadin, 58

al-Sayed, Hassan, 260

el-Sayed, Mohamed, 20

al-Sayed, Nader, 71

Sayigh, Yezid, 91

Schroeder, Gerhard, 281

Scobey, Margaret, 62, 63

Scotland, 171

Scott, Ridley, 103

sectarianism, 7, 8, 9, 13, 22, 37, 171, 182–97

secularism, 64, 75, 77, 90, 117, 118, 119, 121, 122, 123, 146, 147

security forces, police, 1, 5–7, 11–12, 17, 26, 28, 33, 36–9, 42–5, 47, 49, 50–2, 54, 56–91, 114–16, 120, 121, 122–7, 129, 147, 184, 206
brutality, 17, 26, 28, 45–7, 49, 61, 62–3, 80, 121, 122–4
corruption, 20, 52, 62–3, 73, 74, 83
ownership of teams, 20, 184
reform, 36, 54, 67, 71–3, 77, 79, 83, 91, 122–5

Segal, Ze'ev, 158

Sekazza, Ivan, 241–2

Sela Sport, 274

Seleucid Empire (312–63 BC), 152

Selim I the Grim, Caliph of the Ottoman Empire, 117

Selim III, Caliph of the Ottoman Empire, 123

Selinsgrove, Pennsylvania, 93

Sellal, Abdelmalek, 40

Senegal, 242

Sephardi Jews, 154, 155, 159–60, 163

September 11 attacks (2001), 95–6, 108
Serbia, 49, 50–1
al-Serkal, Yousuf Yaqoob Yousuf, 264, 278
Servette FC, 256
Sewell, William, 11–12, 25, 27
sexual harassment, 62
al-Shabaab, 93–4, 99, 102–7, 109
shabiha, 188–90
Shafaqna, 232
Shafi'i Moyhaddin, 104
Shafiq, Ahmed, 81
Shahar, Jacob, 168
Shaheen, Ahmad, 208
Shahrdari Tabriz FC, 205
Shaka'a, Bassam, 158–9
Shalabi, Ahmad, 97
Shalaby, Nora, 61
Shalit, Gilad, 177
Shamarikh, 66
Shanku, Lulu, 190
Sharabi, Hisham, 4, 29, 34, 40
Sharia'a law, 63, 75, 94, 101, 102, 105, 111, 117, 118, 123, 206, 213, 234, 258, 260–1
Shariatmadari, 204
Sharif Sheikh Ahmed, 103
Sharif, Essam, 71
al-Sharif, Manal, 226
Sharif, Solmaz, 232
Sharjah, United Arab Emirates, 1, 212, 217
al-Sharjah, 212
Sharon, Ariel, 155, 156
Sharq, 232
al-Shawa, Rushdi, 151
Sheban, Ahmed, 187
Sheffield United FC, 224
Shehata, Hassan, 58, 109–10, 113, 180

al-Sheikh, Abdel Aziz Ibn Abdallah, 101, 221
al-Sheikh, Muhammad ibn Ibrahim, 98
Shia Islam, 21, 22, 101, 182, 183–4, 192, 193, 194, 209, 215–16, 256, 280
Shikabala, 35
Shirazi, Naser Makarem, 231
Shirin Was a Canary, 231
Shirzanan, 232
Shobeir, Ahmed, 58
shooting, 223
Shu Ismu?, 191
Shubra, Cairo, 61
al-Shurta, 20
Sikhs, 214
Simic, Andrei, 136
Sinai, 6, 86, 90–1
Singapore, 174, 223, 233, 248, 249, 265, 266, 273, 276, 287
Sinop, Turkey, 131
al-Sisi, Abdel Fattah, 2, 20, 36, 83, 85–8, 90, 147, 285
Sivas, Turkey, 134
Siyah Çoraplılar, 132
slogans, 7, 16, 34, 38, 45, 47, 62, 73, 75, 84, 87, 125–6, 130, 147, 148, 161, 165, 200, 201, 206, 207
Smith and Williamson, 273
Sneijder, Wesley, 132
Soccer War (1969), 19
Social Justice Party, 163
social media, 18, 21–2, 35, 58, 61, 69, 73, 75, 79, 83, 88, 101, 118, 144, 147, 185, 191, 216, 231, 260, 280–1
social mobility, 5, 154
social movement theory, 12
socialism, 64, 115
Södertälje, Sweden, 190

soft power, 2, 241, 249, 262
Soheili, Ali, 204
al-Soma, Omar, 191
Somalia, 9, 18, 94, 99, 102–7, 184, 268, 274
Sonatrach, 40
songs, 30, 38, 39, 49, 59, 63, 69, 78, 136–7, 150, 153, 163, 164
Sons Of Iraq, 194–5
Soosay, Dato' Alex, 278, 281
Sorek, Tamir, 151, 156, 157, 256
South Africa, 3, 183
    2010 World Cup, 4, 8, 19, 93, 95, 96, 105–6, 108–9, 110, 148, 174, 202, 283
South Korea, 191, 194, 230, 265, 281
Soviet Union (1922–91), 53, 111, 134, 149–50, 205, 209
Spain, 4–5, 93, 110, 138, 139, 170, 235, 238, 240, 253, 254, 256, 257
Spirit of Soccer, 195
SpongeBob SquarePants, 78
sponsorship system, 243–4, 249, 286
sprinting, 217
Ssebulime, Lori, 93
Stadium of the People, Baghdad, 13
stadiums
    as detention centres, 17
    ecology of, 11–12, 25–7
    electronic ticketing, 140–1, 147
    as grunt schools, 37
    as killing fields, 17–18, 196
    meritocracy, 5
    as military bases, 17, 106
    and propaganda, 1, 14, 18–20, 28, 31, 209
    and protest, 2, 5, 6, 7, 11, 25–7, 39, 42, 67, 129, 147–8, 200–2, 283–5
    punishment in, 11, 13, 17–18

terrorism against, 9, 93–6, 99
stateless peoples, 7, 170–3, 181
Stewart, Jon, 78
stock exchange, 73, 137, 139
Strait of Hormuz, 209, 211
street battle skills, 51, 52–3, 55, 57–68, 71, 115–16, 284
strikes, 78
Stuart, Kenda, 219
student mobilization, 11–12, 26, 28, 31, 36, 54, 88–9, 147, 284–5
Students Against The Coup, 36, 88
Stuxnet computer virus, 212
Suan, Abbas, 149–50, 154, 155
Sudan, 49, 106, 110–11
Suez Canal, 69, 71, 73
Suez Crisis (1956), 4, 172
Sufism, 118
Sugden, John, 171
Şükür, Hakan, 144
Sunday Times, 238, 265
as-Sunnah mosque, Kissimee, 222
Sunni Islam, 117–18, 122, 183, 192, 194, 215, 256
Supreme Council of the Armed Forces (SCAF), 36, 71, 72, 73, 78
Supreme Education Council of Qatar, 258
Supreme Muslim Council, 151
Suqa Holaha, Somalia, 106
Suuqa Bakaaraha, Mogadishu, 104
Sweden, 3, 169–70, 190
swimming, 221, 231
Switzerland, 30, 179, 256, 263, 269–70, 274, 281
Syria, 1, 6, 9, 17, 20, 43, 44, 47, 64, 86, 100, 111, 115, 117–18, 170, 183, 184–91, 206, 207, 210, 221, 262, 265
    1982 Hama massacre, 17
    2004 troops fire on Kurdish Al Jihad SC supporters, 47

2005 withdrawal of troops from Lebanon, 183

2006 al-Tartusi declares 'no objection to soccer', 100

2011 Revolution, 17, 43, 47, 115, 117, 184–90, 221, 262; Saroot joins jihad, 185–8, 190

2012 massacres in Houla and al-Qubair; London Olympics, 9, 188; victory in WAFF Championship, 190–1

2013 bombing of Reyhanlı, Turkey, 117–18

2014 barred from World Cup by FIFA, 187

Syrian Football Association (SFA), 184–5

Syrianska, 190

T24 news, 148

Tabib, Eli, 165

Tabriz, East Azerbaijan, 204–7

al-Tabtabai, Waleed, 217

taekwondo, 196, 217

Tahrir Square, Cairo, 6–7, 20, 26, 30, 50, 52–3, 55, 57–8, 60–7, 70–1, 78, 81, 87, 88, 90, 115, 116, 284

Taj FC, 55, 198–9

Tajikistan, 187

Taksim Square, Istanbul, 2, 36, 115, 118, 121, 123, 125, 126, 127, 128, 129, 130, 131–2, 140, 146, 147, 148

Talabani, Jalal, 47

Talebi, Jalal, 39

Talesnikov, Jan, 166

Taliban, 17–18, 94, 99, 102, 103, 107, 109, 196

Talimciler, Ahmet, 125, 128

Tamim bin Hamad, Emir of Qatar, 247–8, 258–61, 287

Tantawi, Mohamed Hussein, 71, 83

Tanzania, 95

al-Taquri, Bassem, 113

al-Tarifi, Abdul-Aziz, 227

Tartag, Bachir, 42

al-Tartusi, Abu Basir, 100

al-Tawil, Shukri Ali, 97

Taylor, Ian, 34, 48

Tayyar, Şamil, 148

Team, The, 174

tear gas, 57, 58, 60, 66, 114, 115, 116, 124, 129

Teddy Kollek Stadium, Jerusalem, 150, 160, 166

Tehran, Iran, 4, 31, 55, 198, 200–1, 203, 206, 207, 208, 209, 234, 267

Tehran University, 200

Tel Aviv, Israel, 158, 159, 160, 161, 164, 178

television, 46, 105, 117, 132, 140, 148, 184, 186, 188, 191, 197–8, 209, 223, 239–40, 254, 258, 259

temporary marriage, 206

tennis, 217

tennis, 230

Terim, Fatih, 144

terrorism, 93–6, 99, 108, 110, 112–13, 117–18, 126, 153, 162, 165, 166–7, 185, 191, 193, 194, 206, 274

1998 al-Qaeda plot to attack World Cup matches, 94–5; East African embassy bombings, 95

2001 al-Qaeda plot against US embassy in Paris, 112; September 11 attacks, 95–6, 108

2003 Hamas suicide attacks in Israel, 112–13

2004 Madrid bombings, 110; attacks on police in Pattani, Thailand, 112; assassination of Theo van Gogh, 112

2007 bombing of Asian Cup viewers in Baghdad, 191
2009 Jakarta bombings, 95
2010 al-Shabaab Kampala bombings, 93
2012 attack on Ozar Hatorah school in Toulouse, 166–7; bombing near Baghdad Stadium, 194
2013 Reyhanlı bombings, 117–18; bombings of football matches and cafés in Iraq, 194
Thailand, 112, 281
Thaljieh, Honey, 214, 228
al-Thamali, Tamer, 100, 110
al-Thani, Abdullah bin Nasser, 257
al-Thani, Hamad bin Jassim, 246
al-Thani, Hamad bin Khalifa, 242, 258–61, 263, 265
al-Thani, Jassim bin Sosibo, 247
al-Thani, Tamim bin Hamad, 247–8, 258–61, 287
al-Thawadi, Hassan, 237–8
thisisfootballislife blog, 142
Thoreau, Henry David, 237
Three Faiths Forum (3FF), 181
Tiananmen Square protests (1989), 11–12, 26, 28
Tibet, 170
Tigani, Sheikh Sidi, 173
Tilly, Charles, 63, 69
Tilmisani, Umar, 89
Times, The, 30
Timur, Cemile, 236
Tishreen SC, 189
Togo, 55
TOKI (**Toplu Konut Idaresi**), **142**
Tomlinson, Alan, 171
torture, 13, 52, 63, 86, 105, 253, 279
Total, 240

Toulouse, France, 166–7
TP Mazembe, 54
Trabelsi, Nizar, 112
Trabzon, Turkey, 134, 135, 140
Trabzonspor FC, 127, 135, 139, 140, 141
trade unions, 8, 54, 77–8, 83, 123, 127, 159–60, 243, 250, 286
Trafalgar Square, London, 96
Traktor Sazi FC, 204–7
travel restrictions, 110, 174–80, 228
Trevaskis, Gerald, 33
Trimble, David, 182
Trinidad and Tobago, 267–8, 281
Trinidad Guardian, 268
Tripoli, Lebanon, 17
Tripoli, Libya, 15, 16
Tripoli SC, 183
TSV 1860 Munich, 254
Tuama, Salim, 164, 169
Tudjman, Franco, 51
Tulkarem, West Bank, 229
Tunc, Sevecen, 134
Tunis, Tunisia, 53
Tunisia, 6, 20, 26, 29, 34, 43, 46, 49, 50, 53, 54, 58, 59, 68, 91, 94, 112, 187, 203, 221, 234, 239, 264, 283, 284
1998 al-Qaeda plot to attack World Cup match, 94
2001 Nizar Trabelsi arrested in Belgium on terrorism charges, 112
2006 World Cup, 99
2010 violence at Espérance Sportive de Tunis–TP Mazembe match in Congo, 54–5; self-immolation of Mohamed Bouazizi, 43; Revolution, 6, 20, 26, 29, 43, 46, 50, 53, 54, 58, 59, 203, 221, 234, 239, 283, 284

2013 CS Hammam-Lif play in empty stadium, 283

Türk Telekom Arena, Istanbul, 142

Turk, Rifaat 'Jimmy', 158–9

Turkey, 2, 26, 36–7, 47, 86, 114–48, 170, 172, 190, 235–6, 254, 262, 284

   1923 foundation of Republic, 118

   1967 Kayseri riot, 134

   1980 coup d'état, 119, 127, 129, 134; MKE Ankaragücü promoted to premier league, 135; wars between Istanbul supporter groups begin, 127, 129

   1987 Bursa and Konya promoted to premier league, 135

   1991 Beşiktaş fan trampled to death by Galatasaray supporters, 128; Fenerbahçe–Atlético Madrid match cancelled due to power failure, 138

   1993 Galatasaray play Manchester United in UEFA Champions League, 128, 138

   1996 Fenerbahçe defeat Manchester United in UEFA Champions League, 138; national team competes in UEFA Euro Championship, 138

   1997 military memorandum; ousting of Necmettin Erbakan, 119–20

   1998 Gülen self-exiles to United States, 37, 119, 143

   2000 Leeds United supporters killed in Taksim riot, 128; Galatasaray win UEFA Cup and European Super Cup, 138

   2003 women's football league disbanded, 236

   2005 allegations of Erdoğan's nepotism toward Trabzonspor, 135; bankruptcies of Istanbulspor and Adanaspor, 135

   2006 women's football league reconstituted, 236

   2007 assassination of Hrant Dink, 121; Ergenekon investigation begins, 144, 145

   2008 Erdoğan pushes for three-child policy, 118

   2010 Ramazan Kizil sentenced to prison in absentia, 170

   2011 bid for 2020 Olympics, 262; Zekeriya Öz appointed to Galatasaray board, 145; match-fixing scandal, 132, 141–6

   2012 Erdoğan declares abortion constitutes homicide, 118; Fenerbahçe fans accuse Gülen of engineering match-fixing, 144; match-fixing trial; Erdoğan pushes for leniency, 141, 143–6

   2013 Reyhanlı bombings, 117–18; Erdoğan declares *ayran* national drink, 117; Bosporus bridge named after Selim I, 117, 118; police attack Çarşı members with tear gas, 124; kiss-in at Kurtulus metro station, Ankara, 118; Burak Yıldırım killed by Galatasaray fans, 129; Sinop nuclear power plant deal signed, 131; Fenerbahçe fans taunt Didier Drogba with racist chants, 128; Taksim Gezi Park protests, 2, 36, 115–16, 121, 123, 125–32, 140, 146–8, 284; Bülent Arınç backtracks on three-child policy, 118; indictment of Çarşı members, 36, 126–7, 141; TOKI announces plans to build new stadiums and sports facilities, 142; corruption investigation into Gülen movement launched, 146

2014 e-ticketing boycott begins, 140; presidential election, 143, 144; Erdoğan removes Şükür's name from Sancaktepe Stadium, 144

2015 case against Çarşı members dropped, 127; general election, 142, 143

Turkish Football Federation (TFF), 138, 141, 143, 145, 236

Turkish Super League, 135

Turkmens, 193

al-Tuwayjuri, Hamoud, 97

Twitter, 21–2, 58, 69, 73, 144, 260, 280–1

Udinese Calcio, 16–17

Udwan tribe, 44

Uganda, 93–4, 241

Ukraine, 149–50

Ultras, 6, 7, 9, 11, 25–7, 35–7, 47–91, 114–16, 124–7, 129–32, 141, 148, 162, 284–5, 287

Ahlawy, 54, 60, 63, 70, 73, 74, 77, 84, 86, 87

Bassem Youssef, 78

Çarşı, 36, 115–16, 124–7, 129–32, 141, 148

La Familia, 161–7

Nahdawy, 36, 78, 88

Outside Left, 131–2

Salafi, 78

SpongeBob, 78

UltrAslan, 131–2, 136

White Knights (UWK), 48, 51, 60, 61, 68–9, 84–6, 91

UltrAslan, 131–2, 136

unemployment, 48, 65, 68, 69, 161, 235

Union of European Football Associations (UEFA), 138, 140, 145, 153, 179, 220, 239, 255, 268, 276

Union Sportive de la Médina d'El Harrach (USM), 41

Union Sportive Médina d'Alger (USMA), 40

United Arab Emirates (UAE), 1, 8, 19, 193, 203, 211–12, 216–17, 223, 230, 249, 251–8, 259, 262, 264, 266, 285–6

2004 Emirates Airlines Arsenal sponsorship deal, 253

2008 bid for Liverpool, 253; financial crisis, 254

2010 acquisition of Manchester City, 252–5

2011 acquisition of Getafe CF, 254, 257

2012 dispute with Iran after Ahmadinejad visits disputed Hormuz islands, 211; winning of bid to host Asian Cup, 285

2013 Dubai wins bid to host 2020 World Expo, 285

United Investment Bank, 254

United Kingdom, 4, 19, 20, 31, 33, 48, 59, 94, 100, 108, 125, 128, 130, 132, 141, 152–3, 171, 172, 180–1, 182, 188, 214, 243, 245, 252–6, 259, 283

1872 first international match between England and Scotland, 171

1882 introduction of soccer to Egypt, 20

1919 Egyptian Revolution, 4, 31, 74

1936 Arab revolt in Palestine, 152–3

1956 Suez Crisis, 4, 172

1963 Egyptian national team barred from Aden, 33

1993 Manchester United play Galatasaray in UEFA Champions League, 128, 138

1996 Fenerbahçe defeat Manchester United in UEFA Champions League, 138

1998 al-Qaeda plot to attack World Cup match, 94

2000 Leeds United supporters killed in Istanbul riot, 128

2001 BBC *Panorama* reveals ISL cash-for-contract scandal, 274

2002 release of *Bend it like Beckham*, 214

2004 Emirates Airlines Arsenal sponsorship deal, 253

2006 Saved Sect declares football a 'colonial crusader scheme', 100

2008 UAE bid for Liverpool, 253

2010 UAE acquisition of Manchester City, 252–5; Qatari bid for Manchester United, 253

2011 Manchester City win FA Cup, 254

2012 London Olympics, 4, 175, 180–1, 188, 222–3, 232, 233; Bahraini acquisition of Leeds United; Kuwaiti acquisition of Nottingham Forest, 255–6

2013 Prince Abdullah bin Mosaad buys stake in Sheffield United, 224, 255

2014 Ghoncheh Ghavami arrested in Tehran for attending volleyball match, 230

United Nations (UN), 171, 175, 182, 183, 208, 211, 220, 249, 257, 274

United Press International, 1

United States, 8, 12–14, 17, 19, 39, 42–5, 47, 62–3, 93, 94, 103, 119, 121–2, 131, 135, 145, 155, 175, 176, 181, 190, 192–8, 203, 209, 211–12, 222, 238, 239, 241, 243, 252, 258–9, 263, 268, 279–80, 281

1988 recognition of PLO, 43

1990 assassination of Meir Kahane in New York, 161

1993 Battle of Mogadishu, 103–4

1998 al-Qaeda plot to attack World Cup matches, 94–5; loss to Iran in World Cup, 39, 94, 201; East African embassy bombings, 95

2001 al-Qaeda plot against embassy in Paris, 112; September 11 attacks, 95–6, 108; invasion of Afghanistan, 17, 194

2002 Salt Lake City Winter Olympics, 265

2003 invasion of Iraq; de-Baathification program, 13–14, 17, 192, 193, 194–6; Abu Ghraib prisoner abuse scandal, 100

2004 Syrian Kurdish Al Jihad SC supporters pledge allegiance to George W. Bush, 47

2008 87th Infantry plays Sons Of Iraq, 194–5

2011 Obama praises Qatar's Sheikh Hamad, 258–9

2012 State Department report on human rights in Turkey, 121; FFIRI complains about hold up of AFC payments, 198

2015 FIFA corruption case, 3, 8, 238–9, 254, 263, 268, 281

universities, 12, 28, 36, 54, 85, 88–9, 147, 200, 285

University of Florida, 256
Uways, Abdul Halim, 97
Uzan, Cem, 135–6
Uzbekistan, 175–6

van Gogh, Theo, 112
Vanuatu, 281
Varzagan, East Azerbaijan, 206
Vatican, 96
Vázquez Raña, Mario, 1, 279
Velappan, Peter, 265, 271
Velayati, Ali Akbar, 210
Veolia Environment, 240
Vieira, Jorvan, 192, 194
Viera, Valdeir, 38
Vietnam, 241, 251
vilayat-e-faqih, 204
Vinci, 240
VIVA World Cup, 170–1, 173
Vlachos, Hierotheos, 96
volleyball, 230, 232
vuvuzela, 283

al-Waar, 188
Wafd Party, 4
Wahhabism, 22, 101, 222, 262
Wales, 171
Walizada, Abdul Sabor, 196–7
Wall Street Journal, 260
Warner, Jack, 268, 270
Washington Post, The, 196
Wasif, Ahmed, 76
Wasim, Muhammed, 102
wasta (connections), 5
al-Watan, 221
water cannons, 62, 115, 129
Waxman, Dov, 167
'We Pledge', 30
We Too Have No Other Land, 156
al-Wehdat SC, 31, 43–6, 156–7
Weill Cornell Medical College, 249

Werder Bremen, 181
West Asian Football Federation
 (WAFF), 190–1, 217, 219, 220–1
West Azerbaijan Province, Iran, 205
West Bank, Palestine, 44–7, 110,
 112–14, 154, 158, 162, 166, 168,
 174–9, 228–9
West Bank barrier, 162, 175
Western Sahara, 173
White, Jenny, 117
Whitson, Sarah Leah, 244
WikiLeaks, 14, 42, 44–5, 63, 121–2,
 135, 203, 230, 279
wilad sis, 65, 66, 68–9
William Hill, 257
al-Wissi, Sa'ad, 100
women's rights, 2, 4, 7, 21, 37–8, 94,
 118, 120–2, 153, 195, 198, 200–1,
 203, 208, 213–36, 247, 262
working-class, 34, 48, 76, 77, 128,
 129
World Assembly of Muslim Youth
 (WAMY), 102
World Cup, 1, 3, 8, 9, 13, 19, 21, 30,
 37–9, 93, 94–6, 99, 100, 103–6,
 108–9, 110, 134, 172, 174–7, 185,
 187, 194, 200, 201, 202, 237–52,
 253, 258, 260, 261, 263, 265–6,
 274, 283, 287
 1934 Italy, 152
 1938 France, 152
 1954 Switzerland, 30, 134
 1986 Mexico, 1, 13
 1998 France, 13, 37, 39, 94–5,
 200, 201
 2002 Korea-Japan, 38, 201
 2006 Germany, 99, 100, 103, 149,
 175–6, 274
 2010 South Africa, 4, 8, 19, 93,
 95, 96, 105–6, 108–9, 110, 148,
 174, 202, 283

2014 Brazil, 21, 175, 187, 194, 208

2018 Russia, 185, 238, 240

2022 Qatar, 3, 8, 9, 237–52, 258, 260, 261, 263, 265–6, 287

World Sport Group (WSG), 266, 273–6, 277

wrestling, 231

Wuppertaler SV, 112

'Ya Magles Ya Ibn El-Haram' (Essam), 78

Yagmur, Mohammed, 113

Yahya, Karim, 52

Yavuz Sultan Selim Bridge, Turkey, 117, 118

Yediot Ahronoth, 158, 162

Yekutieli, Josef, 152

Yemen, 18, 33, 43, 187, 219, 221

Yenidogan Foods Marketing, 141

Yilmaz, Burak, 132

Yıldırım, Aziz, 142–6

Yıldırım, Burak, 129

Yıldız, Mehmet Derviş, 124

Yıldız Holding, 141

Yılmaz, Mesut, 120

yoghurt, 46, 117

Young Turks, 123, 133

Young, Malcolm, 59

Yousef, Elham 225

Youssef, Bassem, 78

Youth Soccer Festival, 195

YouTube, 21, 61, 101, 185, 216

Yugoslavia, 49, 50–1, 95

Zaghloul, Saad, 4, 31

Zagreb, Croatia, 50–1

Zahir Shah, King of Afghanistan, 197

Zaki, Amr, 19

Zamalek SC, 31, 32, 35, 48, 49, 55–6, 60, 65, 68, 84–7, 107

Zaman, 120, 145

Zappa, Frank, 197

Zapsu, Cüneyd, 122

Zeidani, Sameh, 174

Zeit, Die, 281

Zhang Jilong, 271–2, 277, 278

Zhao Dingxin, 11–12, 25, 27

Zidan, Mohamed, 34

Zidane, Zinedine, 173

Zionism, 100, 149–50, 152–3, 155, 156, 165

Zirie, Firas, 248–9

Zoroastrianism, 218

Zurich, Switzerland, 179